TOWARD
SELF-SUFFICIENCY

A Community for a Transition Period

GEORGE HUNT

TOWARD SELF-SUFFICIENCY
A COMMUNITY FOR A TRANSITION PERIOD

iUniverse books may be ordered through booksellers or by contacting:

iUniverse
1663 Liberty Drive
Bloomington, IN 47403
www.iuniverse.com
1-800-Authors (1-800-288-4677)

Because of the dynamic nature of the Internet, any web addresses or links contained in this book may have changed since publication and may no longer be valid. The views expressed in this work are solely those of the author and do not necessarily reflect the views of the publisher, and the publisher hereby disclaims any responsibility for them.

ISBN: 978-1-5320-5980-3 (sc)
ISBN: 978-1-5320-5981-0 (e)
ISBN: 978-1-5320-6011-3 (sc)

Library of Congress Control Number: 2018912133

Print information available on the last page.

iUniverse rev. date: 11/15/2018

CONTENTS

Dedication...v

Section 1...1

Preface... 3

Pilot Demonstration Project... 7

Introduction: Designing a Community to Prevent Chaos and Provide Opportunities for the Future.. 7

Toward Self-Sufficiency: The Pilot Demonstration Project 11

Demonstration Pilot Community Development Description:..........................16

Housing and Land Use—Option 1 23

Housing and Land Use—Option 2 29

Project Information and Direction...43

Education Potential, Procedures, and Methods...49

Community and Personal Purposes—Why It Is Important.............................64

Reducing Consumerism, Collaboration, Using Local Currencies, and Specific Technologies74

Economic Development Options 81

Governance—Cooperatives, Creative Commons, and the Solidarity Economy.......................87

Section 2 ....**93**

    Advertising and Marketing - What to Do 94

    Transition Design...102

    Other Writings Providing Community Development Information 104

    Agriculture and Landscaping at the Crossroads 143

    Alliance for Science—Cornell University...172

    Our Failing Society... 183

    Summary—Where We Are Now..190

References and Resources.. **196**

Why This Book..**210**

Afterword..**218**

Appendix—Slideshow.. **220**

Endnotes **239**

Index..**245**

DEDICATION

To the three most important women who were in my life. They are always walking with me every day: my mom, Gwen; my wife, Louise; and my daughter, Patricia.

And to my son, Greg.

I Am Alone

I am alone.
I did not ask for this.
First the air was not fit to breathe.
I cried in vain.
They said, "Wait."
Then the soil became just dust.
They said, "Maybe tomorrow."
Finally the bees said, "Goodbye; the flowers are gone."
They said, "We must do something,"
But it was too late.
They said, "I have money to give you now."
All we had asked was for you to love the earth.
It was not heard.
Now we have nothing.
I am alone,
My cries a distant memory.

George Hunt

SECTION 1

PREFACE

A Beginning Solution to Our Current Dilemma

Many books present excellent solutions for our future by suggesting how we can reach a more fulfilling life while living in a world that has less consumption, less greed, and hopefully fewer wars than we have now. They include rewards of a postcapitalist society or a society where liberal democracies can exist but must change or adapt to reduce further decay. Cooperation and collaboration can be a substitute for greed and the continual striving for money. Perhaps we have gone too far already on a path toward a dismal future by demanding more of the earth's nonrenewable resources than it has available for our future use. Humankind has to realize and understand that the natural processes of nature continually functioning around us become teachers leading us in the right path for survival. It cannot be taken for granted anymore. The beauty of nature is all around us. A working relationship with earth's natural processes provides insights and feelings that are genuine and fulfilling. We then do not have to continually reach for the illusive powers of happiness and security; they would already be there with us. What we do now should be in the interests of those who are to be born on this earth and not just for our own short term benefits.

As explained by the author, Molly Larkin, the seventh-generation principle taught by Native Americans "states that in every decision, be it personal, governmental or corporate, we must consider how it will affect our descendants seven generations into the future. So that the pristine sky, field and mountains will still be here for them to enjoy. Western society generally considers a generation to be 25 years; the Lakota Nation considers one generation to be 100 years. This seventh-generation principle was so important to Native American cultures that it was codified in the "Iroquois Great Law of Peace." Molly Larkin (https://www.mollylarkin.com/the-history-u-s-constitution-we-werent-taught-school/). The laws of the Iroquois were also used as a guideline for the writing of the Constitution. Most Native American and indigenous tribes throughout the world embrace this teaching. We seem to have forgotten quite a few things in the last 240 years, and we need an awakening. One of the purposes of this book is to suggest ways we can create a sustainable system for the next hundred years. It becomes a new type of pathway for living.

The suggestions offered in this book provide a means of going in nature's direction by using a design for a small community development that is a pilot demonstration project. The proposed community stresses education and teaching, as well as being an experiment in community relationships for living in a "less stuff" and sustainable environment. To date, its innovative approach has not been replicated anywhere in the world that I know of, and because of this, it can set new standards for community development. The community becomes its own advertising agency for sustainability and self-sufficiency. This is just a beginning solution that can be started now and is adaptable to expand to show values of compassion and a truer understanding of one's self in a world that needs help. History has shown us what can happen when we overshoot our boundaries of sustainability. This book represents the commencement of going on nature's path instead of our own. Let's hope we can get the process started before it is too late.

This project spans a lifetime of collecting ideas. It includes my working for more than fifty years as a landscape architect and a community planner. I graduated from Cornell University in Ithaca, New York, in 1956 after serving in the US Navy. The most interesting projects were those in other countries. With a partner, I designed recreation areas for the Sandals and Beaches resorts in various areas of the Caribbean, and working with a small firm in Jamaica, I completed a master plan for the city of Montego Bay, Jamaica. This was one of my first experiences working in the impoverished areas in another country. It was unique at that time because we established planning districts throughout the city of Montego Bay, held community meetings, and let people of all economic groups determine what they wanted to have provided in each planning district. The planning included housing, transportation, public services, business collaborations, park planning, and more. These town meetings in many cases were the first time Jamaicans living in the poverty areas had a voice and a way to express what they needed and, in turn, what they could contribute. Jamaica is a country of small businesses and entrepreneurs, so the planning had to incorporate ways for these types of businesses to grow and be recognized. The plan received a "Good-Practice Award" from the United Nations for citizen participation and community participation. I also prepared market studies for a resort in the Dominican Republic and in several other countries in which I incorporated some of these concepts. In 1989, I went on an agricultural consulting trip to Hainan, China; Hanoi, Vietnam; and Bangkok, Thailand, to introduce an organic product for soils. To add additional insights to increase my international experience, I attended three conferences about sustainable development at the World Bank and took trips to Greece, Cypress, and Lebanon. I went there to visit my wife who was teaching at a university in Lebanon. I was also a member of ASLA (American Society of Landscape Architects) and this allowed me to expand my knowledge by meeting with other professionals.

In the United States, I owned a small landscape firm in Garland, Texas and we designed projects in more than eleven states, with most of our work being in the Dallas-Fort Worth metroplex. Two years were spent employed with HUD during the urban renewal era, and there I was introduced to poverty in the southwestern part of the United States. I also prepared market and feasibility studies for some of the projects and was later employed by a city agency to help people living in impoverished areas in San Antonio, Texas. It showed me that anyone can be a contributor in one way or another and that listening is one of the most important planning tools. This hands-on work in impoverished and low-income areas allowed me to understand the dynamics occurring there and this led to the design of the pilot demonstration project.

The format for the book is as unique as the project itself. The book is basically in two parts. The first part describes the pilot demonstration project (PDP) community and its many functions and opportunities. It will attempt to solve the social problems that are not recognized by most community projects and will include many ways to make communities more self-sufficient. The project is also aimed to serve people in the middle- and lower-income brackets, but the concepts could be used for anyone. Its purpose is to open people's minds so they can create their own innovative ideas for living. First though, read the section "Why This Book" at the end of this book. It will help you understand what I am attempting to portray. The main purpose is to recognize what dangers are being devised by political factions to undermine our democracy.

PILOT DEMONSTRATION PROJECT

A Suggested Option for Living in the Transition Economy

Introduction: Designing a Community to Prevent Chaos and Provide Opportunities for the Future

Another purpose for writing this book is to offer a feasible program that the United States or other countries can implement to move toward a postcapitalist society. This would be a transition period. It would be a society where people feel wanted and have a purpose in life. It would be not glamorous but far more viable than what we are seeing now. The first thing that has to be done is to show people that our present living situation has to change because we are running out of renewable materials that the earth is providing at rates where they cannot be replenished. I have included a list of books and articles in the references and resources section at the end of the book. Multiple authors can show what is happening to our society and analyze what needs to be changed much better than what can be accomplished in one book. The recommend readings will also provide a good reference for anyone interested in how to fix and understand our present environmental, political, and social problems.

The main intent of the suggestions shown is to create a way to live in an actual built community. This community is called the "Pilot Demonstration Project" (PDP) (once started, it will have a better name). It can provide services and data that will be a start to show what can be accomplished by following a way of development thinking using the processes of nature as guidelines. Innovation is key, and the plan will be made available to make it happen. It is perhaps a utopian dream, but look where most people are now. If we don't understand what we are doing by putting our capitalistic goals ahead of the ability of our future children to have decent lives, then we have no one to blame but ourselves. The project will be an active, continually changing community. We have to help people be aware of what is happening now because of our consumerism binge and our government policies.

Each book I listed as a reference has a letter/number designation, and I will refer to information I am writing about by using that designation and the name of the book. I have put that information adjacent to the material being read so people can expand their knowledge on the subject and get additional information. Copyright laws limit the amount of words and sentences that you can use for quotes from another author. These insertions that I use are just blips and many times out of context with what that author feels is important in their book. Times have changed because of

Amazon books. Now you can look up the book on the internet and look inside the book you are interested in to get additional information (from what you have already read in my book). Then that author of that book may suggest another book that is interesting and worth looking at to obtain other viewpoints. This then, in a way, lengthens what I am writing. The whole purpose is to get people to read more so that they get a broader picture of what is being discussed. This is why I put such a long list of books in the reference section and why I wanted a means that will enable people to understand what expanded information is available within certain categories of subjects. Some of the books are more pertinent than others for explaining our present situation and our possible future, but all of them should be recognized and used for reference. This is against convention, and I hope this explains why it is formatted this way. The same information is available as in a footnote or biographical notes in most books. I think this is an easier way for people to get additional information and you can choose books by topic.

Most of the recommended books on my list, however, were written before the Trump presidency. Trump's present dysfunctional type of government was described in several books as an example of a society in decline or chaos. It is up to the reader to determine whether this is the case. The election in 2016 was basically a negative vote by voters against both parties. The economy had been flat since the 2008 recession, and people wanted change because they felt left out of the system. They definitely got it. Now, to make society start to right itself, there has to be exponential change toward a postcapitalist government or a government that will improve our chaotic form of democracy as it is practiced today. The book *Edge of Chaos*[1] by Dambisa Moyo provides insight on methods that could fix some of our present societal and political problems. It is discussed later in this book and is one of the most comprehensive books explaining why our democracy is failing to deliver manageable economic growth. It recognizes what is happening to our environment, our class structure (including inequality), and our political system. What is happening now is an example of how the elite keep control by offering false promises. President Trump is a master of distraction and is keeping the media talking about him rather than them noting what he is doing to the environment and society. Constructive change has to occur in America in so that it can become the democracy as envisioned by our founding fathers. Also, media has to change by offering some long term ideas and environmental solutions rather than what they are doing now with their constant emphasis on daily news and political agendas. Some of the media is owned by corporations that do not want to rock the boat with their advertisers or change their political philosophy or formats and these policies do not help our progress toward cooperation. The main absurdity is that many Republicans accept Trump's lies, female discretions, and tweets with little questioning. Both parties have been affected by restarting the lemming gene in its members, where everyone behaves the same. This is when they consider the party more important than what is good for the "American People". The recently passed tax bill is a good example of this. The bill was not explained in detail to show how each quintile of the population would be affected and would receive benefits. In some corporations, there will be increases in wages for their bottom-tier personnel, but this is long overdue anyway because of the long period of a flat economy.

Some economists argue this point (of the economy being flat), and it is partly determined by what indicator is used: GDP—gross domestic product; GPI—genuine progress indicator; CPI—consumer price inflation; or PCE—personal consumption indicator. However, many economists have poor batting records (e.g., 2008 recession). The indicator GDP is the measurement most countries use. The GDP is the usual way to measure a country's economy. GDP is the total value of everything produced by all the people and companies in the country. It doesn't matter if they are citizens or foreign-owned companies. If they are located within the country's boundaries, the government counts their production in the GDP. Wikipedia notes the alternative method, GPI, is designed to take fuller account of the well-being of a nation, only a part of which pertains to the size of the nation's economy, by incorporating environmental and social factors that are not measured by GDP. For instance, some models of GPI decrease in value when the poverty rate increases. The GPI separates the concept of societal progress from economic growth, while it is also used in ecological economics, green economics, sustainability, and more inclusive types of economics. It factors in environmental and carbon footprints that businesses produce or eliminate, including the forms of resource depletion, pollution, and long-term environmental damage. This is why the GDP is not a true indicator of the economy. For example, the money spent for a person's medical expenses is part of the GDP estimate, but it is a negative indicator by being an expense to society.

A more serious situation with the Trump administration is the "fox in the henhouse" or an open-door approach for corporate lobbying and decision-making. The EPA, FDA, Department of the Interior, and the Department of Agriculture are the biggest followers of this policy. The government doesn't believe in using truly independent laboratories to help product evaluations but mainly uses information submitted by corporations. Carey Gillam exposes Monsanto and other corporations in her book *Whitewash* (AL1)[2]. The destruction of the environment is carried out by classifying the new (or decreased) standards as reducing regulations with little regard for public safety. This is seduction of the public at its highest level and occurs on a continual basis. Do we really need mining or the invasion of Native American cultural sites at the Bear's Ears Monument? Trump's doing this is called reducing unnecessary regulations in order to make the rich richer and the Koch brothers happier. Another Trump policy is providing subsidies to people and corporations that misuse them. This is usually at the expense of small farmers and businesses. Subsidies also reduce economic growth.

One thing that could be done is to keep a system that can act as a gatekeeper for democracy and prevent the election of extremists that would destroy it. This is so Congress can make decisions and not be bound by party politics and affiliations that would allow this to happen. It would also help if there were limits placed on political spending. Also, a much shorter primary period would be welcomed by everyone. This would include election reform and information concerning who is giving candidates money. It was so much easier when the League of Woman Voters was present to evaluate candidates. To have a functional working democracy voters should be more aware of what is actually happening within their government. There is no need for the election process to take as long as it does other than wearing out the public and enhancing news broadcasts and comedians' salaries. Finally, gerrymandering in all the states should not be designed for one party's advantage (or conservative, liberal, moderate, or progressive viewpoints). This is why there is little change in some districts and elections are determined by certain areas across the country. This is why so many of the people keep getting elected. If the people became more involved, it would help ensure more fairness. Also, the news should discuss how government programs and political decisions affect the inequality within the nation and throughout the world. If decisions were analyzed in these terms, people would understand who Trump is trying to help. It is not the common man. It is a shame that Molly Ivins isn't with us now. If President Trump thinks Steven Colbert is bad, Molly would have kept him up nights wondering why he took this job. This subject will not be discussed again in any detail, because it would take up a whole book (e.g., *Fire and Fury*). The reason it was mentioned here is that most of my book is about how these factors affect communities.

To get back to a more pleasant subject concerning the main intent of my book, the following is a description of an approach for using self-sufficiency techniques in the pilot demonstration project. From now on, we will be going through a transition period caused by environmental inactions. This hopefully will keep us from going past the point of destroying ourselves by not recognizing the detrimental effects of climate change, soil deterioration/erosion, and overuse of our natural resources.

Toward Self-Sufficiency: The Pilot Demonstration Project

The proposed community concept for the pilot demonstration project should be considered for construction now so it can be used as an example of how this type of community would contribute to our life in the future. The purpose of the project is to offer innovative ideas that will demonstrate solutions that could be utilized and adapted for times of recession or abundance. Regardless, we will always need affordable housing. In the latter part of this book, various views of what our society could become are dependent upon many factors dealing with our social systems, use of natural resources, revision of food chains, and various forms of pollution. What we do now determines the living conditions in the future. Present practices of greed, political cronyism, questionable technologies, unstable social systems, overuse of natural resources, expensive or dwindling energy sources, overconsumption, increasing inequality, government debt, environmental degradation, and so on have to be curtailed or reduced. If we don't start considering and acting on these issues now (we are already too late on some), there will be chaos, depressions, and conflicts about food, water, and other resources. How will we act when we have limited energy sources and limited conveniences that we now enjoy? This book will attempt to offer some solutions by the presentation of a community that is a possible viable answer for our future. I hope to provide ideas that will stimulate other ideas to make even stronger communities. Users can be as important as professionals in this regard, since they have valuable considerations that are often overlooked by the designated experts. No project is static, so laws and ordinances that make it so are not acceptable. That is why this type of community will require many exemptions from standard zoning ordinances.

The most important aspect for any community is its social cohesion and the instilling of sharing and collaboration among its members. This is the first step in making it a community that is healthy and viable. Physical structures alone cannot do this. Like nature, the key to success is diversity among its members, and this includes all races, various cultures, young students, the elderly, the handicapped and homeless, occupations, political thought, and so on. Rather than focusing on one's self, the goal is to help others. This proposed community design will make that easier to do. The goal is to give people a chance to define their own purpose in life. Depression is one of our biggest problems, and reaching for drugs to solve it is not the answer. This demonstration project is also economical because it reduces the amount of "stuff" that you think you need. Swapping of stuff can be enjoyable and add variety to life. The project could also reduce dependency on some of the false gods that many people depend on when using social media as their only outlet.

The pilot demonstration project has been designed using several unique concepts that I would like to introduce so they could be included for community development practices. They can be used for affordable housing solutions now and during a recession. Unfortunately, affordable housing solutions are limited due to many different factors. One of these is the lack of funding by HUD and continually higher building and land costs. Most residential designs now are commissioned by builders or individuals for people in the upper-income or middle-income brackets. The designs used and constructed by builders in the United States show few new innovations regarding the homes that they are building. An exception would be using some of the smart housing concepts. Many features being used now are what is trendy each year and mainly regard interior features.

The sense of community is primarily found in master-planned communities featuring swimming pools, some sports activities, and shopping and greenbelts, and these features are not available for many people living in affordable housing communities because of costs.

Social diversity is limited to economic considerations and may include a scattering of affordable housing for persons in the middle-income groups. When people want a larger house, they may add an addition or move to a larger house. Now, due to increasing land costs, we have many McMansions being constructed on small lots. Builders, in order to save money, are not known for preparing the landscape space with decent topsoil, and many times they use subsoil. Because of this, landscape costs for homeowners are more expensive than they need to be. Expansive lawns are the order of the day, and most of them are fertilized with chemicals, over sprayed with pesticides and herbicides, with little regard for water conservation. These factors are some of the reasons for creating the pilot demonstration project.

The summary for the pilot demonstration project (PDP) is shown below, with specific details noted after it.

1. **Demonstration:** Since the proposed community is a demonstration project, it will have different requirements than a typical housing project. The purpose for the project, from a housing perspective, is to obtain enough construction and maintenance data that can be used in other later projects. Will solar panels pay for themselves and over what time frame? Is it better to use wood studs or metal ones? What will the best housing construction products in the future be, considering that some of what we have now will not be available later? For example, will metal materials or wood framing be too expensive or even available? What new technologies are available for power storage or sanitary sewers instead of septic systems and high-pressure lines? What exterior siding or other material is cost-effective now and still has low maintenance costs? What type of landscaping will be applicable for the future? The answer should be organic maintenance, reduced lawn areas, and native plants versus chemical treatments. Organic products and methods will be more sustainable and cost-effective because the soils use natural processes. What sustainable materials and practices are better to use now even if they cost more? These are just some of the questions to be answered. Proper planning now is necessary because of the importance of preparing for the future. The same type of questions will also be considered during the planning of the project for social and environmental potential problems.

2. **Multi-use of Buildings and Products:** To date, this has been a limited consideration in community development, but it will be a major component of the PDP. Due to our uncertain future, this is necessary to keep communities stable. What has happened in Detroit, Michigan, is a good example. Hundreds of houses are vacant due to an economic downturn. It is starting to turn around, and the process is slow and painful, especially for low-income families. One example for housing is in the design of the triplex housing plans. Some of the plans are shown on page 6 in the appendix. In plan 1, the triplex consists of three individual units (A-B-C) ranging between 480 and 500 square feet. Unit A is separated from B and C. Both units A and C can be enlarged to whatever size is desired. Unit 2 shows

how a triplex can be converted to a duplex by just taking down a small section of wall and taking out a movable kitchen to be used somewhere else. This then could be for a single family, with unit A being used by the family and a rental unit or a place for a young or elderly member of the family. As for the multi-use of products, an example would be for several members of the community to use community landscape equipment rather than buying it separately for each residence. Many other examples will be shown later in the book.

3. **Amenities:** The project will have several amenities, and they are described later. Some of these include a community building, small sports park, restaurant, community bank using local currency, library, day care center, and community car rental. These locations are shown on the site plan.

4. **Sharing, Collaboration, Social Programs:** The project is designed around these types of social activities. There are facilities for the elderly, homeless, handicapped, veterans, and people suffering from anxiety and depression. Student housing facilities and medical facilities are also available. The community has car rental and car-sharing opportunities. Special purchasing arrangements can be made with local businesses in regard to discounts and delivery options. The community will have its own businesses, such as landscape and building maintenance, that hire people from the project. Flea market and farmer market facilities are also available. Various types of rental, lease, or home ownership can occur on one lot, and this opens up many more opportunities for the poor to afford housing and start their own businesses. The community will also have its own community money to be used within the project and surrounding area. A government center will be on-site to help people so they do not have to find transportation to go to a government office outside of the project.

5. **Education, Training, and Workshops:** The central area of every community will have training and educational facilities with emphasis on business management, construction trades, agriculture, and landscaping, with other trades available at a later date. The program will be based on a work/study format with very low tuition fees. Student housing will be available on-site for people coming there from other cities or towns. Progress will be evaluated on a person's abilities and not on the number of courses that are completed. Apprentice work will also be available with nearby farmers and general contractors, and the agricultural programs will be based on understanding organic applications, permaculture, and agroecology. Information on these programs is included later in this book.

6. **Support Mechanisms, Governance:** People will not be alone in the community if they need help at any time, because of the social management structure. One of the requirements that will be enforced is that people cannot use drugs (cocaine, heroin, etc.), and if they are caught using them, they will have to leave the community. There may be exceptions for marijuana usage. The project will also have its own type of governance once a certain percentage of the units are occupied, and there will be a nonprofit available for people living in the community to obtain community or other grants. There are many options that could be used, and each individual project would determine its own needs.

This type of community can be anything that you want it to be. People have choices and in turn are recognized as who they are and want to be. People who want privacy can still have it and yet contribute to the community on their own terms. Sharing and collaboration will still be part of the program. The grid plan shown makes the project more affordable, but it has several problems for creating a pleasing aesthetic experience that curved features present. This is why the landscaping, choice of architectural features, and entrance appeal are important for presenting interesting features and vistas that would encourage people to enjoy walking in the community. Affordability, however, is still one of its most desirable features.

This book is divided into two sections. Section 1 discusses the objectives and description of the pilot demonstration project. This is the optimistic section of the book because it describes a way to design a proposed community that would allow people to live in a different type of community than what is available now. It is versatile and innovative enough so that it can adapt to the changing conditions that will occur in the near future. Hopefully, these changes will occur slowly enough that there will be limited problems, but as things appear now, our habits of greed, consumerism, nonproductive wars and destruction, exponential use of natural resources, increasing ecological footprints by the developed nations, depletion of soils, and nonrecognition of climate change by the present administration will hasten our pathway toward chaos to a degree we have never seen before. This community plan should be just a beginning for developing other solutions. Pictures and plans are shown in the appendix and provide a synopsis of the project and its objectives. The land-use plan is shown below with explanations that follow.

In section 2, I attempt to show what is happening both environmentally and socially because of its influence on community design. This is done by using excerpts from books and articles by other authors. This enlarges the scope of the dialogue by encouraging readers to read in depth the writings and comments that would be most interesting to them. It discusses the false power of advertising along with the corruption of our political system. It describes how the mismanagement of our soils can lead to increasing the acidity and temperature of the oceans. This kills the krill, which is one of the main foods for fish. The corals would die, and this destroys the balance of nature in the oceans and land. The permafrost in the arctic could melt and release large amounts of methane that can exponentially speed up climate change. There would be little good topsoil left due to our present agricultural practices, and Monsanto/Bayer would be left with billions of dollars that they can't spend because they are one of the main chaos manufacturers. All this, and I still haven't mentioned the drug companies. I hope the journey through the book will make everyone aware of what is happening regardless of their party affiliation and beliefs. This understanding is needed to bring us together to fight for a common cause—survival. Then, by working together, we can have a safer world for our children.

Schematic Land Use Plan:

30 acres

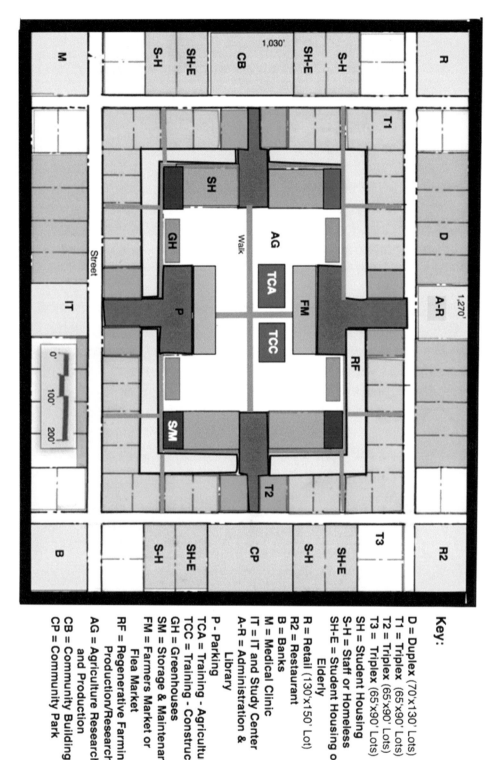

Key:

D = Duplex (70'x130' Lots)
T1 = Triplex (65'x90' Lots)
T2 = Triplex (65'x90' Lots)
T3 = Triplex (65'x90' Lots)
SH = Student Housing
S-H = Staff or Homeless
SH-E = Student Housing or
    Elderly
R = Retail (130'x150' Lot)
R2 = Restaurant
B = Banks
M = Medical Clinic
IT = IT and Study Center
A-R = Administration &
    Library
P - Parking
TCA = Training - Agriculture
TCC = Training - Construction
GH = Greenhouses
SM = Storage & Maintenance
FM = Farmers Market or
    Flea Market
RF = Regenerative Farming
    Production/Research
AG = Agriculture Research
    and Production
CB = Community Building
CP = Community Park

- 15 -

Demonstration Pilot Community Development Description:

A design presentation or schematic land-use plan for the proposed Demonstration Pilot Community is shown here and in other available reports. There are twenty different home designs that could be used, but only a few will be discussed in this book. The homes are shown on pages 7, 8, 9, 10, 11, 12, and 13 and on page 3 in the appendix in the model home area diagram

At this time, the plan is compact in order to reduce costs. The actual site plan for a project could vary considerably according to site conditions, location, financing, market considerations, materials used, available utilities, and so on. Also, the size of the lots could change, with some of them being larger than what is proposed in this plan. It all depends on the final objectives that are selected for any given project. This design approach is an alternative to conventional planning because it is for living in a sustainable manner. A sustainable plan could be designed for other conventional communities by adapting some of the ideas noted in this report as well as others to fit individual circumstances.

Throughout the book, the intention is to acquaint readers and potential sustainable community members with other literature and ideas to make possible a more self-sufficient society. A community like the PDP is necessary for the transition period because it would be very difficult to change from our present capitalist society to a postcapitalist world in a short time. This community must use cooperation and sharing as guiding principles and show how we can be a better society with less consumption. The community members should keep offering design suggestions to the planners and builders during and after the construction period. This process worked in Jamaica because the people felt that they were part of the community, and they wanted to contribute to its development.

There are many examples of buildings that can be used for student and medical housing, with some of them shown on pages 12 and 13 in the appendix. Medical housing has a unique potential for people that have depression and anxiety. This could provide a breakthrough opportunity for studying depression because the facilities are designed specifically for that purpose. The people living in one of these buildings could be students studying one or more courses offered in the community, or elderly persons with depression problems. People needing help with depression issues could live in the project while they are being helped by medical professionals and community members. This in turn could provide research data that would contribute to better understanding of the causes of depression. If this becomes part of the community program, then the medical facility would be enlarged to include the blue duplex units on each side of the medical site (see site plan). One of the student buildings could also be rented out to the medical clinic for specific research.

The design of the building(s) can be changed for a variety of uses. For example, the manager's unit may include a room for two additional occupants, and the large, open space could be used by everyone living there. There would be few or no changes in the building. In this case, a place for studying could be enlarged. The patio areas could also be a vegetable or flower garden, a natural area, or a place for pets. The community will have two or more senior golden retrievers or Labs on site for petting purposes. Elderly persons can have small pets or dogs in their units, and the community will furnish their food and care costs. The paving in the patio areas could also be covered with a canvas that can be retracted. A wood trellis would be another alternative.

The governing framework for the nonprofit would have to be determined by the developer and the people living in the community. One building could be owned by the community nonprofit/ cooperative and in some cases rented out to another nonprofit to conduct their specific type of research. Also, the rights to the ownership of the research conducted on site would have to be determined to see if it would be for sale or common property. This could be a source of income to the nonprofit if that became the purpose of the research. Grants from foundations would also be applied for from foundations, government entities, and so on.

Each living area would be linked to publications, research studies, and videos produced by the community nonprofit on their smartphones or TVs. However, people will be encouraged not to continually use them or social media but to be involved with community activities. The design of the units is small to prevent accumulation of unnecessary stuff. Outside storage would also be available for specific uses. There will be community public meetings at least once a month to share ideas and voice any grievances. Trade fairs and a farmers' market will be open on specific schedules. Also a bartering program using local currencies will be initiated through the community bank. The community emphasis will be on sharing, education, and research. Another building option for student housing is building 9 in the appendix.

The designs and uses shown on the plans, including those in the appendix, can be changed to meet individual markets and site conditions. In the present transition period, the small initial units (about 500 square feet each) and multi-use capabilities of the project homes will reduce waste and allow for changing the uses in each triplex where allowable. The appliances and bathroom fixtures are the same in most units. Differences will occur in the single-family options. Kitchens fixtures, cabinets, and appliances are movable and kept minimal to reduce waste. This will also allow for low-technology applications. Interior designs will vary. Several of the triplexes will be made of different materials to show how they affect maintenance costs and energy uses. Some units will only have window air conditioner units. Fans will be utilized in each of the rooms to reduce electrical consumption. All construction materials will be designed for long-term occupancy, and most of the floors will be stained concrete to reduce costs and maintenance. In the triplex units, the width of the center walkway could be widened or enclosed, and the upper area over the walkway to the roof could be used for storage. There will be more than twenty-five different designs for the elevations of the houses and the style of fencing in order to develop individuality of each dwelling. Different colors will also be one of the options.

The elevations of the triplexes will vary, and some of them will have food gardens on the roof. Solar and wind energy applications will be used in some of the units to evaluate cost comparisons. Trees will make use of passive energy applications and will grow fruit. An example would be to use lower-growing plants of the same species such as crape myrtles or dogwoods. The fences shown will be designed for low maintenance, utilizing masonry materials or metal posts with composite Techwood or other durable materials. There will also be various methods of water collection, sewage treatment, wastewater, and solid waste options. This is detailed later in the report. The number of parking spaces shown could also be eliminated or reduced, depending on the needs of the community and existing ordinances.

The landscape maintenance will be done by a designated nonprofit landscape group (or business) in the community that is trained in ecological maintenance. To demonstrate different options some of the following activities could be used. Different triplex units will have varying amounts of lawn, perennials, and cover crops. There will be two beehives on the property to help with pollination, and flowers will be in bloom most of the year to attract beneficial insects and to provide diversity. Some triplexes will have different soil amendments, bio-stimulants, and organic fertilizers added to show what combinations work best in terms of growth and maintenance. For example, one triplex will not use any additives in order to be a control property for research purposes. Diverse nitrogen-fixing cover crops will be used extensively in the first year instead of lawns. Mapping design exercises will be drawn so that this can be used for a teaching program for students, schools, and homeowners. It also will determine what products work best to achieve the desired results. Most construction and landscaping costs will become part of a databank and closely controlled by community management. The weather will be recorded in detail and soil tests taken to review nutrition needs and organic compounds in the soil. Insect, butterfly, and moth counts will be taken at the appropriate times. Permaculture practices and restoration agriculture will be utilized whenever possible.

A floor plan for one of the triplex plans can be found on page 3 in the appendix the unit on the left is one of the original floor plans of 480 square feet. The unit on the left is a triplex where two units have been converted into a single-family unit with three bedrooms by just removing a small section of wall and moving out one of the kitchens and cabinets. Unit A on the right is an area that can be (1) enlarged; (2) converted into an office, in-law, guest housing, or rental; or (3) an open space where the interior walls are not constructed, to be used as a workspace, office, business space, meeting area, play space, and so on. The walkway area between the units could be enclosed when the unit is located in areas of bad weather. The present eight-foot-wide walkway could be widened for another room and storage. The patio areas could be enclosed with fences for all types of uses in those areas. The unit on the right has been converted from a duplex.

A schematic land plan is shown in the beginning of this book and in the appendix. The main intent is to incorporate as many sustainable design features in the land plan as possible. Initially, the utilities, power, police/fire will be provided by the municipal district where the project is located. However, during the planning stage, it will be determined if some sustainable features can be incorporated into the community. Some of the guidelines for these will be noted in the book *LID—Low Impact Development* (UP38)[3]. Several of these optional features would be in the soft engineering classification which feature some of the following ecological services. Not all of them can be utilized because of the compact design and small size.

- disturbance regulation

- water regulation

- water supply

- soil formation

- erosion control and sediment retention

- waste treatment

- nutrient cycling

- climate regulation

- pollination

- refugia/habitat

- species control

- food production

- raw material production

- genetic resources

LID (UP38)[4] and *The Permaculture City* (UP3)[5] have pictures and details for constructing a low-impact and sustainable development. These books should be utilized along with other books on sustainable development so they are used in conjunction with land planning and individual buildings. Costs will be evaluated between conventional land planning and planning that is sustainable. Once this is done, cost/benefit and harm/benefit analysis will be used to determine how long it will take for each sustainable improvement to pay for itself and if it is feasible from a harm/benefit approach. If some of the improvements cannot be utilized at first, there may be options where a partial installation would make sense for easier future expansion plans. This approach of cost analysis is a unique process, but it is done to obtain enough information to make the most economical yet sustainable designs for future projects.

For the housing, different roof materials will be used. For example, non-petroleum roof materials should only be used for water catchment. Maintenance records will be kept of the different building construction methods. The data obtained will be used to determine what type of buildings are the most efficient, cost-effective, sustainable, and attractive. The data, however, will be affected by landscaping around the buildings, building orientation, weather and other factors. The material selection will also be evaluated in regard to what new technologies would affect its use in the future. This type of evaluation will also be done for paving, fencing, irrigation, landscaping (reduced lawn use and drought-tolerant plants), streets, and utilities. These evaluations will be selected by the tenants and professionals under the authority of the nonprofit governance. This evaluation study will add to the project costs but will offer data not available anywhere else. In a transition and postcapitalist economy, this type of information is necessary to reduce the use of natural resources.

A book that should be used as a guide is *Welcome to Your World—How the Built Environment Shapes Our World* (UP41).[6] It discusses how important it is to have an environment of buildings, landscapes, nature, social needs, and other factors in a community so that it is an enjoyable place in which to live. The built environment should provide a sense of place. This is lacking in most housing areas in the world. She describes the housing in most of our suburbs as boxed, bleached sameness. She states further:

For good and for ill, buildings and cityscapes and landscapes literally shape and help constitute our lives and ourselves. Designing and building enriched environments, ones that are informed by what we now know and are learning about how people experience the places they inhabit, will promote the development of human capabilities. Just as is true with regard to global warming and the earth's environment, nearly every thing we construct today will outlast us to affect those who come after us, sometimes generations and generations of them. Shouldn't a better built environment be the legacy we leave to the world? (p 292).

The proposed Pilot Demonstration Project will try to ascribe to the values noted in this book.

Land Uses and Housing

Following is a description of the housing and land-use improvements. These are just suggestions at this point and will be selected during the planning of the project. The planning professionals will include a developer, architects, landscape architect, ecologists or agroecologists, sociologists, a marketing firm, and a geographer. Others can be added. Every building design should be applicable for more than one use. An example would be the uses of the add-on additions shown in the appendix on page 7. In designing the original home/business, there should be allowances made in the exterior and roof structure to make future additions with minimal expense. Using the multi-use triplex design and other designs will reduce waste and allow people to easily expand their living space without having to move to a larger house. Ownership on a lot could be just one person, rental, lease option (initial first year), condominium, or another combinations. Some of these would require a special permit if it is located in an urban area or its jurisdiction. Option 2 uses are similar to those in option 1 but would include additional or substituted uses for areas with different needs, which could include in-city locations in poverty areas. An alternative could be using the housing designs for infill lots, with just one larger area for the agricultural research and teaching. The selection of designs will be determined by the market study developed for the project and comments from prospective persons who may be living in the community.

The infill housing could be scattered nearby a proposed PDP or located in existing warehouse-type buildings that have been deserted. The uses noted in both options can be interchanged, or different combinations can be used according to each market. The education buildings could be designed so that different subjects could be taught in them. If a workshop area is needed for construction classes and is not available in another building, then it could be set up in one of the triplex units. Everything should be designed for multi-use purposes to allow for changes in the housing market or economic conditions.

The designs for the communities should incorporate all applicable government agencies at the conception of the project. Since it will be different from other projects, they should know what the goals and designs for the proposed community are. They may be able to furnish many forms of instructional and funding assistance. As noted before, government agencies could be located in one of the triplex units. This would be beneficial to all the people needing government assistance, especially the elderly and the homeless. It would keep community members and students from going outside of the community to seek help. The location of a community substation for the police could aid in community relations. The more service facilities located in the project, the closer it would be to self-sufficient.

Our nation is facing problems at our southern border with Mexico, with a large influx of refugees seeking asylum. It can take up to a year to verify that this is a legitimate condition for each family. A proposal is being presented by the government to place some of the families in two bases owned by the Defense Department. What if several PDP community projects were constructed where these families could stay until their cases were approved? This would enable them to

1. work and contribute to the community;

2. become adjusted to our society and learn about our laws;

3. learn the English language by taking courses in English as a second language;

4. have instructions for becoming US citizens and pass the citizenship test once they are approved for asylum;

5. learn new skills or expand their existing skills;

6. have the ability to create jobs in the community unique to their culture;

7. use wage credits to help pay for maintaining the community;

8. grow some of their own foods;

9. be able after a few months to work outside of the community during the day (money earned will be paid back to the community to pay for rent, schooling, food, and utilities—a prearranged amount); and

10. use medical facilities and schools within the community.

If anyone violates established rules of conduct or leaves the community without permission, they will be sent to constricted confinement at another location in the US or sent back to their country of origin. Only one family member will be allowed to work outside of the community. The project will have a security fence and security personnel. Visitors will be allowed in to purchase goods or help the families. Any person who has a criminal background or uses drugs will not be allowed to live there.

If there comes a time when this community is not needed for this purpose, it can be used for affordable housing for the general public. The initial funding can come from reducing government waste or the Defense Department building fewer missiles. Of course, this community would not do the type of research noted earlier in the book.

Note: In the following options (or anywhere in the book), descriptions of the PDP with the words "would," "could," "may," "will," "can," and "should," are used in excess, but it is difficult to describe a future design feature or idea without using them. When using *would,* it means that a design concept or a structure will or should happen. Conversely, using the word *could* or *may* means something may happen or is an optional suggestion. In essence, it may be possible to interchange them, depending on when something happens or doesn't happen, or if it's just an idea. This concept is just that, and what you might want to happen may not be done or may just be an idea for the future. I use *would* or *will* for what I think should be done and *could* and *may* on things that could be a good idea or an option.

Housing and Land Use—Option 1

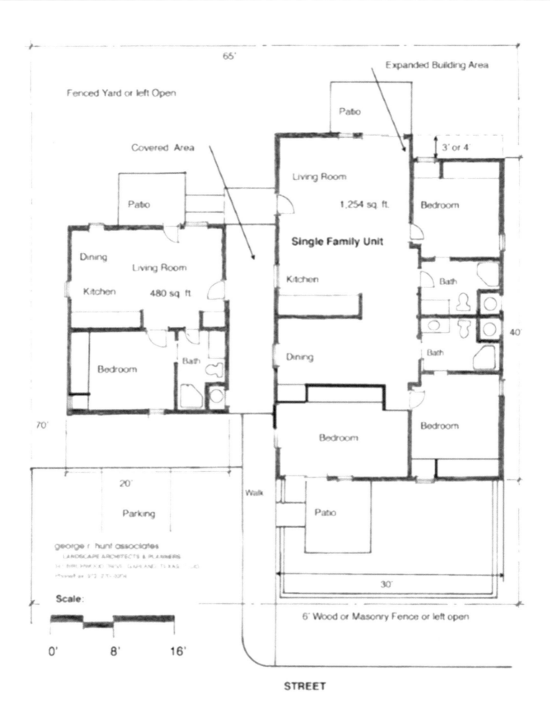

(Other triplex building plans are shown in the appendix. The plan shown above shows how two units are combined into an. expanded single family unit)

The following descriptions for uses are for option 1.

SH—Student Housing (building 9 on page 12, building 1 on page 13, and building 5 on page 11 in the appendix)

This is a multi-use building design that will initially be used for student housing. When it is not occupied by students, some of the rooms could be used for faculty, elderly, or students living in poverty areas. The poverty-area students (including dropouts and those with minor prison time) will have free tuition and housing but will have to work for food and other expenses. Drugs, other than marijuana, will not be tolerated, and each student will sign a paper agreeing to this requirement. The managers' unit in the model home complex will be offices for the community administration until the final administrate building is constructed.

T1—Triplex 1—Option 1 (building 1 on page 6 in the appendix and building shown on this page)

The standard triplex design with each unit about 480 square feet in area. Lot size shown is 90 by 65 feet. This can be enlarged if needed. Unit sizes can change in square footage later when the market is analyzed.

Triplex—Option 2 (building 2 on page 10 in the appendix)

Showing how units B and C have been made into one unit with minimal cost.

T2—Triplex 2—Option 3 (building 3 on page 11 in the appendix)

The community room (A) can be used for business or other approved uses. It also can be used as open space associated with unit B or C. The size of the building can change as needed.

Duplex (building 3 on page 3 in the appendix—on two lots)

These lots would be used for just one duplex design. Lot size is 70 by 130 feet. See model home plan for an example. Other duplex plans are available.

T3—Triplex 3 (modified triplex—enlarged)

Examples of one building type that can be used for many uses, as approved by the community, to add diversity and self-sufficiency.

S-H—Triplex or Optional Design (modified triplex design)

These units would be for staff, homeless, or people living in poverty who want to learn a trade. They would be the triplexes for a total of twelve units. The needs of each group would have to be evaluated in order to make any building designs applicable for the users.

SH-E—Triplex or Optional Design (modified triplex design)

These units would be for student housing or elderly. Total of twelve units. The elderly can cook their own meals or have some brought to them. They will also be offered a chance to obtain local money by babysitting, teaching, or working in one of the community businesses.

R—Retail Store

This would be a small convenience store owned by the community. The store would be used for training purposes for retail management. It could also be part-time work for students. Part of the site would provide automobile gasoline. Local currencies would be used to make products affordable for community members.

R2—Restaurant

This is a store owned and operated by the community, and it would specialize in food from the community farm. It would not sell any GMO food or meat from GMO or antibiotic animals. Again, this restaurant would be used for training purposes for future managers. This is another way to make it a multipurpose facility.

B—Bank

The bank would accept deposits and savings of conventional or community money from community members with no service charge. It would also be community owned. Its main service would be handling local community money and bartering accounts (no interest involved). The cost of the bank operation would be supplied by the community nonprofit. Personnel would be from the community, and school children and community members would be instructed in the ways of using local money. The bank would offer financial advice to community members by offering bank workshops or just postings. These could include simple household advice or world financial news. An alternate plan would be to send out newsletters to community members.

An example of world financial news is an article on the internet "Perfect Storm Global financial system showing danger signs" by a senior OECD economist (Ambrose Evans-Pritchard) on January 23, 2018 (http://www.theweek.co.uk/91129/global-financial-system-facing-perfect-storm):

William White, the Swiss-based head of the OECD's review board and ex-chief economist for the Bank for International Settlements. said: "All the market indicators right now look very similar to what we saw before the Lehman crisis, but the lesson has somehow been forgotten." Saying the financial system had been distorted by quantitative easing and negative interest rates, he said: "There is an intoxicating optimism at the top of every unstable boom when people latch on to good news and convince themselves that risk is fading, but that is precisely when the worst mistakes are made". Compared to 2007-08, says Ambrose Evans-Pritchard in the Telegraph, "this time central banks are holding a particularly ferocious tiger by the tail", as global debt levels have surged by more than 50% of GDP since the financial crisis.

M—Medical Clinic

The clinic would be community owned and rented to doctors who would use it on a part-time basis. The full-time staff could be a registered nurse and an assistant. The nurse will live in the community if possible. She/he would be connected by the internet and video to a nearby doctor's office and a hospital. One office in the clinic could also be available to other doctors (eye, chiropractor, acupuncturist, dental, etc.) by established appointment times. The doctors associated with the clinic will have their own offices nearby the community, and they would also refer patients to other doctors when necessary. This would be like a doctor having house calls. People in the community could call in for appointments to see a doctor within the registered times they are scheduled to be there. Preventive medicine could be emphasized by all the doctors and nurses and the nurse, when not on appointment, will present preventive medicine programs at the community building or in individual homes. The nurse and staff will be paid by the community nonprofit or community insurance. Special programs on nutrition will be offered to all community members by staff personnel.

IT—Technology (or Innovative) Study Center

The study center will have the latest technology for internet capability. It will be available for all community members as needed or by appointment and owned by the community nonprofit. This could reduce the computer needs of the students or community members. The system could be tied to various university systems so that specific data can go back and forth. Research at the PDP, especially in agriculture, will be available to universities in return for permission to use or rent specialized equipment that would be too expensive for the community to own. The research within the community will be independent or with a community-approved university. Most aspects of construction, energy, and agriculture will be constantly tested by community members in terms of the harm/benefit analysis. This information would be available to the public on a basis similar to *Good Housekeeping* or Consumer Reports for a fee. The study center would be open to the community. Other uses and data is available in other reports by George Hunt. The main purpose would be to show students how to evaluate the feasibility of present and future technologies. The IT building would also have a computer program that could be used by all community members to record what items within each household are for sale or needed. It would also note what items are available for bartering, and it could include general community news similar to the "Neighborhood Newsletter" (http://www.neighborhoodnewsletter.org/). The proposed innovative study center will be located in a triplex only.

A-R—Administration and Research Library

When necessary, the community will move its administration building from the model home area to this location. A research library will also be built adjacent to the administration building. It will contain reference books for all of the classes as well as the latest economic news. Community members can suggest what books to include.

P—Parking

Parking areas will be used for community rental cars, with limited spaces for students and visitors. One side of the street will also be used for parking on farmers market days. The material used could be sustainable if it is available and not out of the budget. If one of the streets becomes a green space instead of a street, then the parking area would become a large greenhouse, using vertical hydroponics and soil.

TCA and TCC—Agriculture and Construction Class Buildings

They will include state-of-the-art IT, videos, and classrooms using some of the teaching techniques as discussed in *EarthEd* (SC27).[7]

GH—Agricultural Greenhouses

The greenhouses will be used for crop production and research. One of the greenhouses will be for hydroponics to experiment with soils and hydroponics used together, and three will be for planting research in different soil mediums. One greenhouse will be used for controlled research using different lighting like the type used in the Netherlands, and different shading cloths and fabric could be tested to see what effects they have on plant growth and temperature control. Organic microbe solutions would be used in the irrigation systems to determine if it would be beneficial to increase production.

SM—Equipment Storage and Maintenance Buildings

One of the storage/maintenance buildings will be used for landscaping, and one will be for tools and equipment for sharing purposes. Some of the unit A buildings in a triplex could also be used for storage purposes. An extensive sharing and bartering system would be utilized for all types of equipment and appliances. In addition, specially designed storage units could also be constructed along the back property lines of the lots. A cold storage area for fruits and vegetables could be in one of the triplexes. The product Fresh Paper will also be used for experimental purposes.

FM—Farmers Market and Flea Market Tables and Cover

The farmers market and flea market days will be scheduled by the community as needed. The flea market will be used for swapping, and only local currency will be used for transactions. When not in use for these functions, the space may be used for community personnel and outside community training sessions. The market will also sell value-added canned goods, community crafts, and ethnic clothing. Native landscape plants will also be for sale at all times.

RF—Agricultural and Regenerative or Restoration Crops for Research

This area will be used for growing perennials, cover crops, native plants, and some grains. Especially important will be evaluations of using edible perennials for a food source and the length of time it takes to provide friable soils rich in organic material, fungi, and microorganism communities. Crop rotation will also be practiced to determine the best crops to use. Small native fruit and nut trees may also be used. This area should increase the number of beneficial insects by having beehives on the property. Restoration Agriculture (AL7),[8] Rooted in the Land (E28),[9] and other books on the reference list will be available on-site.

AG—In-Ground Agricultural Research (2.5 acres)

The purpose of this area would be to grow crops using methods as practiced in The Lean Farm (AL3).[10] All growing practices will be recorded and evaluated. A section of the area will also be used for growing plants using heirloom and organic seeds. Special watering needs could be tested as well. The fruits and vegetables produced will be sold at the farmers market and in surrounding areas. The design of this area will correspond to the teaching curriculum that will be used. This will change from year to year to emphasize the use of crop rotations, companion plants, diversity plantings, different methods of water, and other research needs. Records will be kept from year to year for comparison purposes. Other land areas outside of the site can also be utilized if they are available.

CB—Community Building and CP—Community Park

There will be a small community building and swimming pool located in the project. It would be used for entertaining, leisure activities, and special functions for visitors and staff, and community members can reserve it for special functions. This building will be built after input from community members in order for it to meet their needs. It will also have a small kitchen to serve lunches or snacks. The park will be designed by the community members when funds are available and 50 percent of the units are occupied. Lawn and perimeter trees could be planted initially, with any adjustments made at a later date. Maintenance and ownership would be by the community nonprofit. Another option would be to purchase nearby land with a forest or lake for nature walks or sports.

Housing and Land Use—Option 2

The following uses are for option 2. (Possible location in impoverished area.)

D—Duplex (eight buildings—sixteen units)

The duplex units can be selected from a number of available designs. The duplex units are designed so they can be converted into single-family units if the family wants to expand. Uses other than housing would not be allowed within the duplexes. Two parking spaces minimum (in US) would be on each property, or what is allowed by a zoning ordinance. Some of the duplex units will be allocated for guests to be used for overnight stays. The duplex lots are larger lots than those designed for the triplex units and will be able to contain more guests per unit. Consequently, they can be purchased as a duplex, and both units would be under one or two ownerships. If under one ownership, one of the units would be for the owner, and the other one could be rented out, used for overnight guests, or used by a family member. The owner could at a later date convert the duplex into a single-family unit. Another option would be for the owner to sell one or both units. There will be several duplex designs offered where they can be used on one or two lots.

T1—Triplex (thirty-two buildings—ninety-six units maximum)

These triplex units will be designed for housing uses and overnight guest accommodations or a combination of the two. However, none of the units can be used for other uses, and they all have to be for residential use or guests. If one of the owners in the triplex wants to use one of the units for their office for professional use, this can be done by applying for a special permit from the homeowners association (or nonprofit). The size of the units in the triplex can be changed from what is shown, and this can provide more uses and design options. These units would also be easily converted into a duplex or single-family use. The purpose of the project and its location would determine the initial land use, and it can be used for medium to upscale living or for the homeless, elderly, veterans, and so on. A combination of tenants would be optional. Also part of the project would be for profit and nonprofit uses.

T2—Triplex (eight buildings—twenty-four units maximum)

These triplex units can have one unit per triplex for other uses. In the conversion of one of the units for other uses, the bathroom will remain in place so that the unit could be converted back to residential use. These units are located adjacent to an interior drive and parking, so other uses would be applicable in these triplexes. There are many different arrangements for the other uses that could be applicable. Again, the goals and objectives of the project would determine these uses. The community members would review monthly the existing uses allowed in the PDP so that all uses comply with the special permit or community regulations. This aspect of governance will be determined during the planning stages.

T3—Triplex (sixteen buildings—housing optional)

All units will have uses other than housing. If there isn't a market for these uses, some of the units can be used for housing or overnight guests. These units are located adjacent to retail units. An owner could live in one unit in a triplex and have the other units for retail purposes. Two units could be for a swimming pool and recreation area if one is not located in the community building.

SH—Student and Medical Housing (four buildings—twenty-four to forty students—housing design 1)

Student housing is for students from areas outside of the community. Students living within the community in triplex and duplex units would also be eligible for any of the training and classes. Special training classes can also be held in the managers' unit within the student housing building. These classes could be in subjects other than agriculture and construction, with special courses in business management, social marketing, and computer use. The courses that could be offered are endless but should be according to what is relative to the community and applicable for future needs of the students. Special workshops could also be available for overnight guests. The project would appeal to clubs and small organizations because of the types of facilities there. The research at the ITG would be filmed and used for courses and collaboration with universities. After a number of years, online courses could be offered worldwide. There would also be published literature about the research, with its adaption for organic gardening worldwide. Medical housing would be for people needing treatments for depression and anxiety.

S-H—Staff or Homeless (four buildings—twenty-four persons—housing design 1)

Since the building selected is for several different uses, it can be adapted to fit existing market needs. The homeless could be selected for inclusion in the training programs, with homeless veterans having the highest priority. Some of the homeless could work in landscaping, construction, or trades where they have experience. They could also work on-site to pay for training fees. This would be a working program and not just a shelter so that they then would have a trade and be able to find work anywhere. If applicable, people who are mentally ill would be in one building under specialized care, and in certain instances, special resources would be utilized to help drug addicts until their problems are evaluated by specialists.

SH-E—Student Housing or Elderly (four buildings—twenty-four persons—housing design 1)

The elderly could include persons that need housing and may include people living in the general area of the project. They could come from dilapidated homes or have other types of needs. Students in hospitality training would be able to obtain working knowledge in food preparation, nutrition, management, housekeeping, and so on for the elderly. This could be part of the instruction program. The housing units for the elderly would also entail student teaching in care and management. It would also expand their knowledge on building and managing other units of this type, and the elderly units could also use students to care for them as part of a teaching program. This could be a part of a curriculum program so that students understand the needs of the elderly and in turn allow the elderly to participate in some of the classes being offered. This will strengthen the sharing program and allow people to feel good about themselves.

R—Retail Uses

The retail use in this location would be similar to a convenience store but would be operated by the homeowners association in order to have lower prices for community members. Each community member would have a membership card and be eligible for discounts from various stores in the community. Bartering and collaborative programs would also be available. Arrangements would be made with big-box stores for special goods at discounts. The discount stores then be able to use the sales of goods process as a charity donation, and there would be at least one consignment store for bartering of goods within the community. This store could be privately owned or operated by the community nonprofit.

R2—Mixed Auto Uses

This location would be for a small auto mechanic repair facility, with space for hand-washing cars and an optional gasoline pump. It is the only place to wash cars in the project (environmental controls). Very few cars will be needed because bicycle use and community rental cars would be emphasized. This could also be used for training purposes in basic auto repair.

B—Community Branch Bank and Government Offices

The community bank would handle special bartering programs, the community credit union, and special community loans. Community money programs would be started also. The branch bank would be affiliated with a conventional bank and handle regular banking activities. The government offices would be for people to get help without having to leave the community. Government offices could also be located in triplexes if more are needed in the community. See option 1 for additional uses for the bank.

M—Medical Clinic

The functions offered by the medical clinic would have to be determined by the needs of the community and general area. Special nurses would be available for the elderly, homeless, and people with special needs. A special program of study will emphasize ways of encouraging preventive medicine through sustainable practices. Classes will show how all the activities in the community are sustainable and be a pathway for better health. This begins with understanding the soil web and regenerative practices. Again, see option 1 to include other uses.

IT—IT and Innovative Study Center

This study center is a component of the overall training program. It will also be used for agricultural and other research. Special classes will be held to develop innovative thinking in agriculture, construction, social studies, and marketing. Prizes will be awarded for innovative ideas that could be used within the community. It will be in a separate building devoted to this use. It could be in one of the triplex units until the community is fully developed. See option 1 for additional information.

A-R—Administration Facilities and Library

Administrative offices will be located on this site. It will also include offices for the homeowners association if applicable. A research library will provide opportunities for specialized studies and popular publications. The library will be available for anyone living in the community or those who are in training, and people will be taught how to use the internet to get information on selected subjects. The library will be designed after community members have given input regarding what they need.

P—Parking

Parking will be available for visitors to the flea market or farmers market as well as other community activities. Parking will also be available for student housing. Each triplex or duplex will also have its own parking spaces, and parking in the street is optional. The paving in each of the four major parking areas will be different to determine the value and sustainability of each type. Community car rentals will operate from the parking areas and be a sharing program under the jurisdiction of the community nonprofit. Some of the community cars will be donations from the public and will not be new.

TCA—Training Center—Agriculture

This is a training center for regenerative farming and organic agriculture. It will be open to anyone, but community members will have the highest priority. A separate report could be available to show fees and educational programs that are available. There will also be a small kitchen and dining area in each of the training buildings, and these rooms could also be used for meetings and other gathering purposes. Videos will be taken of all training sessions to be used internally and for YouTube productions. Local chefs will be invited to participate in classes to work with students so that they can learn about marketing and nutrition.

C—Workshops—Meeting /Entertaining Building

This building will have a separate kitchen, administrative office, and restrooms. It will be used for workshops, meetings, and other uses. It will be available for anyone in the area. A separate staff will be hired to coordinate activities. See option 1 for additional uses.

GH—Greenhouses (four total)

There will be four greenhouses in the project, and they will be used for training, research, and production. The types and sizes will be determined, but one of the greenhouses will be used for demonstrating new agricultural practices, with a small section to demonstrate vertical farming techniques. Another will be used for aquaculture and sustainable practices, such as practiced on Neversink Farm in the Catskills (https://www.youtube.com/channel/UCp6Ia4JPJTrEJbhQ31EBRmg). The others will be used for agricultural research and propagation. They will produce vegetables, fruit, herbs, medicinal plants, ornamentals, cover crops, and so on. The farmers market on-site will be one of the ways available for marketing, as well as establishing a subscribers' program. Stores, restaurants, and other retail outlets will also be used for marketing, and the agricultural area will be totally organic, along with demonstrations of developing regenerative soils. Another purpose could be to show how these organic techniques can produce healthier foods with higher food densities. Nutrition tests could be a research component. If this is part of the program, some of these tests will be done on-site, and some will be sent off to professional labs. See option 1 for other ideas.

SM—Storage and Maintenance Buildings (four total)

The storage and maintenance buildings will be used for agriculture, construction, and maintenance equipment. Other storage and maintenance buildings may be constructed on individual duplex and triplex lots.

FM—Farmers Market or Flea Market (two total)

Both of these will be in the areas shown. The flea market may also be used for community garage sales, bartering, consignment purposes, and other community functions. Produce grown on-site and in other organic farms could be included in the farmers market. Both areas could be used when there are special occasions. During certain days of the week, the farmers market will have special training sessions for the public in permaculture, organic gardening, and research. There are information forums and websites that provide help for firms wanting to start a farmers market.

RF—Regenerative Farming Production and Research

Special reports are available by George R. Hunt Associates / Natural Regenerative Technologies to show the intent and purposes of using regenerative farming and landscape methods for food production and developing better soil structures. This will also be used for training, research, and production, and the area allocated for this is approximately two acres. This could be a demonstration area to show how bio-stimulants, soil amendments, and other organic products can be used to increase growth and production in plants (agriculture and landscape). It may also show beneficial insects, cover crops, and special soil amendments used to improve the soils to create a balance of fungi, microorganisms, and macroorganisms.

AG—Agriculture Research and Production

This would be a demonstration area for agricultural research and production using many organic methods. Conventional synthetic fertilizers, pesticides, herbicides, and genetically modified plants will not be used. It will show how organic and other products can be used to increase production using natural systems. The IT center will provide access to universities, community colleges, and other experts. A special project will be initiated to help create gardens on school sites. Rain gardens, rainwater storage facilities, and a small demonstration area using plants to clean wastes may also be on the site. Field trips will also be included in the training programs. See option 1 for additional information.

CB—Community and Recreation Building

A community building and swimming pool will be located in this area, or it can be assigned another use if needed. The building will also be used for community meetings. The size of the area is 150 by 200 feet. Only community residents, students, and members can use this facility. It can also be reserved for special functions.

CP—Overnight Guest Recreation Facilities or Community Park

This will be a small playground and recreation area. It could include a small recreation building, spa, and swimming pool to be used by the guests staying overnight. All the activities would be a fantastic market generator for bringing guests/visitors to the project.

Walkways

The brown strips on the plan represent eight-foot-wide walks. There will be benches, lighting, and fitness areas adjacent to some of them.

Other Uses—Triplexes

The following other uses can be used in the T2 and T3 triplex sites. Fifty-four units are available.

- barber or beauty shop
- guest units—rental
- daycare
- consignment store
- bartering
- approved retail uses
- offices and professional use
- landscape maintenance
- artists and crafts
- dry cleaning (sales only)
- specialized training centers
- rental services
- collaborative enterprises
- other uses by special permit from the homeowners association
- fitness center

Other Uses on Selected Triplex Lots

Two or three of the triplex lots will be left vacant to be used for other purposes if needed. One example is shown on page 8 in the appendix. It is a display garden featuring native plants, a water feature, vegetable-growing areas, greenhouse/potting work area, and a cabana. It will showcase sustainable practices using a garden setting. It could also be for public workshops and special community functions as well as a demonstration area for elementary, middle, and high school students. This would be especially valuable to show the public the special values of using native plants in their yards. These facilities could be profit centers for individuals living in the community as well as for the community itself. Part of training programs for young adults and students could also be a source of programs for overnight guests that reflect the culture of the area. Artists could teach workshops, sell their arts or crafts, and provide cooking techniques and demonstrations.

Additional Land Uses

Additional land would make the community more sustainable and add beauty to the project. The areas for these added facilities would have to be determined when a location for the project has been selected. Weather, soil types, views, locations near the site, and availability of existing utilities are just some of the factors to be considered. They could also be used for an expansion of the community project at a later date. Determinations regarding needed extra land will be made during the feasibility process.

Water

A water well could be drilled to provide water for the project. Plants grow better using water from an untreated source. It would also include a purifying system, and this could provide water to the community if other municipal water was not available. If the water was suitable for plants, there would be no need for purification since this type of water would be better for the plants and microorganisms. This could be provided by the community or a private contractor. An option could be to tie into a lake or a stream. In the buildings, the gray water would be separated from the sewage lines, and the cleaners and soap used would have to be sustainable. Also, water-saving fixtures would be used. Some of the buildings could have at least one barrel for rainwater collection. The material for the pipes will also be evaluated. Other options will be reviewed during the planning process to see if the project could supply its own water by methods not mentioned above.

Sewage System

Septic tanks could be used if the project is not located near an existing municipal system. There are other types of systems that are available, and engineers would be hired to determine the best options. Waste and gray water will be separated regardless of what types of sewage systems are used A low-pressure sewage system may be an alternative to using a conventional gravity system if there is a connection to a sewage treatment plant or lift station. Other alternatives may be available, and this would be determined by the location and topography of the site and the absorption rate of the soil. There could be different systems, and this would allow a study of each of the systems as to efficiency, original costs, maintenance costs, and so on. An alternate display project on one residence would be using plants to purify the water. This could be expanded if people wanted to use this system.

Stormwater

Rain gardens could be used throughout the project to reduce stormwater runoff and could be located within the individual yards or along a curb. Native plants, cobblestones, and boulders can be used within the rain gardens. Organic methods of landscaping the soil have better water-holding capacity, so there is less runoff.

The stormwater can be collected and go into a culvert or be collected in a lake on an adjacent property. The lake would be kept clean using organic methods. This water could be used for residential irrigation systems and watering the agricultural crops. The water would not have chlorine or fluoride in it, which would make the plants grow better because these chemicals are toxic to microorganisms in the soil. In conjunction with the rain gardens, there would be minimum lawn areas used whenever possible. Native plants and nitrogen-fixing ground covers could be an option instead of lawns. The streets could be constructed using permeable pavement to further reduce runoff. The runoff from these facilities would go into a sewage system or a separate septic area. Several different methods of stormwater management may be utilized in the project, including special plant and rock areas to see what would be beneficial from a harm/benefit and life cycle analysis. These types of studies are necessary to determine what would be best to use from a sustainability standpoint. This is rarely done, and it would provide guidelines for the future.

Energy

There would be an emphasis on using wind and solar energy to provide electrical energy. This could be solar or wind units on individual buildings or a bank of solar panels on an adjacent property. To be more self-sufficient, the community could be all electric. Gas could be used if gas lines are nearby. Separate gas storage tanks could be used on some properties to provide gas instead of hooking into an underground gas line. Studies would be done to see what was most cost-effective, both monetarily and ecologically. There will also be a community car/truck rental facility adjacent to the site that will allow people to rent used cars for trips outside of the project. In most instances, this would be a less expensive solution than owning a car or truck. Electrical charging units and gas tanks would be available at this location. The use or study of hydrogen would be another alternative.

Some of the homes would have vegetative roofs (crops or other plants), and this would reduce energy costs and provide food. In this instance, some of the roofs would be flat. Trellis (wire) or plants on the south and west sides of a house could further reduce costs because it would reduce heat from building up on the wall surfaces. Large trees could provide the opportunity to make use of passive energy designs, and the trees would be located so as not to shade solar units or roof vegetation, as they require full sunlight. Engineers would be consulted to determine what sustainable options are available. Trees would be located on any severe slopes to prevent runoff. All the information discussed during the planning stage will be documented by text and video to be used in future projects and to show community members details about how decisions were made.

Solid Waste Disposal

A community contract would be made with a private waste firm to haul off solid waste. This is a policy that many small cities and towns are using now. On an adjacent property, there could be a small mulching operation where small limbs and branches (under two inches in size) would be collected along with food scraps and leaves. The branches would be ground up and used for mulch along with the leaves and food scraps for mulch and compost. This mulch will be used by the community, and this may entail a separate pickup by the community. The mulching site will be located within the additional growing area located outside of the community or on a farm that is a co-op member. Kitchen scraps and other organic waste could be kept and separated to be used by farmers in the cooperative or in a mulching operation.

Additional Park and Recreation Areas

Additional park and recreational areas may be needed, especially if an area is available with trees or a small lake or stream, and this could include basketball, softball, soccer, or baseball fields. This additional area could include a building to teach ecological, nutritional, and environmental studies, which would expand the teaching curriculum to make the community a unique experience and a very important facility for the future. The teaching could be coordinated with high schools, colleges, and universities teaching these subjects. The students could be able to get university credits if they wanted to go to a college. This would also apply to a community college. The PDP would have to coordinate with the universities or colleges to determine what courses would be acceptable. It could be approved for federal funding, or the students could get paid for community work (landscaping, etc.) on-site. Trips to a natural site on a farm, park, or a reserve could be included in the training for the pilot demonstration project. Cooperative farms aligned with the community nonprofit could offer opportunities to develop agricultural tourism, and since recreation appeals to everyone, there would be an effort to incorporate inner-city youth in various programs. This could lead to having community gardens in the elementary, junior, and high schools.

Summary of Land Uses

This project is only thirty acres in size, but it could be one of the most unique projects of its type. It includes training for students and adults and a means of teaching people visiting the community how to recognize nature's natural systems as a means of changing our lifestyle to be more sustainable. Its impact is generated by collaboration and cooperation, to show people how they can help each other to enjoy life and preserve our natural systems. This program will help people become successful by helping others as well as helping themselves. Today, in many housing developments, we hardly know our neighbors, and in many cases, this becomes an opportunity for crime. This project is offering its own venture capital for everyone associated with it, especially for members living in the community. In organic landscaping, it is said that we have to teach people how to garden naturally "one yard at a time."

Much of our mono-cropping, which uses dangerous herbicides and synthetic, toxic fertilizers, has lowered the food density in many of our foods. This affects our wildlife and animals as well.

An example is the added nutrition found in chickens and cattle that are grass fed instead of fed on just grain and antibiotics. The fast fix of food processing has increased health problems, costing the United States billions of dollars. The additional data in *Transition to Agro-ecology* (AL13)[11] shows how just a few companies provide many of the processed foods that we eat. They presently control our eating habits. How many times do most people sit down to a pleasurable long meal without the intrusion of TV or social media? Hopefully, a project as shown here can allow people to have a healthier lifestyle and learn how to do it themselves. Studying the relationship between the gut microbiome and the soil biome will also enable people to understand how critical this relationship is. People should become more aware of the nutrition value of what they are eating and drinking. Read the books *The Dirt Cure* (AL20),[12] *Food Forensics* (AL42),[13] and *Real Food-Fake Food* (AL60).[14]

The PDP also becomes a demonstration of how to "work" yourself out of poverty and have a healthier lifestyle by starting with good nutrition. It begins by allowing students, community members, and guests to feel better about themselves. This is by learning how business practices and sustainable natural systems can function together. Our future has to start now on a new path of sustainability and survival.

The method of housing construction will have to be determined because there are many choices, such as wood frame construction with brick, stucco, or wood siding, metal frame construction, concrete block, log houses, and various specialized systems. Use of natural products, such as straw bale, adobe, rammed earth, and burlap bags filled with a gravel/concrete mix, should be considered.

Several different systems should be used to be evaluated for future use. Low-cost energy systems will be designed into the homes. These will be analyzed to see which systems have the most cost-effective benefit analysis. The proposed cost of the project will be determined using several different options. The project will be analyzed to show how it could be adapted for a nonprofit, a for-profit, and a combination of both. The first approach would be to do a for-profit analysis based on just the sale of the buildings. A separate study will determine how to establish the agricultural training programs. This hopefully would include future community members. The profit from the rental of the units for overnight stays will be a separate study. This could be designed as a profit program for the developer or individual homeowners. All of the homes should be sustainable. When selling the homes, the buyer should be made aware of how sustainable features in each home are long-term benefits. Some homes will be constructed without sustainable features so information (maintenance, durability, cost benefits, etc.) can be evaluated.

The location of the project and its surrounding uses are factors to be considered in determining its main function. It could be adjacent to a resort, in a town setting, or in a major urban area. This again shows how it can serve many different functions. The actual locations will determine different cost estimates. A rural or urban area in Mississippi would have different costs than many areas in California. If the project was located near a builder that specializes in manufacturing low-income homes, the housing costs would be lower.

Self-help housing in whole or in part is another option. Since many of the proposed homes are similar, the community would have options as to what they pay to paint the rooms. Prospective buyers would have the option to paint some or all of the rooms themselves (prior to or just after the sale) to save money. Special self-help alternatives would be available for people living in low-income areas. Building a new home is an opportunity to meet your exact design and usability requirements. But from-scratch construction can be a daunting task, especially when it comes to price. This in-depth look at the prices associated with home building will help people make the right budgetary decisions. Once a site is selected, architectural plans will be complete and bids obtained prior to proceeding further.

The following changes or development options could be incorporated into option 1 or 2. The main changes could be to incorporate some hospitality options by having people use part of a triplex for visitor overnight accommodations, similar to Airbnb. Unit A in a triplex would be ideal for this use. The physical facilities would be basically the same. This would allow people to make extra money. The location for the project might be upscaled in order to accommodate the projected market for this type of use. The uniqueness of the project would be a viable market attraction and could provide additional sources of income. This would be determined by several market factors and the people being served. Lower or medium-income persons/families could be in the project, and the guests could volunteer to provide assistance or visit them to understand local culture and enjoy local foods. In fact, this type of project could provide development strategies for many conventional projects in terms of introducing some of the design concepts for their use. Guests could be workshop speakers, visiting students, educators, and so on.

Some options are as follows:

- The overall concept for the PDP is to incorporate overnight accommodations within some of the housing duplex and triplex units. These accommodations would be for persons or families who are staying there for a short time and want to stay in this type of unique facility. An option would be to have a host family provide meals, cleaning, and so on as a means of increasing their income. In foreign countries, they would also include storytelling and other cultural exchanges.

- The project could also include several types of workshops and training sessions for students studying agriculture, organic landscaping, sustainability, and other topics. One of the main topics would be community development and cultural studies. Craft, cooking, photography, and other topics could be taught as applicable for the market. Classes could be organized so that guests could sign up for one-day sessions, and it would also provide an opportunity for the students to learn about what is happing in other areas.

- Guests could be offered special rates if they are able to teach workshops. Organizations could arrange meetings there for small conventions, and building TCC could be used for this purpose.

- Agricultural research is one of the main components of the project, so many guests may want to come to the project to provide their expertise or learn from what is being done. The Small Business Administration may be interested in the project through their SCORE mentoring program.

- Market research would determine the uses for all of the buildings and the best mix of uses between work, retail, housing, and guest units. The project would offer an incentive for people to come there due to the varied facilities that are available for use, learning, and teaching.

- The location would be important in determining what mixed uses would be available. The entire project as shown encompasses thirty acres. Additional space could be added for lakes, agriculture, student housing, and recreation.

- If a company like Airbnb developed the project, it could be used as a tax deduction, due to it being used mainly to help people improve themselves through training and the provision of affordable housing. The project is designed to be used for multiple purposes throughout a long period, so its costs would be easily recoverable. Once the project got started, it could have its own program like Airbnb.

- The student housing, housing for the elderly, and homeless housing could be used for overnight guests when the units are vacant.

- A few of the units or restaurants could host local meetups. These meetups include members from many groups and specialized activities. It would be an important way for people to obtain business or social referrals as well as acquainting themselves with other people in the project.

- Depending where the project is located, they will have rental cars or busses available for guests. Busses could also be used to bring people to the project from hotels or airports.

- The conversion of the units from triplex, to duplex, to single family will allow for a range of guests (number) to stay in the units in order for families to stay together. Special units will also allow for pets. Some of the units will also be designed for the handicapped.

- The enclosed yards could have vegetable gardens, waterfalls, spas, and special landscape features. The landscaping will be maintained using organic methods and materials. Smoking will not be allowed inside of public buildings.

- A new course is being developed at the College of Design at North Carolina State University called Universal by Design. This multidisciplinary course will facilitate understanding of universal handicap and other design concepts and their application in architecture, landscape architecture, graphic design, industrial design, and art and design for the benefit of all individuals. The course will teach the principles and strategies for creating universal outcomes, the limitations of design for accessibility, and the differences between accessible and universal design in all design disciplines. The instructors will explore the international context and design history of universal design. It will demonstrate knowledge of the beneficiary groups of universal design, the social context for universal design, and the designer's responsibility in this regard. Students will be aware of the impact of the environment on human function and will understand the design implications when meeting the needs of people with different abilities and the natural range of human performance that can include variances in sight, hearing, movement, and cognitive processes. When more information is available, the project will design two or three units to display how it could be designed to help the handicapped. A group of handicapped persons will be involved in the evaluation of the design studies. This should be helpful for veterans with disabilities. At least one home will be used as a demonstration unit.

- Other innovative ideas should be incorporated into the project to reflect different opinions. A team of consultants will be utilized to make this happen.

In summary, the following activities would have to occur for the project (PDP) to proceed:

1. Conversations with several potential funders or a combination of funders to review concepts and goals for the project. A nonprofit should be formed prior to this in order to be qualified for grants or partial funding from governments, foundations, private firms or individuals, or nongovernment agencies (NGOs).

2. Funding then would be sought to prepare economic and market feasibility studies for one or more prospective sites. Once a site has been selected, an environmental impact statement will determine if the site meets the standards for a sustainable community. Prior to or during these studies, a team of experts should be selected so the project can proceed to the next steps of design and funding. This would include at least one general contractor or developer, an architect, a landscape architect, a civil engineer (structural engineer if needed), and an agroecologist. Other consultants could be brought in if necessary to establish the research and educational programs. Selected people living in the area or city could be on an ad hoc committee to offer suggestions as to what they feel is needed. This could include farmers that would be interested in establishing a cooperative. Local government planning representatives should be involved from the start.

3. Once the studies are completed, funding will be sought for building the model homes and necessary infrastructure. This would also financing for administration, faculty, and marketing. Most of the sales should occur during the predevelopment stage of the project. People selected to live in the project would have to follow community guidelines for sharing and individual business selections. The diversity within the project is a must in order to make it successful.

4. Since this project is unique, it will have to be approved by the local government under a special permit program. The project will continually change according to the needs of the people, so there should be leeway in zoning. This will be a unique experience for everyone involved.

5. It is hoped that there will be enough money made during its operation by the nonprofit that it can fund its operation and begin to fund a reserve account to establish other communities. During the preparation of the initial studies, this future organizational program will be part of the study. Additional information will also be used to show why this type of community is needed to help our society survive during the coming years. One of the main considerations at the beginning will be how we use energy most

effectively and efficiently. How we do this and adapt accordingly is the biggest question. Finding alternatives to continually using natural resources is at the top of the list.

6. Unless there is a change in the government, most or all of the money obtained would not be federal money.

7. During the final design of the plans, several possible owners will be invited to make comments. Many low-income people have needs that may be different from those usually considered.

8. The main consideration is to keep changing as needed and to be innovative to meet changing conditions.

Another reason this type of community could be a beacon for the future is the continual exponential growth of artificial intelligence (AI) and deep learning. Amazing developments in many different fields will occur using these technologies. Some of these developments will be amazing, and others will be disruptive to the extent that many jobs will be lost. The lower-paying occupations will be the most affected and could cause considerable unrest. Ever-increasing costs of food and essential products, lack of housing, both rental and home ownership, governmental stupidity, and need for additional education will add to the problems. The advantages offered by the pilot demonstration project and others like it may be one of the solutions available for many people.

Site Analysis

Again, analysis of any proposed site will determine what the land-use plan will be, and it could be different from what is proposed in this book. The proposed market studies will be another important component for the final design. The design could also reflect the importance of permaculture, site exposure, drainage, types of soils, transportation patterns, contour configurations, and so on. The diverse needs and ages of people who will be living in the community may also affect its design. The design approach shown in this book is just one optional concept, and uses for lots in the community could change according to needs.

Project Information and Direction

As noted earlier, the main purpose of this book is to offer a way that we can promote the ideals of saving our natural resources and realize what potential pitfalls are awaiting us. A Pew survey taken in October 2017 (http://www.people-press.org/2017/10/05/7-global-warming-and-environment) showed opinions of the American people concerning global warming, environmental regulation, and personal environmentalism. Some of the results are noted below. This is important because it shows what attitudes are prevalent toward environmentalism and how soon some people would be willing to change some of their habits to reduce climate change and other environmental problems.

> An increasing share of Americans – Republicans and Democrats alike – say there is solid evidence that the Earth's average temperature has been getting warmer. But attitudes about global warming and the value of stricter environmental laws remain deeply divided along partisan lines. In fact, the partisan divide about whether stricter environmental laws are worth the cost, or hurt the economy, is now about as wide as the differences over global warming. This marks a major shift from a decade ago, when majorities in both parties said stricter environmental laws were worth the cost.

The New Localism by Katz and Nowak of the Bookings Institute (UP37)[15] shows how a new localism could grow in our cities. It is a book about reimagining power for urban populism. Due to the unique aspect of the pilot demonstration project, it is proposed to have the sales of the project based on a model home concept type of development for pre-sales. A diagram showing one example of a model home sales area is shown on page 13 in the appendix. The project would have options to be a for-profit enterprise, a nonprofit enterprise, or a combination. How each is structured will have to be determined by the funding group. Consequently, the normal feasibility study will have to be adjusted to accommodate one of the following scenarios.

For-Profit: The entire project would be for-profit, with the profit coming from the sale of the buildings and the agricultural training facility. The owners of the buildings would determine how they want to own or rent the spaces. For example, the owner of a triplex could rent out one of the units and perhaps have a business within one of the other triplexes. They could buy the unit for the business or rent it from someone else who bought a triplex to be used just for business purposes. Each owner owning different units would also have the option of renting out units for overnight stays through an organization like Airbnb or another hospitality group established by the nonprofit. Since this is a pilot demonstration project, it could be replicated in several different cities or towns.

Nonprofit: The project could also be a nonprofit enterprise and funded by government agencies, foundations, other nonprofits, or a nonprofit established by a corporation. If this is done, the cost of the project could be tax deductible for the nonprofit corporation. It could also be funded by several of the above entities together, and the expertise from the different organizations or financial entities could benefit the project. If it was a nonprofit, it would cater to more people in the lower-income groups, the elderly, veterans, or the homeless. However, the strength of the development would be in its diversity. People would be able to help each other by collaboration and supporting all the local business enterprises on-site. The project would also encourage associations with people and businesses from the surrounding area.

Combination—For-Profit/Nonprofit: This could combine the advantages of being a for-profit and nonprofit enterprise. Which part of the development would be allocated to each would be determined. It could appeal to a food chain or a hospitality group due to the agricultural production using all organic techniques. The project would also emphasize organic landscape maintenance. All of the activities occurring on-site would provide valuable employment over a long period. Since the work is self-sustaining, it is not subject to as many economic disturbances or cycles. The questions to be answered are when and where to get started in developing the PDP. First it has to be determined what types of governance will be selected and then what options are available for financing. Part of the answer will be determined by its location. If it is in a municipality, then it should be submitted as a special permit for a designated use. The project would not be approved under most zoning ordinances without special conditions being applied and approved.

The facilities and housing being multifunctional could further its protection against recessions. For example, the design of the student housing would allow it to be converted to other uses (elderly housing, single-room rentals, overnight guests, homeless, etc.). Having some of the units or accommodations designated for the homeless would give them not only a place to stay but also a place to work and learn new technologies. It also could be used for corporate employee housing for low-wage workers. This way, they could go to work without traveling long distances and learn another trade at the same time through night classes.

The plan for the PDP would be generally determined by what conditions are projected for the future. From an economic standpoint, perhaps the best summation for the future is provided by Dr. Charles Hall in *Energy and the Wealth of Nations* (CE57).[16] Dr. Hall is an American systems ecologist and ESF Foundation distinguished professor at State University of New York in the College of Environmental Science and Forestry but will soon be retiring. Search for his website and to obtain additional information by using "Charles Hall Energy." His research in biophysical economics is extensive, and on his website, he discusses what he feels should be evaluated in economic approaches for the future. His work represents an excellent summary for what I am attempting to present in this book. An analysis of Dr. Hall's thinking concerning EROI (energy return on investment) can be found in an interview with Chris Martinson on March 6, 2018, titled "Dr. Charles Hall: The Laws of Nature: Trump Economics" (https://www.peakprosperity.com/podcast/113808/dr-charles-hall-laws-nature-trump-economics):

> An example of how energy is involved in a production of a bagel is described as follows: So, if, for example, you buy in New York City, a bagel for a dollar, what that has meant is that that bagel cannot possibly get there without the use of a considerable amount of energy. And that energy is, for example, energy is used in Louisiana to take natural gas and turn it into nitrogen fertilizer, and then it's put in a barge and barged up the Mississippi River to Nebraska, and then a tractor spreads in on a field, and then it plows up the field and plants wheat seeds and later comes along and kills the soil and maybe takes care of the weeds or whatever and certainly harvests it. And then more energy is used to take the harvested wheat and grind it up and turn it into flour. And then they put

it in a sack and put it on a railroad train and ship it to New York City. And there somebody boils a pot of water to cook the bagel—oh, and they use electricity to mix the batter, and then they put the bagel into a pot of boiling water to cook it. And there you have a bagel.

Many of the books in the list have convincing arguments against the theory that "new" technology will save us by conserving resources. A case in point is renewable solar energy. I received a letter from an associate in Japan, and he said that agricultural arable land areas in Japan have declined from 813,000 hectares in 1960 (1 hectare = 2.471 acres) to 450,000 hectares in 2015, of which 41,400 hectares are not even used. The amount of abandoned arable land areas is far greater than that due to the loss of farmers, aging, migration to the cities, and total loss of population as a whole. The numbers are much smaller than in the US, but the problem is bigger in Japan with 120 million people in an area smaller than California, and 73 percent of it is mountains broken into 6,852 islands. Total size of Japan is 37.78 million hectares = 145.93 square miles (1/27 of the US size). Because of the mountainous geography and the greed of power companies, there is a reduction of grid service available to the renewable electric powers. This causes a record number of mega solar farms to go bankrupt in Japan. Non-used solar panels are already causing the poisonous solar panel hazards, and this can become worse than nuclear power plants. This is all that is needed to go along with the Fukushima nuclear plant disaster. It's another example of what can happen when corporations and governments do not evaluate what will happen in the future and focus only on short-term solutions. There is need for a harm/benefit analysis for technology. A start would be establishing mechanisms in society that allow people to care for one another. It could be a society with a purpose rather than one characterized by depression and opioid overdoses. As a society, we have to begin to realize what the future will bring us with reductions in our natural resources. Reductions also include having resources that are too expensive to obtain. An example would be what may happen in the Middle East. Egypt, Syria, and some other countries will have water shortages, degrading soils, and a lack of job opportunities. This will create chaos along with continuing wars. Our present governments have short-term outlooks to set proper government policies. This could further cause problems in the future.

One of the books about our future is *Shrinking the Technosphere* by Dmitry Orlov. The following statement establishes a harm/benefit hierarchy that is used to evaluate any technology to determine its benefit to humankind.

> Technology, in and of itself, is neither good or bad, and is essential for survival and whether it helps us or harms us is a question of whether and how we use it. Our job is to pick and choose carefully, to embrace technologies that liberate and empower us and to look for ways to avoid or eliminate the ones that weaken us, make us dependent on outside interests and forces and can even result in our extinction as a species. (p. 116)[17] The new (re) used aspect is particularly important: if something already exists, then it doesn't need to be remanufactured and therefore causes less harm, because all manufacturing processes deplete nonrenewable natural resources and pollute the environment. (p 120)[18]. If an element or technology is particularly harmful, yet indispensable, consider how it is used rather than what it is in and of itself. For instance, is you are, for the time being stuck in a location where it is impossible to survive without a car, consider not the car itself but how it is being used. (124–125)[19]

In short, each new technology that influences our survival (and some others also) should have this analysis completed prior to being constructed and marketed. It could also be put on the label or in the production booklet. A case to consider is solar power. This is a major renewable technology being promoted throughout the world to reduce fossil fuel use. The benefit would also change if the project was in Texas (sunny) or Upstate New York (long stretches of cloudy weather). Obtaining the energy for the panels would still use up valuable natural resources, so the viable length of time that the panels would be feasible can be calculated in relationship to costs of its share of energy resources over a period of time. Also for consideration are the costs over a certain time of providing these resources because they will keep getting expensive due to being harder to extract from the earth. This gets into the timing of peak production of each resource. If the Trump administration keeps its present policies, the energy reserves will decrease exponentially. For example, shale oil production will not be feasible because of pollution and increasing costs of extraction.

A type of analysis that may be useful is a study of the life cycle of a product or technology. This determines how long a product will last and hopefully exposes any technologies that are built into the product by the manufacturer. This is presently being done in the cell phone market—for example, Apple with smartphones. How often has a car manufacturer used a cheaper car instead of one that would last longer? Gone are the old days when an average person could work on their car using inexpensive parts.

Transition into Postcapitalism

Several books have been written discussing what it would be like to live in a postcapitalist society. This is the ultimate goal, but I feel that society will have to go through a period of hurt before we can get there. I would place the ideas discussed in this book in a transition period between the present capitalist society and the beginning of postcapitalism. In the United States, we are too polarized and susceptible to the whims of technology and an elitist president for major changes to be made. There is a groundswell out there for a change, but we have to be more united in our beliefs for it to become a major movement.

> There is an article in the March/April issue of the *MIT Review* by Elizabeth Wolke titled "A Smarter Smart City":
>
> Described is a project that is underway in a 12 acre warehouse district in Toronto, Canada. Initial planning funding is being provided by a subsidiary of Alphabet—Sidewalk Labs. The neighborhood is called Quayside. The site is owned by Waterfront Toronto—a local development agency founded by Canada's federal, provincial, and municipal governments—and is expected to house 5,000 people. They will be using driverless cars. Sensing and monitoring public activity accurately and frequently will be the key as well as using smart technology. However, this monitoring program is coming under criticism due to privacy issues by its collecting personal data. It will require Sidewalk Labs to clarify this issue.

In contrast, the data to be collected by the pilot demonstration project will be just physical in nature (e.g., cost of utilities, type of construction, agricultural research, economic studies, etc.). Any social data collected will have to be approved by the people living in the community. If this social information is collected (with permission of the people involved) and sold, the profit of any publications would be given to the people who participated in the study.

In America, it will be difficult to determine how long the transition period will last or what it will look like, especially with the present government in office. Of all the books that I will be recommending *How Democracies Die*[20] (CE65) by Levitsky and Ziblatt is one of the most important books to start reading when discussing effects on democracies. Since it was published in 2018, it has information about Donald Trump and how he became president. It is a history of democracies and other forms of government from the time of the writing of the Constitution. Without knowing the history of democracy, we cannot make informed decisions relating to our government and what to expect in the future. The book discusses how Congress and the executive branch reached decisions using mutual toleration and institutional forbearance (patient self-control, restraint, and tolerance). These and other unwritten rules in the Constitution, such as using norms and methods of gatekeeping, were used to prevent or reduce polarization and inequities and led to compromises. It states in conclusion:

To save our democracy, Americans need to restore the basic norms that once protected it. But we must do more than that. We must extend those norms through the whole of society. We must make them truly inclusive. America's democratic norms, at their core, have always been sound. But for much of our history, they were accompanied-indeed, sustained-by radical exclusion. Now those norms must be made to work in an age of racial equality and unprecedented ethnic diversity. Few societies in history have managed to be both multiracial and genuinely democratic. That is our challenge. It is also our opportunity. If we meet it, America will truly be exceptional.[21]

No one knows how long this transition period will last or if we will ever get beyond that point. We can hope by establishing grass root communities and associations to force the powers in office to change so that we will have a fighting chance for survival. Being aware of what is happening politically and socially around us is a start in the right direction. In a transition period, cooperatives are an important part of any development. It is a way to give workers more authority, which is needed to reduce the growth of inequality in developed nations.

Transition periods can also have an effect on societal and monetary values over time. In *MSS Research*, "Indicators of Economic Progress: The Power of Measurement and Human Welfare" (http://www.mssresearch.org/?q=node/626) is an extensive analysis of this topic. A selection from the pdf is as follows:

> The nature and quality of employment required to achieve economic security has also changed dramatically. Manual labor on farms and in factories has been largely replaced by white collar categories of employment which are less physically demanding. In the USA, for example, professional, technical, managerial and other categories of white collar employment rose from 24% to 75% of total employment between 1910 and 2010, while

employment in crafts, manual labor, farming, mining and household services declined from 76% to 25%. These qualitative changes continue. In addition, the qualitative value of employment cannot be assessed strictly in terms of physical working conditions, type of labour or compensation. Types of employment differ widely in terms of the social status and self-esteem they carry, a major reason why the more highly educated shun even undemanding, well-paying jobs that they deem beneath their social status. In our effort to scrupulously account for hidden costs such as environmental degradation and social problems, we should not err in the opposite direction by overlooking the enormous hidden gains that have accrued to the entire society.

Education Potential, Procedures, and Methods

The pilot demonstration project will have education as one its main objectives to enable people to be more self-sufficient. Because of this, some of the following comments on the existing and future demands for extending a new paradigm (a typical example or pattern of something) for education will be explored. It is key to our nation's development.

Many parts of our education system are in chaos, and there is need for a new paradigm that includes more students who presently do not have many options. This is especially true of students living in middle-class and low-income areas. It is sad that many starter jobs are in industries offering minimum wage. The other side of the wooden nickel is that many people do not need to or are not capable of going to college. In order to stay alive, the universities and colleges will have to come up with new ideas. Endowments can only stretch so far, and their tuitions keep going up. Universities find themselves in a bind because of the huge overhead costs (buildings, higher salaries, lower contributions, retirement pensions, etc.). The main way they can catch up is by raising tuition. However, because of higher tuition costs, student enrollment decreases. They have to balance this by offering more scholarships to increase enrollment. More work/study opportunities could be another approach to solve some of the entrapment problems.

The National Center for Education Statistics (NCES), in the article "Undergraduate Retention and Graduation Rates," in May 2018 (https://nces.ed.gov/programs/coe/indicator_ctr.asp} noted:

> For first-time, full-time degree-seeking students who enrolled at 4-year degree-granting institutions in fall 2015, the retention rate (i.e., the percentage of students returning the following fall) was 81 percent. Retention rates were higher at institutions that were more selective (i.e., those with lower admission acceptance rates), regardless of institutional control (public, private nonprofit, or private for-profit). At public 4-year institutions overall, the retention rate was 81 percent. At the least selective public institutions (i.e., those with open admissions), the retention rate was 62 percent, and at the most selective public institutions (i.e., those that accept less than 25 percent of applicants), the retention rate was 96 percent. Similarly, the retention rate for private nonprofit 4-year institutions overall was 82 percent, ranging from 64 percent at institutions with open admissions to 95 percent at institutions that accept less than 25 percent of applicants. The retention rate for private for-profit 4-year institutions overall was 56 percent, ranging from 50 percent at institutions with open admissions to 100 percent at institutions that accept less than 25 percent of applicants.

On Spotlight, on March 19, 2018, an article by Izza Choudhry titled "High School Dropouts More Likely to Go to Prison" (https://slspotlight.com/opinion/2018/03/19/high-school-dropouts-more-likely-to-go-to-prison/) noted:

> Of all of the males in federal and state prisons, 80 percent do not have a high school diploma. There is a direct correlation with a lack of high school education and incarceration. One in ten male dropouts between the ages of 16 to 24 are either in prison or in juvenile detention. Rather than spending tax dollars on incarcerating these dropouts, funding

should be focused on encouraging these individuals to complete their high school education. According to a report by The Hamilton Project, there is nearly a 70 percent chance that an African-American man without his high school diploma will be imprisoned by his mid-thirties. There is a 16.6 percent unemployment rate for African-Americans without a high school diploma, showing that men in this demographic have about the same chance of being incarcerated than being employed.

Also, prisons should change so they become an innovative learning system. Money could be saved and used for educational purposes if the dropout rate was lowered. The reduction of incarceration rates, especially in low-income areas, would be a huge benefit to society and to the people themselves. In the Vera Institute of Justice, "The Price of Prisons, *2015*" (https://www.vera.org/publications/price-of-prisons-2015-state-spending-trends), it stated:

> A common measure used by states to understand this cost is the average cost per inmate," calculated by taking the total state spending on prisons and dividing it by the average daily prison population.[13] This figure represents the amount the state spends annually, on average, to staff and maintain the prisons and provide all prison services. Among the 45 states that provided data (representing 1.29 million of the 1.33 million total people incarcerated in all 50 state prison systems), the total cost per inmate averaged $33,274 and ranged from a low of $14,780 in Alabama to a high of $69,355 in New York. Eight states—Alaska, California, Connecticut, Massachusetts, New Jersey, New York, Rhode Island, and Vermont—had a cost per inmate above $50,000.[14] Eighteen, mostly southern, states had costs less than $25,000, while 19 states had costs between $25,000 and $50,000."

Our society is not changing enough to keep up with what is happening. With our polarization lockup, there is not much hope for change in the near future. Living in a community such as the PDP (with security fences) would be a good alternative because it would be less expensive, and prisoners would get a rounded education. This, however, would not include some hardened prisoners. Strict standards of improvement would have to be designed to make this effective.

A *NJ Med* (https://www.timeshighereducation.com/world ... rankings/world-reputation-rankings-201 ...) survey:

Listed their top 20 countries as leaders in high school education. Number 1 is Finland. The necessary skills needed to establish and maintain a livelihood in the emerging economy may include some of the following:

1. Continually learn new information in life's skills and in the work that you do

2. Creatively apply knowledge and skills that includes a variety of fields

3. Be able to adapt to various circumstances in all work environments

4. Use entrepreneurial skills to handle any task

5. Work collaboratively and effectively with others so you can improve while others also improve

6. Be professional and ethical in all work environments

7. Possess a practical working knowledge of financial and project management in order to understand management decisions

For example, should we teach more entrepreneurship classes in high school and in this community?

In the "Higher Education Solutions" of the Nearly Free University (NFU) (CE43), Charles Hugh Smith shows that there are four broad technology-enabled solutions that would free higher education from its current cartel limitations on opportunities for structured learning and accreditation. The entire book should be read in order to understand how his program could work within the PDP framework and other locations. NFU states:

> That the only dynamic that would make the current higher education system accountable is the introduction of a real competitor (NFU) whose product (diplomas) are issued by organizations outside the cartel (universities, etc.), for example, an accrediting body that accredits students individually based onto test scores and the successful completion of real works projects. (p 15)[22]. Some of the main considerations for improvement are: Accredit the student, not the school. Structure learning such that it no longer depends on larger physical campuses and costly administration. Tailor the curriculum to the needs of the real-world emerging economy and the methods of learning to the individual student. Eliminate the artificial scarcity of admissions and accreditation. (p. 21–23)[23] Sustainable careers in the emerging economy are increasingly an interconnected ecosystem of collaboration rather than a conventionally defined job within a hierarchy. Traditional areas of knowledge are spilling over and overlapping with previously distinct fields of expertise, requires new levels of collaboration." (p. 72)[24]

What universities have that NFU would not have is the large quantity of specialized equipment and research facilities that would not normally be affordable by the NFU with a large grant for that purpose. The value of learning by doing will be the main concept in the proposed pilot demonstration project. This will allow students to determine what they would like to do by being exposed to different work opportunities at the beginning of their studies. The above information on the Nearly Free University is just a brief introduction, and the book presents in detail the options available and how they were determined to be a better system of education. In essence, it demonstrates a viable and realistic education with low overhead. This allows it to be adaptable to changing economic conditions and trends of study. An example of a facility that could be established in the PDP would be innovation study centers. These are unique facilities for a community development to provide, but it is one of the first steps for allowing people to become more aware of what they can contribute to a sustainable future. Again, this establishes a sense of purpose for its participants.

There is also a need for workshops to teach creative thinking, systems designing, and innovation. College education is expensive, and many students are graduating from college with heavy debts, in some cases having limited opportunities for work in their fields of study. Understanding the processes involved in creative thinking is an asset for anyone and could be obtainable at costs much less than that of a college education. It would help people start new businesses or be better managers in larger corporations. Besides that, it can be a lot of fun and allows people to see things around them they hadn't seen before.

Goals and Objectives - Innovative Study Centers Within the PDP

The following goals and objectives represent the first concepts for the center and will be expanded during the planning stages to meet additional criteria. There will be a location in one or more houses constructed (mainly triplexes) for workshops, or houses will rented to persons in order for them to have a space to develop ideas. Each house will be designed with different features to allow for this to happen for different types of businesses. Leaders in the field of teaching creative thinking will be consulted in the planning stages. This study center will also adapt ideas from the *Nearly Free University* and *EarthEd*.

1. There will also be a spiritual and wellness center in one of the buildings in the PDP. This will help people who are lonely or unhappy and could be part of the anti-depression program. There can be one to four innovative centers in each project, each one emphasizing different areas of expertise.

2. There will also be IT linkage from the IT center to individual homes in the development.

3. One of the main purposes is to have a facility that allows people to live in the project and still work by themselves in independent businesses or with other community or cooperative businesses.

4. Some of the homes in the project could be mutually owned by several persons or businesses (fractured housing ownership), and this would allow business executives and managers to live here for short periods and have the opportunity to participate in creative thinking, innovative workshops.

5. The workshops would be given by experts in the field of innovation, and there would be many case studies presented to show how innovations have led to new technology and inventions. Videos would be taken of each workshop and used as examples, if agreed to by the participants. Some workshops may have to be private due to sensitivity of the material or concepts involved.

6. Student housing would also be available on-site for students who want to pursue independent study in the field of innovation and creative thinking. Tuition and fees would be charged for the training and workshops. The management of the nonprofit may allow for free or reduced tuition for first ideas or ideas that would be useful in developing a new business. The nonprofit could be a joint venture partner.

7. The center would be involved with major corporations that recognize and support PDP goals to show the potential of the workshops to their personnel as well as exposing the development as a place where families and personnel could retire.

8. Participants in the workshops could also use the facilities in the project during their stay there. The fees for this would have to be determined. These could be in the units designated for Airbnb use.

9. Business or personnel living in the cooperative would have reduced fees for the workshops or training.

10. Management of the centers would try to obtain funding sources for the development of new ideas. There would also be contacts with legal experts for consultation to help workshop members. The nonprofit would show members how to obtain grants.

11. Special workshops would be presented for the sole purpose of developing technology for persons living in poverty throughout the world. Small sustainable agricultural plots would be tested to determine the most feasible methods of agricultural production for subsistence farmers.

12. Special volunteer programs for high school students will be available as well as demonstration programs for students in the elementary schools.

13. One of the main objectives is to provide exposure of the project to many people and businesses and to show the scope of the complete facilities, including the many special opportunities for working with the homeless and elderly.

14. These centers will provide a service that is not offered anywhere else in this type of setting.

15. The workshops could also include classes in art, music, and photography, as these fields are compatible with innovative thinking and are useful for marketing purposes. They would focus mainly on business development and skills. The people living in the community could also set up their own workshop programs.

16. Included on this site or another site in the area would be an environmental training center so people could understand the methods of sustainability that will be used in the development of the project and can continue using these concepts later. This also could be part of a workshop program.

17. Other ideas are sure to be developed as this subject is explored, but it could be a venture that would help the world understand itself better without the frustrations of some government agencies.

Innovation takes many forms and can be the lifeblood for helping humanity sustain itself in a world that is slowly trying to eliminate itself. Innovation can happen anywhere and by anyone who will let their mind see things that others overlook.

Job Trend Predictions and Student Debt

Predictions for important future areas of study can vary according to whom you talk to. Many future jobs will be associated with work within a community similar to the pilot demonstration project. When talking about future jobs, the answer lies at what point in the future are we talking about. Ten, thirty, or how many years from now? If we continue to ignore the environmental and agriculture problems that we have now, the jobs will be entirely different from what we have available today or in the next five years. The following articles describe information that may affect what trends and ideas occur in the future.

In the book *Systems Thinking for Social Change* by David Peter Stroh (CE19), he asks the question,

How does systems thinking help people achieve sustainable breakthrough change? 1) "First, systems thinking motivates people to change because they discover their role in exacerbating the problems they want to solve, 2) Second, systems thinking catalyzes collaboration because people learn how they collectively create the unsatisfying results they experience, 3) Third, systems thinking focuses people to work on a few coordinated changes over time to achieve systemwide impacts that are significant and sustainable and 4) Fourth, systems thinking stimulates continuous learning, which is an essential characteristic of any meaningful change in complex systems . (p. 21–22)[25] Systems thinking is a language and set of tools meant to illuminate our thinking about how the systems we are all part of actually operate." (p. 206–207)[26]

Next, I am including articles and passages from books that help show some of the problems and shortcomings in our school systems and our work environments. The problems noted illustrate areas that have to be improved, and this is partly caused by the rapid changes occurring in our society that are outpacing the ability of schools and universities to adjust accordingly.

In a post at ZD Net, "10 tips for turning employees into 'intrapreneurs" by Joe McKendrick on January 27, 2013 (https://www.zdnet.com/article/10-tips-for-turning-employees-into-intrapreneurs/) said:

Entrepreneurship doesn't have to mean quitting one's job and risking a house and life savings on a new startup. Full-time employees also can also take on entrepreneurial roles within the confines of their organizations, enriching their jobs while infusing new ideas into the corporate culture. Thus, there's a case to be made for the unique role of "intrapreneurs," or internal entrepreneurs whose ideas may launch new lines of business. In a post at Innovation Excellence, John Webb of Rackspace Hosting provides excellent guidance on how to encourage entrepreneurs, as well as fuel the growth of an intrapreneurial culture in even the most staid organizations. From his original list, here are 10 compelling guidelines: (see article). One example is: "Encourage networking and collaboration:" What's more powerful than a determined intrapreneur? A team of intrapreneurs. Plus, greater networking and collaboration helps intrapreneurs connect with key decision makers in the organization who can help move projects forward.

"Why America Can't Take Its Entrepreneurial Spirit for Granted" is found on the Kauffman Foundation website (no date) (https://www.kauffman.org/blogs/currents/2018/06/why-america-cannot-take-its-entrepreneurial-spirit-for-granted):

This year's Global Entrepreneurship Congress (GEC) in Istanbul, Turkey, (2018) provided the single-best snapshot of what's happening in entrepreneurship from around the world. The energy, enthusiasm, and commitment of each and every country was incredibly impressive and humbling. Here is what we learned while there: "Entrepreneurship has gone mainstream in economic development". When 171 nations gathered to discuss the future of entrepreneurship, it showed that entrepreneurship has moved beyond the fringes of economic development planning. Each country was represented by some officials in the highest levels of their respective governments, with our host country's president appearing at the conference to emphasize the importance of the role entrepreneurs play in building stronger economies. We see this at the Ewing Marion Kauffman Foundation through the policy work we support in Washington and in the states through the Entrepreneurs' Policy Network. Giving entrepreneurs a voice is critical and the Global Entrepreneurship Network (GEN) does it very well.

"Designing the Future of Learning for All Kids" by Julie Scheidegger on May 24, 2018, in Kauffman Foundation Currents (https://www.kauffman.org/blogs/currents/2018/05/designing-the-future-of-learning-for-all-kids) noted:

> Sherman White, Kauffman's director in Education said "posited that designers embrace the challenge to be more thoughtful, bold, creative, and more inclusive. The varied pathways students may choose from shouldn't be determined based on how well learning designers did, or did not, prepare them in the years leading up to high school. Since we can't predict all of the skills needed to succeed in tomorrow's workforce, our charge is to equip students with mental agility ... and a mindset toward a lifetime of continuous learning, retooling, and re-orientation for the ever-adjusting world around them. Ultimately, Whites said that success means "being unable to distinguish or predict life outcomes based on a person's race, gender, or economic status. Let's measure up to the promise we have made to improve academic and life outcomes for all students. And let's begin to invest in amplifying the voices of those who have the greatest stake in all of the work that we do."

The Kauffman Foundation has a pdf, "State of Entrepreneurship 2017," (https://www.supplychain247.com/paper/state_of_entrepreneurship_2017/kauffman_foundation) that can be found on their website. Some of their mega trends are:

The portrait of U.S. Entrepreneurs—80.2 percent white and 64.5 percent male looks a lot different than the overall U.S. populations. Minorities own half as many businesses as non-minorities and their businesses start smaller and stay smaller. These gaps cost the country. In fact if minorities started and owned businesses as the same rate as non-minorities do, the U.S. would have more than 1 million additional employer businesses and an extra 9,5 million jobs in the economy. Adults without high school degrees make up 11.6 percent of the population, but only 3.4 percent of entrepreneurs. Entrepreneurship is an increasing urban phenomenon. Revenue and value creation today can take off dramatically with todays technology, but job growth lags behind.

These statistics show the inequality that exists in the US between racial groups and how there is little funding available to start a business for people living in low-income areas. It also shows the effect this has on the number of jobs available in minority areas. The Kauffman Foundation has many articles about entrepreneurs on their website.

If the purpose of a college education is for students to learn, academe is failing, according to *Academically Adrift: Limited Learning on College Campuses,* (SC84)[27] by Arum and Roksa (http://press.uchicago.edu/ucp/books/book/chicago/A/bo10327226.html):

> Data from student surveys and transcript analysis show that many college students have minimal classwork expectations -- and then it tracks the academic gains (or stagnation) of 2,300 students of traditional college age enrolled at a range of four-year colleges and universities. The students took the Collegiate Learning Assessment (which is designed to measure gains in critical thinking, analytic reasoning and other "higher level" skills taught at college) at various points before and during their college educations, and the results are not encouraging:
>
> - 45 percent of students "did not demonstrate any significant improvement in learning" during the first two years of college.
>
> - 36 percent of students "did not demonstrate any significant improvement in learning" over four years of college.
>
> - Those students who do show improvements tend to show only modest improvements. Students improved on average only 0.18 standard deviations over the first two years of college and 0.47 over four years. (Internet)

"Why Does a College Degree Cost So Much" by John E Schoen (CNBC) (https://www.cnbc.com/2015/06/16/why-college-costs-are-so-high-and-rising.html) (no date) is an article that illustrates college costs. This is a long article and is worth reviewing to get an excellent analysis of college costs:

> The average cost of tuition and fees at a private, non-profit, four-year university this school year was $31,231—up sharply from $1,832 in 1971-1972 (in current dollars). At public, four-year schools, tuition and fees cost about $9,139 this year and in the 1971 school year, they added up to less than $500 in current dollars, according to the College Board. Despite the annual sticker shock, millions of American students and their families still believe it is—and many experts concur, pointing out that college graduates, on average, do still make considerably more than those with just a high school diploma. Since 1971, annual college enrollment has more than doubled in the U.S. to 19.5 million, as of 2013, the latest Census data available. In that year, there were 5.3 million in two-year colleges, 10.5 million in four-year colleges and 3.7 million in graduate school.

On the internet, an article titled "Look at the Shocking Student Loan Debt Statistics for 2018" was provided by Student Loan Hero (https://studentloanhero.com/student-loan-debt-statistics/) on January 24, 2018. Many times, articles on the internet can be found just by typing the source of the article and the title of the subject, and the https does not have to be used. All the articles in the book are able to be sourced in this manner if the https information is not included for the article. First, let's start with a general picture of the student loan debt landscape. "The most recent reports indicate there is:

- $1.48 trillion in total U.S. student loan debt

- 44.2 million Americans with student loan debt with the average debt in 2016 $ 37,172.

- Student loan delinquency rate of 11.2% (90+ days delinquent or in default)

- Average monthly student loan payment (for borrower aged 20 to 30 years): $351

- Median monthly student loan payment (for borrower aged 20 to 30 years): $203

(Data via federalreserve.gov, WSJ, newyorkfed.org here, here and here and clevelandfed.org here)

This type of debt load may increase in the coming years, and if the economy takes a downturn, there may be many problems and defaults. This could also affect students trying to enter college. Now many graduates are taking jobs that are out of their study field and getting lower pay for those types of jobs. This is reflected in college enrollment figures. The article "College Enrollment Dips as More Adults Ditch Degrees for Jobs" by Madeline Farber, December 19, 2016 (http://fortune.com/2016/12/19/college-enrollment-decline/), in *Fortune* magazine, noted:

Students over age 24 account for almost the entire overall decline. When last counted, the population of "older" students was about 6.63 million, according to the Wall Street Journal, and was generally concentrated at community colleges and for-profit schools. Overall, enrollment at four-year, for-profit colleges shrank by 14.5% to 970,267 this fall. At their 2010 peak, about 1.64 million people were enrolled in those schools. By contrast, four-year private, nonprofit schools, reported a 0.6% decline, with 3.79 million students—a decrease that could hurt those schools, as many rely heavily on tuition dollars for revenue, notes the Journal.

Another important book is *EarthEd* by the Worldwatch Institute (SC27).[28] It is comprehensive, and its main thrust is teaching sustainability through nature. Many of the suggestions noted in the book will be used in the pdf. The table of contents should be reviewed by looking inside the book on Amazon. "It again reflects what we need to change in our education system to reach more people economically. They noted that recent political events in the United States and Europe reveal large disparities in scientific knowledge and in the command of the factual evidence about Earth systems, ecology, oceans and so forth. If there is demonization of others in the future, public ecological literacy will become increasingly important to inform and moderate political discourse and to improve governance. This will need leadership at the highest levels."

Education, Training, and Financing in the Pilot Demonstration Project

The agricultural demonstration and research area for agriculture and landscaping is the most important part of the teaching curriculum. Since this part of the PDP is a cooperative, any students and farmers associated with it will have special discount considerations like work/study opportunities. It is hoped that one of the first programs would be to set up functioning cooperatives with farmers in the area of the site. It would also help in marketing of foods and value-added products. Local currency and bartering will be done within the cooperative. Several examples of existing cooperatives will be examined, and one prototype will be selected. Following are some courses that could be offered. They could be structured for both vocational certificates and college degrees.

- Sustainable Agriculture—Components

- Organic Methods of Farming—Introduction

- Bio-Intensive Method

- Permaculture Design

- No Till or Natural Farming

- Farming with Vegetables—Climate and Variables

- Fruit—Grains—Cover Crops

- Soil Structure—Comparisons

- Studies of Synthetic Fertilizers—GMO Crops

- Soil Amendments and Natural Fertilizers

- Bio-Stimulants and Other Chemicals

- Environmental Advantages of Agro-Ecology Methods

- Home Gardening Applications

- Natural Pesticides, Herbicides, and Strategies for Weed Control

- Combinations of Organic Methods, Agricultural Restoration, and Permaculture

- Using Organic Gardening in Large-Acreage Farming

- Soil Biology and Agronomy—Using Mulches

- Studies of Existing Organic and Agro-Ecological Farms—United States

- Studies of Existing Organic and Agro-Ecological Farming Worldwide

- Farming in the Developing World—Examples of Success by Indigenous Farming

- Crop Storage—Transportation—Visiting local Markets and Organic Farms

- List/Study of Distributor Products for Use in Organic Farming—Comparisons

- Research Studies at International Testing Center (several courses)

- Marketing Organic Produce and Management Courses

- Creating Recipes for Health and Then Producing Them

- History of Organic Farming—Literature

- Agro-Ecology—Meaning and Methods

- Using Indigenous and Organic Seeds

- Finding Sources and Information on the Internet

- Use of Video Production for Course Development

- Hydroponics Applications

- Aquaponic Methods and Application in Organic and Agroecology Production

- Self-Sustaining Organic Farming Using Animals, Fish, and Produce

- Free-Range Cattle, Chicken, Goat, Rabbit, and Hog Production Using Agro-Ecology Programs

- Three-Year Research Study Summary

- Field Work at the International Testing Garden

- Community-Supported Agriculture and Other Marketing Programs

- Construction and Home-Made Equipment

- Soil Secrets and MicroLife Products—Changing the Way We Live

These are samples of the courses that could be offered. Any research projects could be filmed and used for courses. Collaboration in online courses with universities could also be an essential part of the program. One year from starting the project, online courses might be offered worldwide if funds are available. There would also be published literature about the research with its adaption for organic gardening. Field trips to recognized farmers practicing natural systems could be available. All courses would emphasize how they are applicable for use in a postcapitalist world or the interim. Some of the courses could also be open source and sold on a user fee basis. Most research results could be for sold or be part of an internet membership program. Teachers could also include cooperative members associated with the PDP, such as the co-op farmers.

The research results, when applicable, could be used by members living in the community to set up businesses. Part of their profit would go back to the nonprofit for additional studies. Students living in the PDP would pay rent and in some cases food expenses. The tuition and other fees would have to be determined when the economic feasibility study is prepared. The other main course structures would be the teaching of construction trades and setting up apprentice programs with general contractors, electricians, plumbers, and so on. These two areas of study (agriculture and construction) will be needed regardless of what happens to the economy. In this case, certain products manufacturers have to be kept in business, if possible. The teaching methods used will incorporate the applicable ideas noted here, and others to be determined when the project gets underway. That is why it is necessary to have key personnel with innovative tendencies, and the strength of the project would be to keep changing as necessary as new situations in research, technologies, and economic conditions appear on the scene.

A book recently published about society's present approach toward educational thinking is very controversial and should be evaluated to see if it would be applicable for the PDF and other educational institutions. It was written by Bryan Caplan, a professor of economics at George Mason University. The book is *The Case Against Education—Why the Education System Is a Waste of Time and Money*. George Mason University is mainly a conservative university, and the author himself states:

> I favor radical reforms nonetheless. Philosophically, I am staunchly libertarian. While not absolutely opposed to taxpayer support for education, I have a strong moral presumption against taxpayer support for anything.[29] Think about what passes for "broadening students' horizons. Teachers expose students to an ossified list of subjects: music, art poetry, drama, foreign language, history, government, dance, sports. Some kids respond eagerly, especially, to music and sports. Yet the greater their excitement, the greater their disappointment: almost no one grows up to be a violinist, painter, poet, actor, historian, politician, ballet dancer or a professional athlete. The alternative? For starters, give students numerous and diverse options.[30]

This is just one comment among many that he discusses in the book. The book is comprehensive, and he uses economic models and tables to explain what he finds wrong with the present education systems in high schools, colleges, universities, and vocational schools. The educational value of degrees for students who are selfish (Does my education pay? Is it worth it?) are compared to the value of degrees to serve society. He discusses the three broad traits that education signals (which are the importance of certain degrees of education or abilities, as seen by employers or colleges for acceptance): intelligence, conscientiousness, and conformity.[31] I should note here that just these few notes do Bryan a disservice because I used just brief excerpts here, and some are out of proper context compared to additional information found in his book. His book is written mainly for people in the field of education because of the quantity of detailed economic data. He mentioned in his book that people should provide some alternative viewpoints to what he is saying. Consequently, I will provide a description of what my agreements and disagreements are with some of his theories and provide additional options for use in the pilot demonstration project.

I agree with him that the graduating requirements in high school and college have to be updated rather than keeping the same requirements that have been in place for over thirty years. This is especially true for high school students not planning on going to college. Standard subjects required by colleges and universities are important for those students planning to be accepted, and college requirements should be used for these students. Courses allowed should be relevant to the student whenever possible. Subjects should be geared initially to increase students' abilities in areas the students want to learn or where they feel they are inadequately prepared. Not enough quality time is spent with individual students to help them on a career path in ninth grade of high school and in freshman year of college. Parents, especially when their children are in high school, should be involved, helping them and the teacher during this orientation period.

If a child has a discipline or a mental problem, everyone associated with the student should know about it so the student can be helped. This is especially important to better understand dropout problems and the effect of the environment on their studies and behavior. The ninth-grade student should have test scores available to see how many and what types of courses they need to be fluent and graduate. A semester course in ninth grade could be allocated to helping students know what options are available to them.

Why do so many people in our society have anxiety and depression? Much of it can be directed back to not selecting or knowing what courses might be best for them (or how to enjoy these courses) in their formative years. Another problem is watering down high school courses for everyone and not having special courses for gifted students. To help students select a major or minor, college freshmen could attend a class that is offered in the fourth or fifth year of their major (or another course if their major is undetermined) for one semester in order to see if what they want to major in is appealing to them. They would take notes and hand these in at the end of the semester. An alternative would be to have an oral test. An automatic grade of B would be given to students if they had an 85 percent attendance record.

Many students do not have any idea of what they want to do because they do not know what options are available. Bryan, in his book, has a list of occupations under the headings of "high usefulness, medium usefulness, and low usefulness." Liberal arts was in the lowest group.[32] He also discusses educational signaling and the importance of what's in a student's résumé and how one's innate ability affects a student's value when being considered for a job or getting into college. One of the problems with this is that all occupations are based on capitalism being the main force in the economy. It does not allow for problems due to agriculture, pollution, lack of resources, climate change, and so on, which in turn affect the types of jobs available. These factors would change many different occupations to a lower value and create a need for additional training for workers. Another idea would be for community colleges to be affiliated with private companies to establish work-study programs. It might take a student longer to graduate but would provide a means of obtaining practical skills and financing some of their college or training costs. It would also help them determine if they enjoyed that type of work.

Several words were absent in Bryan's book, such as compassion, sharing, nature, greed, corruption, sustainability, innovation skills and training, and current political history studies. Knowledge and skills in these subjects add depth and understanding in today's society, especially understanding the inequities caused by some corporations. Conservatives do not want to admit what actions cause the inequities in the political system and the effect they have on social justice and adequate employment opportunities. In fact, inequality is a costly part of our social costs and is unfortunately not a concern of most of the elite. Somehow this is not getting through to politicians and some corporations.

In the book[1][33] it shows how testing data about history and civics discloses that there is severe ignorance among adult Americans on these subjects. The American Revolution Center tested

---

[1]   In the book by David Caplan, The Case Against Education—Why the Education System Is a Waste of Time and Money it shows

1,001 adults about the American Revolution, and 83 percent earned failing grades. Some of the questions asked are noted in a chart in the book. This shows that history and civics should be taught in at least one course in high school and one semester in college. If people aren't aware of what happened in the past, how can they be aware (in a historical context) of what is happening now for their evaluation of present-day and future politics? There is so much misinformation in the news that many people do not know how to evaluate it knowledgeably. Are all votes equal? Yes.

One of the other problems with education is the teaching of conformity with minimal emphasis on developing innovative thought. Conformity is easier on the teacher and does not require the knowledge or aptitude that teaching innovation requires. *Time* listed the top ten college dropouts, and most of them were innovators (http://content.time.com/time/specials/packages/article/0,28804,1988080_1988093_1988082,00.html#). They are Bill Gates, Steve Jobs, Frank Lloyd Wright, Buckminister Fuller, James Cameron, Mark Zuckerberg, Tom Hanks, Harrison Ford, Lady Gaga, and Tiger Woods. They probably received some education from their attendance at a university, but each one had an innovative mind-set or specialized ability that was not totally enriched at college for them to achieve their goals. Special classes in innovation and brainstorming should be a part of most curriculums. How many other students have lost opportunities that could have been enriched by innovative and arts training? This shows that specializing in only the high-usefulness jobs is not the best way to go in many instances.

An example from my own experience was a weekend workshop prepared and organized by the students in the Landscape Architecture Department at Texas A&M, College Station, Texas. The students invited several major principals in landscape architecture to be part of a program. That allowed the professionals to show their work using slides and lectures and to meet with the students. Landscape architects from Texas were also invited each year to help and add their own expertise. Students from all the landscape architecture departments in the nearby states were invited to attend. The students stayed with other students at Texas A&M to reduce expenses and compare courses. In addition, a project was selected for the students to solve. The students worked in five- or seven-person teams and then presented their design ideas on the final day of the workshop. Of course, on Saturday night there was a beer party for everyone, which was also a lot of fun. For me, it was the highlight of the year since it allowed me to make new friends and learn from other professionals and students. It was a sharing of experiences. However, this has been discontinued. It is a great example of teaching innovation. A program similar to this could also be established for other fields of study.

The PDP project has a unique approach for education and training, especially for low- and middle-income families. The main teaching curriculum is based on work-study programs in the main areas of small farm agriculture, construction trades, developing small business enterprises, and innovation studies. There is a market demand in all of these areas of study because there will always be a demand for nutritious food and affordable shelter. Now many cities are noting that the high cost of housing is partially due to lack of qualified labor, and the move to smaller farms is critical to prevent soil erosion and chemical pollution and provide quality food. Also, small businesses are the backbone of our economy and ensure that people are trained for many types of jobs. Since the PDP is just a demonstration project at this time, its impact will be quite small but could be very important in the future.

A webinar by the Alliance for Excellent Education (July 12, 2018), featuring the book *World Class: How to Build a 21st-Century School System*, includes a discussion by the author, Andreas Schleicher, and Bob Wise (AEE). A pdf of the book can be obtained by going to tiny url.com/WorldClassBook. Click on the pdf button below the description of the book to get a pdf of the book for free. It offers solutions and programs from the various nations in the world. It is published through the Organisation for Economic Co-operation and Development (OECD). Some comments about the book are as follows: "For the first time, he's collected 20 years worth of wisdom in one place. World Class should be required reading for policy makers, education leaders and anyone who wants to know how our schools can adapt for the modern world —and help all kids learn to think for themselves " (Amanda Ripley, author of *The Smartest Kids in the World*, a New York Times bestseller. "[Schleicher] ... grasps all the key issues, and does so through keeping his ear to the ground and by working out solutions jointly with a variety of leaders at all levels of the system, and in diverse societies" (Michael Fullan, Global Leadership Director, New Pedagogies for Deep Learning).

Community and Personal Purposes—Why It Is Important

The purpose of the community commons encompasses several objectives that may be necessary for it to be successful. Some of these are listed below, and many more should be added by readers. Some of the objectives have been taken from books, and others are my own from my experiences. I am a landscape architect and community planner who is now entering the twilight zone of life. This allows me the privilege of being optimistic and pessimistic at the same time. The idea for using the triplex design came from my planning experience working on the master plan for Montego Bay, Jamaica. This was done by working with another planner, Arlene Dixon, who was a Jamaican. Throughout Jamaica, many houses were unfinished with just steel sticking up from the walls because they could add more rooms at a later date. By an analysis of this situation, I realized that another approach could be utilized in order for a family to easily expand from a triplex to single family within the same building structure, with very little cost involved.

Another experience there gave me one of the best planning lessons I ever had. We had a community meeting in part of a school that just had one lightbulb. The power for the bulb was an electric line going from the bulb to a connection on a telephone pole. This was then attached to someone else's power source. I never did figure out where they got their water because we were served bottled water. This was education economy at its best. During the meeting, one of the ladies asked me to come over to a window that overlooked a new housing scheme that was built as low-income housing. It was row after row of the same buildings. There was a dearth of aesthetics. She pointed out to me all of the problems this housing generated from a cultural and design standpoint, many things I normally would have overlooked. This was a situation where the people designed most of the plan.

In another project in South San Antonio, I worked in an area that was basically forgotten by the city. Some of the homes did not have sewer or water connections, and many of the buildings were in disrepair. Social standing there was quite complex. One of the homes looked very rundown, but inside it was well appointed and in good repair. This was so the residence looked bad to the tax appraisers who just inspected the houses by driving by. At that time, there were little stickers on the license plates that designated the year for renewal. It was amazing the results you get by mixing mud with glue and pasting the mixture over the sticker. I had many other such episodes that made me realize how much culture is important in designing communities and what people do to save money.

To emphasize additional information available for people in the community, a list and description of books will be used to describe research in culture and other attributes that could be associated with the pilot demonstration project. Other information on the books and articles will be available upon request. Reading or skimming the books of interest will provide other facts in order to see their important relationship to the project. The rest of this section will have information that is relevant to community development because it will show what emotional state the US is in, and any new community should be designed to answer social problems. The first series of topics relates to the problems we have in America. The government claims we have an excellent economy, and this is true for the upper half of society. What is most troubling are the social problems of crime, depression, school and police shootings, and the sharp division between political parties. This separation is becoming one of the worst situations in our history. It is dominating the news, and major problems like the environment are going unnoticed. In this book, with the help of other authors, I will try to make people aware of what is happening.

The URL (internet) address is included with all articles, but many times you can just type in the name of the article, date, and source to get it on the browser. If a date or author is not shown for an article, it is not located in the article. To obtain further information about the books mentioned in the reference list, look up the book on Amazon and then click on the "look inside" option. If certain chapters in the table of contents are highlighted in blue, click on the highlighted area, and you can see some of the information that is shown in that chapter.

The most important goal in this project is finding purpose for a good life as well as a healthy one. This was a theme from an article in the *New York Times* by Dr. Dhruv Khullar on January 1, 2018 (http://onlinelibrary.wiley.com/doi/10.1111/j.1758-0854.2010.01035.x/full):

> Only about a quarter of Americans strongly endorse having a clear sense of purpose and of what makes their lives meaningful, while nearly 40 percent either feel neutral or say they don't and this is both a social and public health problem: Research increasingly suggests that purpose is important for a meaningful life—but also for a healthy life. Purpose and meaning are connected to what researchers call eudaimonic well-being. He also noted "that there are benefits to having a purpose. Some of them are better sleep, fewer strokes and heart attacks and a lower risk of dementia. A sense of purpose gives a broader meaning to life. There becomes less emphasis on consumerism being your main driver or goal as a symbol of success. Success then becomes more what you do and not what you have." Preachers in some evangelical churches should take note of this. This is distinct from, and sometimes inversely related to, happiness (hedonic wellbeing). (https://www.ncbi.nlm.nih.gov/pubmed/11148302).

An article in the *Huffington Post* by Sharon Kim, "Why you Should Never Chase your Passion," on April 4, 2007 *(https:*www.huffingtonpost.com/entry/why-you-should-never-chase-your-passion_us_58e42f04e4b09dbd42f3db97), described:

> What she kept wanting to do had a title with no testimony. She felt like a Louis Vuitton bag, pretty and prestigious on the outside, but worthless on the inside. The gap between where you are and where you want to be is the gap where most people find themselves quitting. It's in this gap where the safer option starts becoming more appealing. And it's in this gap where you realize that maybe your passion, wasn't even a passion to begin with. The minute it gets hard, the minute you feel people starting to judge you, the minute you start believing all the excuses you've been telling yourself, is the minute you've convinced yourself that your passion is no longer worth pursuing. And just like that, you've abandoned the promises your purpose was supposed to bring and you're onto the next best thing.

An article by Caroline Beaton in the *Huffington Post*, "A Little-Known Cause of Millennial Job Burnout" (September 1, 2007 (https://www.huffingtonpost.com/entry/a-little-known-leading-cause-of-millennial-job-burnout_us_59a999a7e4b0d0c16bb524b), noted:

> Americans are working longer hours than any time in the last century. Thirty-six percent of millennials say their stress has increased in the past year, and more than half have lain awake at night from stress in the last month. Yet many of us are also, simultaneously, bored. Gallup found that only 29% of millennials are engaged at work. The University of Kent found that recent graduates rated their administrative, sales and marketing positions — where most land after college — as 7.7 or above out of 10 on boredom. How can we be both bored and stressed? It turns out boredom and burnout are correlated. We see burnout as the result of doing too much and boredom as the result of doing too little. In fact, neither state is related to quantity of activities so much as what we're doing. Boredom stems from uniform, repetitive tasks. No matter how many emails we have to answer, we'll be bored if all our tasks feel similar.

A book concerning happiness is *The Economics of HappineSS* by Mark Anielski (SC22).[34] He discusses the meaning of Genuine Wealth and how you can change so that what you do makes your life worthwhile and you do not rely on habits like excessive consumerism. It provides a chart called the Genuine Wealth balance sheet.

In Quartz on February 24, 2018, by Dan Kopf, in "How Much Money do People Need to be Happy?" (https://qz.com/1211957/how-much-money-do-people-need-to-be-happy/) showed that:

> Take three people. All are unmarried, 33-year-old women who live in the United States. One makes an annual salary of $40,000, another makes $120,000, and the third makes $200,000. Who do you think is the happiest? According to a recently released study (paywall) in the burgeoning field of happiness research, the two higher-earning women are likely to report more satisfaction with their lives than the one who makes $40,000. But, perhaps surprisingly, the psychologists who conducted the study find that the one making $200,000 is probably no happier than the one making $120,000. This is because both the $120,000 and $200,000 women have incomes above $105,000, which according to their research is the point at which greater household income in the US is not associated with greater happiness. The technical term for this cutoff is the income "satiation point." The study is based on a life-satisfaction survey conducted on over 1 million people as part of the Gallup World Poll.

Other information is available that shows that many people in our society are not happy or have not been able to establish a sense of purpose. In the "Science of Loneliness" (https://thewalrus.ca/the-science-of-lonliness), Sam Juric says:

> In recent years, researchers around the world have warned that we are facing a loneliness epidemic. In 2017, the American Psychological Association's annual convention focused on data that reveals loneliness and social isolation pose an equal, if not greater, danger to public health than other, more commonly discussed risk factors such as smoking, obesity, and substance abuse—all factors that, by comparison, take up large amounts of public resources and attention. What's more, in a 2015 study of more than 3 million participants,

researchers at Brigham Young University found that increased social connection is linked to a 50 percent reduced risk of premature death. Put another way: when it comes to a heightened risk of mortality, loneliness is equivalent to smoking 15 cigarettes a day. Today in Canada, one-person households account for over 28 percent of all households, as reported in the 2016 Canadian census. They even surpass the numbers for couples with children, which fell to 26.5 percent in 2016 from 31.5 percent in 2001.

An article on the internet by AARP titled "Social Isolation Looms Large as More Adults Live Alone—Loneliness is a Greater Health Threat than Obesity" (www.aarp.org/health/conditions-treatments/info-2017/loneliness-growing-health-problem-fd.html) (August 8, 2017) noted:

> "Being connected to others socially is widely considered a fundamental human need — crucial to both well-being and survival," she said. "Yet an increasing portion of the U.S. population now experiences isolation regularly." Holt-Lunstad presented data from scores of studies indicating that social isolation, loneliness or living alone has had an impact on the risk of premature death that is as bad or worse than other risk factors, including obesity. "With an increasing aging population, the effect on public health is only anticipated to increase," said Holt-Lunstad. "Indeed, many nations around the world now suggest we are facing a 'loneliness epidemic.' The challenge we face now is what can be done about it." She recommended that schoolchildren get social-skills training and that doctors include social connectedness in medical screenings. And she advised adults to prepare for retirement socially as well as financially because many social ties are forged in the workplace.

Since most of the people that would be living in the community (PDP) would be "generation me" or millennials, we would need to find out more about this group to see how they might react or accept this type of community living. One of the suggestions I found in one article would be to have a four-day workweek so there is more time for social interaction. This should be considered and is a personal option for anyone wanting to do it. The best book for millennial research is *Generation Me* by Jean M. Twenge, PhD (SC68).[35] Just a few notes will be made here, but the information is pertinent for how the community would have to be designed in order for the project to keep these social needs recognized. Persons with problems should be accepted for living in the community because that is what the community is about. Generally, millennials' generational time is (1982–1999), making the age group in 2018 nineteen years of age to forty-two years. The book noted that in 2016 there were an estimated 83.1 million persons in this group. It is now larger than baby boomers (1943–1960). These are just a few comments from the book, and it should be read completely to put everything in the proper context. Many of the suggestions made in the book will be considered in determining the design alternatives in the pilot demonstration project.

One of the considerations for creating happiness is to have enough money (local and regular currency) and not live in dire poverty. Poverty keeps people from reaching their potential through having poor learning environments, especially in high school. Many students drop out of high school and are destined for low-paying jobs. This is why it is important to have training in vocational studies in occupations that will provide fulfillment and allow them to have a better life. President Trump's slogan is "Make America great again." The only problem—it was directed at the 1 percent and some of the corporations.

The number of people living in poverty is increasing each year, and increasing inequity is one of the problems. The following article in the *Washington Post* on December 21, 2017, by Premilla Nadasen (https://www.washingtonpost.com/news/made-by-history/wp/2017/12/21/ext ...) said:

> But could extreme poverty also be a feature of what is (although perhaps not for long) one of the richest and most powerful nations in the world? Quite possibly. To answer the question, the United Nations launched an investigation of extreme poverty in the United States. To quote the U.N. report: "The American Dream is rapidly becoming the American Illusion, as the U.S. ... now has the lowest rate of social mobility of any of the rich countries." In 1981, the top 1 percent of adults earned on average 27 times more than the bottom 50 percent of adults. Today the top 1 percent earn 81 times more than the bottom 50 percent.

The American Academy of Pediatrics has a pdf on the internet titled "Poverty and Child Health in the United States," from March 2016. It is located on AAP News-Gateway (http://pediatrics.aappublications.org/content/early/2016/03/07/peds.2016-0339). It is a long article, and part of it noted:

> Child poverty is associated with lifelong hardship. Poor developmental and psychosocial outcomes are accompanied by a significant financial burden, not just for the children and families who experience them but also for the rest of society. Children who do not complete high school, for example, are more likely to become teenage parents, to be unemployed, and to be incarcerated, all of which exact heavy social and economic costs. A growing body of research shows that child poverty is associated with neuroendocrine dysregulation that may alter brain function and may contribute to the development of chronic cardiovascular, immune, and psychiatric disorders. The economic cost of child poverty to society can be estimated by anticipating future lost productivity and increased social expenditure. A study compiled before 2008 projected a total cost of approximately $500 billion each year through decreased productivity and increased costs of crime and health care,[7] nearly 4% of the gross domestic product. Other studies of "opportunity youth," young people 16 to 24 years of age who are neither employed nor in school, derived similar results, generating cohort aggregate lifetime costs in the trillions.

There has to be a way to help people in poverty and not with just food stamps. People need to establish a sense of honest values and an opportunity to help themselves. For example, the food stamp program could be revised so that it is restricted to just necessary foods, preferably healthy ones. As noted above, the cost to society of people living in poverty could be reduced by the adoption of more realistic programs that create opportunities. Sharing and collaboration should be a start. We have to reduce the poverty thinking by a minority of people, that they do not have to work and try to get as much money from the government as possible. This also applies to Congress. They need to set a better example, especially when they leave the government and then work for lobbyists and legal firms. It's the old saying, "Well they do it, so why can't I?" The same applies to the president when he tells so many lies within an atmosphere of chaos. When the environment is in dire straits, he creates diversions like the NFL kneeling as a critical problem in our society. Does wearing a US flag pin on your lapel makes you a patriotic American? Oh, the symbols we create to deceive.

These are just a few comments in the above article, and it should be read in full to put everything in the proper context. The growth of extreme poverty is an indicator that we shouldn't be talking about how to slash spending on social programs but how to expand services and better meet the needs of the vulnerable among us. We can do this by incorporating them into the solution process. One and a half million American households live in extreme poverty today, nearly twice as many as twenty years ago. As an example in a beginning step, the *San Francisco Chronicle* will lead an effort to flood the Bay Area with stories and news reports on the city's homelessness crisis. Working with local television, print, and online news outlets, this coordinated effort will create a wave of coverage about this pressing issue, hopefully forcing the public and area politicians to put some major energy and resources into finding real, lasting solutions. Are you a homeless services organization? The free *Homeless Services eBook* is full of expert advice that comes from years of helping human services organizations.

Needless to say, the United States has had deteriorating social problems for a long time, and many of them are not helped by social agencies or other governmental agencies, mainly due to lack of available funding and viable programs that work. Another social problem that is prevalent with capitalism is corporate greed. For example, Derek Burnett in an article in *Reader's Digest*, "Corporate Greed: These Companies Deceived America For Profit—And You Probably Helped Them" (https://www.rd.com/culture/corporate-greed/), noted that some of the world's most respected corporations went out of their way to deceive us. The list included Volkswagen, Luminosity, Coca-Cola, Theanos, and Exxon Mobile. There are many more examples, such as banks (Wells Fargo), Big Pharma, Enron, Monsanto, and so on. This could be a book in itself. He showed what each of the companies did to deceive people. One example was Mobile-Exxon.

> The pitch: "The risk of climate change is real and it warrants action. Ninety percent of emissions come from the consumption of fossil fuels." Does this quote come from a fringe environmentalist? Nope. It's from an ExxonMobil spokesperson speaking to us earlier this year. The oil giant has seen the light: The greenhouse effect imperils Earth. The hitch: Thirty-five years ago, executives at ExxonMobil (then Exxon) considered how climate change could factor into decisions about new fossil fuel extraction, according to an e-mail from a former employee. Yet they continued to fund groups and individuals who debunked global warming. Last fall, the Union of Concerned Scientists released a trove of documents revealing just how deliberately the fossil fuel industry attempted to sway the public. One 1998 memo by the American Petroleum Institute, an industry group that is bankrolled by ExxonMobil and other oil and natural gas companies, laid out a strategy to get the public to "realize" the "uncertainties of climate change. "It would target high school science teachers, conduct a media campaign, and distribute "information kits" that included peer-reviewed papers emphasizing "uncertainty" in climate science.

Even the present government is part of the process by their weakening of environmental regulations to help businesses. This will be addressed later in more detail. An additional concern is the number of people who are depressed and suffering from anxiety. There are many reasons for this, and it is related to many different social conditions. The book *Lost Connections* by Johann Hari (SC80) is one of most pertinent books of our time. It emphasizes how prevalent depression and anxiety are in our society. He noted:

Between 2011 and 2012, the polling company Gallup conducted the most detailed study ever carried out of how people across the world feel about their work. They studied millions of workers across 142 countries. They found that 13 percent of us say we are "engaged" in our jobs—which means they are "enthusiastic about, and committed to their work and contribute to their organization in a positive manner." Against them, 63 percent say they are "not engaged," which is defined as "sleeping through their workday, putting time—but not their energy or passion—into their work." And a further 24 percent are "actively disengaged." They, Gallup explained, "aren't just unhappy at work; they're busy acting out their unhappiness. Every day, these workers undermine what their engaged co-workers accomplish … Actively disengaged employees are out more or less to damage their company." (p. 64)[36]

This book is fascinating read, and since there is so much data being presented, it is difficult to do it justice with just one paragraph. One part of the work by Hari refers to "Disconnection: Nine Causes of Depression and Anxiety," and the response toward solutions is "Reconnection." The book presents guidelines and data that should be read in order to understand what is occurring in our society in regard to evaluating methods of reducing depression and anxiety. It has been found in many studies that nutrition is one of the keys to lowering depression.

An article, "What Foods are Good for Depression?" from July 16, 2017, by Jon Johnson in *Medical News Today*, presented research information on the correlation between diet and depression (https://www.medicalnewstoday.com/articles/318428.php):

A recent study posted to BMC Medicine demonstrated that a group of people with moderate to severe depression improved their mood and signs of depression by eating a more healthful diet. The study was the first to prove that diet alone could reduce depression symptoms. The dieters followed a specific program for 12 weeks that included one-on-one counseling with a dietitian. The treatment diet encouraged eating whole foods while discouraging things such as refined foods, sweets, and fried food. Dieters showed greatly reduced symptoms when compared to other groups. In addition, more than 32 percent of participants experienced remission, so were no longer considered depressed.

There are many more articles available on the internet about depression, and they should be read to understand more about this condition. Just don't believe some of what the drug companies are telling you. This has been detailed here because it represents societal problems that can affect our work habits, personalities, happiness, and relationships. This is why in the PDP community, so much attention is given to social activities such as sharing. As an example, how many people are burdened with doing the same monotonous thing every day at work, with little opportunity to better one's self?

The Pilot Demonstration Project: A Breakthrough Opportunity for Depression Research

After reading articles on depression, I realized that the pilot demonstration project could help people by offering opportunities for a different way of life. They could become immersed in a society that is more compassionate and sharing, more relaxing, and have an opportunity to discover their potential. People within the PDF will be diversified in regard to race, nationality, age, income, sex, disabilities, and skills. They can live in or outside of the project, take classes or work, but must be willing to work with others or share. Restrictions would be that you would be open to new ideas and not polarized and unwilling to change. People with different types of depression and anxiety problems and disabilities will be welcomed, because one of the goals of the PDF is to discover solutions. There will be many learning opportunities as well as teaching opportunities. The project will have extended boundaries by working with members of the cooperative farms. Special funding will also be available for veterans and their families (especially those who are homeless). The other question to be answered is: could this type of community be a substitute for a universal basic income for relieving stress for people in poverty? I feel that this is another way for people to lose their dignity, as it's just another money program. Instead, people have to have a feeling of accomplishment in what they do in bettering themselves. The social program in the PDP allows people to keep their dignity and not feel that they are dependent on the government. It is associated with one person helping another.

If the proper doctors are available (as noted previously in the book), this project would be ideal for extensive research for certain types of depression. The people would be easily accessible at all times and be able to work and be around community members. There would be sharing both ways. The nonprofit will have the personnel to apply for grants, especially for veterans. After some training, people could work on the cooperative farms and be apprentices in the construction industry so that they can increase their earning potential. Sharing and collaborative activities will make a difference in how people think of themselves and others. At least it would be an attempt to reduce the polarity and inequality that exist now. There could be constant research and evaluations by the people living in the community in order to provide new ideas and make the project relative to the needs of the people. Hopefully, this type of project could spread to other locations, and each new location would present new restraints and social conditions.

There are many ways the project can create income to expand the various programs available. An important goal would be to develop a means to redesign the food supply system and use regenerative agroecology for food production. This can be demonstrated in the project. We are limited in the amount of time left to understand how to prevent extensive erosion, the use of pesticides, herbicides, and chemical fertilizers that destroy the soils and insects and the destruction by storms relating to global warming. Under the Trump administration, the environment is being destroyed at an accelerated rate by giving large corporations the go-ahead to use natural resources free of charge. The sad thing is that these problems are hardly mentioned in corporate-owned media. We need to reverse this trend.

"Depressed? Anxious? Blame Neoliberalism" is an article in the magazine *In These Times*, March 2018, by Johann Hart. Following is an excerpt:

> The public debate for decades now concerning depression has focused on biological factors, like the notion that depression is caused by low serotonin, a myth that has shown to be demonstrably false. Neoliberalism poses many problems, but perhaps the most neglected is that it has supercharged our current crisis of depression and anxiety. All human beings have natural psychological needs: to feel we belong, to feel we are secure, to feel we are valued, to feel we have a secure future we can begin to understand. These are ingrained in all of us all. Neoliberalism does a very poor job of meeting these

psychological needs, in part because its theory of human nature doesn't match with human nature. and all humans crave connection-to other people, to meaning, to the natural world.

Recognizing Adolescent Depression: In an article in the Mental Health America website, "Depression in Teens," it noted that adolescent depression is increasing at an alarming rate. Recent surveys indicate that as many as one in five teens suffers from clinical depression. This is a serious problem that calls for prompt, appropriate treatment. Depression can take several forms, including bipolar disorder (formally called manic depression), which is a condition of alternating between periods of euphoria and depression.

> Unrealistic academic, social, or family expectations can create a strong sense of rejection and can lead to deep disappointment. When things go wrong at school or at home, teens often overreact. Depression can be difficult to diagnose in teens because adults may expect teens to act moody. Also, adolescents do not always understand or express their feelings very well. They may not be aware of the symptoms of depression and may not seek help. Teens may experiment with drugs or alcohol or become sexually promiscuous to avoid feelings of depression. Teens also may express their depression through hostile, aggressive, risk-taking behavior. But such behaviors only lead to new problems, deeper levels of depression and destroyed relationships with friends, family, law enforcement or school officials.

Two or more of the triplex units in the PDP could be allocated for people who are distressed. They will be included in group talks and also work within the community as a form of treatment. This would not only help the persons with depression but also offer a different setting for research.

Depression and Eating: Dr. Mercola's newsletter of March 22, 2018, is titled "Abdominal Obesity Linked to Anxiety and Depression" (https://articles.mercola.com/sites/articles/archive/2018/03/22/abdominal-obesity-linked-to-anxiety-depression.aspx). It discusses:

> Depression and anxiety are two leading mental health problems that have seen a dramatic rise in incidence in recent years. Worldwide, depression is now the leading cause of ill health and disability, with rates rising 18 percent in the decade between 2005 and 2015. In the U.S., more than 16 million people struggle with the condition, and 1 in 4 women in their 40s and 50s are on antidepressant drugs. This, despite the fact that antidepressants have been proven to work no better than placebo. Eight to 14 percent of pregnant women are also on antidepressants, even though studies have linked their use during pregnancy to birth defects. Meanwhile, data from the National Institute of Mental Health suggests the prevalence of anxiety disorders — which include generalized anxiety disorder, social anxiety and panic disorder — may be as high as 40 million in the U.S. — about 18 percent of the population over the age of 18 — making it the most common mental illness in the nation, and 800 percent more prevalent than all forms of cancer.

With the high depression rate in the United States, there may be a link to overeating to compensate for the feeling of depression. An interesting article published by Healthline on May 26, 2017, by Ana Gotter titled "Coping with Depression and Overeating" (https://www.healthline.com/health/depression-and-overeating) discusses:

The link between depression and overeating. They noted that a 2012 study has shown why both stress and eating poorly are linked to an increased risk for anxiety and depression. According to the Anxiety and Depression Association of America, people with obesity who have binge eating disorders typically struggle with some sort of mental illness, including anxiety or depression. Both conditions have the ability to cause the other: If overeating leads to weight gain and an inability to control binge eating, depression may follow. Depression itself may also trigger overeating as a coping mechanism.

"Suicide rising across the U.S." is an article on Center of Disease Control and Prevention website from June 2018 (https://www.cdc.gov/vitalsigns/suicide/index.html). It noted:

> 1). Suicide rates went up more than 30% in half of the states since 1999, 2) Nearly 45,000 lives lost to suicide in 2016, and 3) More than half (54%) of people who died by suicide did not have a known mental health condition. Many factors contribute to suicide among those with and without mental health conditions: Relationship problem (42%), Problematic substance use (28%), Crisis in the past or upcoming two weeks (29%), Criminal legal problem (9%), Physical health problem (22%), Loss of housing (4%) and Job/Financial problem (16%). Note: Persons who died by suicide may have had multiple circumstances. Data on mental health conditions and other factors are from coroner/medical examiner and law enforcement reports. It is possible that mental health conditions or other circumstances could have been present and not diagnosed, known, or reported. Suicide rates are one of the factors that show the social stability of a society and we in the United States have to be more aware of people in trouble.

An article in the *Washington Post* by Heather Long (March 30, 2018), titled "The unhappy states of America: Despite an improving economy, Americans are glum" (https://www.washingtonpost. com/news/wonk/wp/2018/03/30/the-unhappy-states-of-america-despite-an-improving-economy-americans-are-glum/?utm_term=.b382671107ce), notes the following:

> The Gallup-Sharecare Well-Being Index started in 2008 as a way to assess how Americans are doing beyond the usual financial and economic metrics. Every year, Gallup interviews more than 160,000 adults in the United States and asks them about their sense of purpose, their social relationships, their financial security, their health and their connectedness to their community. In a surprise to the researchers, 2017 turned out to be the worst year for well-being on record. The overall index score was even lower than during the financial crisis, and, for the first time in the decade that Gallup has done this poll, no state in the country showed a statistically significant increase in well-being.

The fact that there are so many people that commit suicide who do not have signs of mental health problems is very disturbing. There seems to be a link between suicide and depression that should be studied. There is much work to be done by all of us to solve these social problems. The first step is to be aware that they are there. Making caps stating "Make America Great Again" is not a realistic start. We at least need sincere compassion.

Reducing Consumerism, Collaboration, Using Local Currencies, and Specific Technologies

Reducing Consumerism

Right now, it is hard for people to reduce consumerism due to advertising's blitz of all types of products. Then there is the perceived prestige of keeping up with the Joneses, needing of the next new technology and a host of other excuses, because many people think consumerism is a way to obtain happiness. Reading some of the books in the resource list, you can discover that this isn't necessarily so. The way to reduce consumerism is to ignore what you think you want (want is different from need—with the exception being your wife's/husband's birthday), and one way of reducing buying is to buy something after a few days of thinking it over and not having it be a spur-of-the-moment decision. There may be an exception to this rule if you are a collector and see a one-of-a-kind object that speaks to you.

The book *The More of Less* by Joshua Becker, 2016, (SC76) discusses what steps can be made to reduce excessive spending habits. A summary can be found on the internet.

> Excessive consumption leads to bigger houses, faster cars, trendier clothes, fancier technology, and overfilled drawers. It promises, happiness but never delivers. Why is that? Because consumption never fully delivers on its promise of fulfillment or happiness. Instead, it steals our freedom and results only in an unquenchable desire for more. It brings burdens and regret. It distracts us from the very things that do bring us joy. Now, resisting consumerism won't give us happiness in itself. What matters is what we fill the empty space with. But we have to start somewhere. (p. 47)[37]. He notes the tools of the trade advertisers use to trap us into buying, such as 1- Loyalty points and cards, 2- Retail-Stores credit cards, 3- Scarcity mind-set, 4- Instant markdown, 5- decoy pricing, 6- Loss leader, 7- samples and 8- Architectural layouts. (p. 58–61)[38]

The author then details the types and attitudes of consumerism in each of the generations.

I wish I had read this book earlier because I am now living in a house filled with books, crafts, clothing, and excess furniture. My wife and daughter were both professors, and we all had a fetish for collecting clothing, art, and books. Now some of it we cannot give away. My sister had a good answer to this problem she sold her house, put the furniture in my brother's barn, and moved to Panama near a beach.

The book *The Price of Everything,* by Eduardo Porter, (SC88) has a subtitle "Solving the Mystery of Why We Pay What We Do."

> Herein lies the central claim of this book: every choice we make is shaped by the prices of the options laid out before us—what we assess to be their relative costs—measured up against their benefits. Sometimes the trade-offs are transparent and straightforward—such as when we pick the beer on sale over our favorite brand. But the Indian scavenger girl may not be aware of the nature of her transaction. Knowing where to look for the

prices steering our lives—and undress ending the influence of our actions on the prices arrayed before us—will not only help us better our decisions. The prices we face as individuals and societies—how they change as we follow one path or another—provide a powerful vantage point upon the unfolding of history. (p 3–4)[39] Children in many cases are influenced by what they see on television. "Peanuts," took to my mind the most precise stab at the underlying epistemological problem "My life has no purpose, no direct, no aim, no meaning, and yet I'm happy. I can't figure it out. What am I doing right?" (p 64)[40]

Additional information about consumerism is located in the section "Advertising and Marketing—What to Do."

Collaboration

The planning for collaborative communities such as the PDP is based on the economics of sustainability and profitability within the individual community. In order for this to be successful, each employment base should be analyzed prior to or during its development. This consists of four parts: the (1) service employment that would be generated to maintain the community public functions, (2) the employment for the businesses and activities within the community, (3) the work that is available in the surrounding area outside of the community, and (4) the need for specialized temporary labor in the construction trades and other trades as applicable. The number of jobs in each part would depend on the projected size of the community and the functions within it in terms of employment. Planning this initially would be a unique practice, but it would create a longer-term sustainable community.

Site planning would minimize the need of the automobile by limiting the width of streets and having community automobiles and busses available for use. Energy use could be reduced by individual energy-efficient and passive housing designs and landscaping to allow for heating and cooling. Alternative energy could be used and would be adaptable for incorporating new technologies that use little energy. Bike trails and open greenbelts and parks make walking and biking an efficient and enjoyable means of transportation.

Collaborative functions could further reduce family expenses and allow for people to generate extra income, while seniors would have opportunities to work and enjoy the recreational facilities. There would not be large institutional housing developments for them. It is known that most seniors are ideal babysitters. The community would then have group buying power to further reduce family expenditures. There could be IT linkage for all the homes, where people could list what they needed or to sell or give to others. This would also list job opportunities for community members. Many of the businesses would be cooperatives in one form or another in which community members could make additional income.

The community would also emphasize being a teaching community, and there would be vocational instruction and other training available within the individual cooperatives. Local coordination with government agencies, NGOs, nearby school districts, community colleges, and universities are other options to pursue. A community association or the nonprofit could design applicable ordinances for the community and govern like a village or town government. They would furnish and collect utility fees and other use fees as allowed. All ordinances could be voted on each year and could require at least a 60 percent (or other percent) approval. This would have to be designed during the planning process, and its location would be a factor.

Following are some additional ideas that could be incorporated into a collaborative community to make it more sustainable in providing continuous employment and recognition of the importance of the environment and eco accountability.

The main purpose of this new collaborative community is to provide a community that will be self-sufficient over a long period (or a short period if we don't do anything about our environmental and agricultural problems). In review, some of the primary factors suggested are as follows:

1. That persons and families be interviewed to determine their willingness to live in this type of community. This would also determine what skills they have and their aspirations for additional skills or occupations to pursue.

2. That the design of the community will include the determination (approximately) of the type of community, types of businesses, and public facilities to be included and the types and number of jobs that required to serve the community through an estimated period of time.

3. That the income from the community in fees, profits on sales, rent, and so on will be partially sufficient to pay back money expended for the financing of the community development or to provide additional services. Grants would also be part of the income stream. A feasibility study and market study will be required to establish orderly development activities.

4. That some of the families living in the community will have the option of working outside of the PDP.

Local Currencies

As noted before, in order to create many of the various services in this report, there needs to be a nonprofit established in order to obtain grants and other types of funding. There is information in books and on the internet showing how to do this. Also, some banking systems may be available as a source of funds. If they aren't there, history will be of value. Look on the internet under "local currencies" (Vancity Savings Credit Union—see Wikipedia). Other interesting companies and banks to review are: Mountain Equipment Co-Op, Corporation 20/20, Upstream 21, Mondragon Cooperative Corporation (MCC) in Spain Business Alliance for Local Living Economies (BALLE), Grameen Bank (Micro-Loans), the JAK Members Bank in Sweden (see Wikipedia), and the State Bank of North Dakota, the only state-owned bank in the United States. In order to understand what the bank does, the following information is from an interview with the magazine *Mother Jones*. "How the Nation's Only State-Owned Bank Became the Envy of Wall Street" by Josh Harkinson, March 27, 2009 (https://www.motherjones.com/politics/2009/03/how-nations-only-state-owned-bank-became-envy-wall-street/):

The Bank of North Dakota is the only state-owned bank in America—what Republicans might call an idiosyncratic bastion of socialism. It also earned a record profit last year even as its private-sector corollaries lost billions. To be sure, it owes some of its unusual success to North Dakota's well-insulated economy, which is heavy on agricultural staples and light on housing speculation. But that has not stopped out-of-state politicos from beating a path to chilly Bismarck in search of advice. Could opening state-owned banks across America get us out of the financial crisis? It certainly might help, says Ellen Brown, author of the book, Web of Debt, who writes that the Bank of North Dakota, with its $4 billion under management, has avoided the credit freeze by "creating its own credit, leading the nation in establishing state economic sovereignty."

An excellent book, *Money* (SC49) by Thomas Greco, provides a history of local currencies and an explanation of the common forms and institutions that are used today. It shows how communities can get funded through trade exchanges and other means. Greco states:

That the entire machinery of money and finance has now been appropriated to serve the interests of centralized powers. The key element in any strategy to transform society must therefore be the liberation of money and the exchange process. If money is liberated, commerce will be liberated; if commerce is liberated, the people will be empowered to the full extent of their abilities to serve one another; the liberation of capital and land and the popular control of politics will follow as a matter of course. Once equitable exchange mechanisms have been established, it will no longer be possible for the privileged few to appropriate the major portion of the land, productive resources and political power. (p. 13)[41]

This is why it is vital that the PDP becomes independent from the control of the present money system. Bartering, sharing, and using local currencies are some ways that this can be done.

Thomas Greco, in another book, *The End of Money and the Future of Civilization* (SC 50), asks:

What needs to happen to reverse the destructive and despotic trends, and prevent our sliding into a modernistic feudalism? In my opinion, we need (at a minimum) to find ways of achieving a number of goals: 10 Power and control need to be centralized, 2) Wealth must be more fairly distributed, 3) Local economies must be nurtured, 4) The commons, especially the credit commons, must be restored, 5) Monopolies must be eliminated or circumvented, 6) The basic necessities of life- especially water, air, food, and energy-must be brought under popular control and 7) Ecological restoration must be a high priority. (p. 230)[42]

These statements represent a common theme, and by instituting most of the goals of the PDP, we can get on the pathway to there.

Creating Wealth (SC16)[43] explores the use of natural capital and local currency options that are different from the other sources and political power books. These are too involved to discuss further but should be consulted during the planning stages. Local currency is one of the best ways to bring communities together and encourage sharing within the community. This would be very valuable for transitional and postcapitalist societies. In fact, some local currencies could be tied to the activities and actions of the local and farmers' cooperatives. This way, the value of money would not be tied to the national economy in times of a recession.

Specific Technologies and Observations

There are many new technologies coming out monthly, and they should be reviewed and evaluated to see if they are applicable for community development. One concept would be LucidEnergy (https://thinkprogress.org/its-not-a-pipe-dream-clean-energy-from-water-pipe ...).

> There's one place with near-constant running water that can be tapped for energy without causing environmental problems: cities' drinking water pipes. LucidEnergy, a Portland, Oregon-based startup that launched in 2007, is starting to capture the energy of water pipes, beginning with a pilot project in Riverside, California and now with a full-scale project in Portland. Gregg Semler, president and CEO of LucidEnergy, said his team originally went into the business of hydropower by looking at ways to capture energy from streams. But they soon realized that it was difficult to predict the flow of a stream, and that generating hydropower could be environmentally degrading. Pipes, on the other hand, are existing-man made infrastructure, so equipping them to be power producers doesn't present any environmental concerns. They also pump water daily at a fairly constant rate, which allows for a consistent flow of energy.

This is but one company, and there are many more out there.

One source of information would be a magazine (including digital) titled *MIT Technology Review*. One thing I could never understand is why people can't design a system of storing the energy caused by the circular movement of wheels on a car. Could a generator be fitted on each wheel?

Many of the books noted about postcapitalism should be reviewed to discover new technology as well as the shifting economic situation to determine if there any trends toward postcapitalism. The government's position on climate change and reduction or eliminating safety and environmental regulations may move us faster in that direction. Would corporations be in another form, such as cooperatives, worker-owned companies, or just going without, because the natural resources have been used up? Could we live on polluted water and grass? Many people say the answer is technology and artificial intelligence. If the mistakes we are making now aren't artificial, what would you call it—Trumpism?

The book that explains what is happening to us is *Immoderate Greatness—Why Civilizations Fail* (CE61)[44] by William Ophuis. It is only 103 pages, but it offers an explicit description of why civilizations fail and how we now are heading that way. In "Biophysical Limits," he explains why ecological exhaustion, exponential growth, expedited entropy, and excessive complexity are factors that provide limits as to what we can do as a civilization. Added to this are our human errors of moral decay and practical failure. His conclusion on pages 68 and 69 provides an alternative to civilization as it is currently conceived. His analysis, in my opinion, is the most conceivable of any I have read. Please read his book to better understand what I am talking about.

Another evaluation to consider from an economic standpoint is the proper meaning of value. Value must be recognized in order to make all parties associated with creating value (in a corporation or public entity) understand what is needed in the changing conditions we are entering. The book *The Value of Everything—Making and Taking in the Global Economy* (CE64) discusses this in detail.

> At the heart of today's financial and economic crisis is a problem hiding in plain sight. In modern capitalism, value-extraction is rewarded more highly than value-value creation (which is) the productive process that drives a healthy economy and society. From companies driven solely to maximize shareholder value to astronomically high prices of medicines justified through big Pharma's value pricing, we misidentify taking with making, and have lost sight of what value really means. Yet, argues Mariana Mazzucato, if we are to reform capitalism we urgently need to rethink where wealth comes from. Which activities create it, which extract it, which destroy it? Answers to these questions are key if we want to replace the current system with a type of capitalism that works for us all. (Back cover)[45]

. In a newsletter by Sovereign Man (Simon Black) published on September 7, 2018, he described the dire situation of America's pension plans (https://mail.google.com/mail/u/0/?tab=wm#inbox/ FMfcgxvzKQsXKKfLvnFxLBzSpplvhdGX):

> Right now many pension funds around the world simply don't have enough assets to cover the retirement obligations they owe to millions of workers. In the US alone, federal, state, and local governments, pensions are about $7 trillion short of the funding they need to pay out all the benefits they've promised. (And that does't include another $49 trillion in unfunded social security obligations). America's private pensions are in bad shape too --a total of around 1,400 corporate pensions are a combined $553 billion in the hole. In 2015, the total worldwide gap in pension funding was $70 trillion according to the World Economic Forum. The WEC said that the worldwide pension shortfall is on track to reach $400 trillion by 2050. There just not enough young people being born to pay out benefits for retirees. By 2060, 40% of the population will be over 65.

There is additional information in the newsletter. Many people who will be dependent on pensions may face a dismal future. This and our present debt load add to the complexity of times ahead. Add this to our other problems, such as lack of natural resources, soil erosion, climate change, and lack of affordable housing (rent and ownership), our present good (?) economy does little to comfort our children. No wonder we are suffering from anxiety and depression. Now Trump is extolling that we are in one of the highest economic periods in history with high economic growth, plentiful job openings, low unemployment, and high numbers on the stock market. This is true, but it applies mainly to the top 20 percent of the economic ladder. This is the group of people he is catering to, to the detriment of others. Previous articles have shown how the middle class is shrinking, and the wages for the lower 50 percent have stayed level in the past twenty years. An article in the *Washington Post*, on May 25, 2018, by Heather Long, titled "The alarming statistics that show the U.S. economy isn't as good as it seems," discusses this point. (https://www.washingtonpost.com/news/wonk/wp/2018/05/25/the-alarming-statistics-that-show-the-u-s-economy-isnt-as-good-as-it-seems/?utm_term=.5b74c403001f):

In the past week, two reports — a new Federal Reserve survey of more than 12,200 Americans about their finances and a new United Way report on financial hardship — reveal just how unstable life remains for a large number of people. Here's a rundown of the key findings:

Forty percent of American adults don't have enough savings to cover a $400 emergency expense such as an unexpected medical bill, car problem or home repair. Forty-three percent of households can't afford the basics to live, meaning they aren't earning enough to cover the combined costs of housing, food, child care, health care, transportation and a cellphone, according to the United Way study. Researchers looked at the data by county to adjust for lower costs in some parts of the country. More than a quarter of adults skipped necessary medical care last year because they couldn't afford it. Twenty-two percent of adults aren't able to pay all of their bills every month. Only 38 percent of non-retired Americans think their retirement savings is "on track." Only 65 percent of African Americans and 66 percent of Hispanics say they are "doing okay" financially vs. 77 percent of whites.

Economic Development Options

There are about four economic development options that society can review at this time. We are late in deciding what direction to take, due to many uncertain circumstances. Detailed information found in the list of books will provide insights into each of them. The options can be taken all at once, or they might be combined using specific restraints. The important thing is that the public is made aware that these options even exist and that critical environmental and economic decisions are made to prevent problems that could cause catastrophic results.

1. Our Present Situation—The Capitalist Society

We can continue on the same path with token green solutions added to make it look like the resource depletion and climate change problems are being addressed. Residential tips on saving water is one example. This is needed but will not affect the overall path to sustainability at the scale that is required. Many environmentalists feel that climate change cannot be reduced in a capitalistic society. The book *Extreme Cities* (E46)[46] shows the effects of climate change and disasters on cities. One example is that the cost of disaster relief in the United States in 2017 was over $300 billion. Another example were the rains occurring in India and Bangladesh.

On CNN, an article, "A third of Bangladesh under water as flood devastation widens" by Steve George, August 1, 2017 (https://www.cnn.com/2017/09/01/asia/bangladesh-south-asia-floods/index.html), noted:

> In Bangladesh and India, the International Federation of Red Cross and Red Crescent Societies (IFRC) estimates that at least 1,200 have died and more than 41 million people have been affected by monsoon rains and severe flooding as of June this year. The rains are now moving northwest towards Pakistan. At its peak on August 11, the equivalent to almost a week's worth of average rainfall during the summer monsoon season was dumped across parts of Bangladesh in the space of a few hours, according to the country's Meteorological Department, forcing villagers in low-lying northern areas to grab what few possessions they could carry and flee their homes in search of higher ground. And still the rains keep coming. In Bangladesh alone, floods have so far claimed the lives of 142 people, and impacted over 8.5 million.

The problem is that the change we got in the election could be called overshooting. Inequality is increasing along with racism. Our fix-it Congress has only a 20 percent approval rating even when they say they are doing what they can for the American people. This is while they are hiding all the perks they are getting. Extensive lobbying, corporation and government corruption, need for finance reform for elections, threats of war, refugee and immigration problems—these are just a few items that need to be addressed. Many of these and other problems are noted in the book *This Changes Everything* (E44)[47] by Naomi Klein. Since so many things are growing exponentially, there isn't much time left to save ourselves from total chaos. Our present rate of consumerism has to be reduced regardless of what else is happening. If chaos does occur, what do we do with a lot of our structures if they become vacant and we can't afford to pick up the waste we have generated?

In the book *Limits to Growth* (CE9), it is noted that:

Each unit of industrial output consumes nonrenewable resources. Technological advance in the model will gradually reduce the amount of resources needed per unit of industrial production, all else being equal. But the model does not allow industry to manufacture material goods out of nothing. As nonrenewable resources diminish, the efficiency of resource capital declines—one unit of capital delivers fewer and fewer resources to the industrial sector. The book shows different scenarios (1–10) showing the effects of technology, population growth, etc on society, etc. This is an expanded analysis of what I am showing here. (p. 144)[48]

2. Capitalist Society with Improving Technology to Solve Problems

Many people feel that technology improvements will keep society from declining. Many books disagree with this assumption, including *Shrinking the Technosphere* (E38)[49] and *The Immoderate Greatness* (CE61).[50] These books should be read in order to understand their reasoning. In one section of the book *Shrinking the Technosphere,* it states that companies should evaluate the harm/benefit ratio for existing and new technologies. He shows a list of thirty-two harmful and beneficial conditions that would be applicable. To this I would include a time and cost study of cradle to grave or cradle-to-cradle study of costs and environmental damage potential. Some technologies act in opposition to each other, and one of them can be to offset the other.

3. Society with Reduced Consumption and Minimal Nonrenewable Resources

Several of the books mentioned earlier provide scenarios of what this would entail and the consequences thereof. The problem will get worse the longer we wait, especially when we ignore climate change, the broken food supply chain, and other nonrenewable depletions. Our economic footprint must be reduced by making people know what they are doing to the earth. The book *Our Ecological Footprint* (E9)[51] explains this process in detail. To obtain updated information, go to the website Global Footprint Network, and it will have data on the ecological footprints of most of the countries in the world (https://www.footprintnetwork.org/our-work/ecological-footprint/):

The Ecological Footprint is a measure of the "load" imposed by a given population on nature. It represents the land area necessary to sustain current levels of resource consumption and waste discharge by that population. Updated information can be found on the Global Footprint Network. For example, in 2014 the United States had a population of 319 million and a GDP per person of $50,283 while India had a population of 1.2 billion and a GDP per person of $500. The ecological footprint for the United States was 8.4 global hectares(gha) (1 hectare=2.47 acres) per person and a biocapacity reserve of -4.8 gha and in India the ecological footprint was 1.1 gha and its biocapacity reserve was -1.1 gha. In 2015 the U.S had reached its yearly bio capacity by July and the rest of the year was a deficit.

The United States is way over what it should be due to consumption, fossil fuel use, and so on.

4. A Society Collapsed and in Chaos

This is what we don't want to happen.

What we do now as a worldly society will determine which of these four options we find ourselves in. It will be determined by the time it takes us to recognize our social and environmental problems. We are seeing faster changes happen now than ever before due to the pace of technology development and exponential growth factors. It is up to us to decide now since we are one of the leading developed countries in the world. One of the purposes of this book is to show everyone the options and reasons to make these various decisions.

The book *Four Futures* (SC67) presents its interpretation of life after capitalism:

> There are four suggestions noted and they are, (1) Communism: Equality and Abundance, (2) Rentism: Hierarchy and Abundance, (3) Socialism: Equality and Scarcity and (4) Exterminism: Hierarchy and Scarcity. It notes that we can't go back to the past, and we can't even hold on to what we have now. Something new is coming—and indeed, in some way, all four futures are already here. The above information and reflections presents what is the existing and projected conditions for our society.[52]

Next, I will present several arguments as to why we should have this pilot demonstration project in order to prepare for the future, while offering an existing livable platform of how to do it. In summary, the elimination of poverty requires recognition of limits, so that we do not increase inequality instead of faster growth, including limits to growth in per capita resource use, limits to population growth in all countries, and limits to the growth of greed and power. Presently, we are not recognizing (or not wanting to recognize) that current growth will exceed earth's carrying capacity. Wikipedia (https://en.wikipedia.org/wiki/Carrying_capacity) defines carrying capacity as:

> The carrying capacity of a biological species in an environment is the maximum population size of the species that the environment can sustain indefinitely, given the food, habitat, water, and other necessities available in the environment. In population biology, carrying capacity is defined as the environment's maximal load, which is different from the concept of population equilibrium. Its effect on population dynamics may be approximated in a logistic model, although this simplification ignores the possibility of overshoot which real systems may exhibit. The carrying capacity of an environment may vary for different species and may change over time due to a variety of factors including: food availability, water supply, environmental conditions and living space.

Again, one of the main objectives of this project is to show how a new type of sharing and sustainable city prototype can function and be a viable solution for living in the capitalist, transition, and postcapitalist societies. Unless something is done relatively soon, there could be grave consequences. The earth is running out of natural resources. Presently, "growth" is the outcry that most businesses say when they need to keep increasing in order to maintain our present society. The feedback loops are negative and increasing to the point that our society is getting too complex to keep it functioning. By using up our resources, creating waste, and increasing air pollution and social inequities, we are rapidly declining as a civilization. Shortsighted beliefs in our present way of doing things will be our downfall. Earlier, it was shown why we need a society that is both economically and socially different from the capitalist society we are living in now. If we are at all ethical, we must provide a healthy earth for future generations.

In the *Community Resilience Reader* (UP2), it noted that sustainable consumption must call for:

1. Absolute reductions in the material goods and energy we consume and a shift in values away from material wealth and consumerism toward new measures of progress and well-being.

2. Technological innovation and efficiency gains that help us refine the production process, creating less impact on the planet. Recognition that consumption will need to increase for individuals and communities whose needs are not being met.

3. A transformation of our economy from one defined by continuous growth to one that functions within the very real limits of a finite planet.

4. A shift in values away from material wealth and consumerism toward new measures of progress and well-being.

5. Recognition that consumption will need to increase for those individuals and communities whose needs are not being met. (p. 262)[53]

The pilot demonstration project will highlight alternative economic and business models that minimize environmental impacts and show inclusive and equitable community economies. Some of the goals for the PDP will correspond with a list provided in the *Community Resilience Reader* (UP2). These are noted as follows (Rosemary Cooper):

1. Reduction of the amount of materials consumed: Smaller homes, more efficiently made products, absolute reductions in the amount of goods purchased, streamlining or eliminating product packaging, food waste prevention and the reuse of products and materials:

2. Repair and maintenance of products to extend their useful life: Repair businesses, repair cafes and fix-it clinics, the -do-it-yourself (DIY) repair movement and the sharing of products, services, and land, including via borrowing and renting: Tool and other lending libraries, clothing swaps, food gleaning programs, community gardens.

3. Use of durable, long-lasting and upgradable products and materials: More durably made goods, goods that are more repairable, leasing versus purchasing, extended product warranties and the use of lower-impact, equitably sourced products made using materials and resources that are rapidly renewable, able to be replenished, and less toxic than conventional materials: (p. 264)[54]

See the books *The Mesh* (SC20)[55] and *What Is Mine Is Yours* (SC21)[56] for additional information on how the processes of sharing and collaboration are working now.

I cannot note in this book all of the great ideas expressed by all of the authors, and I hope what I have included here is not that far out of context. The concept and value of the pilot demonstration project will be elaborated on and expanded in detail so that people see that is an option leading to self-sufficiency. I will include the following topics:

1. Governance—cooperatives, creative commons, and the solidarity economy

2. Advertising and marketing of the project and its ideals and goals

3. Environmental and economic opinions in the United States

In each of the categories, there will be several options or scenarios presented for evaluation. Some may not be applicable for certain locations due to existing site conditions or established laws and ordinances. Also, combinations of the options may be applicable, and it is up to the developer or nonprofit to determine what would work according to budget restraints and other factors. If funding becomes available, then an economic and environmental feasibility study will be made for certain approved options. The additional goal of this book is to stimulate other ideas that could work. Since there is so much information available, it is difficult to include it in one book. That is why so many books are listed in the reference list. Many of the books noted were written several years ago. This is especially true for books about culture and nature. An example would be books by Schumacher, Steele, Thoreau, Muir, Carson, Jacobs, Leopold, and McHarg, to mention a few.

My viewpoints about nature were in part developed by my father continually reading me *The Bears of Blue River* by Charles Major. By the time we finished all of the many readings, I think he knew it by heart. My mother was an uncertified naturalist and stressed how much we owed to nature. It didn't hurt that we lived in Skaneateles, a beautiful small town in Upstate New York on one of the finger lakes. We also had white-tail deer wander through the lot, and I could walk to a stream in the woods nearby and fish for trout and watch polliwogs grow. I could sit for hours just enjoying the beauty of nature. I also worked on my grandfather's farm (which was next door to the house) and at a florist that grew their own flowers in greenhouses. The following poem expresses the feelings I have about "Home."

It seems so long ago, and yet there is nothing left now but the old homestead.
The harvest of memories have long since gone into the recesses of my mind,
There to be found when I think of times long past.
I am often walking with my mother guiding me in a path that was always true,
For her spirit reminds me each day to be a child in every way.
For children see things that are long forgot, only to be remembered in our dreams.
By these windows we grew up, not knowing how much it would mean to be in a place so filled with love.
Now we move from place to place, hoping for the chance to enjoy all the times past.
The windows are broken now, unable to keep these memories inside but let them escape to be with us in what we do.
The boards have lost their paint; the fireplace no longer spreads its warmth.

We can still hear the voices of the spirits that dwelt within,
Calling again to show us the way from which we sometimes wander,
Only to be drawn back into a circle of love that was always there,
And lasting until we have to join them deep in the recesses of our spirit.
For this we are forever grateful of all the memories that were there,
Which remind us now of the past and help guide us in what we do.
For we are no more, or much less, than the strength of our memories
That carry us wherever we go and remind us of the place we use to know.
George Hunt, "What Do You See"—Memories

Governance—Cooperatives, Creative Commons, and the Solidarity Economy

There are many options available for determining the type of governance for this type of community. Some stretch conventional thinking and existing laws. The consumer society we are in encourages "not in my backyard" (NIMBY) thinking, and this further exacerbates inequity. In a way, this thinking is understandable, but it harms society. This does not encourage society to have lasting strength to endure what may happen if we continue to ignore the use of nonrenewable resources. Remember, pollution does not distinguish between the elite and the other 80 percent. On top of this, we should not go to developing countries to get their resources, leaving more poverty and pollution there. The book *New Confessions of an Economic Hit Man* (CE59)[57] provides many examples of how the developed world has caused misery in third world countries. The structural adjustment programs of the World Bank is one example.

Option 1: The Conventional Approach

The conventional method of obtaining development approval is to submit a plan and documentation to a governing body such as a village, town, county, or city (in US). They review it to see if it corresponds to existing zoning (except in Houston and some other entities). The staff reviews the application and with its recommendations sends it to a planning commission for approval, and this may require a public hearing. After this planning commission meeting, adjustments are made, and it is scheduled for a public meeting before the city council. It then is approved (with additional requirements if deemed necessary) or disapproved. This can be a fast or slow process depending on the complexity of the application and in what city or county the project is located. What I am suggesting may be too complex for some municipalities. Hopefully, the governing entity recognizes that the plan submitted constitutes sustainable development and is a demonstration project. This is why I included certain books in the urban planning references. The attitude of people who believe that more growth is necessary could be hard to overcome. *Better Not Bigger* (UP6) is one of the best books available provide an alternative viewpoint to having more growth:

> The standard refrain of many public offices is that "growth is a given." It's not a question of whether we'll grow, but they say, but how. This sort of resignation that growth is inevitable is simplistic at best. At worst, it shows a callous attitude toward the legitimate concerns of citizens and a reckless disregard for the long-term consequences of endless urban growth. (p. 8)[58]. Responsible policies toward growth will foster strong, healthy communities that will remain great places to live for generations to come. (p. 9)[59]

This book is intended to be a resource for individuals and groups who want to get off the treadmill of urban growth. It provides insights, ideas, information, tools, and techniques to make the transition away from growth-oriented and growth-addicted communities and toward stability. It brings together some of the best available information on these topics and is written for those who are seeking a more balanced, informed, and productive discussion about growth. Overall, the message is intended to be one of optimism and empowerment.

A classic book on this subject from a social and economic standpoint was written in 1973 by E. F. Shumacher, *Small Is Beautiful* (CE60). The book covers many subject, such as production and materialism, but its main focus is how we treat people in poverty, both in the US and foreign countries. One paragraph notes:

> We shrink back from the truth if we believe that the destructive forces off the modern world can be "brought under control" simply by mobilizing more resources-of wealth, education, and research-to fight pollution, to preserve wildlife, to discover new sources of energy, and to arrive at more effective agreement on peaceful coexistence. Needless to say, wealth, education, research and many other things are needed for any civilization, but what is needed today is a revision of the ends which these means are meant to serve. And this implies, above all else, the development of a life-style which accords to material things their proper, legitimate place, which is secondary and not primary. The logic of production" is neither the logic of life no that of society. (p. 178)[60]

If only we as a civilization had listened to him; we would not have as many problems in our country. Another book on this subject is *The Permaculture City* (UP3) by Toby Hemenway:

> Urban permaculture takes what we have learned in the garden and applies it to a much broader range of human experience. We're not just gardening plants but people, neighborhoods, and even cultures. Permaculture is applied ecology; that is, it is a design approach based on finding and applying. Tour own creations some of the guiding axioms at work in the natural ecosystems. We search for the principals that generate life's resilience, immense productivity, diversity, interconnectedness, and elegance. Life's wisdom can teach us to build sorely needed replacements for industrial production's murderous conditions, nonrenewable fuel, and toxic, landfills-clogging products. But nature can do more than improve how we make things. It can also teach us how to cooperate, make decisions, and arrive at good solutions. The most straightforward, easily comprehended way to learn nature's approach is by mimicking he form and processes of the natural environment. (p. ix–x)[61]

The PDP will have to demonstrate various practices that show how the growth problem is reduced or solved. It can begin by having people reduce consumption habits. This will increase the acceptance of smaller homes. The sustainable practices will reduce environmental problems, and local foods will be more nutritious. Sharing and collaboration could change the need for many items and reduce waste, and solar and passive energy designs will reduce electrical needs. The elimination of costs associated with automobiles could save people money. An example would be to have the community shop for all types of insurance and get group rates for community members. Water can be collected or designed to function as rain gardens. Jobs will be available in the community through small business development as well as community businesses. Community babysitting services will be convenient for families, and recreational facilities could increase the marking potential of the project. The teaching and education programs could allow people to better themselves without having to go long distances outside of the community to do so. Medical services will be available, and the multi-use aspect of all the buildings will keep the community viable, less expensive, and changeable so they can adapt to changing conditions. IT work stations will allow people to have technology that they couldn't otherwise afford.

Inexpensive social functions will bind the community together. Community money could offer opportunities that are not available in other communities. This is a short list, and many more can be designed for uses that will reduce the growth spiral that is causing inequities all over the world. This will be a nature-inspired community rather than a community that fights nature.

One thing that makes it easier for city governments to approve plans like the PDP is that they do not receive many applications for affordable housing, especially in a single community. After approval of the submitted plan, the only governing restrictions are what the developer places on the property (normally to maintain an elite status) or to have a homeowners association act as a form of governance. Most of the developments using conventional processes are based on capitalism and are encouraged by most cities. The *Hightower Lowdown* (volume 19, number 12, December 2017) noted the following (article edited to make it shorter):

> Last year, "Good Jobs" first tracked 386 incentive deals since 1976 that gave at least $50 million to a corporation and then tallied the number of jobs created. The average cost per job was $ 658,427 each. Some other examples showed that New York gave a $ 258-million subsidy to Yahoo and got 125 jobs-costing taxpayers 2 million per job. Louisiana handed $ 234 million to Valero Energy and got 125 jobs—$ 15.6 million per job. Oregon awarded $ 2 billion to Nike and got 500 jobs—$ 4 million per job. This situation happens quite often, but not to the extent proposed by Amazon. In times of a downturn a company that was given these concessions may decide to reduce payroll or move out of its "new" location? Do the taxpayers get their money back? What guarantees should the company offer the city if this happens? This process is a oneway street with the taxpayers going in the wrong direction.

The *Lowdown* is published once a month and is available by an inexpensive subscription. This entire article shows how Amazon is deceiving the public by wanting excessive concessions and claiming job opportunities that in turn are offset by job losses. At these rates, as noted above, job procurement would be at the head of the list. This type of information should be available so that people know what is happening around them and how they could be affected by government decisions. Remember this example when discussing the ethics of some corporations. This is one reason why there should be limits to the growth of our materialistic society.

Option 2: The Formation of a Community Commons Concept

The following discussion is from *Post-Capitalist Entrepreneurship* (CE1)[62] and notes that essentially the commons are resources that are shared with express or unwritten rules for ensuring the survival and growth of physical, digital, or cultural spaces. There is a long section in the book showing extensive information about the rights of the commons.

In the book, the author suggests the applicable benefit corporations and associations that should be considered for society are B corporations, platform cooperatives, alternative currencies (cryptocurrencies), distributed autonomous organizations, and alternative financing. He also has suggestions about what to look for in the future global economy, where the postcapitalist entrepreneurship can thrive in a reframing of the economy, where it is local and primarily urban while maintaining strong regional and global connections. Corporations using sustainable management—for example, the three bottom lines principle—and aligned with one of the applicable benefit corporation structures noted above could be a part of a transition or postcapitalist society. They would have to pay a nature fund for any natural resources used or pollution of the air, water, and so on.

Gwendolyn Hallsmith's book *The Key to Sustainable Cities* (SC24)[63] says options for sustainable cities can be a framework for other options of governance to be considered. It requires a new attitude for social development so that we do not keep using growth and capitalism concepts as our master. This is the least we can do for future generations.

> The book uses the principals of system dynamics to demonstrate how yesterday's solutions have turned into problems cities are facing today. The book points to a new approach to city planning that builds on assets as a starting point for city to develop healthy social, governance, economic, and environmental systems. It helps communities understand the forces that support unsustainable systems, gives them new ways to look at problems, and outlines tools for designing new strategies to improve their environmental, economic, and social performance by using powerful local leverage points for change. (on back cover by author)[64]

Option 3: Solidarity Economy

The solidarity economy is a collaborative economic concept that has been practiced in various parts of the world. An excellent description is noted in a twelve-page paper by Ethan Miller (2010) and can be found on the internet at "Solidarity Economy—Key Concepts and Issues—Ethan Miller." It also can be located at the US Solidarity Economy Network (www.ussen.org). Following is an excerpt from the paper:

> One of the great strengths and innovations of the solidarity economy movement is its ability to move beyond the factionalism that has so often weakened historical efforts to imagine and build other economies. Indeed, when faced with the question of economic alternatives, many activists have often been tempted to build or to seek a blueprint, a Big Plan, for how "the economy" should operate. While such "blueprints" for alternative economic structures can be very useful as tools for clarifying and motivating our work. This concept emphasizes a program that should be utilized in the proposed community. The entire paper should be read to get the full impact of the concept. Whatever is done, there should be many people involved to create the design and organization of the project.

Another connection in relationship to this is Grassroots Economic Organizing (catalyzing worker co-ops and the solidarity economy). They have many available papers and are willing to help with projects.

Option 4: Pilot Demonstration Governance

In developing the PDP, there has to be a determination of what type of governance would be applicable and then see what options are available for financing. Part of the answer will be determined by its location. If it is in a municipality, then it should be submitted as a special permit for a designated use. The project would not be approved at this time under most zoning ordinances without special conditions being applied and approved.

The developer would be a nonprofit organization. A charity's organizing document must limit the organization's purposes to exempt purposes set forth in section 501(c)(3) and must not expressly empower it to engage, other than as an insubstantial part of its activities, in activities that do not further those purposes. This requirement may be met if the purposes stated in the organizing document are limited by reference to section 501(c)(3). For development of the project in foreign countries, there would have to be a new analysis to see what is required legally. In addition, an organization's assets must be permanently dedicated to an exempt purpose. This means that if an organization dissolves, its assets must be distributed for an exempt purpose described in section 501(c)(3), or to the federal government, or to a state or local government for a public purpose. To establish that an organization's assets will be permanently dedicated to an exempt purpose, the organizing document should contain a provision ensuring their distribution for an exempt purpose if the organization dissolves. In certain situations, reliance may be placed upon state law to establish permanent dedication of assets for exempt purpose.

As noted earlier, the people selected to live in the project will be screened in order for it to function as designed for this specific concept. Many will work in the project, and others may have jobs outside of it. Now with computers, it is easier to work from home, and the working group noted above could finalize the social networking and job possibilities for the community. This process would adjust and change continually. Once 25 percent (or another percentage) of families are living in the project, a governing council could be established. Any major decisions that have to be made will be voted on by every adult, with a majority vote needed for approval of changes to a governing document. The original nonprofit (which can have changing personnel) could have the option to veto if the decisions violate the original bylaws. The bylaws will be established prior to any sales being made, and the PDP will be different from any other project because of all the research that has to take place.

In the site plan, the central agricultural research and educational area is to be part of a cooperative. A cooperative (also known as co-operative, co-op, or coop) is "an autonomous association of persons united voluntarily to meet their common economic, social, and cultural needs and aspirations through a jointly-owned and democratically-controlled enterprise." Cooperatives may include (Wikipedia) (https://en.wikipedia.org/wiki/Cooperative):

- businesses owned and managed by the people who use their services (a consumer cooperative)

- organizations managed by the people who work there (worker cooperatives)

- organizations managed by the people to whom they provide accommodation (housing cooperatives)

- hybrids such as worker cooperatives that are also consumer cooperatives or credit unions

- multi-stakeholder cooperatives such as those that bring together civil society and local actors to deliver community needs

- second- and third-tier cooperatives whose members are other cooperatives

- non-profit community organizations

Information about cooperatives can be found on the internet and YouTube. On Slideshare (https://www.slideshare.net/jobitonio/concepts-and-types of cooperatives), Jo Bitonio, professor/ program coordinator at Private and State Universities, listed different forms of cooperatives, such as Tubao Credit Cooperatives, Consumers Cooperatives, Producers Cooperatives, Marketing Cooperatives, Service Advocacy Cooperatives, Agrarian Reform Cooperatives, Cooperative Banks, Dairy Cooperatives, Education Cooperative, Electric Cooperative, Financial Service Cooperative, Fishermen Cooperative, Health Services Cooperatives, Insurance Cooperatives, Transport Cooperatives, Water Services Cooperatives, Workers Cooperatives, and other types as determined by an authority.

The nonprofit formed would be able to obtain funding from private investors, foundations, governments, and other sources through the cooperative network. Cooperatives (CE1) ownership is distributed across members and can also include different types, such as platform cooperatives (PC), which are more frequently about facilitating access to resources already produced and commons-based peer production (CBPP), which is generally about creating networks of coproduction and co-consumption. Various types will be utilized by the proposed community to fit various purposes.

When determining whether to form a cooperative, it would be helpful to review the article published by Chron titled "Advantages and Disadvantages of Business Cooperatives," by Kevin Johnston, June 27, 2018 (https://smallbusiness.chron.com/advantages-disadvantages-business-cooperatives-24608.html). The disadvantages can be adjusted if needed by use of bylaws and innovational ideas. Another example of a successful cooperative is the Mondragon cooperative in Spain. The Mondragon Corporation is a corporation and a federation of worker cooperatives based in the Basque region of Spain. It was founded in the town of Mondragon in 1956 by graduates of a local technical college. Its first product was paraffin heaters.

SECTION 2

Advertising and Marketing - What to Do

The project must develop a marketing system that can compete with the consumer advertising that is on TV, in newspapers, on the internet, and in magazines and flyers. This is a large order but one that must be done in order for our society to understand the problems with capitalism as it is being practiced. Not all corporations have ethical problems or damage the environment and society, but finding them would be quite a task because of the way most corporations have to do adhere to their legal objectives.

An article titled "Advertising—The Art of Capitalism" by Alla Zaykova (December 12, 2015) (https//midnghtmedia musings.wordpress.com/2015/12/12/advertising-the-art.) is included here in part because it is important information on how advertising is relative in a capitalistic society:

> Academic discourses usually position advertising as a tool of the capitalist countries to legitimize and reinforce its socio-political arrangements. Advertising does this by presenting consumption as an answer to all material and social needs. Fetishism of commodities infuses objects with powers objects cannot possess and "capitalist realism" presents an idyllic view of the world that is desirable, but impossible to achieve and which celebrates the capitalist way of life.

In *No Logo*, Naomi Klein (SC69)[65] presents a history of modern advertising that includes an analysis of how people have used it over a period of time. To present what she emphasizes in the book can be understood by reading the table of contents:

> (from table of contents) No Space (New Branded World, The Brand Expands, Alt.Everything, The Branding of Learning, Patriarchy Gets Funky), No Choice (Corporate Censorship, Brand Bombing, Mergers and Synergy), No Jobs (The Discarded Factory, Threats and Temps, Breeding Disloyalty), No Logo (Culture Jamming, Reclaim the Streets, Bad Mood Rising, The Brand Boomerang, A Tale of Three Logos, Local Foreign Policy, Beyond the Brand, Consumerism Versus Citizenship, Two Years on the Streets).

She gives a picture of advertising that would be helpful in designing an approach for promoting what is important in creating a sustainable and just world.

An interesting book is *Frenemies: The Epic Disruption of the Ad Business (and Everything else)* by Ken Auletta (SC90). It is an analysis of the present state of advertising and some of the problems and successes in advertising. A quote from the book notes:

> That among the hidden efforts of advertisers, critics most often latch on to how marketing manipulates our emotions. Industry leaders don't deny this, they extol it. Jack Haber, who retired as CMO of Colgate in 2017, says, "I'm a believer that consumers make decisions emotionally." As proof he cites Daniel Kahneman's esteemed best-selling book, Thinking, Fast and slow, to demonstrate that most human decisions pivot on emotion. "If you look at how people make decisions to buy things, people make decisions emotionally. That's why we try to build an emotional connection to a brand." This emotion can make people

buy things that they don't need or pay too high a price because they didn't want to spend time shopping. Low income families or depressed persons are especially vulnerable. (p. 184–185)[66]

The book also discusses ad blockers, mobile phone advertising, Facebook, Apple, and Google. The word "frenemies" refers to how one's friend can turn into a competitor. Anyone interested in these topics should read the book.

I feel that an advertising agency gets the most money for a questionable quality of work as compared to almost any other type of company. They are very intelligent in deception and stupid on content. I would like to know what grade level they are shooting for in their advertising. It's probably higher when they use a dog in the ad. (I am partial to golden retrievers.)

For example, anyone who would like to get pertinent information on a car would be out of luck. None of their ads provide performance facts because car companies would get in trouble from a marketing standpoint. If facts were mentioned, each company would have to keep improving to beat the facts provided by other companies. A car might actually last longer, with fewer replacement parts needed during its lifetime. In a postcapitalist society, cars that we have now probably would not be around, or they may have technologies that are more sustainable. Perhaps using hydrogen power will be the new frontier. There are also the ads that say that the people that they have used in the ad are people and not actors, but they did not note that the people are coached in what to say.

The worst ads are those sponsored by Big Pharma. When you time their ads, the side effects of advertised drugs versus the values offered by the product, the side effects are usually longer. Using some products for cosmetic purposes may cause death—for example, to cure pimples or some other minor ailment that could be fixed by a good diet. Notice that during the discussion of side effects, you are drowned out with nature or a pleasurable experience. Speaking of Big Pharma, there is a nonprofit called Worst Pills-Best Pills that offers an inexpensive monthly newsletter and can be a lifesaver. One of the drugs a doctor prescribed for me was on the list in the worst category and might have killed me if I had taken it. The good thing about the drug, however, was that it only cost $230 a month. They also noted in their March 2018 newsletter: (https://www.worstpills.org/login.cfm?redirected=1&page=/member/back_issues.cfm&qString=):

> That drug companies just raised their prices by 3% to 10%. Before this pharmaceutical companies were one of the few categories of corporations that made a yearly profit over 20%. At the high end of this range they increased the prices of Viagara, Lipitor, Zoloft, and Chantix.

Would this be enough to reduce sexual activities and smoking? There is also the differential between the cost of drugs in the United States and some other countries, as will be detailed later in the book. The relationships between some doctors and the drug companies also needs to be looked at, but don't go to the FDA for help. They are one of "the fox in the hen house" agencies. This is quite a world we live in. Who do you trust in government? Clue: it is a short answer.

We are discovering that many drugs are causing more problems with side effects than what their value is as a drug. Have you ever wondered what surveys were used to obtain their conclusions and who did the surveys (usually the drug manufacturers)? Was approval of a drug based on the fast-track method? And why is the same drug less expensive in other countries? I doubt even the men and women dressed in black visiting doctors' offices to sell the drug products could answer these questions. Perhaps the doctor couldn't either.

An article in Consumer Reports, "Find out if your doctor takes payments from drug companies—New government data show more than 500,000 U.S. physicians have industry ties," published September 30, 2014, (https://www.consumerreports.org/cro/news/2014/09/find-out-if-your-doctor-takes-payments-from-drug-companies/index.htm) noted:

> First, research shows these payments influence doctors in their choice of treatments. Second, our national telephone polls have consistently found that a strong majority of consumers are concerned about these cozy relationships. Our polls have also revealed that the bulk of consumers think doctors should inform their patients about payments they've received from a company whose drugs they are about to prescribe. "A major conflict of interest is at work when a physician has accepted payments from a drug or device-making company whose products he or she then prescribes or implants," says Marvin Lipman, M.D., Consumer Reports senior medical adviser. "The Sunshine Act will be embarrassing to some and infuriating to others, but is an excellent step toward consumer protection." The data, which is being released by the Centers for Medicare and Medicaid Services on 546,000 physicians on payments totaling more than $3.5 billion.

This would be illegal in many other professions. This pattern is the same as in the illegal drug market. The drugs are free and dispensed to get people to try them. This is because people asked the doctor about these drugs. They saw them being advertised on TV, and once people started taking them, they worked or the side effects took over. The drug companies are mainly marketing toward older audiences that are suffering from more serious ailments and diseases. Many people feel that the negative risks go along with a powerful remedy for a serious disease because it has to be powerful. One of the biggest tragedies is the opioid epidemic that has been going on for so many years. On the internet, there are many references to this. Presently, there are over a hundred lawsuits by states, cities, and counties of drug manufactures and some doctors for manufacturing and overprescribing opioids. The medical and drug industry should answer for what they have done.

"New York City Files $500 Million Lawsuit Against Drug Companies Over Opioid Deaths" (https://www.nbcnewyork.com/news/local/NYC-Opioids-Heroin-Epidemic-Big-Pharma-Suit-470722263.html) stated:

> The lawsuit aims to recover expenses the city will incur in combating the crisis. In 2016, more than 1,000 people in New York City died of an opioid overdose, according to official data — the highest number on record. "More New Yorkers have died from opioid overdoses than car crashes and homicides combined in recent years. 'Big Pharma' helped to fuel this epidemic by deceptively peddling these dangerous drugs and hooking millions of Americans in exchange for profit," Mayor Bill de Blasio said in a statement.

The lawsuit alleges the opioid epidemic was caused by manufacturers' marketing and by distributors sending prescription painkillers into New York City. That in turn placed a burden on the city for increased substance use treatment services, ambulatory services, emergency department services, inpatient hospital services, medical examiner costs, criminal justice costs and law enforcement costs.

The unfortunate part is the number of people who died. Where was the FDA? The medical industry seems to place more attention on treatment than prevention. How many times have you gone into a doctor's office for your fifteen-minute session and they just gave you a pill? To add to this, most doctors have not studied nutrition to understand how it relates to health. Lack of proper nutrition causes many of our health problems, especially when the main diet is processed foods. Again, in order to make the medical institution money, a doctor's appointment time in many cases is shorter than it should be. This is different in each hospital. When hospitals compete against each other, they each buy the most expensive equipment available. This raises the price of medical costs and an overload of some equipment. Sometimes this affects the number of x-rays and other tests you get because the hospitals have to protect themselves against lawsuits and help pay for the equipment. As will be noted later in the book, pharmaceutical medicine is the third largest medical killer behind heart attacks and cancer. The billing practices are also in shambles, not to mention the state of medical insurance. Medical insurance mixed with politics is a dangerous concoction. The medical and drug systems are indeed broken, and remember it represents an entry in the GDP as an asset and not an expense.

Kaiser Health News published an article by Bruce Horovitz and Julie Appleby on March 16, 2017, titled "Prescription drug costs are up, so are TV ads promoting them" (https://www.usatoday.com/story/money/2017/03/16/prescription-drug-costs-up-tv-ads/99203878/):

> The aim of direct-to-consumer (DTC) advertising: getting patients or their family members to remember a drug's name and ask by name for a prescription. Spending on such commercials grew 62% since 2012, even as ad spending for most other product types was flat. "Pharmaceutical advertising has grown more in the past four years than any other leading ad category," said Jon Swallen, chief research officer at Kantar Media, a consulting firm that tracks multimedia advertising. It exceeded $6 billion last year, with television picking up the lion's share, according to Kantar data. Shows are heavy with drug ads, the Kantar data shows. But the proliferation of drug advertisements has generated new controversy, in part because the ads inevitably promote high-priced drugs, some of which doctors say have limited practical utility for the average patient-viewer. The cost of Lyrica, is about $400 for 60 capsules, for example. Critics say the ads encourage patients to ask their doctors for expensive, often marginal — and sometimes inappropriate — drugs that are fueling spiraling health care spending.

Again, notice that "ask the doctor" is an often-used phrase, and this is opposed by the American Medical Association. What if big Ag had an ad saying, "Ask Monsanto"? This is like telling a doctor that the drug companies know something that the doctor isn't aware of concerning the proposed drug. There may be a lot of truth to that. Are the drug companies for public good? They say that they can help people by giving individuals who contact them a break on prices. However, let's look behind the bushes.

An article on November 17, 2016, by Grace Song and the Penn Wharton PPI, "How Big Pharma Manipulates the Public Good" (https://publicpolicy.wharton.upenn.edu/live/news/1554-how-big pharma-manipilates ...), presents another picture. Its setting is in a courtroom, and the case involved AstraZeneca, the FDA, and a dozen or so generic drug companies. The lawsuit was over Crestor, AstraZeneca's popular cholesterol drug, and involved AstraZeneca's attempt to stop generic versions of Crestor from entering the market once its patent expired on July 8. It is interesting and gives you insight into how some drug companies manipulate their definition of "public good." Another article on January 19, 2017, by Rachel Thomas, from the Seven Pillars Institute, titled "Pharmaceutical Industry Ethics" (https://sevenpillarsinstitute.org/pharmaceutical-industry-ethics/) states:

> Many industry features intended to promote development and distribution of drugs lead to perverse incentives for suppliers. Operating costs for pharmaceutical companies are extremely high especially: funding research and development, fighting legal battles, and distributing through insurers. However, the creation of new treatments for diseases is a public good, so governments tend to incentivize research through patent laws and subsidies. After investing in developing a new drug, a company has the exclusive right to sell and profit from the product. While these laws aim to promote medical progress, they create a monopoly over potentially lifesaving drugs, allowing suppliers to charge monopolistic (high) prices. Although patent laws are necessary to incentivize the development of new drugs, they support monopolies and prevent competition in the industry. A monopoly over products allows a company to fix prices, helped by inelastic demand, earning the company substantial profits. By definition, monopolistic markets do not offer free access to competitors.

A very informative article (twenty pages) written by Emily Miller and published on January 25, 2018, by Drugwatch, titled "U.S. Drug Prices vs, The World" (https://www.drugwatch.com/featured/us-drug-prices-higher-vs-world/) states:

> "The drug prices in the U.S. for the exact same drugs are often exponentially higher than they are in Canada and in every other country," said Gabriel Levitt, president of PharmacyChecker.com, a company that verifies overseas pharmacies and compares prices for different drugs. "The savings that Americans can get right now can average about 70 percent when you look at the lowest prices in Canada versus prices that Americans pay at local pharmacies here." What's more, a PharmacyChecker.com analysis found 70 percent of the most popular, non-controlled, brand name drugs sold in the U.S. (as identified by IMS Health data in 2015) are manufactured outside the U.S., then imported and sold to Americans at a higher price compared to patients in other countries. Take Nexium, for example. AstraZeneca manufactures the stomach-acid drug in Sweden and sells it to consumers in the U.S., Canada, U.K., Australia, New Zealand, India and Turkey. One 40 mg pill costs $7.78 in the U.S. compared to $3.37 in Canada. The price drops even more to $2.21 in the U.K., Australia and New Zealand. In India and Turkey, the same pill costs less than 37 cents.

One thing is certain about the pharmaceutical industry: they are getting their money's worth from lobbyists. However, President Trump said he would do something about these inequities, and I hope it comes to pass.

"Requiring Prices in Drug Ads: Would It Do Any Good? Is It Even Legal?" is an article that was in the *New York Times* on May 19, 2018 (https://www.nytimes.com/2018/05/19/us/politics/drug-prices-ads.html):

> If President Trump has his way, television viewers who see commercials for the drug Keytruda will learn not only that it can help lung cancer patients, but also that it carries a price tag of $13,500 a month, or $162,000 a year. Viewers who see advertisements for Neulasta, a drug that reduces the risk of infections after chemotherapy, would learn that the list price for each injection is $6,200. And magazine readers would see a new bit of information in ads for Humira, the world's best-selling drug, prescribed for rheumatoid arthritis and other autoimmune diseases: its list price, which has been widely reported as approximately $50,000 a year. Neulasta, is a drug that reduces the risk of infections after chemotherapy. If President Trump has his way, viewers would learn that the list price for each injection is $6,200. But what the administration presents as a simple matter of transparency has raised a torrent of questions from consumers, doctors, drugmakers and advertising professionals. Would it be legal? How would it work? Would it actually drive down drug prices? Would it be counterproductive, since high prices could discourage patients from considering helpful medicines?

Now that we have learned that the drug industry and advertising are bedfellows, it is time to get back to examining the advertising industry. In the book *Understanding Media* (1964) (SC61), Marshall McLuhan wrote about a news item that captures a good deal of the meaning of the automobile as it relates to social life (I will lay odds that it was a Texan):

> It was terrific. There I was in my white Continental, and I was wearing a pure-silk, pure-white, embroidered cowboy shirt, and black gabardine trousers. Beside me in the car was my jet-black Great Dane imported from Europe, named Dana von Krupp. You just can't do any better than that. (p 194)[67]. McLuhan did not have a pleasant view of advertising even in the 1960's. Many people have expressed uneasiness about the advertising enterprise in our time. To put the matter abruptly, the advertising industry is a crude attempt to extend the principals of automation to every aspect of society. Ideally, advertising aims act as the goal of a programmed harmony among all human methods, it stretches out toward the ultimate electronic goal of a collective consciousness. When all production and all consumption are brought into a pre-established harmony with all desire and all effort, then advertising will have liquidated itself by its own success. (written in 1964) (p 202)[68]

In closing, I will quote from Marshall McLuhan's book *The Mechanical Bride: Folklore of Industrial Man* (1951) (SC91):

> This was his first major publication and it carried an unsettling message: "Ours is the first age in which many thousands of the best-trained individual minds have made it a full time business to get inside the collective mind … in order to manipulate, exploit, control. … It was 1951. And this was the book that would establish McLuhan's reputation as one

of the foremost and wittiest critics of modern mass communications. (from inside back cover) When discussing books touted as an aid when climbing the corporate ladder, he observes how "the more equality there is in the race for inequality, the more intense the race and the less inequality which results from the consequent rewards. That means less and less distinction for more and more men of distinction." (p. xi)[69]

I wish he were here now; we would have so much more material that he could work with.

When my wife and I first came to Dallas, we were fortunate enough to attend a lecture at the University of Dallas by the top six philosophers of that time. Marshall McLuhan was one of them. It was one of the most inspiring days of my life. *The Mechanical Bride* is a fascinating book and very prophetic concerning the state of advertising then and how it applies to the situation now. It is one of the most humorous books that I have ever read.

We need to develop an advertising platform in order to let people know what is happing in our government and the environment. Information about what is happening in this world should be organized in a manner that would have the most acceptance by the public. This should appeal to persons who believe in the tenets of reducing pollution, decreasing consumerism, and sustainability. Of course, this would be dismissed by President Trump as "false news." This is from someone that is setting a record for lying.

The pilot demonstration project would provide actual data to show how an alternate lifestyle and worldview is needed to prevent chaos. This will take time because of the dominance of the existing capitalist society, which in many cases uses greed as a mantra. If we have a recession, additional disasters and reduction of available money, the messages we are sponsoring will be accepted by more people. Emphasis should also be made to appeal to those who are affected by increasing inequity throughout the world. The last presidential election in the United States was determined by negative votes. People were looking for a change from big-city politics, and it happened. There is a need for change in another direction rather than increasing the power of the elite at the expense of the lower 80 percent. This could include putting emphasis on cleaning up government. Topics could include election finance reform, gerrymandering, representatives in all areas of government elected with more progressive viewpoints, and a more informed electorate.

Conversations among many people should also include the best way of doing this environmental messaging as well as the most opportune time to do it. Without an advertising strategy, this effort could be a waste of money. Perhaps we could use the Consumer Reports format. This would allow for any information to be reliable and backed up by acceptable independent sources. One example would be showing how a harm/benefit analysis could be done for an existing or new technology. Time is also running short for working with people that overuse the smartphones and social media, with little regard for reading and speaking on a variety of subjects. Understanding the relativity of history as to what is happening belongs to a small minority. IT is too ingrained as a habit.

One of our fixations is putting emphasis on certain celebrities. There seem to be two types of celebrities. Some news and other programs have considerable time allocated for interviews with celebrities. This is popular with many people in their audience and shows how powerful the present brand of consumerism of using an identity with a personality. There are those who are self-aggrandizing and do little toward helping others, and there are those who use their celebrity status to help humanity. We need to recognize the latter more because they can be a powerful force in establishing an example for good. One example is the TV program *Big Brother*. The show stresses competition to obtain money at any cost. The script showed people becoming friends, and then one of the friends goes against the other to get ahead. Another case in point is the heavy reliance on war games and the enjoyment some people get from destroying other people while using these games. This is acceptable now because you supposedly win by the amount of the skill you obtained by sitting in front of the console for hours.

Another problem related to advertising is how browsers are infringing on those of us who do not care for ads when using the internet. In some cases on Firefox, certain emails cannot be printed because you are using an ad blocker. To remove the ad blocker, you have to go through several steps. This now lets the ads flow in with all their messages to make us consume even more. It's bad enough when your purchasing choices are tracked and then sold to advertisers. If you use mobile technology, you do not have a private life. And for this service of letting them know what you like, you get zero money from the advertisers. In the old days, this was called a racket. If you buy something that you think you want because of advertising and then find out it was defective or you didn't need it after all, you are doubly damaged because now you are targeted for this type of product. Google now has an ad filter on their ad blocker that allows some ads to filter through to your website. Do they get extra money from the advertisers whose ads are selected for viewing? I am going to have to look up the definition of "free choice" because I don't think it is around anymore.

Transition Design

My first introduction to transition design was through the book *Designs for the Pluriverse* by Arturo Escobar (CE53).[70] This led to reading about the transition design thinking by Ezio Manzini in his book *Design, When Everybody Designs* (UP40).[71] Transition design is a different way of thinking than what is being presently practiced. It is humanity based so that everyone is a designer. In discussing this, I apologize to both authors for my interpretations of their concepts. The presuppositions for this are from *The Designs for the Pluriverse* (CE53):

1. Every community practices the design of itself: its organizations, its social relations, its practices, its realization to the environment.

2. Every design activity must start with the strong supposition that people are practitioners of their own knowledge and from there must examine how people themselves understand their reality. What the community designs, in the first instance, is an inquiring or learning system about itself. As designers, we may become co-researchers with the community, but it is the latter that investigates its own reality in the codes process.

3. Every design process involves a statement of problems and possibilities that enable the designer and the group to generate agreements about objectives and to decide among alternative courses of action. The results should be a series of scenarios and possible paths for the transformation of practices or the creation of new ones. (p. 184–185)[72]

It is autonomous (having the right or power of self-government or undertaken or carried on without outside control) and design oriented and has the realization of the communal (of or relating to a community) good.

I would add one other presupposition to the above agenda. This would be to determine the relationship between the experts and the other persons involved. From a practicing landscape architect's standpoint, there are always the questions of costs, specific engineering, site analysis, architectural design, liabilities, cultural patterns and desires, and so on that affect the approval or disapproval of ideas or concepts. Rules and roles of the parties involved should be a beginning topic. The first step would be to have the people be the designers, with input from "the experts" as necessary.

We have been in a transitional period for a considerable number of years (there are variable times suggested by different authors), and we will continue to be in it until there is a sustainable society (hopefully). What it will look like and how long it will take—no one knows. Climate change, the status of our available nonrenewable natural resources, pollution and soil degradation, weather, war, the intelligence of governments, cultural and social changes, and population growth will be some of the determinants. Right now, the intelligence of governments ranks right up there as a major determinant. When designing communities, the attitudes of society are paramount.

Ezio Manzini's book *Design—When Everybody Designs* (UP40) is the most complete book on transition design that I have read (although this is a low number), and I would recommend that any designer, regardless of their design experience, read the book. If I designed another community, I would make sure everyone involved had a copy of Manzini's book. He states the following:

> Design mode means the outcome of combining three human gifts: critical sense (the ability to look at the state of things and recognize what cannot, or should be, acceptable), creativity (the ability to imagine something that does not yet exist, and practical sense (the ability recognize feasible ways of getting things to happen). (p. 31)[73] Design is concerned with making sense of things-how they ought to be in order to create new meaningful entities. It also collaborates actively and proactively in the social constructing of meaning. And therefore, of quality, values, and beauty. (p. 35)[74]. To make human systems more enduring, therefore, we should enhance the complexity of technical systems. That is, we should foster the coexistence of solutions based on different logics and different rationales. In addition, we should consider the varied complexity of energy, production, market, economy, and the "genetic richness of an artificial ecosystem: a richness that guarantees its capacity to continue involving in the face of wider changes in context. (p. 192)[75]

The only thing I would mention is that design is always changing and not static, especially when dealing with social and natural concepts. This is not what government entities normally approve. Most zoning ordinances are cumbersome and hard to change. This means for any project to be successful, it must include these players in the program initially. Another way would be to have a general concept completed and then include government officials in further meetings. Another way would be to give each of them Ezio's book.

One of the design options to explore is found in the book *Democracy at Work—A Cure for Capitalism*[76] by Richard Wolff (CE37). In the book, he suggests using a new workers' organizational paradigm called workers' self-directed enterprise (WSDE). This would take the place of the typical cooperative management and governing structure. It is different from worker-owned or worker-managed enterprises. This type of management creates democracy, and we desperately need it. This would be adapted for use in the pilot demonstration project.

Other Writings Providing Community Development Information

This section of the book has other articles and references that help clarify what is happening in the world in the areas of economics, agriculture, social structure, and the environment. They are equally significant, and many cover pertinent information that would contribute to a functioning project such as the PDP. This is especially true for the books authored by Charles Hugh Smith (CHS). The topics are varied but mainly refer to the meanings and relationships of money, work, leisure, status, and jobs. What I am noting in this section is that comments from the books mentioned here are short and out of context and order. This does a disservice to the many authors, but I hope it encourages people to buy the books and see the information on the internet. They reflect and explain what is coming in terms of how people might react to the economic and environmental options.

Another option would be to make a list of websites for free publication to show information that corresponds to the type of thinking that is represented in this book. A couple of examples would be "Resilience" and "Peak Prosperity Weekly," but there are many more on the internet, especially in YouTube, and many others are noted in this book. The topics and excerpts are not in any specific order. The writings by others are just provided by this author, and it is up to the reader to research them and determine their accuracy. This will allow readers of the book the opportunity to see and understand various points of view.

Trump Popularity among Republicans: President Trump's ratings among Republicans is at an all-time high, as published by Atarexik on June 24, 2018 (https://www.ataraxik.com/2018/06/24/trumps-approval-rating-republican/). This provides an interesting insight about the reasons for polarity in politics today. It states:

> In the New York Times this morning, Jeremy W. Peters wrote about polarization in modern American politics, and how the approval rating of the president is extremely high. In the very beginning, Peters tells the story of Gina Anders, a woman doesn't support Trump but finds herself defending him anyway, not out of a duty to contrarianism, but merely as a counter-reaction to the hysteria of his opponents. To women such as Anders, the reaction to Trump is worse than the actual policies implemented. Anders explained that "all nuance and all complexity – and these are complex issues – are completely lost." "It makes me angry at them, which causes me to want to defend him to them even more." This is a common experience for individuals now, who feel as though the hysteria on the "left" – for lack of a better word – have totally misrepresented issues and blown things way out of proportion (3). Because of the mischaracterization of Trump, people who despite the president often have a sense of self-righteousness, as if they are on the right side, allowing themselves to berate anyone who may agree with him on whatever issue.

This is a very important observation that should be recognized by everyone, especially Democrats. I may be somewhat guilty in my comments about the government, but I am trying to base my comments on facts as much as possible. There is no disputing that President Trump is a liar, but I feel it is out of line for someone to deny restaurant service or scream at someone who works for Trump. Now it seems that the vitriol on both sides is extreme and is not helping matters. I like to put a little humor into my comments to lighten the load of possible disasters coming. It is a shame that this type of reasoning, as shown in the article, determines how people rationalize what they are doing. It's easier to disapprove of both the Republicans and Democrats, because there is room for two rotten apples to fit in a pail, with room left for some good apples to be added later. I just hope there is some sanity left in our country by the time this book gets published.

Culture and Economics: The first thirty-six pages of "Money and Work Unchained" (SC77[77] Adam Taggert, December 14, 2017) by Charles Hugh Smith can be obtained on the internet (https://www.oftwominds.com/Money-Work-free.pdf). I will try to show how the writings from this book would be a guide for better community project options for work. The book describes relationships among the meanings of work and is defined by the author:

> "What we will be exploring is unchaining work from our preconceptions of work and unchaining money from our preconceptions of money." The ideas presented will help people understand what is happening in our present society. It would also establish guidelines for community thinking. Humanity and the planet we inhabit deserve a system of money as well as paid work that isn't unfair, unjust, predatory, parasitic, exploitive and destructive. Such a system is now within reach. The danger is that if we don't fully understand work, money, wealth and capital, we may find ourselves in a behavioral sink of purples despair with no income at all. Rather than entering a paradise of paid leisure, we might find ourselves in a nightmare of social dysfunction that extends far beyond financial destitution, deep into a toxic poverty of purpose and meaning. (p. 2)

"Why Urban Villages are on the Rise around the World" by Amanda Abrams (Sharable) (www.resilience.org/stories/2018-02-12/why-urban-villages-are-on-the-rise-around-the-world/) provides examples of sharing urban villages that are ongoing or being started throughout the world. It showcases how this type of approach would change urban living so that everyone is a participant. An example is the Participation City in London:

> With groundbreaking funding totaling $8.5 million, the project — which began in November — aims to work with over 25,000 people, creating 250 projects, and 100 businesses. It may feature many of the projects that occurred in West Norwood, but will also include retrofitting an old warehouse to create a makerspace where businesses in food, manufacturing, or retail can incubate and flourish.

Immigration—Trump's Gulags: "A visit to one of Trump's child-gulags reveals prison conditions and propaganda posters" is an article in *Daily Kos* written by Mark Summer on June 14, 2018 (https://www.dailykos.com/stories/2018/6/14/1771865/-A-visit-to-one-of-Trump-s-child-gulags-reveals-prison-conditions-and-propaganda-posters):

> For the first time, journalists have been allowed to visit one of the camps where children—most of them the children of applicants seeking to legally enter the United States on sanctuary applications—have been taken away from parents and warehoused. And it's not as bad as you think it is. It's worse. MSNBC reporter Jason Soboroff was one of those who visited a facility in Brownsville, Texas, that is known as Casa Padre. In this location,

1,469 boys were housed inside the concrete blocks of a former Walmart. What Soboroff found wasn't just an overcrowded warren of cells, and boys lined up to receive rations. He found a facility where children are given treatment usually reserved for the most dangerous inmates at a federal prison. They're kept locked in for 22 hours each day, and given one hour of "structured time" and only a single hour of "free time" outdoors. Each boy gets 40 square feet of living space, which is the same as the minimum standard Texas uses for allocating space in a maximum security prison. One thing that MSNBC also noted was that only the insistence on oversight by Democratic congressmen gained them access. The standard procedure of the facility when approached by a reporter was to call the police.

This is an injustice, and if we and Congress allow this to continue, our complacency is part of the problem. This is happening in many areas across the country and reminds one of what was happening in Germany before World War II. The unfortunate thing about this is that few people in the government are speaking out against this in a constructive manner and offering possible solutions. We really need a fair immigration policy instead of the present blame game. The posters shown hanging on the walls make this even more insulting. Would you like to see pictures of Trump staring down at you 24-7? This is like having Halloween every day of the year. Presently, the children have to recite the Pledge of Allegiance in English every morning. Hopefully, pressure from the people will stop this practice. The Republicans' answer is to blame it on the Democrats.

Coca-Cola: *Fortune* magazine on January 5, 2017, published an article called "Coca-Cola Sued for Alleged Deceptive Marketing" (http://fortune.com/2017/01/05/coca-cola-sued-soda-marketing/) that noted:

> The lawsuit, filed in a California district court by the non-profit group Praxis Project, alleges Coca-Cola (ko, -0.47%) "deceives consumers about their health impact." Praxis Project further alleged American Beverage Association, a trade group that Coke and other beverage companies fund, assists in the effort to purportedly mislead the public about the health implications of soda, which some studies have linked to type 2 diabetes and obesity. The lawsuit against Coca-Cola is in part stating that the Praxis Project lawsuit, which is calling for a jury trial, aims to prove Coke violated the Fair Advertising Law in its marketing and wants the defendants to fund a "corrective public education campaign to reduce the consumption of sugar-sweetened beverages." It also calls for the defendants to prominently post on their websites the "consumption of sugar-sweetened beverages can lead to obesity, diabetes and cardiovascular disease"—a request that echoes the public health warnings that tobacco makers have been forced to add to their packaging for many years.

Of course, Coca-Cola is denying the charges. This is just one example among many.

Internet: "Declining Majority of Online Adults Say the Internet Has Been Good for Society" is the topic of a Pew survey from April 30, 2018. This is by Aaron Smith and Kenneth Olmstead (http://www.pewinternet.org/2018/04/30/declining-majority-of-online-adults-say-the-internet-has-been-good-for-society/):

This shift in opinion regarding the ultimate social impact of the internet is particularly stark among older Americans, despite the fact that older adults have been especially rapid adopters of consumer technologies such as social media and smartphones in recent years. Today 64% of online adults ages 65 and older say the internet has been a mostly good thing for society. That represents a 14-point decline from the 78% who said this in 2014. The attitudes of younger adults have remained more consistent over that time: 74% of internet users ages 18 to 29 say the internet has been mostly good for society, comparable to the 79% who said so in 2014. As was true in our 2014 survey, college graduates are more likely than those with lower levels of educational attainment to say the internet has had a positive impact on society (and less likely to say it has had a negative impact). Among online adults with a college degree, 81% say the impact of the internet on society has been mostly good and just 7% say it has been mostly bad. By contrast, 65% of those with a high school diploma or less say the internet has had a mostly good impact on society, and 17% say its impact has been mostly bad.

Sexual Harassment and Power: "Men, Power, and Sexual Harassment—Why Powerful Men Sexually Harass Women" was an article on ThoughtCo written by Linda Bowen on March 18, 2017 (https://www.thoughtco.com/men-power-and-sexual-harassment-):

> Dutch sociobiologist Johan van der Dennen believes power itself is corrupting. In a May 2011 interview with SPIEGEL ONLINE about the relationship between sex and power, he speculates that powerful men may behave differently because they can: Powerful men have a both an overactive libido as compared to 'normal' men, but they are also more willing to gamble that they can get away with their sexual activities ... [I]n my opinion, it is the position of power itself that makes men arrogant, narcissistic, egocentric, oversexed, paranoid, despotic, and craving even more power, though there are exceptions to this rule. Powerful men generally have a keen eye for female beauty and attractiveness ... Every "willing" woman confirms the power of the powerful man ... It is not too speculative to think that powerful men live in a sexualized or eroticized world. Not only do they expect to have sex whenever they fancy, but they also expect that every woman is always willing to provide this service, and enjoy it. They are ... opportunistic and just take what they want. It probably comes as a complete surprise when somebody does not comply.

Low Income Households: The United Way completed a 110-page study (2014) of household incomes in fifteen states. It is "UW-(ALICE)." They have developed Household Survival Budgets for each state under ALICE. It was named after Alice, who is a hardworking member of the community and is employed yet does not earn enough to afford the basic necessities of life. Alice earns above the federal poverty level but does not earn enough to afford a bare-bones household budget of housing, child care, food, transportation, and health care.

> The United Way ALICE Report uses new measures to provide a more accurate picture of financial insecurity at the state, county, and municipal level. The average for the 15 states is as follows: Total Households: 45,425,396 (39% of all U.S. households), Households Below ALICE Threshold: 40%. (Average), Household Survival Budget-Single Adult. $20,038, Household Survival Budget-Family of Four: $55,381 and Percent of Jobs paying Less Than $20/Hr.: 61% (average). This is not the economic picture presented by the government. In part this reflects the mood and frustrations of the people with many living from paycheck to paycheck. To further the problem, the new tax bill just gave the elite moneys with a trickling compensation for middle and lower income families.

Hopefully some of the ideas expressed in this report can remedy the present situation.

Corporations: One of the prevalent questions today is, What is the best way to restructure corporations so that they have goals other than just to make money? In the case of Monsanto, they are not only making money, but they are harming the earth and people. John Perkins in *The New Confessions of an Economic Hit Man* (CE59) suggests the following:

> Some argue that we need to rid the planet of corporations; however, the likelihood of this happening-at least in my lifetime-is extremely low. I think, instead, we need to take the shamanic approach (it is a dream of love-for ourselves, for each other, for nature, and for the planet. It is a dream that tells us to replace the old dream of a death economy with a new dream of life economy) to transform-shapelift-the attitudes and goals of those who own and manage the corporations. Corporations are highly effective at channeling brilliant ideas into concrete action. But their dream of maximizing profits without regard for the environmental and social costs, their orientation toward pillaging resources and promoting debt and materialism, has been disastrous. It is time for a new dream that is based on saving the earth, the public, and future generations-not just humans but all beings. (p. 291)[78]

The legal requirements of corporations having to make money for stockholders as the number-one consideration should be lowered in priority so they can be adjusted to what was said above. CEOs making absurd salaries, regardless of their accomplishments, is crazy. A factory worker making twenty to thirty dollars an hour doing repetitive work is not going to be too excited about enhancing the income of excessively highly paid management that they never see. But in many cases, that is their only option other than two jobs or the spouse working. Doing this requires extra clothing, transportation, babysitting costs, medical costs, and so on. On top of this are cases of sexual harassment. Welcome to our present society.

The Bayer-Monsanto Merger: "Empowering a Life-Destroying Cartel" was on the *Global Research News Hour*, episode 221, May 20, 2018 (https://www.globalresearch.ca/the-bayer-monsanto-merger-empowering-a-life-destroying-cartel/5641082). It was written by Michael Welch, Dr. Vandana Shiva, Nick Meyer, and Ellen Brown, and this is the first of a series of articles. They noted:

> That the U.S. Department of Justice recently cleared the path for a merger takeover of Monsanto and Bayer worth more than $60 billion. When the partnership attains U.S. anti-trust approval (likely within days) a new entity will emerge, commanding more than a quarter of the combined world market for seeds and pesticides. Critics argue that the power of these economic giants is such that they have captured regulatory agencies. Limitless financial resources permit these and similar companies to buy off academics, media and politicians. According to a recent poll of 48 U.S. States, 94% of farmers are concerned about the merger, with 83 percent being very concerned. Their top three concerns: market dominance to push other products, control over farmers' data, and increased pressure to rely on chemical based farming practices.

The main thing to do now is to realize what they are doing to the earth and not use their products or GM foods and plants. Put pressure on politicians to pass a GM labeling law that makes sense and not one suggested by the USDA. Also have the news mention environmental and agricultural issues instead of spending time promoting stupid celebrity shows.

A weed killer that could be used is Mirimichi. This product kills a large variety of weeds even in cold weather. The active ingredient is Ammonium Nonanoate. MicroLife, which sells Mirimichi, also has a variety of insecticides and fungicides that are safe to use. Contact your landscape nursery to inquire. Available on the internet are several articles about controlling weeds without using chemicals. There are some benefits of weeds such as purslane and dandelions. Weeds mainly are found in poor, nonnutrient soils and are the first plants to grow on bare soils. Nature does this to provide food for microorganisms and fungi.

CRISPR: in The Readout, an article titled "Wall Street freaked out about CRISPR again" on June 12, 2018, by Biopharm America (https://us11.campaign-archive. com/?u=f8609630ae206654824f897b6&id=69a3474b4a), it stated:

> Investors' bullishness on the potential of gene editing has made a trio of startups into multibillion-dollar enterprises. But the latest blowup, courtesy of a pair of scientific papers, provides a jarring reminder to the market: Until this newfangled technology is proved safe in actual humans, investing in CRISPR stocks a head-spinning experience. The three big CRISPR companies lost nearly $500 million in value Monday after two freshly published papers warned that gene-edited cells could be breeding grounds for cancer. Each paper is based on preclinical research, and scientists said the finding is hardly a death knell for the nascent field of CRISPR. CRISPR (/ˈkrɪspər/) is a family of DNA sequences in bacteria and archaea. The sequences contain snippets of DNA from viruses that have attacked the prokaryote. These snippets are used by the prokaryote to detect and destroy DNA from similar viruses during subsequent attacks. These sequences play a key role in a prokaryotic defense system, and form the basis of a technology known as CRISPR/Cas9 that effectively and specifically changes genes within organisms.

The Meaning of Human Existence (E39) by Edward O. Wilson presents a view of who we are from one of the foremost biologists and naturalists. One of the statements noted in the book is as follows:

The great religions are also, and tragically, sources of ceaseless, and unnecessary suffering. They are impediments to the grasp of reality needed to solve most of the social problems in the real world. Their exquisitely human flaw is tribalism. The instinctual force of tribalism in the genesis of religiosity is far stronger than the yearning for spirituality. People deeply need membership in a group whether religious or secular. From a lifetime of emotional experience, they know that happiness and indeed survival itself, require that they bond with others who share some amount of genetic kinship language, language, moral beliefs, geographical location, social purpose and dress-code preferably all of these but at least two or three for most purposes. (p. 150–151)[79]

Monsanto Again: An article in *Sustainable Pulse* on June 4, 2018, titled "Monsanto Relied on These 'Partners' to Attack Top Cancer Scientists"

(https://sustainablepulse.com/2018/06/04/monsanto-relied-on-these-partners-to-attack-top-cancer-scientists/?utm_source=newsletter&utm_medium=email&utm_campaign=gmos_and_pesticides_global_breaking_news&utm_term=2018-06-13) stated:

> This fact sheet describes the contents of Monsanto's confidential public relations plan to discredit the World Health Organization's cancer research unit, the International Agency for Research on Cancer (IARC), in order to protect the reputation of Roundup weedkiller. In March 2015, the international group of experts on the IARC panel judged glyphosate, the key ingredient in Roundup, to be probably carcinogenic to humans. The Monsanto plan names more than a dozen "industry partner" groups that company executives planned to "inform / inoculate / engage" in their efforts to protect the reputation of Roundup, prevent the "unfounded" cancer claims from becoming popular opinion, and "provide cover for regulatory agencies." Partners included academics as well as chemical and food industry front groups, trade groups and lobby groups. One example: Henry I. Miller, MD, a fellow at the Hoover Institution and founding director of the FDA's Office of Biotechnology, has a long documented history of working with corporations to defend hazardous products.

Immigration: CREDO (via Daily Kos, campaigns@dailykos.com, via sg.actionnetwork.org) had an article, "Trump nominates member of hate group to oversee refugee resettlement" on June 12, 2018 (https://mail.google.com/mail/u/0/?tab=wm#inbox/163fa8f19fc0e1ec). They are asking people to write to Congress to tear down the nomination.

> Ronald Mortensen has spread racist smears about immigrants, declared that undocumented immigrants routinely commit felonies, claimed foreign nationals carry serious disease into the United States and railed against Dreamers – implying most are criminals and demanding all pay restitution for their supposed crimes. And he put it all in writing as a fellow for an anti-immigrant think tank that the Southern Poverty Law Center has called a hate group.[2] Now, xenophobe-in-chief Donald Trump has nominated Mortensen to lead the U.S. government's efforts to aid refugees. Mortensen has smeared all immigrants as "murderers, identity thieves, gang bangers, and other assorted thugs."[3] He is a fellow for the Center for Immigration Studies, a favorite organization of racist Trump adviser Stephen Miller that has already funneled other hate-mongers into the administration and which the Southern Poverty Law Center has labeled a hate group for its efforts to demonize immigrants and people of color. Mortensen's work has even been shared approvingly by outright white nationalist figures.

This is a good test for Congress to see if they approve him. What does it say about President Trump to have even nominated him? Was he to be snuck in through the back door of the White House? The United States would be much better off if the president played golf all day. That I could vote for. So much for draining the swamp. I dearly wish the swamp would come back; at least it would create a wetland.

Koch Brothers: If you really want a good scare, read the volume 20, number 3, March/April 2018 issue of the *Hightower Lowdown*. It shows what the Koch brothers are doing to get their agenda into our government policy. Talk about being controlled by the rich. Some of the notes made in the article:

> (1) The Brother's Koch want nothing less than to supplant America's core democratic principal of majority rule-the willow the people- with their core plutocratic principal of inviolable property rights-domination by the wealthy minority (2) Some of their goals are: a) Killing all restrictions on political spending buy corporations and the rich. (3) Suppressing the voting rights of students, people of color, the elderly, and others who tend to oppose Republican policies and candidates. (4). Eliminating the right of consumers, workers, and others to sue corporations, forcing them instead into corporate-controlled arbitration. (5). Ripping to shreds the social safety net including food stamps, jobless benefits, Social Security, and Medicare/Medicaid. (6). Axing regulations to protect people and our environment from corporate abuse. (7) "Preempting" the right of local people to pass laws that corporations oppose. (8). Subverting democracy through gerrymandering and (9 Packing courts with pro-corporate judges. Koch Industries has annual sales topping $115 billion. Their $122.4 billion combined wealth is higher than Gates, Buffett and Zuckerberg.

Much of the information in the article was provided by Lisa Graves, co-director of Documented (documentedinvestigations.org) and senior fellow at the Center for Media and Democracy. CMD's Koch Exposed (www.exposedbycmd.org/koch/) has additional information. He listed Robert Maguire at the Center for Responsive Politics (openserets.org). They track campaign money.

After reading this, it is easy to see why Koch Industries feels the way they do. They have a terrible pollution record. On the internet, there are several articles about their pollution record. One of the most inclusive ones is by Polluter Watch (http://polluterwatch.org/koch-industries) (no date or author). The article lists how they are polluting the United States and other activities as to political donations. Following is just part of the information in their article:

The Political Economy Research Institute ranks Koch Industries as the fourteenth worst air polluter in the U.S. in their Toxic Release Inventory (link is external). CARMA reports (link is external) that Koch releases about 200,000 tons of atmospheric carbon dioxide annually. In late 2000, the company was charged with covering up the illegal releases of 91 tons of the known carcinogen benzene from its refinery in Corpus Christi. Initially facing a 97-count indictment and potential fines of $350 million, Koch cut a deal with then-Attorney General John Ashcroft to drop all major charges in exchange for a guilty plea for falsifying documents, and a $20 million settlement. Koch Industries and the Koch family spend millions of dollars on lobbyists (link is external) to fight climate and energy legislation, millions more on politicians (link is external), and still more millions on organizations denying climate change (link is external). Through the Charles G. Koch Charitable Foundation as well as Koch Industries and the other Koch family foundations (link is external), numerous and substantial donations go to organizations that deny, skepticize or belittle the significance of global warming.

Another factor to consider is that the Koch influence and the Trump administration will delay any action to prevent erosion damage to our soils, make headway on climate change, and reduce additional depletion of our natural resources. We are too late now in our environmental actions to reduce problems, and this will cause even greater problems beyond the point of viable solutions. Greed is taking the place of better judgment.

If you are interested in any of the topics written in this book, go to the internet and YouTube and get different viewpoints.

In her preface in *Dark Money* (CE56), Jane Meyer had several comments related to the thinking of the president regarding proposed legislation and his beginning associations with the Koch brothers.

> The fact of the matter was that while Trump might have been elected by those he described as "the forgotten" men, he would have to deal with a Republican Party that had been shaped substantially by the billionaires of the Radical Right. He would have to work with a vice president once funded by the Kochs and a Congress dominated by members who owed their political careers to the Kochs. The Kochs' dark money, which they had directed their successors to keep spending long after they had passed away, would continue to exert disproportionate influence over American politics for years to come. (p. xxii)[80]

Roundup Testing: Dr. Mercola, in an article on May 23, 2018, titled "Latest Update on Toxicity of Popular Weed Killer and Proposed Rule for Labeling of GMOs" (https://articles.mercola.com/sites/articles/archive/2018/05/23/popular-weed-killer-toxicity-proposed-gmo-labeling-rules-updates.aspx), provided updated information about Roundup. They noted:

> 1) Testing by the U.S. National Toxicology Program reveals glyphosate formulations such as Roundup® "significantly altered" the viability of human cells by disrupting the functionality of cell membranes. 2) government researchers warn that the Roundup® formula is far more toxic than glyphosate in isolation, due to the synergistic interactions between various chemicals, 3) new testing may soon be started by the Ramazzini Institute in Italy on the chemical's chronic toxicity potential and carcinogenicity, 4) now some companies are considering using plant vaccines and this could lead to dangerous consequences and 5) there are many problems with the proposed legislation by the USDA (United States Department of Agriculture) for licensing GMO foods. It seems the USDA is unnecessarily complicating things and using new terms to confuse the public in order to help the biotech industry.

In addition, the development of superweeds and its long-term toxicity in the soil are not mentioned, but they are an important part of the equation—how damaging Roundup is through its creation of chemical-resistant plants. Would you want your children and dogs playing on the lawn after Roundup has been applied when better organic products are available?

President Trump: The book *It's Even Worse Than You Think—What the Trump Administration is Doing to America* by David Cay Johnston (CE58) is, as Booklist said, "A precise and fiery indictment of an unstable, unethical president." The Seattle Review of Books' comment was "Essential … It holds Trump accountable for all his lies." The subjects in the table of contents are as follows:

> The Trump Factor, Kleptocracy Rising, Refusals to Pay, Appointees, Jobs Hiding in the Budget, A Mighty Job Creator, Forgetting the Forgotten Man, Washington Apprentice, Taxes The Tax Expert, Trump's Tax Return, Trump's Wall, Fossil Fuels and Climate and Science Denial Polluters. Paradise, Go FOIA Yourself, Interior Purging, Stripping Science, Stocking the Science, Global Affairs Diplomatic Trade, Digital Delusions, Education Promises and Performances, Bankers Before Brains, Law and Order, Veterans, Race and Guns, Immigration Above the Law, Wounding the Veterans, The Road to Charlottesville, Immigration, Conclusion The Con Unravels,[81]

Read the book and understand what we have gotten ourselves into.

Computers and iPhones: Another article and video by Crystal White and Anne Cox, titled "The dumbing down of society—the constant urge to be plugged in," was on Blasting News-Lifestyle (also Peak Prosperity) on May 14, 2018 (https://us.blastingnews.com/lifestyle/2018/05/the-dumbing-down-of-society-the-constant-urge-to-be-plugged-in-002570369.html). The authors are concerned about people staring at screens. Cell phones, laptops, computers, and tablets have taken precedence over actual interaction. Topics in the article are as follows:

> 1) Negative effects on family time, 2) Avoid the inevitable doom of our teens, 3) Cyberbullying, 4) What about our marriages?, 5) There are possible remedies, and 6) Take a look in the mirror. They further note that long hours in front of a screen causes many ill effects and then lists them. The article ends with the statement that the internet is an amazing tool. But even as it has shrunk the world and brought us together, it's threatened to push us further apart.

My opinion is that you have to be selective in the type of things you read and do on the internet. Facebook and Google, along with advertising, can be destructive, and there are many ways that your privacy can be compromised. Another problem is your opinions and buying habits being tracked. You can never tell when you are going to be hacked by Russia. The internet should be a learning experience and not a social crutch.

The Biology of Greed: This was part of a blog updated on May 25, 2011, in the Huffington Post by John Selby, using the title "Is there a Cure for Greed?" (https://www.huffingtonpost.com/john-selby/is-there-a-cure-for-greed_b_480181.html):

> Greed isn't the product of our forebrain's logical deductive cognitive-emotive process. The greed impulse originates in the primitive fear center, in the amygdale and related reptilian parts of the brain. If we're going to curb greed in banking, investing, etc, we must first admit that we all possess the greed bug. Unless we shine the light of reason and higher awareness directly at this selfish reactionary pattern of the human mind, there's no hope of changing it—because significant change always starts from within. What to

do: Perhaps we need a Presidential Commission On Greed—one that examines the root psychological dynamic of greedy behavior, and how to change this behavior. America was founded on the notion that all its citizens can aspire to be filthy rich—but is this really our highest goal? We usually perceive our country as the most generous culture on earth (which in many ways we are) and yet we allow our own economic system to be driven overmuch by greed. As a result, investment bubbles continue to swell and burst, and the average middle-class family continues to bear the brunt of the resulting hardship.

I just hope people, governments, and corporations realize what they are doing when they use this power—before it destroys the earth. An example is that, from most Republicans, there has not been an outcry about what the secretary of the EPA is doing to our environment. The political lemming effect is a powerful tool in today's society.

Assessment of Life on Earth: The Guardian on May 21, 2018, published an article written by Daimian Carrington, its environmental editor, titled "Humans just 0.01% of all life but have destroyed 83% of wild animals—study" (https://www.theguardian.com/environment/2018/may/21/human-race-just-001-of-all-life-but-has-destroyed-over-80-of-wild-mammals-study). The study was published in the Proceedings of the National Academy of Sciences:

> The new work is the first comprehensive estimate of the weight of every class of living creature and overturns some long-held assumptions. Bacteria is a major life form—13% of everything—but plants overshadow everything, representing 82% of all living matter. All other creatures, from insects to fungi, to fish and animals make up just 5% of the world's biomass. The transformation of the planet by human activity has led scientists to the brink of declaring a new geological era—the Anthropocene. The new work reveals that farmed poultry today makes up 70% of all birds on the planet, with just 30% being wild. 60% of all mammals on Earth are livestock, mostly cattle and pigs, 36% are human and just 4% are wild animals.

This shows the impact that humankind has had on the world. Our eating habits and consumption patterns will have to change if we want to reduce our water shortages and pollution activities of agribusinesses.

Taxonomy of Work, Jobs, Corporations, Status Quo: Another book by Charles Hugh Smith is *Get a Job, Build a Real Career and Defy a Bewildering Economy* (SC78). It would be a must-read for the people living in the PDP in order to help themselves and better help others. The core concept in the book is that certain kinds of work offer little in the way of social value, the connectedness that humans crave as part of our hierarchy of needs. It will help people understand how to make work more fulfilling and create their own social values. Many retraining programs do not offer this type of information. A statement from the book describes corporations (from a description from one of his other books):

> In my book "Resistance, Revolution, Liberation: A Model for Positive Change," I outline the following five basic types of capitalism (though variations of these are equally visible in monarchies, theocracies and socialism). They are 1) Extractive, 2) Exploitative, 3) Enterprise, 4) Marketing and 5) Corporate/State. In this book he describes each of them in more

detail. For example, an Exploitative Capitalism is based on the monopolistic control of labor and other productive assets such as land. A classic example is a plantation with indentured labor. (p. 24)[82]

The type of corporation many times describes how it relates to jobs and how the corporation treats people.

Another book by Charles Hugh Smith, *Why our Status Quo Failed and is Beyond Reform* (SC79), notes:

> Though we're assured our status quo offers equal opportunity to all, the reality is our status quo exists to protect the privileges of the few at the expense of the many. (p 1). Why has the status quo failed? Let's begin by examining the six separate problems-they are all aspects of one world-system. 1) Entrenched poverty, 2) An economic model of expanding consumption in a world of finite resources, 3) An economic model that relies on wages to distribute the outcome of an economy, 4). A political-economic model of centralized banks/states managing economies, 5). An economic model that depends on ever-expanding credit, i.e. borrowing from the future, to fund today's consumption, and a 6). A crisis of purpose and meaning. (p.3)[83] for example, entrenched poverty is characterized by a chronic shortage of the tools needed to create prosperity. (p 5)[84]. The end state of unsustainable systems is collapse. Though collapse may appear to be sudden and chaotic, we can discern key structures that guide the processes of collapse. (To continue) (p. 79)[85]

This book summarizes much of what has been stated in my book. I have expressed before that we need corporations only if they adopt a set of ethics and adhere to sustainable practices. Is there any reason that Koch Industries would reform? No, unless things got so bad that they had no other choice but to reform—or if we run out of natural resources. Many other corporations now fit into that same category.

Marketing: An article in *Yes* magazine, titled "Today's Young Adults Want to Redesign Capitalism. But into What?" on April 5, 2018, (http://www.yesmagazine.org/new-economy/todays-young-adults-want-to-redesign) by Joseph Blasi and Douglas L. Kruse said:

> There's growing evidence that today's young adults, ranging in age from 18 to 29 or so, are strongly dissatisfied with our political and economic system and specifically, growing numbers are rejecting capitalism. A troubling 2016 Harvard University survey found that 51 percent of American youth aged 18 to 29 no longer support capitalism and 75 percent said they do not identify or like the core concepts of capitalism. Some of the objections were that they felt that capitalism was unfair, there were conflicts between the rich and poor, but the majority do not feel that socialism can fix the problem.

There is more interesting information in the article, including topics of interest like profit sharing and employee ownership.

Shale Production: An analysis of the price of shale oil production in the United States is noted in the article "Prospect of shale wave looms over resurgent oil prices" by Tony Seskus, January 18, 2018 (https://www.cbc.ca/news/business/shale-oil-prices-1.4491116). This shows problems in the market as well as future projections.

Another article about shale production is "Why is the Shale Industry Still Not Profitable?" by Nick Cunningham (https://www.resilience.org/stories/2018-01-30/shale-industry-still-not-profitable/). This is an updated article on industry conditions. Richard Heinberg made the following comments in the article:

> Riyadh-based Al Rajhi Capital dug into the financials of a long list of U.S. shale companies, and found that "despite rising prices most firms under our study are still in losses with no signs of improvement." The average return on asset for U.S. shale companies "is still a measly 0.8 percent," the financial services company wrote in its report. One factor that has worked against some shale drillers is that the advantage of hedging future production has all but disappeared. In FY15 and FY16, the companies surveyed realized revenue gains on the order of $15 and $9 per barrel, respectively, by locking in future production at higher prices than what ended up prevailing in the market. But, that advantage has vanished. In the third quarter of 2017, the same companies only earned an extra $1 per barrel on average by hedging.

"EIA: U.S Oil Abundance for Now—But Don't Peek Behind That Curtain, Shale Reality Check: Drilling Into the U.S. Government's Rosy Projections for Shale Gas and Tight Oil Production Through 2050" by Richard Heinberg of the Post Carbon Institute and David Hughes, February 4, 2018 (http://www.postcarbon.org/eia-dont-peek-behind-that-curtain/), said:

> Explores four big questions crucial to the realization of the EIA's forecasts. 1) How much of the industry's recent per-well drilling productivity improvement is a result of better technology, and how much is due to high-grading the best-quality parts of individual plays? 2) Can technological advancement in the industry continue to raise productivity indefinitely? 3) What will be the ultimate cumulative production from all U.S. tight oil and shale gas wells? 4) What about profitability? So far, overall, the industry has lost money on tight oil production, and shale gas has done little better. That's even with most recent drilling being focused in core areas. The industry and its investors assume that if productivity continues to increase, and oil prices rise, profitability will eventually materialize. But what levels of oil and gas prices would be required to profitably extract fuels in the large non-core areas that the EIA assumes will eventually be tapped after "sweet spots" are drilled and exhausted? The AEO offers little in the way of realistic analysis on this point.

These articles show what the problems are in the industry and questions the long-term availability of oil and gas in the United States. It strengthens the credibility of what is noted in this book about this issue and questions the government's rosy projections for the future. This can have serious ramifications concerning our future supply of oil and is something people should be aware of when determining their long-term plans.

Grassroots Empowerment and Sharing in Cities. The article "Fearless Cities" by Jerry Gellaly and Marios Riveria (www.resilience.org/stories/2018--01-19/fearless-cities/) features citizen platforms, sharing, and social ecology. Following is from the beginning of the article:

> Fear and uncertainty seem to have settled into our societies, not only among citizens, but also political leaders and transnational corporations who see their capitals and centers of power stagger in the face of the combined effects of slowing global economic growth, imminent energy decline and increasing climate chaos and in this context, we are witnessing a multitude of responses. The first response attempts to regain control and security through new forms of authoritarianism and protectionism and the second response, fueled by techno-optimism, sees no limit to our capacity to invent our way out of global crisis through what has been described as a 'fourth industrial revolution' and this approach is advocated by organizations such as the World Economic Forum, along with a multitude of transnational corporations, financial powers and governments.

The article "Worker Cooperatives Offer Real Alternatives to Trump's Retrograde Economic Vision" (www.resilience.org/stories/2018-02-02/worker-cooperatives-offer-real-alternatives-trumps-retrograde-economic-vision/) by Sarah Aziza (Imaging Nonviolence) said:

> While the struggle for living wages and steady work is a real concern for millions of Americans, these high-profile gestures are emblematic of a persistent, fallacious narrative. It is one that touts an era of bygone American prosperity, which Trump, and those like him, promise can be restored through top-down, reactionary policies. Not only does this telling obscure or scapegoat communities of color — which are often disproportionately affected by the loss of manufacturing work and the suppression of wages — it also erases the agency of the American worker, who is left at the mercy of politicians and corporate executives.

The agricultural and landscape activity in the PDP will form a worker's cooperative, which will include students, people living in the community, and local farmers. The farmers will be included in production and teaching as applicable. The community nonprofit will organize the funding.

Another approach shows that the commons-based co-ops are distinguished from collective capitalism by their commitment to creating and expanding common goods for the whole of society; in platform co-ops, it is the platforms themselves that are the commons, needed to enable and manage the exchanges that may be needed.

Workers' Rights: The Economics Foundation noted in "Why Workers' Rights are Good for the Economy" (http://neweconomics.org/2018/01/workers-rights-good-economy/?header=La ...) by Adrian Bua:

> When economic decision-making power is in the hands of the public rather than corporate interests, economies tend to have lower rates of inequality, and higher levels of productivity. These are the findings of the new international Economic Democracy Index, launched at NEF this month. The Economic Democracy Index is an innovative tool which measures and compares democratic participation and economic rights across 32 OECD countries and it reveals important new insights for our understanding of what makes an economy prosperous.

Climate Change: Longreads noted in "We Should be Talking About the Effect of Climate Change on Cities" (https://longreads.com/2017/10/19/we-should-be-talking-about-the effect-of-..) by Ashley Dawson:

> In 2015, the Manua Loa Observatory in Hawaii reported that the daily mean concentration of CO_2 in the atmosphere had surpassed 400 parts per million (ppm) for the first time; each year Arctic sea ice levels grow lower and lower; permafrost in areas like Siberia and Alaska is melting, releasing dangerous quantities of methane into the atmosphere; and each year brings more violent storms and more severe droughts to different parts of the world. One recent announcement merits particular attention, however: in the summer of 2014, a team of NASA scientists announced conclusive evidence that the retreat of ice in the Amundsen Sea sector of West Antarctica had become unstoppable. This melting alone, they concluded, will drive global sea levels up by over 1 meter (3 feet). Two great tides are converging on the world's cities, generating an unprecedented urban climax. The first of these is a human tide. In 2007, humanity became a predominantly city-dwelling species. Of the approximately 7 billion humans current living, 3.3 billion live in cities. But if the human condition is now an urban one, this urban humanity is not spread evenly across the world's cities.

Product Labeling: There is a question now concerning how accurate product labeling is when the label "organic" is used. Dr. Mercola in an article titled "Regenerative Agriculture—The Next Big Thing" (https://articles.mercola.com/sites/articles/archive/2018/03/27/regenerative-agriculture/) noted:

> That organic standards have been watered down, in some cases to the point of no longer fulfilling even the most basic criteria. Standards are continually being usurped by Big Agriculture, especially Monsanto. He listed several terms, such as regenerative agriculture, and suggested the term "Biodynamic" may be the best way for certification. In organic certification at least 10% of the farm has to be organic. In Biodynamic certification 100% of the farm has to be biodynamic. Biodynamic farming is a spiritual-ethical-ecological approach to agriculture. It has superior harvests while healing the earth.

Consumerism and Discontent: An article in *New Internationalist* by Tim Jackson (https://plus.google.com/share?url=https://newint.org/blog/2017/09/14/consumerism-Disappointment) presents an argument that shows how consumerism thrives on discontentment. The article is fascinating, as one comment notes:

> "Discontentment is the motivation for our restless desire to spend. Consumer products must promise paradise. But they must systematically deliver much, much less. They must fail us, not occasionally, as psychologists have observed, but continuously. The success of consumer society lies not in meeting our needs but in its spectacular ability to repeatedly disappoint us."

Racism: Another interesting article in *New Internationalist* (go to their website and be content reading all day) called "How Black Lives Matter" by Jamilah King (https://newint.org/features/2018/03/01/black-lives-matter-change-politics) discusses the politics of the present black movements.

Climate Change: A pertinent article on climate change was in the *New Internationalist* that suggested that storms do not discriminate but make landfall on societies that do. "Why natural disasters are not natural" by Daniel Macmillen and Voskoboynik describes another viewpoint on climate change (https://newint.org/features/web-exclusive/2017/09/15/social-climate-disasters). One comment is "that the storms also show the presence of past structural injustice. In the Caribbean, the arrival of Hurricane Irma exposed the poverty of many islands, compounded through histories of colonial neglect and processes of economic conversion into tax havens and secrecy jurisdictions. While the hurricane was ripping through houses and lives in the region, Richard Branson was waiting in a concrete wine cellar in his home on a private Caribbean island, describing those hours as a party." Oh, to be rich and famous.

Managing Corporate Change: *Changing Course* (UP19) is an excellent book about businesses and the environment:

> It notes that an increasing number of corporate leaders think it makes good sense by integrating the principals of sustainable development. They recognize that there can be no long-term economic growth unless it is environmentally sustainable, 2) maintain credibility with society, which is necessary to sustain business operations, 3) confirm that products, services, and processes must all contribute to a sustainable world, 4) create open dialog with stakeholders, thereby identifying problems and opportunities as we'll as building creditability through their responses, 5) provide meaning for employees beyond salaries, which result in the development of capabilities and growth in productivity and 6) maintain entrepreneurial freedom through voluntary initiatives rather than regulatory coercion. (p. 84)[86]

I guess the Trump administration and Monsanto didn't read this book.

Artificial Intelligence: **"In the Age of AI"** by Roberto Veronese in *Method*, on June 16, 2017 (https://medium.com/method-perspectives/designing-for-education-in-the-age-of-ai-25b1d51db7b9):

> The way we acquire knowledge and skills is going to fundamentally change due to the introduction of new technologies supporting flexible and personalized learning models. Artificial intelligence and machine learning are playing a transformational role in the world of education as well as in many other industries. Their adoption promises to offer the efficacy of one-to-one tutoring at an unprecedented scale and in the context of an open, collaborative, lifelong learning experience. Recently the World Economic Forum estimated that 65% of children entering primary school today will ultimately end up working in jobs that currently don't exist. We can assume those jobs will be cognitively demanding and require higher-order skills such as the ability to comprehend the context and not just the content, as well as creatively defining problems rather than reflexively solving for them. In an hyperconnected society where the nature of work is increasingly collaborative, social and argumentative capabilities will be even more important.

US Federal Reserve: "A Great Irony—The U.S. Federal Reserve" on Peak Prosperity, February 17, 2018, by Chris Martinson (https://www.peakprosperity.com/blog/113760/worst-threat-we-face-right-here-home) noted:

The ironic parody of all the current US concern over the possibility of Russian meddling in US elections is that virtually nobody from either political party seems the slightest bit concerned that the US is actually recreating the very worst mistakes of the now-defunct Soviet empire. In point of fact, the Federal Reserve has done far more self-inflicted harm to long-term US interests than anything that Russia has been accused of, let alone been proven to have done. At this point, there's no contest between the two and if the damage inflicted by the Federal Reserve had been done by a terrorist organization, it would for certain be public enemy #1.

Diets: An article relevant to diets is by Stuart Wolpert, from April 3, 2007, titles "Dieting Does Not Work" (http://newsroom.ucla.edu/releases/Dieting-Does-Not-Work-UCLA-Researchers-7832). UCLA researchers report:

Will you lose weight and keep it off if you diet? No, probably not, UCLA researchers report in the April issue of American Psychologist, the journal of the American Psychological Association. "You can initially lose 5 to 10 percent of your weight on any number of diets, but then the weight comes back," said Traci Mann, UCLA associate professor of psychology and lead author of the study. "We found that the majority of people regained all the weight, plus more. Sustained weight loss was found only in a small minority of participants, while complete weight regain was found in the majority. Diets do not lead to sustained weight loss or health benefits for the majority of people." Several studies indicate that dieting is actually a consistent predictor of future weight gain. Other articles on the internet present studies to this effect. The consensus is to eat a more balanced group of foods, do not overeat the wrong kinds of food or too much sugar and have an adequate exercise program. One of the main factors in our growing obesity and heart failure problems is the consumption of sugar.

This is reflective of the advertising for the soft drink industry, as ads encourage you to drink soft drinks to make a meal better. There is no nutrition in a soft drink, and one type of soft drink fills you up with sugar, and the diet drink may cause weight gain and other problems. What one won't do, the other will. In other words, advertising is getting people to spend their money on doubtful causes. This is an area where people cause their own problems by (1) eating too much, (2) eating the wrong foods, (3) not exercising enough (even walking), and (4) and spending money on diets that do not do very much from a healthful standpoint. Our lack of willpower and common sense is doing us all in.

Food Nutrition—Soils: On top of these problems is what is happing to our foods due to the use of chemicals, degradation of soils, water contamination, and so on. It is getting to the point where we might not be able to get healthy foods. Why?

- In an article on Scientific American by Martin Pool (no date), "Dirt Poor: Have Fruits and Vegetables Become Less Nutritious?" (https://www.scientificamerican.com/article/soil-depletion-and-nutrient-loss/), Dr. Davis at U. Texas in Austin (2004) did a study:

"Efforts to breed new varieties of crops that provide greater yield, pest resistance and climate adaptability have allowed crops to grow bigger and more rapidly," reported Davis, "but their ability to manufacture or uptake nutrients has not kept pace with their rapid growth." There have likely been declines in other nutrients, too. It further lists nutrient losses in other plants with the main cause the degradation and poor management of soils. Efforts to breed new varieties of crops that provide greater yield, pest resistance and climate adaptability have allowed crops to grow bigger and more rapidly," reported Davis, "but their ability to manufacture or uptake nutrients has not kept pace with their rapid growth." There have likely been declines in other nutrients, too, he said, such as magnesium, zinc and vitamins B-6 and E, but they were not studied in 1950 and more research is needed to find out how much less we are getting of these key vitamins and minerals.

- The nutrition value of plants grown hydroponically should be studied and analyzed. Plants grown in good soil with trace minerals, microbes, and so on provide what the body needs for proper nutrition and taste. Plants grown in fertilized liquids do not provide these functions. With the large hydroponic greenhouses being used now, the nutrition value of food becomes very important, and tests should be done to compare the nutritional value of foods grown using hydroponics and those grown in soil. The difficulty in doing this is that several different types of soil have to be used for testing because the amount of biology and fungi in the soil determines the amount of nutrition in the plant. If the soil has certain trace minerals in it, the plants and fruit you eat will have them also.

- The University of California, Riverside published an article by Bettye Miller on March 14, 2017, titles "How Unregulated Household Chemicals Harm Us" (https://www.universityofcalifornia.edu/news/how-and-why-unregulated-toxic-chemicals-harm-us):

She notes that generations of toxic chemicals in everyday use—from ingredients in cosmetics and paint to nonstick cookware and upholstery—have sickened or killed thousands of Americans. Why? In the book "Tragic Failures," (AL73) Carl Cranor states: What's the difference between prescription drugs and those other everyday chemicals? In two words: the law. In a few more words: the law creates and invites ignorance about toxicants, risking our health and permitting substantial harm. "A third reason is that the laws create ignorance about potential toxicants, provide substantial incentives for companies to remain ignorant about their own products, and, because of the legal structures, provide many incentives for companies to create doubt about the science or demand ideal science in fiercely opposing any actions that might threaten their products or reduce their profits,"

As an example, many other books on my list describe the harm that Roundup does to people and soils.

- An article in *Nature Ecology and Evolution* on February 16, 2018, titled "Resistance is Complex" (https://www.nature.com/articles/s41559-018-0495-5) notes:

  The evolution of resistance has consequences for both food security and healthcare. To meet this challenge we need large-scale data to distinguish between what is evolutionarily plausible and what actually occurs in the field and the clinic. Another example from agriculture comes from genetically modified crops that express insecticidal proteins from the bacterium Bacillus thuringiensis. 'Bt crops', which include cotton, corn and soybean, have been a global commercial success since they were developed two decades ago. However, unsurprisingly, many insect pests have evolved resistance, with nearly half of Bt crop varieties experiencing resistant pests by 2016[2]. The key to those cases that have not experienced substantial resistance evolution is a combination of management strategy and genetics. Further spread of resistance to glyphosate could have significant economic consequences for food security and thus human health, which must be considered together with further investigation into the controversial question of whether the herbicide is carcinogenic.

Our government is not doing anything about these problems; in fact, they are compounding problems by eliminating safety regulations on protecting the environment by allowing industries more opportunities to do what they want regardless of how damaging it would be. By the way, the Koch brothers and lobbyists are leading this movement by monetary contributions. The power of money is everywhere except in low-income neighborhoods.

"We are between the rock and the hard bottom" in terms of health in the United States. These are only a few of the problems that we have now, and it will take a long time to fix some of them. We should study some of these articles because some of the fixes can be done by individuals. Right now, it is hard to tell what fix is most critical, but recognizing climate change and the harm to our soils are some of the first.

"Technology and its Discontents" by Steven Gorelick (Local Futures), February 9, 2018 (www. resilience.org/stories-02-09/technology-and-its discontents/), discusses the problems with some of our technologies. The full article shows the problems with the use of smartphones:

  According to The American Journal of Psychiatry, "Internet addiction is resistant to treatment, entails significant risks, and has high relapse rates" and the risks are highest among the young: a study of 14-24 year-olds in the UK found that social media "exacerbate children's and young people's body image worries, and worsen bullying, sleep problems and feelings of anxiety, depression and loneliness". Not surprisingly, a 2017 study in the US found that the suicide rate among teenagers has risen in tandem with their ownership of smart phones. Digital technologies are a threat to democracy in ways that go deeper than even Vladimir Putin might hope, since there is also evidence that a child's use of computers negatively affects their neurological development.

The author includes references for the above information. The PDP has to show people the values and problems associated with the internet and social media. The dependence on social media is a social problem. People feel that it offers acceptance to them when they are communicating. It also generates unstable competition to see who has the most social connections. It does not help that the main thoughts from President Trump are beamed to us through Twitter. Most people are so absorbed by the continuous chaos and ineptitude in Washington that they do not know about or pay attention to the more important matters, such as the environment and existing social conditions. The media and most corporations do not help. This is why one of the main purposes of the PDP is to market information that is described in this book.

Wi-Fi—Harmful? Dr. Mercola wrote in an article titled "Wi-Fried—Is Wireless Technology Dooming a Generation to Ill Health? That External Interference Can Disrupt Your Body's Natural Bioelectric Signals, published March 31, 2018 (https://articles.mercola.com/sites/articles/archive/2018/03/31/emf-exposure-wireless-technology.aspx):

> Many of these mobile phones are smartphones, with apps that frequently receive and transmit pulsed electromagnetic signals. The human body also has natural electromagnetic fields (EMFs), as many of your bodily processes involves the transmission of electric signals, and as noted by Demasi, "External interference can disrupt those signals." In a 2016 article, Jerry Phillips, Ph.D., a biochemist and director of the Excel Science Center at the University of Colorado, explained how living cells react to RF radiation: "The signal couples with ... cells, although nobody really knows what the nature of that coupling is. Some effects of that reaction can be things like movement of calcium across membranes, the production of free radicals or a change in the expression of genes in the cell. Suddenly important proteins are being expressed at times and places and in amounts that they shouldn't be, and that has a dramatic effect on the function of the cells. And some of these changes are consistent with what's seen when cells undergo conversion from normal to malignant."

There are many opinions about this, and it should be recognized as a potential problem to keep track of. It is one of those questions that may need more time to be evaluated.

"Unprecedented Crime" is a review by Howard Breen from February 16, 2018 (https://www.resilience.org/stories/2018-02-16/unprecedented-crime-review/):

> In a time when common sense human survival is really becoming uncommon with worsening existential threats in the White House and in our atmosphere and oceans with each passing hour, British Columbia writers Dr. Peter Carter and Elizabeth Woodworth, as honest brokers of factual scientific information, expose for readers the moral and intellectual bankruptcy of Big Oil glory days and their approaching end of days while Dr. James Hansen (the former NASA scientist, pioneering climate-prophet) provides a Foreword that is sure to give you the first twists and turns between nightmares and hope to be found in the book. Climate change is impersonal, and usually glacially slow. However, there are uber-rich, faceless corporate villains lurking behind the rise in planet temperature are those who strive to ensure we all, in varying degrees, and are part of the problem by keeping the planet fossil-addicted. "Unprecedented Crime" deftly arguing

that climate denial is not just immoral, that it is a willful act of global-scale violence, an unimaginably senseless and cruel act of climate battery against today's vulnerable, and dispossessed, a fate which will surely only deepen.

Sustainability: "Can farming save Puerto Rico's future? As climate change alters how and where food is grown, Puerto Rico's agro-ecology brigades are a model for sustainable farming," from the Food and Environment Reporting Network by Audrea Lim, June 11, 2018 (https://thefern. org/2018/06/can-farming-save-puerto-ricos-future/). This is an interesting website to subscribe to because it is mainly about how people work together using sustainable practices.

> Our climate is changing, and our approaches to activism and politics have to change with it. That's why FERN, in partnership with The Nation, is launching Taking Heat, a series of dispatches from the front lines of the climate justice movement by journalist Audrea Lim. Lim will explore the ways the communities that stand to lose the most as a result of climate change are also becoming leaders in the climate resistance—from the farms of Puerto Rico to the tar sands of Canada, from the streets of Los Angeles to Kentucky coal country, communities are coming together to fight for a just transition to a greener and more equitable economy. At a time when extreme weather events and climate policy impasse are increasingly dominating the environmental news, Taking Heat will focus on the ways climate change intersects with other social and political issues, showcasing the ingenious and inventive ways people are already reworking our economy and society. There will be new dispatches every few weeks.

"How Societies Collapse" or "The Eerie Parallels Between Rome, Nazi Germany, and America" by Umaie Haque Eudaemonia on January 30, 2018, (https://eand.co/how-societies-collapse-91fcd98f03d3) noted:

> Societies collapse in much the same way—there is something like a universal way of collapse. Yet the whole problem begins with the fact that human beings, having needy egos, find their own downfall difficult to accept. Perhaps you yourself will object—you are a mighty citizen of a proud society. Ah. Do you think the Incas, Mayas, Romans, or Nazis ever thought they obeyed the laws of history? Of course not. Becoming a powerful society makes us vulnerable to collapse because it leaves us puffed up with hubris. "We shall never fall!", we cry, "our thousand-year reign has barely begun!" Do you see how this all fits together, like pieces of a puzzle? It is ignorance of this great and terrible cycle that underpins so much human suffering that perhaps it is the single greatest evil in history. And yet our first tendency is to deny that it is happening to us, isn't it? So every step is harder and harder to uptake—a gravity created by our own weaknesses: our needs for superiority, for belonging, for infantile security.

Housing: The 2018 summer issue (no. 86) of *Yes* magazine, "The Affordable Housing Issue," is an excellent issue to purchase about the current state of housing. Some of the articles are (1) "Why Can't Everyone Have a Home," (2) "Just the Facts: Affordable for Whom?" (3) "5 Ways Communities are Creating Affordable Homes," (4) "How to Protect a Renter Nation," (5) and "Make them Pay: The Global Wealth-Hiding, Ultra Rich Elites."

Affordable Housing: The National Low-Income Housing Coalition has a PDF on the internet, "The Gap: The Affordable Housing Gap Analysis 2017" (http://nlihc.org/sites/default/files/Gap-Report_2017.pdf) from March 2017, which provides information about "A Shortage of Affordable Homes." The information is extensive, and anyone interested in this subject should read its full content. A brief excerpt:

- 11.4 million ELI (extremely low income) renter households accounted for 26% of all U.S. renter households and nearly 10% of all households.

- The U.S. has a shortage of 7.4 million affordable and available rental homes for ELI renter households, resulting in 35 affordable and available units nits for every 100 ELI renter households. Seventy-one percent of ELI renter households are severely cost-burdened, spending more than half of their income on rent and utilities. These 8.1 million severely cost-burdened households account for 72.6% of all severely cost-burdened renter households in the U.S.

- Thirty-three percent of very low income (VLI) renter households; 8.2% of low income (LI) renter households, and 2.4% of middle income (MI) renter households are severely cost-burdened.

Unemployment: Daily Reckoning on March 11, 2018, published the article "Economic Numbers Are Less Than Meets the Eye" by James Rickards (https://dailyreckoning.com/economic-numbers-less-meet-eye/):

In May the official U.S Bureau of Labor Statistics reported that unemployment had dropped to 3.9%, the lowest in almost 20 years. This rate is based on a total workforce of 160 million people, of whom 153 million are employed and 6.3 million unemployed. Of the 153 million with jobs, 5 million are working part time involuntarily; they would prefer full-time jobs but can't find them or have their hours cut by current employers. Another 1.4 million workers wanted jobs and had searched for a job in the prior year but are not included in the labor force because they had not searched in the prior four weeks. If their numbers were counted as unemployed the unemployment rate would be 5%. There are millions of people between 25-54 capable of work who are not included in the workforce. The Labor Force Participation Rate measures the total number of workers divided by the number of "potential" workers. The LFPR rate plunged to 62.8% in April 2018. If they were added back to the unemployment calculation the unemployment rate would be close to 10%.

There is much more in-depth information than what can be listed here, but this explains in part the slow growth and stagnant wages that have characterized the US economy since June 2009.

"The Town that Found a Potent Cure for Illness: Community" (www.resilience.org/stories/2018-02-21/the-town-thats-found-a-potent-cure-for-illness/) by George Monbiot:

> Frome in Somerset has seen a dramatic fall in emergency hospital admissions since it began a collective project to combat isolation. There are lessons for the rest of the country and it could, if the results stand up, be one of the most dramatic medical breakthroughs of recent decades. It could transform treatment regimes, save lives, and save health services a fortune. Is it a drug? A device? A surgical procedure? No, it's a newfangled intervention called community. The Pilot Demonstration Project will utilize this information to establish a program in the community and also set up a comparable study program. So, with the help of the NHS group Health Connections Mendip and the town council, her practice set up a directory of agencies and community groups. This let them see where the gaps were, which they then filled with new groups for people with particular conditions. They employed "health connectors" to help people plan their care, and most interestingly trained voluntary "community connectors" to help their patients find the support they needed.

This approach may be applicable for foundation or government funding.

"The drugs do work: anti-depressants should be given to a million more Britons, largest ever review claims." The research involved almost 120,000 patients. Credit: Getty, Laura Donnelly (Science Section, *Telegraph* U.K.), February 21, 2018 (https://www.telegraph.co.uk/science/2018/02/21/drugs-do-work-anti-depressants-should-given-million-britons/):

> At least a million more Britons should be put on antidepressants, the authors of the largest ever review of the drugs today conclude. The research led by Oxford University, and published in The Lancet, examined 522 trials involving 21 types of medication over almost four decades. All were found to be effective, yet its authors warned that just one in six patients suffering from depression are receiving treatment. Researchers said too many GPs were "squeamish" about offering medication for depression, when they would not hesitate to ensure patients received treatment for cancer or heart disease.

This is really scary. It is hard to believe that so many people in our society are depressed. It appears that we should look into what causes depression rather than depending on pills. Also, doctors should have a broader education by leaving their ivory towers and look around at our society. The system is really broken.

"Adolescence research must grow up": Young people get a raw deal from society. Targeted study and approaches as part of a new global effort are urgently needed to help them. Many adolescents would benefit from a global research effort to focus on the issues that affect young lives. Credit: Nina Leen/The LIFE Picture Collection/Getty Nature 554, 403 (2018) (doi: 10.1038/d41586-018-02185-w):

> When it comes to science- and evidence-based approaches to welfare, adolescence has been ignored for too long. In a special package, we examine the complexity and promise of adolescence, and assess problems this age group faces, as well as solutions, through

the lens of disciplines from medicine and social science to education and neuroscience. The need has never been greater: 10–24-year-olds now make up a record 25% of the global populatio

This is why we need to establish relationships in the PDP, to help them create a purpose that will help them throughout their lives.

"Sacrifice Zones in Rural and Non-Metro USA: Fertile Soil for Authoritarian Populism" by Marc Edelman from Open Democracy (www.resilience.org/stories/2018-02-21/ sacrifice-zones-rural-non-metro--usa-fertile-soil-authoritarian-populism/):

> Sacrifice zones – abandoned, economically shattered places – are spreading in historically white rural areas and small towns across the United States. Rural decline fosters regressive authoritarian politics and this is the fourth article in a series on 'confronting authoritarian populism and the rural world', linked to the Emancipatory Rural Politics Initiative (ERPI). 'The United States is coming to resemble two separate countries, one rural and one urban,' political analyst David Graham proclaimed in a 2017 article in The Atlantic. Viewing the map of 2016 presidential election results, it is hard to avoid a similar conclusion. Donald Trump carried over 2,500 largely rural counties and Hillary Clinton, who won the popular vote, less than 500 mostly urban ones.

This is the best analysis of how Trump got elected. This is important information for the PDP community because it will allow people to know about and address what has to be done. It should address the problems and offer solutions. The structuring of the bank as local and the use of sharing and local currencies are one example. It should also be noted in the information sent out from the PDP.

"Farewell to Development" by Arturo Escobar (www.resilience.org/stories/2018-02-23/farewell-to-development/). For additional information, see the book *Designs for the Pluriverse* (CE53).

> Two key elements define the concept of "post-development." The first questions the central premises of development, including economic growth and material progress. Post-development challenges the idea that all countries must develop along Western capitalist lines according to these dictates. The second, which emerged in the mid-1990s, is that African, Asian, and Latin American nations can and should put forward alternatives to development that incorporate non-Western concepts of what constitutes a thriving society. Those of us who subscribed to this view believed that other ways of theorizing— of liberating the imagination to enable other definitions of possible futures—were critical to changing the discourse in the Global South.

The PDP could also be a part of the Tradition Town movement. Additional information can be found on the website "Tradition Towns USA." Its guiding principles are represented by the Seven Guiding Principles of Transition.

"America's best scientists stood up to the Trump administration" in the *Guardian* (https://www. theguardian.com/environment/climate-consensus-97-per-cent/2018/apr/25/americas-best-scientists-stood-up-to-the-trump-administration) (no authors name):

> Over 600 NAS members called out 'the Trump Administration's denigration of scientific expertise. Everyone in the Trump administration seems hell-bent on damaging the planet. Recently, climate change denier Jim Bridenstine was confirmed by Senate Republicans to lead Nasa – one of the two most important climate science organizations in the country. Trump has brought with him a swamp filled with anti-science staff whose goal is to handicap the US and permanently remove us from any leadership role in the world. To be clear, Trump, Pruitt, the entire administration, and those who support him will inherit a terrible legacy that we will not forget. These people will be known for willfully trying to destroy the planet that we rely on for health and prosperity. For those who voted for Trump and who vote for other deniers of climate change, you can no longer say "I just didn't know." It is never too late to change course. But it is untenable to say you care about future generations yet still support politicians and policies that lead to future destruction. You have to choose one or the other; there is no middle ground, and we need to quit pretending there is.

Moral Education: In November 1993, Dr. Farzam Arbab presented a letter about what needs to be done with moral education in a society that is rapidly shifting from an established sociopolitical system to a new system not yet fully defined and articulated. His paper was titled "Living in a Rapidly Changing Society: Transition to Maturity." It can be found on the internet using this title (http://www.bahai.org/documents/essays/arbab-dr-farzam/living-rapidly-changing-society-transition-maturity). One statement from the report notes:

> In this past century and a half, every country and region in the world has seen old structures swept away through radical reform or revolution. Yet, it is an historical fact that these attempts have, by and large failed to generate this sense of purpose, the values and the standards of behavior that are essential for the creation of a new society. As a result, for decades humanity has been living in a state of crisis that seems to deepen almost daily. Some traditionalists want us to go back to our old ways. (p. 1) The fact is, however, that return to the standards of the past is not possible, for the forces released during this period have set in motion a process of transformation that is clearly irreversible. (p 1) (People) will have to express more fully the virtues inherent in mankind, and weed out our faults, harmful habits and tendencies inherited from their environment. Above all, they will have to lengthier strength to processes that counteract the negative forces undermining the foundations of human existence and align themselves with the forces leading mankind to the fulfillment of its destiny. (p. 4)

"Our laws make slaves of nature. It's not just humans who need rights" in the Guardian on May 23, 2018, by Mari Margill (https://www.theguardian.com/commentisfree/2018/may/23/ laws-slaves-nature-humans-rights-environment-amazon):

> To make progress in this area, we must break away from legal strictures that were never intended to apply to nature, such as legal personhood, and establish a new structure that addresses what nature needs. Perhaps we can call this framework legal naturehood. A recent symposium at Tulane Law School, in New Orleans, brought together academics, lawyers and activists to develop a set of guidelines for recognizing and enforcing legal rights of nature, known as the rights-of-nature principles. These define the basic rights that nature needs, including rights to existence, regeneration and restoration. Further, they call for monetary damages derived from violations of these rights to be used solely to protect and restore nature to its pre-damaged state. In addition, they outline a means for nature to defend its own rights – like children unable to speak for themselves in court – by being the named "real party in interest" in administrative and court proceedings. The principles build on laws and judicial decisions that have begun to accumulate in this new area of law, laying the groundwork for what legal naturehood could look like.

Natural Systems: To fully understand how natural systems around us function, we should read *The Hidden Life of Trees* (E50). The following passage is from the book:

> Four decades ago scientists noted something on the African savannah. The giraffes there were feeding on umbrella thorn acacias, and the trees didn't like this one bit. It took the acacias mere minutes to start pumping toxic substances into their leaves to rid themselves of large herbivores. The giraffes got the message and moved on to other trees in the vicinity. But did they move on to trees close by? No, for the time being, they walked right by a few trees and resumed their meal only when they had moved a 100 yards away. The reason for this behavior is astonishing. The acacia trees that were being eaten gave off a warning gas (specifically, ethylene) that signaled to neighboring trees of the same species that a crisis was at hand. Right away, all the forewarned trees also pumped toxins into their leaves to prepare themselves. The giraffes were wise to this game and therefore moved farther away to a part of the savannah where they could find trees that were oblivious to what was going on. (Forward)[87]

The book also shows how plants use underground fungi for food and communications. When plants have aphids, they send out pheromones to attract beneficial insects to eat the aphids. Restoring the wolf population in Yellowstone National Park allowed the park to balance itself by reducing the elk population, because the elk were eating trees on waterways, causing erosion and other problems. Trees can identify which species of insects are attacking them and put up defenses accordingly. The mother tree can help its offspring by feeding them and helping them with sickness during periods of stress. This is why we do not need chemical fertilizers, herbicides, and pesticides, because they do not let natural processes work as they should. Chemicals cause our problems, yet we are told by the chemical companies that if more harmful insects show up and weeds become resistant to one kind of chemical, then the only answer is using stronger and more toxic chemicals to solve the problems. Somebody forgot to tell them that nature has been around a little longer than the chemical companies. Monocropping destroys nature's balance by preventing diversity, which encourages natural systems. We are now able to produce food locally to provide most of our food needs at a lower price. The poisoning of our soils and erosion still continues and must be eliminated. An example would be health problems caused by Monsanto and corrupted government activities.

Post Capitalism by Paul Mason (SC82) presents a program to get to a postcapitalist way of life. The following quotes indicate the theme of the book:

Over the past two decades, millions of people have resisted neoliberalism (capitalism) but in general the resistance failed. Beyond all the tactical mistakes, and the repression, the reason is simple: free-market capitalism is a clear and powerful idea, while the forces opposing it looked like they were defending something old, worse and incoherent. (p. xii)[88] Non-market forms of production and exchanges exploit the basic human tendency to collaborate—to exchange gifts of intangible value—which has always existed but at the margins of economic life. This is more than simply a rebalancing between public goods and private goods: it is a whole new and revolutionary thing. The proliferation of these non-market economic activities is making it possible for a cooperative, socially just society to emerge. (p. 143)[89] (In economics, non-market forces are those acting on economic factors from outside the market system. They include organizing and correcting factors that provide order to market and other societal institutions and organizations – economic, political, social and cultural – so that they may function efficiently and effectively as well as repair) Wikipedia

The development of as many nonmarket forms of commerce, banking, agriculture, construction, and product design as possible is critical to the success of the PDP. This way, it can be more self-sufficient and independent from the existing capitalistic economy. In conjunction with this would be greater involvement with worker-designed activities.

"Home Care Cooperatives and the Future of Work" by Reed Ingalls (resilience.org/stories/2018-03-12/home-care-cooperaives-future-work/) is an article that demonstrates the superiority of the worker-cooperative model in the home health care industry. One of the founders of this type of home care is Capital Home Care Cooperative.

Environment: The book *Drawdown* (E40) is one of the most comprehensive environmental plans ever proposed to reverse global warming. It is edited by Paul Harken. The foreword states:

> Sometimes, when a concept or institution reaches its logical conclusion, the world looks at the results and cries: "Never Again." For really bad ideas—from totalitarianism to fossil fuel dependence—saying "never again" isn't enough. Humanity needs other, better ideas to take their place. That's where we are today. We know we can't avoid the cataclysmic impacts of global warming by only focusing on achieving zero net carbon emissions; we must also rapidly re-sequester carbon. Drawdown—by identifying and researching dynamic, innovative solutions—creates the playbook for this urgent goal.[90]

The subjects in the contents are energy, food, women and girls, buildings and cities, land use, transport, materials, and coming attractions. It noted that almost all the solutions compiled and analyzed in the book lead to regenerative economic outcomes that create security, produce jobs, improve health, save money, facilitate mobility, eliminate hunger, prevent pollution, restore soil, clean rivers, and more. It is fully illustrated and provides an introduction about several other books that could be read to increase your knowledge on multiple topics.

Nutrition: Books on nutrition help explain what is wrong with the foods we eat and how to make them better and available. Several books on nutrition are listed in the (AL) part in the reference list. They are all excellent books and will help you understand why you are gaining weight, getting diabetes, and just feeling lousy. Most of them recommend getting local foods from the farmers market. The PDP will have a system of food trucks to deliver fresh foods to neighborhoods, their own farmers market, and a cooperative group of farmers to help in the effort.

Urban Growth: All city officials and other decision makers should read the book *Better Not Bigger* (UP6). This is an oldie but relative to what our needs are today.

> The purpose of the book is to be a resource for individuals and groups who want to get off the treadmill of urban growth for it provides insights, ideas, information, tools and techniques to make the transition away from growth-oriented and growth -oriented and growth-addicted communities and toward stability. In growth management there are two kinds of growth. One is how growth should occur and the other one is whether growth should occur. (p. 9)[91] Additional public policies that has the potential to moderate growth are: infrastructure spending restrictions, limiting speculative development, consumption limits, carrying capacity limits and ecological footprints. (p. 131)[92]

He also listed the twelve myths of growth and what works by putting the brakes on growth. At the end is a summary for sustainable development.

Systems Design: Part of any analysis considers systems design using various feedback loops. One of the best introductory books is *Systems Thinking for Social Change* by David Peter Stroh (CE19).

It noted that to tell a systems story, people need to make three shifts (p. 32)[93]

1. From seeing just their part of the system to seeing more of the whole system—including why and how it currently operates as well as what is being done to change it.

2. From hoping that others will change to seeing how they can first change themselves.

3. From focusing on individual events (crises, fires) to understanding and redesigning the deeper system structures that give rise to these events

There are several other books available discussing systems that add to understanding how they are more applicable now in all of our and nature's activities. In the past, we solved or understood problems using linear thinking. To understand nature, you have to see how its systems fit together. For example, if a plant has aphids, it puts out a signal to attract insects that eat the aphids. A plant can also communicate through its roots with the help of fungi. Designing within the way that natural systems work is an approach that uses many different design fields.

Nature's Innovations: Innovation inspired by nature are described by Janine Benyus in *Biomimicry* (AL23). In 1997, this book enlightened many people and made us understand how nature is the leading innovator. It explains all of the topics I have discussed. There are so many interesting topics in the book to select quotes from, but I settled on this:

As adults, we need to put down our books about nature and actually get into a rainstorm, be startled by the deer we startle, climb a tree like a chameleon. It's good for the soul to go where humans do not have a great say about what happens. Between these trips to the "big outside," we need only open our hearts to the smaller encounters: the smell of old sunlight in a leaf pile, the chrysalis of a butterfly inside our mailbox, the glimpse of that earthworm that helps us grow tomatoes. This literal immersion in nature prepares us for the figurative immersion. This is where we take our reasoned minds and stuff them back in our bodies, realizing that there is no membrane separating us from the natural world. (p. 288)[94]

Remembrances: *Mountain Fragrance* by Rita Taylor (SC83) is a wonderful book describing the lands and culture of South Korea. She was an English professor there for many years.

> What made my experience of Korea, a country which like most others that is caught up in all the racket and noise of contemporary life so special? Perhaps it is the following realization: No matter how tentatively we may be able to intuit or touch the inner beauty of a culture, that is, that part of a culture or collective path which remains untouched by the hectic activity of outside life and multitudinous impressions, but which nevertheless is in continuing transition—this reaching to its inner nature is like experiencing the sudden fragrance from a mountain. The very intransigence and subtleness of it nevertheless presents us with a feeling of an echo of everything that we perceive inwardly as eternal. (p 1)[95] When I first arrived in Korea, I met a most interesting woman who was teaching English in the same city where I lived. The moment I met her in the doorway of a friend's apartment I knew that she was special. ... (p. 89)[96]

Nature: If nature had to vote for her favorite group in the United States, it would be the Native Americans. They have the greatest reverence for Mother Earth, and they understand how nature provides substances for us, all in her way. Unfortunately, their history shows they are one of the most persecuted groups in the United States. I received a flyer from the Southwestern Reservation Aid, Washington, DC, a program of partnership with Native Americans, and they pointed out a few facts people should be aware of:

> 1) Indian reservations were established because the government's objective was to rid the country of its "Indian problem" and open land for site settlers. 2) The locations put reservations in areas it regarded as being unfit for white settlers—isolated and arid places unsuitable for agriculture and far from towns, transportation and the growing economy. 3) Most reservations if you see them today would show a proud people who are living in near third-world conditions. Poverty is extreme. Many people are living in run down houses and trailers, many which are without electricity, telephone, running water or a sewage system. Most reservations are so isolated that the added costs of transporting supplies into and out of the reservation make local production impractical. 4) Between 35-85% of the Native Americans who live on most reservations are unemployed. To find

work, many must move away from the reservation and leave their families behind. 5) Even the most basic services-healthcare, stores and schools-are often an hour or so way. 6) Fewer than 15% of the 566 federally-recognized tribes operate prosperous casinos and give payouts to tribal members. Today, the land reserved for Native Americans has shrunk to just 2.3% of the land originally promised.

"Indian Lands, Indian Subsidies, and the Bureau of Indian Affairs" is an article that was written by Chris Edwards in February 1, 2012 (https://www.downsizinggovernment.org/interior/indian-lands-indian-subsidies). Part of the article notes:

> The federal government runs a large array of programs for the roughly 1 million American Indians who live on reservations. Many of the programs are housed within the Department of the Interior's Bureau of Indian Affairs (BIA) and Bureau of Indian Education (BIE). These two agencies have about 9,000 employees and spend $2.9 billion annually. Since the 1970s, the federal government has promoted Indian "self-determination," but tribes still receive federal subsidies and are burdened by layers of federal regulations. In addition, the government continues to oversee 55 million acres of land held in trust for Indians and tribes. Unfortunately, Indians who live on reservations are still very dependent on the federal government. Indians and the federal government have a long, complex, and often sordid relationship. The government has taken many actions depriving Indians of their lands, resources, and freedom. A former top BIA official admitted that federal policies have sometimes been "ghastly," including the government's "futile and destructive efforts to annihilate Indian cultures."

The history of the government not living up to its promises is as bad as some of our political history. We are not getting our money's worth with government subsidies for Native Americans because they are still living in poverty. If the subsidies worked, you should see some improvement. You have to realize that some of the subsidy money is in the form of surplus fattening foods that have caused high rates of diabetes on reservations. The government's Indian Health Service (IHS) is doing a credible job in reducing diabetes, but this is a pattern of government giving people a problem in order to have another government entity try to correct that problem. This represents our long-range thinking in this country.

Poverty conditions on some reservations cause high levels of alcohol abuse (thus stereotypes), constant stress, infant mortality, youth suicide, kidney disease, and so on. It appears that our government wants to keep Native Americans dependent and not address the underlying causes of poverty. Infoplease noted that there were 559,796 native people in the United States (2015). This would mean that every person received an average $5,175 yearly from the US government. This money doesn't do much other than help people stay alive. One of the answers is for the creation of facilities that can be placed on an Indian reservation or adjacent to it that will create jobs in order to make the reservation self-sufficient and self-sustainable. This is complicated because of existing laws pertaining to what can be built within a reservation.

> (Wikipedia—Indian Reservations). Indian Country today consists of tripartite government—i. e., federal, state and/or local, and tribal. Where state and local governments may exert some, but limited, law-and-order authority, tribal sovereignty is diminished.

This situation prevails in connection with Indian gaming because federal legislation makes the state a party to any contractual or statutory agreement. Finally, other-occupancy on reservations may be by virtue of tribal or individual tenure. There are many churches on reservations; most would occupy tribal land by consent of the federal government or the tribe. BIA agency offices, hospitals, schools, and other facilities usually occupy residual federal parcels within reservations. Many reservations include one or more sections (about 640 acres) of school lands, but those lands typically remain part of the reservation (e.g., Enabling Act of 1910 at Section 20. As a general practice, such lands may sit idle or be grazed by tribal ranchers.

A plan is needed so that the reservations can create meaningful jobs and build facilities that will improve conditions there. In conjunction with this, Native Americans can create social strategies that will have meaning to them. This should be clarified in the plan.

On another subject, before donating money to organizations professing that they need money for individual Native American schools, it should be researched to see if large marketing firms have been hired to obtain money. Some of the marketing firms get an overly high percentage of the donations. Most schools on reservations cannot afford to do this type of marketing, and they really need the money. Oh, regarding nature's voting program that I noted at the beginning of this essay, the Trump administration could not vote because they do not have the knowledge at the EPA to qualify at this time.

Social Challenges—Indian Nations: Wikipedia—American Indians Today/Current problems (https://en.wikibooks.org/wiki/American_Indians_Today/Current_problems) noted in part:

In the reservations but also outside the Native Americans have to deal with further worrying social developments: of all ethnic groups in the USA the American Indians have the:

- highest rate of school drop outs (about 54%),

- highest rate of child mortality,

- highest rate of suicide

- highest rate of teenage suicide (18.5 per 100,000),

- highest rate of teenage pregnancy,

- lowest life expectancy (55 years)

Drug abuse and alcoholism have become mass problems among the American Indians. For those the confrontation with unemployment, environmental destruction, the decay of the reservations and the lack of positive future prospects and leisure time activities to distract them situation, are probably hard to bear. Furthermore in the recent years gang violence in the reservations has increased, fueled by weak law enforcement, youth unemployment and the lack of activities for young Indians and with the results of vandalism and theft.

This is a major crisis in the United States that should be recognized and addressed. A new paradigm should be started on one of the reservations that will recognize all of the housing, employment, and social problems so that the people can live with dignity and have a purpose. So often, it is assumed that just giving money is all that is needed. Native Americans do need the money because of their poor living conditions; they need much more than that in order to be independent and able to choose their own destiny. If we do not recognize and fix what the underlying causes of the problems are, we just go around in circles, accomplishing very little. Perhaps something like the pilot demonstration project could be a start, as it could give them the opportunity to show us how to live in this transition period. This could be their donation to us. If we can spend money on war, surely there should be some for our people. We just have mixed-up priorities.

Agriculture: *The Soil Will Save Us* by Kristin Ohlson (AL56),[97] is an excellent first book to read to better understand why regenerating our soils is one of the first steps to save our society. This can be done and must be started soon. The author takes the reader around the world to show how farmers are restoring the soil and what this means for better and longer food production. No synthetic fertilizers, pesticides, or Monsanto. For example, you can see how Gabe Brown, a farmer and activist near Bismarck, South Dakota, can push a four-foot long, half-inch reinforcing bar into the ground with his hand. Some of his pastures have more than twenty different varieties of grasses and perennials to be used for animals, soil regeneration, and crop rotation. These are the processes that help restore the soil while preventing erosion and water runoff. After reading many books like this, I am astounded that there aren't many more people who understand what is needed to make the world a better place. Many people want change, deservingly so, but we may be looking in the wrong direction. If not for us, then for our children and their children.

History: The book *Collapse* (E20) by Jared Diamond is more relevant now than when it was written in 2005. It gave us a path to follow through the annals of history, and like many things, it has been ignored by most of society. The back cover states:

> Who hasn't gazed upon the abandoned temples of Angkor Wat or the jungle-choked city of the Maya and wondered, could the same fate happen to us? Jared Diamond explores how humankind's use of the environment reveal the truth behind the world's great collapses, from the Anasazi of North America to the Vikings of Greenland to modern Montana. What emerges is a fundamental pattern of environmental catastrophe-one whose warning signs surround us today and that we ignore at our peril. Blending the most recent scientific advances and a vast historical perspective into a narrative that is impossible to put down, Collapse exposes the deepest mysteries of the past even as it offers hope for the future.[98]

Housing Costs: Simon Black writes the Sovereign Man newsletter on the internet, and his June 4, 2018, letter was about problems that the middle class were facing in the United States (https://mail.google.com/mail/u/0/#inbox/163cb99e645ba2a4). Part of the letter discussed housing costs:

Housing prices have obviously increased over time. But what's really interesting is how much more rapidly home prices have increased over wages. In late 2011, for example, the average home cost around 3.56 times the average salary in the US, according to data published by the Federal Reserve Bank of St. Louis. By the end of 2017, the average home cost 4.73 times the average salary, even though mortgage rates were essentially unchanged. In other words, even when you adjust for the fact that people are earning more, housing became 33% more expensive in just six years-- and that doesn't account for increases in property taxes, home owners association dues, insurance premiums, etc. It's the same with rent: back in 2000, the average monthly rent in the United States was 7.38 times the average weekly wage. By 2017, rents had risen to 8.66 times the average weekly wage, an increase of 17%. So even though people are technically earning more money, their money buys them less and less house. Medical care costs show the same trend: in 2000, average annual medical care spending in the United States accounted for 10.8% of the average salary.

Bank Scandals: In another letter by Simon Black, on June 6, 2018, he wrote:

> The front-page headline told the story of yet another banking scandal: "Cartel case nets six bankers" The article was about how six prominent investment bankers in Australia colluded to defraud investors. This comes the day after Australia's financial regulator hit Commonwealth Bank with an AUD $700 million (~USD $525 million) fine for aiding criminal organizations to launder money. And earlier this week the United States government slammed French bank Société Générale with a $1 billion fine for rigging interest rates and bribing Libyan government officials. Bear in mind that the ink isn't even dry yet on the $1 billion check that Wells Fargo wrote last week as a penalty to settle its previous scandal, where they defrauded 570,000 clients in a car insurance scam. I'll (Simon) pause and acknowledge the obvious-- banks are constantly screwing their consumers and violating the public trust. It's been proven time and time again that banks lie, cheat, steal, and otherwise do whatever they have to do to make more money at our expense. They manipulate markets. They make wild bets with their customers' savings. They engage in accounting tricks to make themselves appear financially healthier than they really are.

This is only part of the letter. When you make so much on a scandal, the fine is just a drop in the bucket. It may eventually happen that when you deal with a banker, you need to get a signed ethics statement. However, he does not mention how the banks are sacrificing their profits by offering such high interest rates on their savings accounts. Savings use to be a cornerstone of a healthy economy, but now money should be put somewhere else. Fifty cents' interest a month means you have thousands of dollars in a savings account. If I was a banker, I would be embarrassed to even suggest having one. This is home to the power of their money.

Water Shortages: Now the city of Cape Town, South Africa, has had such a severe drought

(https://news.nationalgeographic.com/2018/02/cape-town-running-out-of-water-drought-taps-shutoff-other-cities/) that they will run out of water sometime in 2018. This may be a sign of things to come. Feeding the elite now could starve our children later in many parts of the world.

National Geographic published an article, "Why Cape Town is Running Out of Water," on March 5, 2018, by Craig Welch (https://news.nationalgeographic.com/2018/02/cape-town-running-out-of-water-drought-taps-shutoff-other-cities/). This is an example of climate change, and the shortage is caused by a prolonged drought and population growth:

> Not only does the City of Cape Town (four million people) have water problems, but the farmers will have to start relying on rain-fed crops in an area where there is no rain. The city. is prepping 200 emergency water stations with each one serving almost 20,000 residents. When "Day Zero" hits people will only be able to consume 25 liters per day, about 1/12 the amount an average American uses per day. Unemployment tops 25%. The city for years has had a water management plan in place, but did not plan for this long a drought. Now reservoirs stand at 26% capacity and the taps will be cut off and the taps will be cut off at 13.5%. Cape Town is a lush city with water features and landscaping, could find itself not watering yards and public landscaping.

Now several areas around the world are starting to have water problems. If this happened in other countries, you might have unscrupulous water vendors selling water in plastic bottles at high prices, and several businesses and residents would have to leave the city due to lack of business or income. Property values would decline. Agriculture would not be able to meet the demands of the people due to the lack of water. Food production would have to be more local, with small gardens at home, and whether they could be watered is another question. Politics could intervene, and there could be favoritism as to who could get water. This would increase more inequality and perhaps incite riots. The poor always suffer more in these circumstances because they are on the bottom of the economic ladder. This could be an indicator of what could happen in the transition period if we don't start doing something to make our earth more sustainable.

Most of the following information is taken from the book *Post Carbon Reader—Managing the 21st Century Sustainability Crisis* (E14). It is a compilation of essays mainly by fellows of the Post Carbon Institute. This is noted here in order that references can be made to the various institute fellows so that additional information can be obtained from the book itself and the various institutions that are represented. The information is quite extensive, and the book offers insight of what to expect in the future in regard to sustainability and economics. In certain instances, additional information will be provided that is found in each individual essay. The post carbon era refers to the time when there will be reductions in the availability of fossil fuels for energy use. It discusses what changes will be necessary in order to subsist in this type of economy.

Five basic assumptions were made by the Fellows of the Post Carbon Institute:

1. We have hit the "limits to growth".

2. No issue can be addressed in isolation.

3. We must focus on responses, not just solutions.

4. We must prepare for uncertainty.

5. We can do something. (p. xv-xvi)[99]

The purpose of this short analysis of *The Post Carbon Reader* is to provide sustainability information. It also includes information on areas of expertise for reference. Many of the suggestions noted in the book could be utilized in the development of a collaborative community to make it sustainable and adaptable. The growing population figures show why new innovations in approaches to community development have to change to meet new demands and economic conditions.

Democracy: In an article titled "America's Version of Capitalism is Incompatible with Democracy" by Eric Levitz, May 2018, in New York Intelligencer and Peak Prosperity Weekly (https://nymag. com/daily/intelligencer/2018/05/americas-brand-of-capitalism-is-incompatible-with-democracy. html), he suggested:

> An ever-greater share of economic gains concentrates in ever-fewer hands, while the barriers to converting private wealth into public power grow fewer and farther between. Politicians become unresponsive to popular preferences and needs. Voters lose faith in elections — and then, a strongman steps forward to say that he, alone, can fix it. All this contraindicates the democracy movement's prescription: If our republic's true sickness is its inegalitarian economic system, then that illness won't be cured by cross-ideological coalitions. Quite the contrary: What's needed is a movement that mobilizes working people in numbers large enough to demand a new deal from capital. Thus, if the liberal intelligentsia wishes to save American democracy, it should devote the lion's share of its energies to brainstorming how such a movement can be brought into being — and what changes that movement should make to our nation's political economy, once it takes power.

Agriculture: "37 Million Bees Found Dead After Planting Large GMO Corn Field" is an article in the daily Native News and Peak Prosperity Weekly (http://dailynativenews.site/2018/03/37-million-bees-found-dead-after-planting-large-gmo-corn-field). It noted:

> Millions of bees dropped dead after GMO corn was planted few weeks ago in Ontario, Canada. The local bee keeper, Dave Schuit who produces honey in Elmwood lost about 37 million bees which are about 600 hives. "Once the corn started to get planted our bees died by the millions," Schuit said. While many bee keepers blame neonicotinoids, or "neonics." for colony collapse of bees and many countries in EU have banned neonicotinoid class of pesticides, the US Department of Agriculture fails to ban insecticides known as neonicotinoids, manufactured by Bayer CropScience Inc. Two of Bayer's best-selling pesticides, Imidacloprid and Clothianidin, are known to get into pollen and nectar, and can damage beneficial insects such as bees. The marketing of these drugs also coincided with the occurrence of large-scale bee deaths in many European countries and the United States. A new study published in the Journal Proceedings of the National Academy of Sciences revealed that neonicotinoid pesticides kill honeybees by damaging their immune system and making them unable to fight diseases and bacteria.

Cozy Relationships—Drug companies and Congress: "'60 Minutes' just laid out the ugliest truth about the opioid crisis" by Linette Lopez, October 16, 2017, (http://www.businessinsider.com/60-minutes-opioid-whistleblower-2017-10) stated in part:

Joseph Rannazzisi, the former head of the Drug Enforcement Administration's division in charge of regulating the drug industry. Rannazzisi says he was pushed out of the agency in 2015 for aggressively going after the companies responsible for flooding pharmacies all across the country with opioid medications — primarily the distributors McKesson, Cardinal Health, and Amerisource Bergen. They control over 80% of the distribution market in the US. Rannazzisi, a lawyer, was helping to form a legal strategy that would hold companies accountable when they knowingly sent opioids to doctors and pharmacies that sold the drugs illegally. This force of white-collar drug dealers, more than anything else, is what sparked the crisis. The drug companies spent over 248.7 million dollars lobbying Congress.

This information is just the tip of the iceberg, so read the article and see how drug distributors and Congress are helping fuel the opioid epidemic. The bill passed by Congress and signed by President Obama made it more difficult to prosecute drug offenders and some doctors. On top of this, the drug companies have hired large numbers of people who worked for the Drug Enforcement Agency. This, it appears, is the easiest way for them to get inside information. The deaths from opioid use are multiplying rapidly, while the drug distributors are continually getting richer. Some doctors' hands aren't clean either. How much longer will this keep going with nothing being done? Why do we keep electing the same people to Congress? The American people should not be blameless because very few of them are doing anything about it.

Climate Change: A new report warns that dire climate warnings are not dire enough (August 20, 2018, by Jon Queally, Common Dreams, https://www.commondreams.org/news/2018/08/20/we-are-climbing-rapidly-out-humankinds-safe-zone-new-report-warns-dire-climate):

> "Climate change is now reaching the end-game, where very soon humanity must choose between taking unprecedented action, or accepting that it has been left too late and bear the consequences." In the new report—titled "What Lies Beneath: The Understatement of Existential Climate Risk" (pdf)-40 pages—authors David Splatt and Ian Dunlop, researchers with the National Centre for Climate Restoration (Breakthrough), an independent think tank based in Australia, argue that the existential threats posed by the climate crisis have still not penetrated the collective psyche of humanity and that world leaders, even those demanding aggressive action, have not shown the kind of urgency or imagination that the scale of the pending catastrophe presents.

Genetically Modified Children—New Film Unveils the "Monstrous" Child Deformities Caused by Agrochemicals in Argentina: This topic is an example of how advertising and marketing can be used for destructive activities. This article and video show how the companies of Philip Morris and Bayer-Monsanto have ruined the lives of tobacco and soy farmers in Argentina. It is in an article published on August 27, 2018, by Waking Times and Dr. Mercola (https://www.wakingtimes.com/2018/08/27/genetically-modified-children-new-film-unveils-the-monstrous-child-deformities-caused-by-agrochemicals-in-argentina/):

> The shocking film "Genetically Modified Children" unveils the horrors of decades of chemical-intensive agricultural practices in Argentina, where the majority of crops are genetically modified (GM) and routinely doused in dangerous agrochemicals, and the

chokehold big tobacco companies such as Philip Morris and chemical and seed giants have on poverty-stricken farmers desperate to earn a living. The film, produced by Juliette Igier and Stephanie Lebrun, shows the devastating health effects the region's agricultural sector is having on children, an increasing number of whom are being born with monstrous physical deformities. Some of the children's cases are so severe that, without a medical intervention, will result in death before the age of 5. This was started with advertising that convinced the government to allow Roundup© to be allowed into the country.

It describes the trap the tobacco farmers are placed in by growing tobacco for company that purchases the tobacco for Philip Morris at low prices. Philip Morris will not buy the tobacco unless they use GM tobacco, Roundup, and other dangerous chemicals. The farmers have to mix the chemicals by hand and spray the crops, which exposes them to the chemicals. Wives handling the clothes and washing them in a creek (which is their drinking water) then become exposed to the chemicals themselves. The chemicals in the body cause changes in the genes, which go to the gentle organs. Consequently, many children are born with extreme deformities. To increase the problems, the Argentinian government won't help them because they make money on import taxes. It is a Ponzi scheme of destruction. Monsanto does about the same thing by over-spraying transgenic soy beans with Roundup. The farmers barely make a living due to the high cost of seeds and chemicals the farmers have to buy. Why consider GM seeds and chemicals when organic methods are better for everyone?

When designing communities, the attitudes of society are paramount. One of the factors associated with community is understanding existing social attitudes within societies. Presently in America, our society is out of balance, and inequities are constantly increasing to the point that we are afflicted with many divisions within its structure. They are even evident within families. Trump's method of governing is one of the causes. This is explained in the following article by Rebecca Morin, August 9, 2018, on Politico, titled "Trump praises Texas AG's lawsuit to repeal DACA" (https://www.politico.com/story/2018/08/09/texas-daca-trump-lawsuit-771014). It states in part:

> President Donald Trump on Thursday praised a lawsuit led by Texas to repeal an Obama-era program that grants work permits to undocumented immigrants brought to the U.S. as children, saying he hopes the legal action is "successful." The lawsuit, which was filed against the Trump administration over the Deferred Action for Childhood Arrivals program in May, was argued in federal court in Texas on Wednesday by the state's attorney general, Ken Paxton. "Ken just filed a very interesting lawsuit, which I think is going to be very successful," Trump said on Thursday in New Jersey during a roundtable discussion on prison reform that included several governors and state attorneys general. Alabama, Arkansas, Louisiana, Nebraska, South Carolina and West Virginia have also signed on to the lawsuit, which was filed in U.S. District Court in Brownsville, Texas. In the action, the states argue that DACA leads to additional costs in health care, law enforcement and education, in addition to increased competition for jobs.

This is just one example among many. The main thing is that it should be discussed by Congress and voted on as soon as possible. Keeping people in flux, not knowing what to expect, is unfair. One point to consider is that if these people left, there would be a tremendous shortage of jobs in many different vocations, and purchasing costs of goods would be higher.

A book that emphasizes democratic reform is *Edge of Chaos* by Dambisa Moyo (CE67). She emphasized that there should be long-term economic and political policies that evaluate the demands of today's voters for benefits and perks and those of future generations:

> All of the ten proposed reforms in this book seek to address two central concerns: first, fixing and removing the myopia embedded in the democratic process, and second, improving the effectiveness and quality of policymaking, so as to tackle the headwinds that are threatening the global economy today by enacting long-term policies that drive economic growth. By binding the government, extending political terms, and increasing pay, politician's outlooks are better aligned to achieving long-term goals, thus addressing the myopia (nearsightedness or lack of imagination) problem. Restricting campaign contributions similarly limits the influence of outside interests that could discourage politicians from taking a longer term view. Intensified political competition and fewer safe seats mean more politicians have to demonstrate their quality to the electorate.[100] (p 218–219)

It is an analysis of how our present democracy is failing to deliver economic growth now and in the future unless certain steps are taken to correct our economy and the types of globalism we are engaged in. It describes the "headwinds" that will cause our economy to become chaotic and fail if they aren't addressed properly at this time. Most of the problems are due to our present political situation. We all should be acquainted with this problem. She shows there is a feasible way to obtain economic growth without depleting our resources or harming the environment. Anyone planning to vote should read the book because it is easy to read and one of the best studies about economics. To do what she suggests we have to reform the way we practice a democracy in chaos.

However, these thoughts about what is happening with our politics are not new. Mark Twain had a few comments of his own. ThoughtCo. was kind enough to place them on the internet, "Mark Twain Quotes" by Daniel Kurtzmanl on November 10, 2017 (https://www.thoughtco.com/mark-twain-quotes-2734314?print). Some are shown below, but there are many more in the article.

> "There is no distinctly native American criminal class except Congress."

> "Fleas can be taught nearly anything that a Congressman can."

> "I am quite sure now that often, very often, in matters concerning religion and politics a man's reasoning powers are not above the monkeys."

> "All Congresses and Parliaments have a Kindly feeling for idiots, and a compassion for them, on account of personal experience and heredity"

> "Anger is an acid that can do more harm to the vessel in which it is stored than to anything which it is poured."

History: The book that explains what is happening to us is *Immoderate Greatness—Why Civilizations Fail* (CE61)[101] by William Ophuls. It is only 103 pages, but it offers an explicit description of why civilizations fail and how we now are heading that way. In "Biophysical Limits," he explains why ecological exhaustion, exponential growth, expedited entropy, and excessive complexity are factors that provide limits as to what we can do as a civilization. Added to this are our human errors of moral decay and practical failure. His conclusion on pages 68 and 69 provides an alternative to civilization as it is currently conceived. His analysis, in my opinion, is the most conceivable that I have read in any of the books I have discussed, "We Are Climbing Rapidly out of Humanity's Safe Zone."

> Crime, mass murders, and increased numbers of people with mental health problems are on the list of society's problems. Capitalism, racism, wars, and the importance of individuality are leading the charge. The purpose of this report is to show some unique methods and practices that can lead society in a more positive and sustainable direction. The question of whether or not it is too late is up for discussion. The lists of books noted above are only a partial list out of many others that could be added. The books listed could also be placed in multiple categories due to their mixed content. Societal corrections have to be made soon in order to give future generations a chance to have an acceptable life.

Globalism: The book that describes the polarity that globalism causes throughout the world is *Us vs Them - The Failure of Globalism* (CE70) by Ian Bremmer. All around us, even at parties, it can be Us Vs. Them. Just look at the latest Supreme

Court hearing.

> This book is about the consequences . When human beings feel threatened, we identify the danger and look for allies. We use the enemy, real or imagined, to rally friends to our side. This book is about ongoing political, economic, and technological changes around the world and the widening divisions they will create between the next waves of winners and losers. It's about the ways in which people will define these threats as fights for survival that pit versions of "us" against various forms of "them." It's about the walks governments will build to protect insiders from outsiders and the state from its people. And it is about what we can do about it.[102] (P6)

Agriculture and Landscaping at the Crossroads

In evaluating happiness and the food chain economy, the publication "Localization, Essential Steps to Economic Happiness" by Helena Norberg-Hodge (www.localfutures.org) explains how our economic system centralizes power and creates intense competition for artificially scarce educational opportunities and jobs, while at the same time reaching into the psyches of young children, perverting a universal need for love and acceptance into a need to consume. It emphasizes how localization of the economy can renew connections—to one another, to communities, and to the living world around us. Our present economy can waste resources in many different ways. For example, the present economy can have "redundant trade."

The book also discusses globalization costs and the disruption of globalization in people's lives. The small farmers, the poor, and the disfranchised suffer from its effects, while the elite and corporations go to the bank more often. An article by the Economic Policy Institute, "NAFTA's Impact on U.S. Workers" on December 9, 2013, by Jeff Faux (https://www.epi.org/blog/naftas-impact-workers/) noted:

> NAFTA affected U.S. workers in four principal ways. First, it caused the loss of some 700,000 jobs as production moved to Mexico. Most of these losses came in California, Texas, Michigan, and other states where manufacturing is concentrated. The vast majority of workers who lost jobs from NAFTA suffered a permanent loss of income. Second, NAFTA strengthened the ability of U.S. employers to force workers to accept lower wages and benefits. As soon as NAFTA became law, corporate managers began telling their workers that their companies intended to move to Mexico unless the workers lowered the cost of their labor. Third, the destructive effect of NAFTA on the Mexican agricultural and small business sectors dislocated several million Mexican workers and their families, and was a major cause in the dramatic increase in undocumented workers flowing into the U.S. labor market. Fourth, and ultimately most important, NAFTA was the template for rules of the emerging global economy, in which the benefits would flow to capital and the costs to labor.

The article has additional information applicable to NAFTA and should be read so that you can obtain a full picture of its consequences. If this trend continues, unemployment will increase here, and that would cause many problems. Add automation, and these problems will leave us trying to find an explanation for what's causing it. In this case, knowing the Trump administration, it would be to blame China, Canada or the Obama administration. It is always good to have these excuses in your back pocket. Compound this with the audacity of Amazon to ask for so many freebies for their new offices to be built in the United States. As political parties from both the left and right embrace the wishes of corporate and banking interests, voting can become all but meaningless. Corporate interests become ever richer thanks to globalization, because they are able to increase their expenditures on lobbyists, campaign contributions, and political advertising. Someday Congress may decide to close some of these loopholes. However, it seems any Republican who is in office now and is saying anything about what Trump is doing is retiring. Referring to Koch's contributions to Congress, it is pretty obvious what is happening in those "hallowed halls."

Agroecology: The book *Transition to Agro-Ecology* by Jelleke de Nooy van Tol (AL13)[103] is one of the best books on the subject, and it notes the problems and possible solutions. This book lets you see (1) how different modern agricultural systems have spun out of control due to lack of adequate feedback systems; (2) how there are many farmers, organizations, and programs all over the world giving us good examples of the new normal and sustainable methods of agriculture and food production; and (3) how we can learn from the latter group how to let this transition happen.

Agroecology (an umbrella for organic agriculture, conservation, or restorative agriculture and permaculture) is the application of ecological principles to the production of food, fuel, fiber, and pharmaceuticals and to the management of agriculture and the growing of crops as an ecological system. Another reason there is such slow acceptance for agroecology is that many universities are linked to agribusiness by the courses being offered at major agricultural universities. For example, at Texas A&M, there is only one course that mentions organic farming and conservation agriculture, and none for agroecology. They offer undergraduate and master's degrees in agribusiness. They are advocates for chemical fertilizers, pesticides, and herbicides to solve problems rather than using natural systems. Many universities do not change because of the grants they receive from agribusiness and the government. Presently, in the United States, most government subsidies go to agribusinesses. The USDA put on a conference this spring, and guess who was listed as a majority of speakers? Big agribusiness. Monsanto and other players have an open door to Mr. Perdue's office. There is no mention of organic and agroecology methods of farming. It makes you wonder how he got that position. I guess it's knowing people in high-income places. No wonder the government has to spend so much money for security to guard him.

In contrast, the University of California at Santa Cruz and the Center for Agroecology and Sustainable Food Systems is the leader in agroecology studies. The mission of the Center for Agroecology and Sustainable Food Systems (CASFS or the Center) is to research, develop, and advance sustainable food and agricultural systems that are environmentally sound, economically viable, socially responsible, nonexploitative, and serve as a foundation for future generations. Through their research, education, and outreach programs, the Center works to create agriculture and food systems that sustain both human communities and the environments in which they live. Stephen R. Gliessman, a professor at the University of California at Santa Cruz, has published a textbook, *Agroecology, The Ecology of Sustainable Food Systems* (2nd edition) (AL30),[104] and this is an excellent source for understanding how natural process are a major part of what makes agroecology work. Also, in the preface of the book, he lists some other books on the subject of agroecology. To fully understand this approach, I would recommend reading one or both of these books. The most important factor to understand is how to improve soils by utilizing protection of the soil food web and learning about restoration agriculture.

Several books explain in detail the properties of an organic and improved soil (AL5, AL7, Al13, AL15, AL20, AL27, AL29, AL34, AL35, AL56, etc.). The main thing to realize is that conventional agribusiness practices destroy the microbes and fungi in the soil and cause nitrogen pollution in waterways or excess nitrogen for plants, which disrupts their natural way of growing. Also, excess soil compaction, water runoff, and lowering of organic content in soils causes massive erosion problems. It does not allow for carbon sequestration in the soil to absorb carbon dioxide. The practices of using heavy equipment, tilling, and keeping the land fallow (bare) during parts of the year also lead to erosion. Agroecology and restorative agriculture prevents these problems and allows plants to survive with less water. This is why it is so important to teach the proper methods of agriculture using the natural way in the pilot demonstration project.

A problem that needs to be recognized is the use of Roundup, which is manufactured by Monsanto. It is used mainly with GMO plants because they are resistant to it when it is sprayed on the fields to kill weeds. However, it seems to cause cancer and other health problems (witness many lawsuits against Monsanto because of this). They, of course, deny the accusations. The website "Sustainable Pulse" has weekly reports on Roundup, and one (https://sustainablepulse.com/2018/01/08/shocking-sudy-shows-glyphosate-herbicides) posted said:

> "Shocking Study Shows Glyphosate (which is in Roundup®) Herbicides Contain Toxic Levels of Arsenic" This study was published in Toxicology Reports. Monsanto was only testing (some in house) glyphosate (at least what they told us) instead of Roundup® which has additional chemicals, listed as inert ingredients, that cause harm.

Prof. Gille-Eric Seralini from the University of Caen, Normandy, France, and his colleagues Dr. Nicolas Defarge and Dr. Joel Apiroux have discovered several new findings that crush the pesticide industry's claim that the "inert" ingredients in glyphosate-based herbicides do not need regulating (https://sustainablepulse.com/2018/01/08/shocking-study-shows-glyposate):

- Glyphosate-based herbicides are shown to contain heavy metals such as arsenic, chromium, cobalt, lead and nickel, which are known to be toxic and endocrine disruptors. These are not declared and are normally banned due to their toxicity.

- Tested on plants, herbicide formulants such as POEA are toxic in isolation, while glyphosate alone is not toxic to plants at normal agricultural levels, but apparently only at higher levels.

Corn ranks high on lists of food products most likely to contain GMOs, or genetically modified organisms. The website Non-GMO Project—GMO Facts (https://www.nongmoproject.org/gmo-facts/) (no author-date) noted:

> Because GMOs are novel life forms, biotechnology companies have been able to obtain patents to control the use and distribution of their genetically engineered seeds. As a result, the companies that make GMOs now have the power to sue farmers whose fields have been contaminated with GMOs, even when it is the result of the drift of pollen from neighboring fields. Genetically modified crops therefore pose a serious threat to farmer sovereignty and to the national food security of any country where they are grown. More than 80% of all genetically modified crops grown worldwide have been engineered for herbicide tolerance. As a result, the use of toxic herbicides, such as Roundup®, has increased fifteen fold since GMOs were first introduced. In March 2015, the World Health Organization determined that the herbicide glyphosate (the key ingredient in Roundup®)

is "probably carcinogenic to humans." Genetically modified crops also are responsible for the emergence of "superweeds" and "superbugs," which can only be killed with ever more toxic poisons such as 2,4-D (a major ingredient in Agent Orange). Most GMOs are a direct extension of chemical agriculture.

Corn: Scientific American published the article "It's Time to Rethink America's Corn System" by Johnathan Foley, March 5, 2013 (https://www.scientificamerican.com/article/time-to-rethink-corn/). It noted:

> It is important to distinguish corn the crop from corn the system. As a crop, corn is highly productive, flexible and successful. It has been a pillar of American agriculture for decades, and there is no doubt that it will be a crucial part of American agriculture in the future. However, many are beginning to question corn as a system: The current corn system is not a good thing for America for four major reasons. The American corn system is inefficient at feeding people. 1)The corn system uses a large amount of natural resources, 2) The corn system is highly vulnerable to shocks 3) The corn system operates at a big cost to taxpayers and 4) the corn system receives more subsides from the U.S. government than any other crop, including direct payments, crop insurance payments and mandates to produce ethanol. In all, U.S. crop subsidies to corn totaled roughly $90 billion between 1995 and 2010—not including ethanol subsidies and mandates, which helped drive up the price of corn.

In the book *Restoration Agriculture* (AL7), Mark Shepard noted:

> That although corn packs a tremendous caloric wallop per acre, it hardly qualifies as a nutritional food. There is not much nutrition in corn and it would not be feasible to use it to feed the world. If you did there would be problems with getting nutritional diseases from lack of proper nutrition. Corn is low in calcium, but high in magnesium and phosphorus and this causes a deficiency in calcium. If corn was the main food then there would be deficiencies in folic acid, vitamin B12, retinol and vitamin E. Niacin (Vitamin B3) is locked up in the corn and lack of niacin can cause pellagra. Much of the annual crops do not enter into the human food chain. If a human being eats 10 pounds of corn only about 1 pound becomes human flesh. The remainder is used as the energy for metabolism or is flushed down the toilet. Another problem is when animals (mainly cows) are fed on grain instead of their natural food which is grass. If 10,500 pounds of corn was fed to a cow all you would get would be 569 pounds of beef. Only 5.4% of calories of corn become calories for human nutrition. This is a hell of a way to go into the future. (p. 154–159)[105]

Roundup in Court: Sustainable Pulse posted an article on May 7, 2018, "US Judge Gives Green Light to Misleading Roundup Label Lawsuit against Monsanto" (https://sustainablepulse.com/2018/05/07/us-judge-gives-green-light-to-misleading-roundup-label-lawsuit-against-monsanto/):

> Beyond Pesticides (BP) and The Organic Consumers Association (OCA) today responded to a federal judge's ruling against Monsanto Co.'s motion to dismiss the groups' lawsuit, filed in April, 2017. "In the face of EPA's poor regulation of pesticides, misleading pesticide product labeling cannot be left unchecked. The court's decision to allow our case to move forward, in denying Monsanto's motion to dismiss, is critical to showing that the

company is deceiving the public with a safety claim on its Roundup (glyphosate) label. Its advertising and labeling claim that Roundup 'targets an enzyme found in plants but not in people or pets' is false, given the devastating harm that glyphosate has on beneficial bacteria in the gut biome. The disruption of the gut biome is associated with a host of 21st century diseases, including asthma, autism, bacterial vaginosis, cardiovascular disease, cancer, Crohn's disease, depression, inflammatory bowel disease, leaky gut syndrome, multiple sclerosis, obesity, Type 1 and 2 diabetes, and Parkinson's.

Additional comments are found in the books on food nutrition. Since 1990, food has lost some of its nutritional value. Makes you want to eat four meals a day. This is really profitable for the snack food industry.

Another concern with the use of Roundup is that after a small period of time, it causes super weeds (normal weeds that grow very large) to grow. These super weeds cost farmers considerable time and money to try to get rid of them. Besides, the soil where Roundup was used becomes toxic, and it takes over a year or two for organic treatments with amendments to start making the soil healthier. Also, from a personal standpoint, large grasshoppers like the super weeds. More food for the money. The book *Whitewash* (AL1)[106] is a history of Monsanto's activities and should be read in order to understand how they are able to do what they do. In contrast, plants have their own defense mechanisms. They can communicate to help each other grow, warn against insect intruders and get beneficial insects to come and eat destructive insects, get nutrients from roots of plants' microorganisms and fungi, structure themselves to get the most light exposure (if they need to do so), and a host of other activities. It's best to let the plants handle their own affairs.

The "New Normal" approach is about recovering and restoring the connections and interactions between soil, water, plants, animals, food, health, and us. We should assist smallholder or indigenous farmers to get access to resources, not in the least the use of compost and carbon for their soils. We should scale up existing good practices and appropriate technologies. Programs should be continued for sustainable land management to eradicate soil erosion and encourage financial capacity building for smallholder farming all over the world. An organic regenerative farming future cannot be attained without conserving biodiversity and the associated ecosystem services. This is true not only for nature itself but also for farmers and ranchers and all of us who depend on the natural world. Using nature is not an expensive input cost for indigenous and other farmers. In contrast, using GMO-laden plants is an expensive input cost. Not since the age of dinosaurs has the world been on the verge of losing so many species in so little time. With growing resource needs and a warming world, losses are predicted to intensify.

What Is Agricultural Biodiversity? A definition is found on the Convention on Biological Diversity's (CBD) website (www.cbd.int/agro/whatis.shtml). The following dimensions of agricultural biodiversity can be identified:

1) Genetic resources for food and agriculture: Plant genetic resources, including crops, wild plants harvested and managed for food, trees on farms, pasture and rangeland species, Animal genetic resources, including domesticated animals, wild animals hunted

for food, wild and farmed fish and other aquatic organisms, Microbial and fungal genetic resources. These constitute the main units of production in agriculture, and include cultivated and domesticated species, managed wild plants and animals, as well as wild relatives of cultivated and domesticated species. 2) Components of biodiversity that support ecosystem services. These include a diverse range of organisms that contribute, at various scales to, inter alia, nutrient cycling, pest and disease regulation, pollination, pollution and sediment regulation, maintenance of the hydrological cycle, erosion control, and climate regulation and carbon sequestration. 3) Abiotic factors, such as local climatic and chemical factors and the physical structure and functioning of ecosystems, 4) Socio-economic and cultural dimensions. Agricultural biodiversity is largely shaped and maintained by human activities.

The National Organic Standards Board (NOSB) is a federal advisory committee that advises the NOP (National Organic Program). NOP Regulation—Preamble: "We have amended the definition of organic production to require that a producer must conserve biodiversity on his or her operation. The use of 'conserve' establishes that the producer must initiate practices to support biodiversity and avoid, to the extent practicable, any activities that would diminish it. Compliance with the requirement to conserve biodiversity requires that a producer incorporate practices in his or her organic system plan that are beneficial to biodiversity on his or her operation."

Miscellaneous: Information on the soil food web can be found on the **Soil Food Web** website

(http://www.soilfoodweb.com.au/index.php?option=com_content&view=article&id=46&Itemid=54):

> Although not apparent to the naked eye, a healthy soils a dynamic living system that is teeming with life. Most of the organisms that live in the soil are beneficial micro-organisms such as fungi, bacteria, protozoa, and nematodes. While seemingly insignificant, they are represented in the millions in any given soil, providing a range of important services that promote plant growth and vigor. The collective term for all of these organisms is the 'soil food web'. The interactions amongst these organisms can provide plants with many of the requirements that they need to survive and flourish which includes the availability & retention of nutrients, disease suppression, and the building of soil structure. The use of chemicals to kill pathogens and pests can also kill the beneficial organisms. The result is a sterile environment conducive to further disease and nutrient deficiencies. The quick fix often leads to a grower's dependency on more and more artificial chemical and fertilizers to maintain his crops as with each application he is killing the natural soil food web. This could be compared to developing a drug dependency and the need to enter rehabilitation to kick the habit.

The soil food web is one of the most important topics to comprehend to see why the use of chemical fertilizers (salts), pesticides, and herbicides are some of the worst products to use. For example, it is better to do nothing than use Weed and Feed for lawns and plants. These products are toxic to the soil web participants and the existing natural systems. There are many more books in the references that provide additional information on the soil food web.

"Ryan Zinke Is Opening Up Public Lands. Just Not at Home" is the title of an article in the *NY Times* by Julie Turkowitz from April 18, 2018 (https://www.nytimes.com/2018/04/16/us/ryan-zinke-montana.html):

> Mr. Zinke has emerged as a leading figure, along with the Environmental Protection Agency, in the environmental rollbacks that have endeared President Trump to the fossil fuel industry and outraged conservationists. In the last year, Mr. Zinke has torn up Obama-era rules related to oil, gas and mineral extraction and overseen the largest reduction of federal land protection in the nation's history, including an effort to slash the size of Bears Ears National Monument. But here in Montana, where support for drilling in certain beloved areas can be a career killer, Mr. Zinke has struck a different note. And as he faces allegations that he has violated travel and ethics rules, an examination of his Interior Department record shows that his pro-development bent has not always applied to his home state. But as Mr. Trump's chief public lands administrator, Mr. Zinke has favored the fossil fuel companies that have increasingly made up his donor base, overhauling restrictions on methane emissions, fast-tracking the oil-and-gas leasing process, and pushing to open nearly the entire outer continental shelf for energy development.

Of course, this would make grazing legal and allow amending the site's proclamations to allow fishery management decisions. I guess Native American culture doesn't mean anything to this government, or Secretary Zinke doesn't read any books other than what certain corporations write.

"The Ultimate Guide to GMOs: Discovering the Myths and Truths About Genetically Modified Organisms" (https://media.mercola.com/assets/pdf/ebook/ultimate-gmo-guide.pdf), a publication (pdf) by Dr. Joseph Mercola, can be downloaded from the internet. It is a brief history of Monsanto and contains factual information about GMOs. He also publishes a daily newsletter (free) which discusses topics associated with health.

Example of Sustainable Farming: Kyusei Nature Farming is a farming method that was initially advocated by Mokichi Okada of Japan, the founder of Sekai Kyusei Kyo in 1935. It is based on his belief that "The world can be transformed into a paradise by eradicating disease, poverty and conflict." This philosophy of Mokichi Okada for saving the world is a treasure that should be shared by the whole world regardless of religions and ideologies. A manual titled "Kyusei Nature Farming and Technology of Effective Microorganisms—Guidelines for Practical Use" was produced by APNAN and INFRC, edited by Ravi Sangakkara, revised edition 1999 (http://www.apnan.org/APNAN%20Manual.pdf). This is a comprehensive manual about this type of farming. The editor called it an ideal type of agriculture. Its principles are as follows:

1. Production of safe and nutritious food to enhance human health

2. Development of economic and spiritual benefits to both producers, farmers ad consumers

3. Sustainability and ease of practice by every person

4. Conservation of the environment

5. Production of sufficient food of high quality for increasing populations

"Inefficient Productivity or Productive Inefficiency?" This is an article from the internet (www.resilience.org/stories/2018-02-06/inefficient-productivity-or-productive-inefficiency?) by Gunnar Rundgren (RR) and Garden Earth. The article states:

> New research demonstrates – again – how deceptive the concepts of productivity and efficiency are in agriculture. Huge increases in labor productivity and modest increases in land productivity are gained by a massive increase of use of external resources, while natural capital is depleted. Is that efficient? There is a growing body of research (Spain) measuring resource flows to better understand the impact of developments and it is argued that only if economic growth can become substantially decoupled from material use, waste, and emissions, it can be sustainable. The metabolism of Spanish agriculture has changed through the increased use of mechanization, irrigation, chemical fertilizers and massive use of imported animal feed, to mention the most important drivers. We are told again and again that modern agriculture and the Green revolution are wonders of efficiency and productivity but when one look closer into the Spanish figures they give a different picture.

How to Break into Organic Farming—Rodale Institute: Rodale is one the best-known research institutions for organic agriculture. It is a nonprofit, and the following provides information for how to work with them (www.resilience.org/stories/2018-02-01/how-to-break-into-organic-farming-interview-with-rodale-institute/):

> Organic methods and production would probably increase if agro-ecology methods were used. Many young people are interested in farming and they understand the benefits it provides socially and environmentally, yet struggle with entering a lifestyle that takes a while to get started, requires significant monetary investments, and is filled with uncertainty (especially the first five years). With farming, these risks are very real but can have great rewards once overcome. To help alleviate these fears and promote the process, longevity, and sustainability aspects to farming, programs like the Veteran Farmer Training Program are arising that help address these issues. Programs like the National Incubator Farm Training Initiative, Dairy Grazing Apprenticeship program, Organic Certification reimbursement, Young Farmers Coalition, Organic Farming Certification Program, and apprenticeship training programs nationwide are becoming more and more prevalent in the beginning farming community.

This type of information would be part of the curriculum in the PDP so that students could relate to what is happening in the United States and the rest of the world. Research could also be conducted to incorporate data to show how the food system could be changed to be more efficient and productive. For example, it could compare the costs for growing a crop locally (including natural resource, gas, etc. costs) to what it would cost by bringing in that crop from long distances. This could then be part of the marketing plan to show people the comparisons of procurement, and the research would show more than just yields data. It should also be noted that the seeds to be used are not GMO seeds and that there are several companies offering organic seeds for sale. Try to select a seller/grower that grows seed that is adaptable to where you live. This is true of flower seeds also. The Rodale Institute also has a monthly magazine.

Poisoning Our Children (AL65) is a book discussing the use of chemicals and pesticides in the marketplace. In the description of the book on Amazon.com, it provided the following synopsis:

> Learn the truth behind:
>
> -The Rigorously Tested Myth. Are pesticides tested for safety before going on the market?
>
> -The Very Small Amount Myth. Can even a small amount of chemical residue be harmful?
>
> - The Breakdown Myth: Do pesticides rapidly biodegrade, and are the breakdown products truly harmless?
>
> - The Reliable Regulatory Authority Myth. Do the regulatory authorities review unbiased evidence before declaring a product safe?
>
> - The Pesticides Are Essential to Farming Myth. Are pesticides the only thing keeping our planet from starvation?

Sadly, parents must educate themselves on this serious danger to the health and development of our most vulnerable population, our children.[107]

Books (AL1), (AL36), AL42), (AL51), (AL60), (AL61), and (AL64) also relate to this subject.

"How polluters are writing the rules at the EPA" is an article written by Brett Hartll on July 6, 2017, on The Hill (http://thehill.com/blogs/pundits-blog/energy-environment/340879-how-polluters-are-writing-the-rules-at-the-epa). It states: (This was written prior to Pruitt's resignation)

> From undoing limits on toxic effluent discharges from power plants to dismantling the Clean Power Plan and the Clean Water Rule, special interests have achieved huge, substantive reversals in policy since President Trump and Pruitt came to power. A few weeks after secretly meeting with Dow Chemical, Pruitt reversed the EPA's own scientific recommendation and allowed the pesticide chlorpyrifos to stay on the market. And after receiving a letter from Dow in April asking the EPA to stop its assessment of the impacts of pesticides on endangered species, Pruitt obliged. In the sense that Pruitt is allowing special interests to dictate policy and make changes to policy on the substance, he has "settled" far more than any other administrator of the EPA at a similar point in an administration. The big difference, of course, is that he doesn't even wait for industry to win in court, or even necessarily file a lawsuit. He just does what industry tells him to do, before the ink's even dry on their requests.

Another potential for poisoning the earth is discussed in the following article in the *Washington Post* by Chris Mooney, "The Arctic is full of toxic mercury" (https://www.washingtonpost.com/news/energy-environment/wp/2018/02/05 ...):

> We already knew that thawing Arctic permafrost would release powerful greenhouse gases. On Monday, scientists revealed it could also release massive amounts of mercury — a potent neurotoxin and serious threat to human health. Permafrost, the Arctic's frozen soil, acts as a massive ice trap that keeps carbon stuck in the ground and out of the atmosphere — where, it is released as carbon dioxide, the greenhouse gas would drive global warming and as humans warm the climate, they risk thawing that permafrost and

releasing but U.S. government scientists on Monday revealed that the permafrost also contains large volumes of mercury, a toxic element humans have already been pumping into the air by burning coal.

"Major Study Shows Species Loss Destroys Essential Ecosystems" (www.resilience.org/stories/2017-12-07/major-study-shows-species-loss-destroys-essential-ecosystems/) (Jan Angus—Climate and Capitalism):

> 80,000 measurements were taken by interdisciplinary working groups from Germany, Austria, Switzerland, and the Netherlands. In more than 500 test plots, they planted varying numbers of plant species, from monocultures to mixtures of 60 species. By doing so, researchers could prove how the diversity of species affected the capacity of the ground to absorb, store, or release water. "No other experiment to date has examined the nutrient cycle with such rigor", says Prof. Wolfgang W. Wilcke from the Institute of Geoecology at the KIT in Karlsruhe. Better ecosystem services through biodiversity 1). High-diversity areas achieved better carbon storage. 2). The number of insects and other species was significantly higher. 3). Reciprocal interactions between species such as pollination took place more frequently.4). Higher-diversity meadows transported surface water into the soil better and 5). High-diversity ecosystems were more stable in the case of disruptions such as droughts or floods than low-diversity ecosystems.

Why Use Natural Systems for Landscape Planning and Maintenance of Residential and Business Properties?

It is vital for the pilot demonstration project to utilize diversity by having people of various economic and social backgrounds living there. The innovative project planning, landscape designs, collaborative activities, and the variations of housing designs to accommodate alternative and passive energy use also add to the project's diversity. At least 85 percent of the landscape planting will use native plants and plants that support maximum wildlife use. This approach will then be part of the teaching process because some of the homes will be planted using conventional practices (including chemical fertilization and planting practices) in order to be control sites. The methods of planting native plants and trees require different techniques in order to encourage fungi and microbial growth. Most landscape companies do not do this. Lawns require more bacteria in the soil, while most trees are dominated by fungi. The PDP will be able to show how these soil processes work, using growing data and visuals. The value of using natural systems to build up the soil is that the cost of maintenance decreases each year after the plants have been planted, and the soil structure keeps improving each year. The evaluation of maintenance costs will also be part of the education program. All this could be used in video and slide presentations for workshops. Speakers will be sought from universities that practice agroecology and other specialized organizations (farmers, nonprofits, arborists, practicing professionals in all applicable fields, etc.). They would also contribute to the PDP to make it recognized in the world. By using the project as a demonstration facility, it will market the natural system approach so that more people understand its value.

The PDP would also work with existing wildlife and educational centers to establish joint programs. In Dallas, Texas, there is an Audubon Center and the Heard Museum. One of the main reservoirs, the John Bunker Sands Wetland Center, east of Dallas, provides tours and offers programs to elementary, middle, and high schools. It shows how to use natural processes in water reclamation and wildlife management and focuses on wetland ecology, plant ecology, bird migrations, and water conservation. It is the largest man-made wetland in the United States, covering over 1,800 acres. It obtains its water from a 90 percent polluted (effluent) river, cleanses it, and pipes 165 million gallons of water to Lake Lavon to be used for municipal water. Its overall size is 1.4 miles by 3.7 miles. The approximate number of wetland plants is approximately 1.6 million. This is a very viable option instead of the usual lake reservoirs. A small system could be used near the PDP to serve as an example of the system.

The following information pertains to the application of proper practices for landscape purposes. The commercial fertilizers, pesticides, and herbicides advertised on TV (and by some lawn maintenance companies) should not be used. Some of the herbicides have glyphosate, and this is dangerous to children and pets. Besides, natural system applications cost less because the microbes and fungi are increasing to provide more nutrients for the plants.

The main question is, why not use natural systems (agroecology) or organic methods? This approach utilizes nature's natural processes. The key is establishing a natural balance. The natural system along with organic landscape planting and maintenance is less expensive after the first year because fewer biologicals and fertilizers are required on a yearly program. This is the beginning of substantial savings in the amount of water used for watering the lawn, plants, and trees because the soil is looser and can absorb more runoff due to the microorganisms and fungi in the soil. It also means less pollution. Results of doing this can be visible in a few months. Since there is such a variation of existing natural system dynamics on each property, there have to be individual approaches for each client. Movements in shade patterns, drainage flows, soil and plant conditions/health, past maintenance history, microclimate factors, and disease potential are some of the factors to be considered.

The most important concern is the condition and health of the soil on the property. The microorganisms, fungi, earthworms, nematodes, and other living creatures in the soil are part of the soil food web. They make nutrients available to the plant. Without their being leached through a cation exchange capacity process, it rebuilds the damaged soil structure (hardpan/compaction) by opening up air pores in the soil to keep the microorganisms healthy. They can then perform their symbiotic relationships with the plants and suppress diseases. This creates healthy pest-resistant plants and increases the soil's water-holding capacity. The fungi in the soil can extend the root capacity of plants by over 150 times in some instances. By using natural systems, you are feeding the soil and not just the plant. The microbes, fungi, and other living forms in the soil feed the plant, and the plant in turn feeds them.

The Living Landscape (AL67)[108] shows how the home landscape can be essential in creating a diversified landscape and ecological benefits for homes and neighborhoods. For example, residential homeowners have been infatuated with large areas of lawn. In a way, this is similar to monocropping in agriculture. Many lawns require large amounts of water, and much of this is wasted. The EPA has a leaflet about outdoor water use in the United States.

Lawns: (https://en.wikipedia.org/wiki/Lawn):

> In the United States, 50 to 70% of residential water is used for landscaping, most of it to water lawns. A 2005 NASA study "conservatively" estimated there was 128,000 square kilometers (49,000 sq. mi.; 32,000,000 acres) of irrigated lawn in the US, three times the area of irrigated corn. That means about 200 gallons of fresh, usually drinking-quality water per person per day would be required to keep up our nation's lawn surface area. Lawn maintenance may use inorganic fertilizers and synthetic pesticides which causes great harm; they may permanently linger in the environment, and they negatively affect the health of all nearby organisms, as many are carcinogens and endocrine disruptors. The United States Environmental Protection Agency has estimated nearly 70,000,000 pounds (32,000,000 kg) of active pesticide ingredients are used on suburban lawns each year in the United States. It has also been estimated that more herbicides are applied per acre of lawn than are used by most farmers to grow crops. A hectare of lawn in Nashville, Tennessee, produce greenhouse gases equivalent to 697 to 2,443 kg of carbon dioxide a year.

Commercial and residential irrigation water goes to waste due to evaporation, runoff, or overwatering. Following are some common outdoor water inefficiencies. Many people water their lawns too often and for too long, and this causes the over saturating of the soil, which can kill plants due to lack of oxygen in the pores in the soil. It's usually not necessary to water grass every day. Instead, test your lawn by stepping on a patch of grass; if it springs back, it doesn't need water. Regular maintenance of an irrigation system can help ensure that water is distributed evenly on the lawn and does not overspray onto paved areas. Look for an irrigation contractor certified in system maintenance and auditing to keep your system working efficiently. Alternatively, a water-based irrigation controller can do the scheduling for you, providing the right amount of water to your plants automatically, if it is adjusted and designed properly. Landscaping with plants that are not adaptive to your climate increases water use and costs. Instead, use native plants or species adapted to the local climate, which reduces outdoor water use.

WaterSense, a voluntary public-private partnership program sponsored by the US Environmental Protection Agency, seeks to help homeowners and businesses improve water efficiency and reduce their costs by promoting efficient irrigation technologies, such as weather-based irrigation controllers and certification programs for irrigation contractors. For more information, visit www.epa.gov/watersense. Reducing lawn locations to those that are used for pathways and outdoor play would also create diversity and reduce water use. The reduced areas can be filled with native plants, mulch, or cobblestones/gravel. The species of grass used makes a difference. For example, in Texas, buffalo grass uses less water than St. Augustine.

The book *Living Landscapes* (AL67) notes in chapter 3:

> That some of the ecological benefits for humans are carbon sequestration, shading and evaporative cooling, watershed protection, moderation of extreme weather and air-filtration. The ecological benefits for wildlife are the support for pollinator communities, connection of viable habitats, and providing plants that allows for maximum use by caterpillars so there is a sufficient food supply for birds. The birds also eats lots of insects and are always an attractive addition to any garden. This ecological balance of natural systems eliminates the need for chemical fertilizers, herbicides and pesticides. (p. 112)[109]

Agricultural Myths: In *Scientific American,* the article "3 Big Myths about Modern Agriculture" from April 5, 2017, by David R. Montgomery (https://www.scientificamerican.com/article/3-big-myths-about-modern-agriculture1/) named the myths as (1) large-scale agriculture feeds the world today, (2) large farms are more efficient, and (3) conventional farming is necessary to feed the world. Comments from the article are:

> We've all heard proponents of conventional agriculture claim that organic farming is a recipe for global starvation because it produces lower yields. The most extensive yield comparison to date, a 2015 meta-analysis of 115 studies, found that organic production averaged almost 20 percent less than conventionally grown crops, a finding similar to those of prior studies. But the study went a step further, comparing crop yields on conventional farms to those on organic farms where cover crops were planted and crops were rotated to build soil health. These techniques shrank the yield gap to below 10 percent. I now see adopting farming practices that build soil health as the key to a stable and resilient agriculture. And the farmers I visited had cracked this code, adapting no-till methods, cover cropping and complex rotations to their particular soil, environmental and socioeconomic conditions. Creating demonstration farms would help, as would carrying out system-scale research to evaluate what works best to adapt specific practices to general principles in different settings.

This article is a synopsis of the problems we are facing in our food production systems when we rely on agribusinesses to produce our food supply. The answer is regenerative agriculture programs where the soil is restored.

The Costs of our Food and Other Information: One of the most comprehensive books about agriculture is the 2014 book *Global Eating Disorder* (AL66) by Gunnar Rundgren. Part 1 includes chapters 2 through 9 and discusses the progression of agriculture from 12,000 BC to the present. The data noted is referenced in the book and will not be noted here. The book has to be read to get its full impact. Many statistics are found throughout the book that give considerably more information than what is shown here:

> The food chain now favors the big supermarkets because they can dictate what they want, mainly higher processed foods, at the peril of the farmer. In the United States in 2011, out of each dollar spent on food, the farm sector got 10.8¢, food processing 22¢, packaging 4¢, transport 3.5¢, retail 12.2¢, food services 31.2¢ (food distributors), energy 5.5¢, finance and insurance 6.1¢, advertising 2.4¢, and legal and accounting 2.1¢. The famers share has gone down by more than thirty percent in just 20 years, and the share

for the farmers and their employees work is now less than 2.7¢, more or less the same as advertising costs of the food industry. As much money is spent on convincing us to eat branded products as to remunerate the people who actually produce the food in the field. (p 92)[110] Using regenerative processes will not ensure we have good and wholesome food, but we certainly will be closer when we have embedded our food system in ecology rather than in the economy. (p. 349)[111]

There are extra costs in the food chain when agribusinesses import food from long distances. As shown above, the distributors are the main expense within the total costs of the food dollar, and unlike the farmer, they are not susceptible to weather conditions and other problems that the farmer has to contend with. The farmer now has a chance to make more money due to selling products locally, local distribution on their own, and growing more nutritional products. They can do this by using and understanding the systems that are in place. Diversity will increase, which will encourage the growth of pollinators, and the soils will be healthier due to better management practices. Local production can also reduce food deserts. Other studies show that subsidies are the only thing that makes farms profitable at this time. Now it is the large corporations that control the food chain, and this is another problem for farmers. They ignore that they are destroying the environment. Consequently, the small farmer does not receive the share of subsidies that large agribusiness receives. The PDP should evaluate a new approach to provide methods for the project and aligned cooperative farmers to obtain more money. The present system shortchanges the farmer, and the distributor profits. In the statement from the book, a farmer receives very little for his crop in relationship to other participants in the food chain. Farming locally would reduce many of the other costs, especially the food distributors. In the example, the food distributors receive eleven times the amount of money that the farmer does. In addition, he uses energy and causes air pollution while providing food that is not as fresh as the local farmer's. Note: Gunnar Rundgren has 987 footnotes documenting sources.

The book discusses food waste, managing the planet, efficiency and productivity (deceptive words), relationships to history, the food puzzle, the agricultural treadmill, fueling and farming, and the importance of soils, cars, animals, and people. The chapters on solutions (and where do we go from here) are especially helpful for establishing methods for regenerative farming practices (agroecology, restoration, etc.). The last part of the book looks at alternative pathways for a better food and farming future. Discussed are (1) technical solutions, mainly about farming; (2) where food might come from; (3) how we can change our consumption patterns; (4) economic alternatives in a wider sense; and (5) the policies needed to get us there. The land ethic simply enlarges the boundaries of the community to include soils, waters, plants, and animals, or collectively the land. We just have to know now how to see it and then use it for the benefit of society.

The problem today is not lack of food but the inability to access it. Cereal production has tripled, while the global population has almost doubled. Developing countries in the south spend 50 percent to 60 percent of their income to purchase food, a figure that can rise to 80 percent in the poorest countries. The increase in the price of food has made it so that people are continually hungry. If this continues, there might be uprisings in some of these countries. In the north, most people do not realize how bad the food supply problem is throughout the world.

2018 Farm Bill: To make matters worse, take the case of the 2018 proposed farm bill. This was defeated in the first vote, so it is unknown how it will be changed, if at all. Most of the organic and small farmers, along with many environmental groups, opposed it. In an article on the internet, May 15, 2018, the Wild Farm Alliance posted "Take Action: Oppose the House Farm Bill" (https://www.wildfarmalliance.org/take_action). It listed ten reasons to tell your representative to oppose the House Farm Bill (Post WFA and title):

Some of the reasons were 1) Helps the big get bigger and the rich get richer, 2) Cripples conservation programs, 3) More hungry and food insecure families, 4) Less local food, 5) Struggling rural communities, 6) Uncertain future for beginning farmers and ranchers, 7) No closer to equity for farmers of color, 8) Public research and seed breeding falls behind, 9) No risk management improvements for farmers and 10) Food safety support takes a back seat. This information was adapted from the National Sustainable Agriculture Coalition (NSAC). The NSAC noted as it stood, H.R. 2 (farm bill) would have gone down in history as the most anti-family farm and anti-environment farm bill of all time. The bill sought to unravel critical conservation, local food, business development, and organic agriculture programs with long track records of success. H.R. 2 also would have created a multitude of new loopholes, allowing unlimited, unchecked taxpayer subsidies for the wealthiest mega-farms. These provisions would have led to consolidation in the countryside, and further exacerbated the challenges that beginning farmers and small and mid-sized family farms face every day.).

The NSAC also publishes (free) the following information in "Grassroots Guide to Federal Farm and Food Programs" (http://sustainableagriculture.net/publications/grassrootsguide/):

> This guide does as its title suggests: it walks you through dozens of the federal programs and policies most important to sustainable agriculture and how they can be used by farmers, ranchers, and grassroots organizations nationwide. This guide is organized into nine chapters, along with a quick-reference overview chart, glossary, and other resources – all accessible on the left sidebar of this page: Quick Reference Chart, Preface, Beginning & Socially Disadvantaged Farmers, Conservation & Environment, Credit & Crop Insurance, Food Safety, Local & Regional Food Systems, Organic Production, Renewable Energy, Rural Development, Sustainable & Organic Research,

Seed Companies: "Out of Hand: Farmers face the consequences of a consolidated seed industry" from the National Family Farm Coalition (https://www.beginningfarmers.org/out-of-hand-farmers-face-the-consequences-of-a-consolidated-seed-industry/):

> The report outlines events that led to extensive concentration, including weak antitrust law enforcement and Supreme Court decisions that allowed genetically engineered crops and other plant products to be patented. These factors have created unprecedented ownership and control over plant genetic resources in major field crops. Five of the top 6 agrochemical companies are also on the list of the biggest seed companies. Monsanto is the world's largest seed company and fourth largest pesticide company. The WTO states that seeds, genes, plants, animals and combinations thereof are all patentable. Patent laws in the United States even restrict the right of independent researchers to carry out research, e.g. on the safety and performance of a GMO crop, without the consent of the patent holder—de facto allowing companies such as Monsanto to determine the safety of their products.

The Loss of Diversity Causes and Consequences: The following was written by Paul R. Ehrlich, professor of biological sciences at Stanford University (https://www.ncbi.nlm.nih.gov/books/NBK219310/):

> The primary cause of the decay of organic diversity is not direct human exploitation or malevolence, but the habitat destruction that inevitably results from the expansion of human populations and human activities. Many of the less cuddly, less spectacular organisms that Homo sapiens is wiping out are more important to the human future than are most of the publicized endangered species. People need plants and insects more than they need leopards and whales (which is not to denigrate the value of the latter two). The extirpation of populations and species of organisms exerts its primary impact on society through the impairment of ecosystem services. All plants, animals, and microorganisms exchange gases with their environments and are thus directly or indirectly involved in maintaining the mix of gases in the atmosphere. Changes in that mix (such as increases in carbon dioxide, nitrogen oxides, and methane) can lead to rapid climate change and, in turn, agricultural disaster. As physicist John Holdren put it, a carbon dioxide-induced climatic change could lead to the deaths by famine of as many as a billion people before 2020.

A silvicultural system is the process of tending, harvesting, and regenerating a forest. Different objectives in forest management (e.g., conservation in an ancient seminatural woodland versus production of timber from a conifer plantation or the inclusion of livestock) are likely to lead to the adoption of different restoration systems where livestock eat grass, native fruits, nuts, and so on. The manure and stomping on the ground by the livestock help fertilize and maintain the forest. Another strength in this food equation is making use of more perennials. This is an excellent example of diversity.

If developing countries were encouraged to use natural approaches for their food production, they would be able to sustain themselves better and not have to pay for expensive imports, such as fertilizers. The book *Drawdown* (E40) provides solutions for incorporating good practices in the food supply. One of the articles was "The man who stopped the desert" by Mark Hertsgaard. It describes how Yacuba Sawadogo used his indigenous knowledge to restore the desert in Burkina Faso.

> Mark noted that people are growing three things: trees, crops and wisdom. Foreign aid, sacks of GM corn, and handouts come and go, but if we are to successfully address global warming, we should learn to trust the capacity of the people everywhere to understand the consequences and imagine place-based solutions on a collaborative basis, and not force solutions around them, however well intended. A plan for reducing hunger can be incorporated into our society but without agribusiness and using their human and natural resources for our gain in doing it. Strengthening the better use of local production and distribution is one of the first steps. (p. 118–120)[112]

Who Will Feed Us: Several studies have shown that growing foods organically can have a smaller, same, or greater yield than conventional agribusiness farming. An interesting and vital study by the ETC Group is titled "Who Will Feed Us." This can be found by just entering the title on your browser (http://www.etcgroup.org/content/poster-who-will-feed-us-industrial-food-chain-or-peasant-food-webs).

Most of the report is included here because of its importance. The data references are not included here but can be found in the original report from the internet.

1. Peasants are the main or sole food providers to more than 70% of the world's people, and peasants produce this food with less (often much less) than 25% of the resources – including land, water, fossil fuels – use to get all of the world's food the table.

2. The Industrial Food Chain (Agribusiness or Industrial Chain) at least 75% of the world's agricultural resources and is a major source of GHG emissions, but provides food to less than 30% of the world's people.

3. For every $1 consumers pay to Food Chain retailers, society pays another $2 for the Chain's health and environmental damages.

4. The total bill for the Food Chain's direct and indirect cost is 5 times governments' annual military expenditure.

5. The Industrial Chain lacks the agility to respond to climate change. Its R&D is not only distorted but also declining as it concentrates on the global food market. The Peasant Food Web nurtures 9-100 times the biodiversity used by the Food Chain, across plants, livestock, fish and forests. Peasants have the knowledge, innovative energy and networks needed to respond to climate change; they have the operational scope and scale; and they are closest to the hungry and malnourished.

Where do most people get their food?

It is estimated that 70% or about 5 billion people of the world's population depend on the Peasant Food Web (PFW or Web) for most or all of their food. Rural peoples who look to "famine foods" in the seasons of scarcity prior to harvests will survive thanks to the Web's protection of agricultural biological diversity.

Who produces the most food?

The Web feeds about 70% of humanity and produces 70% of the world's available food in calories and weight.

What happens to all the food produced by the chain (industrial agriculture)? 44% of the Chain's crop calories are wasted in meat production. More than 50% of the Chain's crop calories are used as livestock feed, but only about 12% of those calories (or 6% of total calories) are then converted into food for people. Another 9% of the Chain's crop calories go to biofuels or other nonfood products. At least 5% of the Chain's calories are lost in transportation, storage and processing. About 8% of the Chain's calories are wasted in households. Only 24% are eaten by people.

Who is using up our agricultural resources?

The Web uses less than 5% of agricultural lands to grow the food that nourishes them. ETC estimates that the Web uses approximately 10% of agriculture's fossil energy and no more than 20%. Of agriculture's total water demand with far less damage to soils and forests. The Chain uses more than 5% of the world's agricultural land and in the process annually destroys 75 billion tons of topsoil and controls the market environment that cuts down 7.5 million hectares of forest. The Chain accounts for at least 90% of agriculture's fossil fuel use, 80% of freshwater used, and leaves us with a bill of $.3 trillion (for food and damages). It also leaves 3.9 billion people underfed or malnourished.

Who breeds our food crops?

80-90% of peasants seeds are saved, shared or locally traded. Importantly for adapting to climate change, peasants protect and sometimes interbreed 50,000-60,000 wild relatives of cultivated species at no cost, with potential economic value of $196 billion. Commercial breeders actually work with only 3 crop species. In fact, one crop, maize receives 45% of all private R&D spending. The Chain's brewing is also expensive: a single GM variety costs $ 36 million to get to market.

Who breeds our livestock?

Peasants have domesticated at least 34 livestock species and continue to nurture and breed more than 8. The chain focuses almost exclusively on 5 livestock species, cattle, poultry, pigs, sheep and goats. The web has worked on 8,774 rare breeds while the chain on 100 commercial breeds.

Who looks after livestock health?

Peasants and pastoralists breed and protect livestock that have enormous resilience and resistance. In the chain livestock vulnerability has created a huge industry. Global animal pharmaceutical sales total 23.9 billion p/a (per annum), and 10 companies control 83%. Antibiotic resistance costs the US $55 billions p/a. Antibiotic resistance is a threat that may be equal to climate change.

Who safeguards our fisheries?

Artisanal sustainable techniques harvest 25% of the total marine catch. The chain catches 6 marine species and "farms" 5 others. 91% of ocean fish stocks are overexploited or at maximum exploitation. Since the 1970s there has been a 39% decline in marine populations and a whopping 76% drop in freshwater species harvested. 1/3 of seafood sold in US shops and restaurants is wrongly labeled. Despite this, governments annually donate $ 35 billion in fuel subsidies and cheap insurance to commercial trawlers.

What is happening to food diversity?

Peasant-led crop and livestock breeding promotes diversity for both food security and nutrition. Women, who do much of the seed selection and breeding, especially focus on improving nutrition, seed and food preservation, and cooking characteristics. Diversified agroecology farming is based on the maximization of synergies between species. For example, in Kenya the push-pull mixing of maize and pasture for dairy has doubled the production of both milk and maize and rice–duck synergies in Bangladesh increased rice productivity by 20% in 5 years. Since 1961, in markets controlled by the Chain, there has been a 36% "implosion"in the number of species preferred by processors and retailers (fewer millets, pulses and tubers; more maize, soybeans and salad vegetables). While these species haven't disappeared, their use has withered. Within species, there has been a 75% loss in the genetic diversity available to science for plant breeding. (Like the species, the genetic diversity is not necessarily extinct but has "disappeared" from common usage and may be found on only a few farms.) Beyond species and genetic loss, the nutritional qualities of Chain-bred varieties have declined 5–40% depending on the species.

Who controls agricultural inputs?

The Web uses mostly local inputs: locally-bred crop varieties and livestock breeds shared with the community; manure; and sustainable (often traditional) technologies to counter pests. Nearly 90% of the seeds that peasant farmers use come from their seed-saving or are bartered with neighbors in local markets. The Chain relies on the $41 billion commercial seed market – 55% controlled by 3 companies (Monsanto, DuPont and Syngenta). Industrial farmers are dependent on GM-targeted pesticides bought from 3 companies (Syngenta, BASF and Bayer) who control 51% of global sales worth $63 billion. There have been more than 200 takeovers of smaller seed companies since the introduction of GM seeds 20years ago, and if the unprecedented mega-mergers being negotiated now are successful, the 3 surviving giants may monopolize 60% of commercial seeds and 71% of pesticides. This will give them still- greater control over the combined market for herbicide-tolerant GM plant varieties. If mega-mergers go through, 3 corporations will control 60% of seeds and 71% of agrochemicals.

Who protects our forests and forest foods?

Peasant livelihoods depend on 80,000 forest species, and 2.7 billion people cook with fuelwood. Of these, more than 1 billion people use 513 million hectares of officially "protected areas" for food and livelihood security. In total, 80% of the Global South looks to forests for timber, fuel, food, medicine, clothing and tools. In one recent survey, Indigenous peoples in Guatemala, Bolivia and Brazil were found to be 6–22 times more effective at safeguarding "protected areas" than governments. Although peasants are accused of deforestation, in Indonesia, the fastest forest clearing nation in the world, about 90% of the palm oil driven deforestation is attributed to large private enterprises selling to even bigger transnational food processors. In Latin America, industrial livestock increase causes 71% of forest loss. The Chain – and governments – have done a terrible job of monitoring forests, largely due to underreporting. According to UNEP, 50–90% of commercial tropical timber removal may be illegal and under-reported. Satellites miscalculated the Amazon's biomass by 25%. Between 1990 and 2010, the rate of tropical forest loss accelerated by 62% instead of slowing by 25% as claimed. Science only recently learned that the life expectancy of tropical trees has decreased 33% since the 1980s: trees are growing faster but dying sooner. These miscalculations mean that since the 1990s, the amount of carbon stored in the Amazon p/a dropped from 2 billion to 1 billion tonnes.

Who safeguards our soil?

Less than 1/2 of peasant lands may use some synthetic fertilizer. Normally, peasants use manure, so-called crop wastes and soil micro-organisms to fix 70–140 million tonnes of nitrogen p/a, roughly equivalent to $90 billion in nitrogen fertilizer sales. Peasants have their own soil protection

strategies – tree windbreaks, nitrogen-fixing and deep-rooted crops or mixed crop-livestock systems. Artisanal fishers protect biologically diverse and invaluable mangrove ecosystems, seagrass meadows and peatlands. In contrast, the Chain is responsible for almost all of the 75 billion tonnes of soil lost p/a, with damages costing $400 billion p/a. The Chain dominates more than 75% of global agricultural land, and uses most of the world's synthetic fertilizer, which costs an additional $365 billion in environmental damages p/a. The synthetic fertilizer industry's annual sales are $175 billion for every $1 spent on fertilizer, more than $4 are incurred in soil and environmental damages. Only 1/2 of synthetic fertilizers reach the crop, and the Chain has no incentive to reduce the waste.80% of the Chain's synthetic fertilizer goes toward livestock, and 80% of the Chain's agricultural land is used for livestock production. The Chain warns that with population and wealth increase, the demand for meat and dairy products will climb 70% by 2050, requiring every ha of arable land, leaving no room for land for direct human consumption– unless they can deploy their new technologies.

Who cares for our threatened crop pollinators and microbes?

In the Web, wild pollinators, including more than 20,000 species of bees and other insects, birds and bats, are protected partly because indigenous and peasant producers depend on the same habitats for hunting and gathering. These pollinators also pollinate 75% of the main global (often industrial) food crops. The Chain destroys natural pollinators, and 1/3 of its crops now depend on expensive commercial beehives. $235–577 billion pa in productivity is threatened by a collapse in pollinator populations linked to insecticide abuse. The Chain's solution? "Terminator" (gene editing) technologies that sterilize crops so they don't need pollination (but farmers will have to buy new seeds for every sowing). Only 1-5% of a pesticide application acts on the target pest, drastically damaging the ecosystem and jeopardizing our health. Genetically-uniform crops and livestock, combined with synthetic fertilizers and pesticides, have decimated beneficial agricultural microbes, which damages soils, reduces feed efficiency and makes animals vulnerable. Fertilizer Nitrogen deposition reduces peatlands' capacity to store carbon by killing bog-building moss Sphagnum. This strategy of mass production has also accelerated antibiotics use in humans and animals, reducing the diversity of bacteria in human and livestock microbiomes, and is believed to contribute to physical and mental health problems.

Who wastes our water?

Peasants and Indigenous Peoples know the importance of water for life and have used holistic methods such as rainwater harvesting (which reduces irrigation needs by 50%) and crop rotation that increases water availability up to 20%. 4 times fewer nitrates leach into groundwater from organic farms than from the Chain's fields. Agriculture uses 70% of the world's freshwater withdrawals but the Chain soaks up most of it through irrigation, livestock and processing. 1/3 of major aquifers are distressed and approximately 2/3 are being depleted. Livestock production alone accounts for 27% of our water use. The Chain's focus on meat means producing animal calories that need 5 times more water than calories from vegetables. Coca-Cola's water footprint (direct and indirect) is sufficient to meet the personal needs of 2 billion people. The globalization of food systems means that the food we eat uses water from someone else's country (e.g. 75% of UK food-related water use is extraterritorial.

Who needs more fossil carbon?

The Web uses 9 times less energy than the Chain to produce the same 1kg of rice, and 3 times less for maize. Overall, the Chain requires 10 kcal of energy to produce 1 kcal of food energy while peasants spend 4 kcal energy to produce 1 kcal of food energy. Despite climate change, the Chain continues to use 3–5% of the world's annual natural gas supply to manufacture synthetic fertilizers. liters of fossil fuel are used in producing and distributing nitrogen fertilizers (per ha). 50% of the energy the Chain uses to grow wheat is to manufacture the crop's fertilizers and pesticides. The average American uses 2000L of oil equivalents p/a to put food on the table.

Who processes and who preserves food?

"Preserving" is a strategy to survive lean times. Indigenous Peoples invented virtually every known method of preservation (drying, smoking, salting, pickling, fermenting and freezing) long before the Chain invented vacuum sealing. Peasants and Indigenous Peoples developed more than 117 fermentation strategies that secured important vitamins and minerals. At least 2 billion people in the South depend on artisanal processing. The Chain's goal is not to "preserve" but to "process" foods into more profitable packages. Processed foods make up 75% of Chain sales, a 92% jump to $2.2 trillion p/a since 2002.3000 food additives are used by US processors today, compared to 704 additives 60 years ago. These additives don't stop killing microbes when we eat them and could be contributing to additional gastro-intestinal problems. Nanoparticles such as titanium dioxide, silicon oxide and zinc oxide are added to hundreds of processed foods and consumed in growing amounts without adequate safety regulations. Commercial processing not only undermines local markets, but also reduces diversity and encourages unhealthy eating, contributing to obesity. Commercial processing also leads to pollution: an estimated 8 million tonnes of plastic leaks into the ocean p/a, about 1/3 of which is discarded by the Chain. If unabated, by 2050 the ocean will contain more plastic than fish by weight.

Where is the waste?

Food loss in the Web is a significant problem. In the world's most impoverished regions (sub-Saharan Africa and South Asia), 6–11 kg of food per person p/a is wasted at the household level. Beyond the household in these regions, 120–150 kg is lost per person p/a in other parts of the Web. Minimal investments in improved storage and transport could cut these losses deeply and immediately. While this food is lost to humans, at least a portion is spread back into the soil or fed to livestock. Waste in the Chain is serious and inexcusable. Less than 5% of the Chain's agricultural R&D addresses post-harvest losses. Of the 4 billion tonnes of food the Chain produces p/a, 33–50% is wasted along the Chain, costing consumers $2.49 trillion p/a. The average American or European wastes 280–300 kg of food annually. In the US alone, 350 million barrels of oil and 40 trillion liters of water p/a are wasted producing food that is never eaten. The Chain takes pride in its efficiency, but concedes that only 1/2 of its synthetic fertilizers (and even less of its pesticides) reach the crop at one end of the Chain and that barely 1/2 of its food is consumed at the other end.

Do we need all of the food we consume?

Because of subsidies that lead to over supply, the Chain produces more food than is needed for healthy nutrition, and a lot of food that is unhealthy or harmful to eat, making 30% of the world obese or overweight (more than are hungry). For example, Americans eat 25% more than they need. If everyone in the world ate as much as the average American, it would be like adding 1 billion extra mouths to feed. In OECD countries, obesity cuts life expectancy by approximately 10 years – roughly the same impact as smoking. The impacts of obesity cost $2 trillion p/a globally. The Chain will contribute to a predicted doubling of the number of people who are overweight or obese, up to 4 billion by 2030, and a 50% increase in the number of people with diabetes by 2040

What does the chain cost?

For every $1 global consumers pay to the Chain, we incur $2 of costs for managing the Chain's destruction: the "field-to-fork" waste of food we never eat (about 33% of the Chain's total production) as well as the cost involved in the food we overeat (about 17% of the Chain's total production). The Chain's total cost includes not only the direct bill to consumers, but also the indirect costs to governments and society for health and environmental damages (which equal more than 1/2 of the Chain's direct food bill). Additionally, 75% of the Chain's food is processed, and of dubious value. We could save people, our climate and trillions of dollars by supporting the Web. Here is the math: The direct food bill paid annually by consumers is $7.55 trillion. The direct food bill includes $2.49 trillion lost or wasted along the Chain and the $1.26 trillion price tag for overconsumption, which together total $3.75 trillion (or 50%) of the direct bill paid for food. Beyond the direct food bill, there is an additional $4.8 trillion indirect cost for social, health and environmental damages caused by the Chain, which brings the true global bill to $12.37 trillion. The cost of waste, overconsumption and indirect damages incurred by the Chain amounts to $8.56 trillion, meaning 69% of the Chain's total cost is counter-productive. For comparison, the Chain's real total cost equals 5 times the world's annual military expenditure. All this to feed 30% of humanity. Still, these figures don't consider the catastrophic risk of epidemic zoonoses: diseases transmitted from diverse (including wild) animals to domesticated (genetically-uniform) livestock or transmitted in foods. According to UNEP, if a global epidemic arises it could cost trillions.

Who encourages cultural diversity?

Indigenous Peoples discovered, protected or domesticated, and bred and nurtured every food species we use. The Web sees cultural diversity (different ways of knowing) as inherent to agriculture and in ensuring environmental sustainability. Cultural values influence production, consumption and our respect for Earth. As an economic strategy, diversity ensures more variety and possibilities of having enough to eat at all times than the uniformity demanded by the Chain. The Chain regards cultural diversity as an obstacle to market monopoly by dismissing the thousands of diverse ways of related to the Earth, it also contributes to the expected loss of 3,500 of the world's 7,000 languages (and cultures) in the 21st century. Food and environmental security is threatened when1/3 of South American soils are occupied by no one speaking an indigenous language capable of accessing the indigenous knowledge of the land. As men learn the language of the conqueror, women's intimate knowledge of flora, fauna and food disappears. Pachamama could help us if it weren't for macho papas. Monoculture food systems disconnect consumers from peasants and land, changing our food choices and customs and accelerating the loss of diversity. The Chain homogenizes modes of life, production and consumption even though our climates, living conditions and livelihoods make new and different nutritional demands on our bodies. For all the talk of Big Data and Artificial Intelligence, our generation may be the first in history to lose more life-supporting knowledge than it gains.

Who protects livelihoods and human rights?

Around the world, organic farms provide 30% more livelihoods than Chain farms. In general, organic farm labour achieves higher returns per worker. More than 2.6 billion livelihoods worldwide are derived from farming, fishing and pastoralism and at least 2/3 of households in the Global South (often led by women) grow some food. The Chain respects neither livelihoods nor Human Rights: The Chain has wiped out most family farms in industrialized countries to focus on so-called "modern" farms that employ 50 million workers, while driving rural families to cities. The Chain has exposed the remaining peasants and plantation workers to health risks from machinery and pesticides. Pesticides poison 3 million people p/a, leading to 220,000 deaths p/a.Robots are eliminating agricultural workers – 1 out of every 3 bowls of rice eaten in Japan is already sprayed by drones, and driverless tractors and combines are expected in rice paddies and fields in the early 2020s. 52% of US fast food workers rely on food stamps. Allowing such low wages is an indirect subsidy of $7 billion p/a to the Chain. The Chain's labour practices violate Human Rights, including cases of slavery (e.g. Brazilian sugarcane production and shrimp aquaculture in Thailand and Bangladesh), and close to 100 million child laborers. The ILO estimates that 60% of child laborers work in agriculture, including on palm oil and sugarcane plantations in countries like India and the Philippines, and in cocoa farms in West Africa. Violence against peasants and workers is tragically escalating as people are being driven off their land and criminalized or killed for saving their seed and feeding their families.

Who really innovates?

Oligopolies dominate almost every link in the Chain, and innovation is suffering. E.g. without condoning the Chain's use of pesticides, 70 new active pesticidal ingredients were developed in 2000 but only 28 in 2012. Since 1995, the cost of bringing a new pesticide to market has increased 88%. Why? It costs less to use PR to hype innovation than to spend on R&D. The agri-chemical majors know it is cheaper (by half) to adapt plants to chemicals than to adapt chemicals to crops: $136 million to breed a GM plant in the USA; $286 million to market a new pesticide. History shows that people can adapt their food strategies quickly when necessary. In Silicon Valley terms, the key is "crowd-sourced diversity. "Before modern transport and communication, African peasants adapted a new species, maize, to most of the continent's ecosystems in a century; Peasants in Papua New Guinea adapted sweet potatoes as food and forage from mangroves to mountain tops across 600 cultures, also in a century; In the 1800s, US farmers adapted a wheat variety from New York to the Midwest, across growing conditions comparable to those projected with climate change throughout the 21st century.

Why aren't the chains assumptions challenged?

The presumption that the Chain is feeding the world, and must continue to do so, goes largely unchallenged because we are dependent upon the limited statistics and interpretations volunteered by agribusiness. Even as we are told that "agribusiness as usual" is unstoppable, less and less information about the reality of markets and market share is made public. Since the late 1970s, individual companies and industry analysts have grown more secretive. This is partly because business analysts are consolidating as data itself becomes more profitable and proprietary. But the scope of "proprietary business information" is widening because – at any price – companies want neither the public nor politicians to know what they know. As a result, policymakers accept that myths such as the 'inevitable' increases in meat and dairy consumption and the need for agricultural chemicals are unchallengeable, and watchdog organizations can't access data to disprove the myths.

Further, statisticians and investment analysts rarely talk to peasants. So-called Big Data ignores the essential Little – or Local – Data: the holistic analysis used by the Web. Government and industry data is unreliable: grossly underestimating the global marine catch by at least 25% and severely miscalculating deforestation caused by feed crops and livestock because 50-90% of tropical logging is conducted illegally.

Then, too, the Chain's biggest companies are routinely and increasingly fudging their figures. The Economist estimates that the gap between real profits and the optimistic results spun by company accounts is distorted by 20%. While a lot of miscalculation is due to the complex nature of food and food systems, the Chain benefits from the misinformation.

What policy changes are needed?

Food Sovereignty through the Peasant Food Web is the basis for the world's food security, and supporting the Web is our only realistic choice in the face of climate change. But 'peasants as usual' are not an option. Agriculture is 12,000 years old. By the end of the century, we may face climatic conditions the world hasn't seen in 3 million years. Peasants will not be able to feed the world without major changes. With the right policies, land and rights, peasant-led agroecological strategies could double or even triple rural employment, substantially reduce the pressure for urban migration, significantly improve nutritional quality and availability and eliminate hunger while slashing agriculture's GHG emissions by more than 90%. For the billions of peasants in the Peasant Food Web to continue feeding themselves and others, policies are needed that would:

1. Ensure agrarian reform including the right to territories (land, water, forests, fishing, foraging, hunting),

2. Restore the right to freely save, plant, exchange, sell and breed seeds and livestock,

3. Remove regulations blocking local markets and diversity,

4. Reorient public R&D to respond to peasants' directions,

5. Institute fair trade, determined by peasant-led policies,

6. Establish fair wages and working conditions for food and agricultural workers.

Sources and comments

See original report from the internet.

Peasant agriculture is reliable and resilient. In a normal or abnormal year, on good or poor soils, women and men working with diverse crops, fish ponds and livestock will produce more food per hectare than industrial farms. Using agroecological strategies, the Web will consistently produce more, at less risk to people and the planet. In a normal year, with sufficient money, machines and labour, on good soils, using high-yielding varieties or breeds of commercial crops, livestock species or fish monocultures, the Chain may be able to produce more commercial mass per hectare than peasant-bred varieties of the same species. However, in recent decades, yields have stagnated for 4 of the Chain's major crops (maize, rice, wheat and soybeans), which together account for 57% of the Chain's crop calories). The Chain's crop genetic uniformity caused the devastating Corn Leaf Blight in the USA in 1970; a new wheat rust is threatening the crop in Africa and around the world; black sigatoga is destroying genetically-uniform banana plantation Tungro and leafhopper infestations devastated Southeast Asian rice; and crops from coffee to oranges and rubber remain impressively vulnerable today because of their uniformity.

Before the Chain, genetic uniformity caused the 1840s Irish Potato Famine that killed one million people and forced another million to migrate. Nevertheless, the Chain is supported by $50 billion in public and private sector research. There is little data on the funding for peasant-directed research or agroecology but it is less than 1% of the Chain's R&D. While cutting public R&D support for the private sector would benefit both people and planet, shifting that funding to agroecology would be game-changing.

The etc group also has additional information on the following topics:

Seeds & Genetic Diversity
Farmers' Rights & Food Sovereignty
Biodiversity & Cultural Diversity
Genomics & Biotechnology
Climate & Geoengineering
Corporate Monopolies
Related Fora:
Food and Agriculture: FAO, CGIAR, CFS
Social Movements: World Social Forum
Regional: EU, Asia Pacific, Africa, Americas
Climate: UNFCCC, IPCC

The information included in this report shows how dominant corporations and politics have become in establishing policies that are detrimental to most of us. If the corporations were more ethical and sustainable, there would be a different situation. For example, meat, especially cattle, would have to cost more due to the amount of natural resources they consume, and sustainable methods of raising cattle should be utilized rather than what is being done now. Present methods of fattening cattle and crowding necessitates the use of antibiotics. Cattle can sustain pasture and soil vitality by constantly moving the proper number of cattle from one pasture to another. Grazing animals can have either a positive or negative effect on water quality, depending on the way their grazing patterns are controlled. Proper grazing management favors pasture productivity and reduces the potential for soil erosion and manure runoff. Healthy and vigorous canopy cover protects and enhances water quality by lessening the impact of precipitation that dislodges soil particles, thereby reducing the amount of sediment in surface runoff. This is just one example of how agricultural methods have to be changed to protect our environment and provide more nutritious meat without antibiotics.

On YouTube, a video presented by Graeme Sait, titled *Humus*—The Essential Ingredient and Mastering Mineral Balance in the Soil, shows how important it is to save and produce humus in our soils. Agribusiness management causes a reduction of humus, resulting in erosion and the depletion of soils.

> Humus is a stable carbon source for sequestration and its formation by photosynthesis and decay in plants reduces the amount of carbon dioxide in the atmosphere. It is more important than the cutting car emissions. If this continues the amount of agricultural production areas will decrease, there will be more carbon dioxide in the air caused by use of fossil fuels and the oceans will become more acidic. The higher the acid content in the ocean will cause the death of corals (which we are presently witnessing), krill and phytoplankton. Krill feed on phytoplankton, microscopic, single-celled plants that drift near the ocean's surface and live off carbon dioxide and the sun's rays. They in turn are the main staple in the diets of literally hundreds of different animals, from fish, to birds, to baleen whales (National Geographic). If the coral, krill and phytoplankton are killed by an increase of lower pH (acid) then the food chain in the ocean will suffer and this could kill fish and other creatures because one of their main food sources isn't available. In turn millions of people would lose one of their main sources of food.

This would be a worldly crisis. When this might happen depends on if we continue the same agribusiness farming (ten to thirty years by some estimates) or start agroecology practices. Many books and articles describe how humus is formed and its value to the earth's ecology.

Just reading about these problems will not get them improved. We need to create a movement against the chemical companies or at least boycott their products, such as Monsanto's Roundup. It doesn't help that Bill Gates, Howard Buffett, and some universities back the present agribusiness practices. This is for our children and our children's children. We can start on our own properties by not using chemical fertilizers, pesticides, and herbicides. This would be a start in carbon sequestration.

"Roundup for Breakfast? Weed Killer Found in Kids' Cereals, Other Oat-Based Foods" (https://t.co/QDKM9gYxSW) is an article from August 26, 2018, found on Eco Watch Community:

> Monsanto's—and now Bayer's—glyphosate problem is also a headache for General Mills. The Cheerios-maker could face a class action lawsuit alleging the company failed to warn consumers about traces of the controversial herbicide in its products. A Florida woman filed the lawsuit Thursday in Miami federal court, according to Reuters. The move comes about a week after a California jury awarded $289 million to a school groundskeeper who claimed Monsanto's blockbuster weedkiller Roundup gave him cancer. Plaintiff Mounira Doss cited the Environmental Working Group's (EWG) widely circulated report last week that found Cheerios contained 470 to 530 parts per billion (ppb) of glyphosate, Food Navigator reported. The U.S. Environmental Protection Agency (EPA) sets its tolerance for glyphosate at 30,000 ppb in grains and cereals but the EWG sets their health benchmark at 160 ppb. Reuters reported Thursday that the German pharmaceutical giant is facing 8,000 U.S. lawsuits alone, up from the 5,200 it previously disclosed.

Also look up the Environmental Working Group's analysis to find information about other cereals. Remember the EPA under the Trump administration skewers information toward big agribusiness, so it is hard to know how reliable they are. The problem is caused by farmers spraying Roundup on the oats just before harvesting so that they are easier to harvest.

A film has been made from the book *Food, Inc.*[113] due to its exposure of some of the worst practices in agriculture in the United States. It consists of a series of articles edited by Karl Weber. A few of the titles follow:

"Organics—Healthy Food, and So Much More" by Gary Hirshberg

"Food Science, and the Challenge of World Hunger" by Peter Pringle

"The Ethanol Scam: Burning Food to Make Motor Fuel" by Robertl Bryce

"The Financial Crisis and World Hunger" by Muhammad Yunus

"Cheap Food: Workers Pay the Price" by Pesticide Action Network

"The Climate Crisis; at the End of Our Fork" by Anna Lappé

"Declare Your Independence" by Joel Salatin.

"Produce for the People: A Prescription for Health" by Preston Making

Many of these articles describe what industrial agricultural corporations are doing in the United States. Many practices, such as poor treatment of agricultural workers, are still occurring. Our buying of cheap food condones the practices. The government's agriculture programs have to be changed so that the smaller farmer can make a living and not have to sell crops below cost, depend on small subsidies, and have to work other jobs outside of farming. They are still subject to extreme weather that can destroy their crops. Distributors who make more money than the farmer (or grower) do not have this problem.

Ben Hirshberg has written an interesting, small book titled *Traditional Nutrition* (AL81). It describes areas throughout the world where the healthiest people live. It discusses their nutrition and some of their social characteristics. One of the most interesting areas was on the Greek island of Ikaria. It is ninety-nine square miles in size and home to about ten thousand people. A brief description is as follows:

> These Greeks seem live happy-go-lucky lives full of good food, good wine, and lots of time socializing. Oh, and they stay up late, wake up late, and take frequent naps. The average Ikarian day might start at 11am. As a result, not many businesses open before then. Breakfast might be goat's milk, honey and sourdough bread or traditional Greek yogurt and honey. About 40% of the island is technically unemployed, but everyone has a family garden to work in.

Families have their own vineyards as well. When an Ikarian tells you that he is going to come over for lunch, usually beans, potatoes, greens and maybe some fish or meat, he'll arrive at ten in the morning or six in the evening. Few clocks work on the island. They walk quite often during the day and take some homemade wine to a friend's house at night and may not get home until 2 in the morning. They aren't particularly concerned with how much money they have, and they're more than happy to give what they have to those in need. Crime is also more or less nonexistent.[114]

Talk about a contrast with living in America—surrounded by nature 24/7, not likely to be involved in any armed conflict or government intervention, probably no (or just a few) automobiles but plenty of food and wine. Friendship and sharing are the main components of their social structure, and with this, most everyone is healthy over a long period. I am going to get my airline ticket now.

Where Do We Go from Here?

Although I grew up next to my grandfather's farm and my father had a three-quarter-acre garden, I was not involved with its operation and had very little labor participation. Other than reading, I am not qualified to answer the question "Where do we go from here?" It should be answered by experts I have mentioned. Joel Salatin, who operates a unique farm, Polyface Farm in Swoope, Virginia, would be one of the first people I would contact. He is a noted authority on "beyond organic" farming and has given lectures throughout the world. He can also be found on YouTube. His book describing his farm operation and the history of Polyface Farms is titled *Your Successful Farm Business—Production, Profit. Pleasure*[115] (AL78). Other experts are Conor Crickmore of Neversink Farms (who has lectures on YouTube), Mark Shepard *(Restoration Agriculture)*, Gabe Brown, Brown's Ranch, Bismarck, ND, Dan Barber (*The Third Plate*), Stone Barnes Center for Food and Agriculture, Stephen R. Gliessman (*Agroecology)*, University of California, Santa Cruz, Wes Jackson, Land Institute, Wendell Berry (author/farmer), Michael Pollan (author), and many more, which I apologize for not mentioning.

The first book I would recommend on the topic of agriculture is Michael Pollan's *The Omnivore's Dilemma* [116] (AL79). It describes of industrial agriculture (agribusiness) and big organic (Polyface Farms and mixture of organic and industrial agriculture). Another way of describing the book is comparing corn (monocropping) and feedlots and prairie grasses. Forestry is also mentioned in the last chapters describing hunter-gatherers. Following are some comments from the introduction:

> Each food chain described does about the same thing: linking us, to how we eat, to the fertility of the earth and the energy of the sun. Ecology also teaches that all life on earth can be viewed as a competition among species for the solar energy captured by green plants and stored in the form of complex carbon molecules. A food chain is a system for passing those calories on to species that lack the plants ability to synthesize them from sunlight. The industrial revolution of the food chain, dating to the close of World War II, has actually changed the fundamental rules of this game. Industrial agriculture has supplemented a complete reliance on the sun for our calories with something new under the sun: a food chain that draws most of its energy from fossil foods instead.

The readings featured in this book advocate the establishment of small farms being located locally by urban areas, if possible, to reduce pollution and transportation costs. Now the term "organic is questionable because standards have been reduced, and many products labeled organic are not truly organic because of the way they are grown and treated with chemicals. This is because some agribusinesses have gotten into the act of growing plants labeled organic. With the large amounts of land devoted to corn and soybeans (mainly GM), how do you change the monocropping of corn when the large amounts of land are quite a distance from any major market? Some of the options would be to start growing a mixed prairie on some of the land, reduce some of the land to a farm like Polyface Farms, initiate a restorative agriculture permaculture farm and crop rotation plans, climate use of chemicals and GM plants, or have more pasture land for grass-fed cattle.

New, light equipment could also be designed for one-inch-deep tilling using a propeller blade. Equipment should be made lighter so the soil isn't compacted. Decisions should be made to determine which plants would be best to use when the market is a certain distance away. A logical plan should be designed to help solve these problems.

Alliance for Science—Cornell University

Before getting into this topic, I would like to quote a passage from N Scott Momaday: "You say that I use the land, and I reply, yes, it is true; but it is not the first truth. The first truth is that I love the land; I see that it is beautiful; I delight in it; I am alive in it."

Before discussing the Alliance for Science at Cornell University's College of Agriculture and Life Sciences (CALS), I would like to confirm that my disagreements are only with the Alliance for Science and not any of the other departments at CALS. They are excellent, and many of them utilize sustainable practices (with the exception of those that sponsor GMOs, chemical fertilizers, pesticides, herbicides, and the continuation of large agribusiness practices). For example, the magazine of CALS *periodiCALS*, volume 8, issue 1, 2018, described several programs that are ongoing there. Some of them are as follows:

1. The promotion of cassava development in Africa by improving breeding practices, improving flowering, and using a genomic selection to develop disease-resistant varieties that also increase yield and respond to the needs of smallholder farmers and processors. They obtained new funding of $35 million from the Bill and Melinda Gates foundation and UK Aid.

2. A new $1.2 million lab to study the hemlock woolly adelgid that threatens eastern forests.

3. A removable implant that may control type 1 diabetes.

4. Study of chronic fatigue syndrome.

5. Bird and conservation research in the Department of Natural Resources.

6. Studying the effects of plastic debris on the health of corals and looking for solutions.

7. How birds are revealing links between connectedness, stress, and health.

8. Helping the farmers that are growing apple trees for hard cider.

9. Food scientist works to improve nutrition, understanding gastrointestinal disease.

These are just a few of the research studies occurring at CALS, so most of the other departments are not like the Alliance for Science. Sustainability is the basis for the argument against the use of GMOs. The main question is the manner of the discussion about GMOs, pesticides, and Roundup that is occurring at the Alliance for Science. Monsanto wants to get credible universities to substantiate what they are doing by publishing research according to their guidelines. They do this with the money carrot so universities have funds for their expensive research departments or other uses. One example was in 2014 when the Melinda and Bill Gates Foundation gave Cornell University in Ithaca, New York, a $5.6 million grant to establish the Alliance for Science to promote the use of GMOs in Africa and other parts of the world. The head of the Gates Foundation's agricultural research and development team is Rob Horsch, who spent decades of his career at Monsanto. They also received another $6.4 million grant (*Cornell Chronicle* by Joan

Conrow) (http://news.cornell.edu/stories/2017/09/gates-grant-seeds-cornell-alliance-science-10m-campaign). These are probably not neutral grants.

"Why is the Gates foundation investing in GM giant Monsanto?" is an article published in the Guardian (https://www.theguardian.com/global-development/poverty-matters/2010/sep/29/gates-foundation-gm-monsanto):

> The Bill and Melinda Gates Foundation, which is sponsoring the Guardian's Global development site is being heavily criticized in Africa and the US for getting into bed not just with notorious GM company Monsanto, but also with agribusiness commodity giant Cargill. Trouble began when a US financial website published the foundation's annual investment portfolio, which showed it had bought 500,000 Monsanto shares worth around $23m. This was a substantial increase in the last six months and while it is just small change for Bill and Melinda, it has been enough to let loose their fiercest critics. Seattle-based Agra Watch—a project of the Community Alliance for Global Justice—was outraged. "Monsanto has a history of blatant disregard for the interests and well being of small farmers around the world ... [This] casts serious doubt on the foundation's heavy funding of agricultural development in Africa," it thundered.

In January 2016 (https://usrtk.org/gmo/what-bill-gates-isnt-saying-about-gmos/), Bill Gates said "that GMOs change genes in the plant, with a thorough safety procedure, reduces the amount of pesticide you need, raises productivity and can help with malnutrition by getting vitamin fortification."

Another article titled "Why is Cornell University hosting a GMO propaganda campaign" in the *Ecologist* (https://theecologist.org/2016/jan/22/why-cornell-university-hosting-gmo-propaganda-campaign) shows responses from Cornell (CALS):

> CALS called the FOIA (Freedom of Information Acts) requests a "witch hunt", yet documents obtained via these FOIA requests generated news stories in about academics who were working with industry PR operatives on campaigns to promote GMOs. Eric Lipton, who explained how Monsanto, facing consumer skepticism about GMOs, "retooled their lobbying and public relations strategy to spotlight a rarefied group of advocates: academics, brought in for the gloss of impartiality and weight of authority that come with a professor's pedigree." In one case, reported by Laura Krantz in the Boston Globe, a Monsanto executive told Harvard professor Calestous Juma to write a paper about how GMOs are needed to feed Africa. "Monsanto not only suggested the topic to professor Calestous Juma. It went so far as to provide a summary of what the paper could say and a suggested headline. The company then connected the professor with a marketing company to pump it out over the Internet as part of Monsanto's strategy to win over the public and lawmakers", Krantz wrote. Juma said he took no money from Monsanto but noted he has received funding from the Gates Foundation.

I am only presenting my opinions on this subject, and I will leave it up to the readers to form their own opinions.

On the Advancement for Science website, a blog titled "The Perils of GMO Research-Scientist Speaks Out" (https://allianceforscience.cornell.edu/blog/2018/05/perils-gmo-research-scientist-speaks/) said:

> Golden Rice is a vitamin A-fortified rice developed specifically for Asian countries where it has the potential to alleviate the problem of vitamin-A deficiency (the leading cause of preventable blindness in children). The scientist behind the project, Ingo Potrykus, started the research in 1991 and produced the first Golden Rice plants in 1999 – a remarkable achievement that saw him grace the cover of Time magazine. (Potrykus retired from my university that year.) Almost 20 years later, his creation, a plant variety that has repeatedly passed regulatory safety testing, is still not available to the children who need it most. The United States Food and Drug Administration (FDA) has approved Golden Rice, marking the third positive international assessment for the genetically engineered biofortified crop. Previously, Food Standards Australia, New Zealand and Health Canada gave Golden Rice the stamp of approval in February and March 2018 respectively. (https://allianceforscience.cornell.edu/blog/2018/05/us-fda-approves-golden-rice/)

In another blog on Mother Jones, Tom Phillpott, on February 3, 2016 (https://www.motherjones.com/food/2016/02/golden-rice-still-showing-promise-still-not-field-ready/), said:

> That what they are doing is beneficial, their vitamin-enhanced claims have failed to get off the ground and the problems with the use of golden rice to cure Vitamin A Deficiency (VAD) does not make sense for substantiating this claim. For starters, Friends of the Earth and MASIPAG agree that merely planting Golden Rice will not solve the VAD crisis. "Golden Rice may seem like a realistic solution for Vitamin A Deficiency (VAD), but those opposed say the project is deeply flawed. They point out that there are multiple recourses for malnutrition planned and currently in place, that are cheaper and do not require GMOs, and that should make golden rice unnecessary. For example, UNICEF employs a vitamin A supplementation programs that improves a child's survival rate by 12-24% with the price of only a few cents. In addition, golden rice may specifically target the deficiency of vitamin A but it could not address the countless additional social, economic, and cultural factors that contribute to vitamin A deficiencies.

In *Independent Science News for Food and Agriculture,* on October 25, 2017, the article "Goodbye to Golden Rice? GM Trait Leads to Drastic Yield Loss and 'Metabolic Meltdown'" by Allison Wilson, PhD, (https://www.independentsciencenews.org/health/goodbye-golden-rice-gm-trait-leads-to-drastic-yield-loss) stated:

> In India GR2-R1 Swarna rice had pale green leaves, various root defects, and extra side shoots (tillers). The plants also flowered later, were half the height, and half as fertile. Yield was one-third of non-GMO Swarna. "What the Indian researchers show is that the Golden Rice transgenes given to them by Syngenta caused a metabolic meltdown," says Jonathan Latham, Executive Director of the Bioscience Resource Project. "The classic criticisms of genetic engineering as a plant breeding tool have always been, first, that introduced DNA will disrupt native gene sequences and, second, that unpredictable disruption of normal metabolism may result from introducing new functions. Golden Rice exemplifies these flaws to perfection."

The Agriculture, Food, and Human Values Society's eighteen-page pdf titled "Disembedding grain: Golden Rice, the Green Revolution, and heirloom seeds in the Philippines," by Glenn Davis Stone and Dominic Glover (http://pages.wustl.edu/filespages/imce/stone/stone_glover_2016_golden_rice. pdf) shows what happens when using Golden rice in the Philippines. It is an involved study, and students and others should read the entire article. They also note that there is a growing popularity regarding the use of heirloom seeds, which are free of GMOs.

An article in Independent Science News, on June 3, 2018, by Allison Wilson, PhD, and Jonathan Latham, PhD, "GMO Golden Rice Offers No Nutritional Benefits Says FDA" (https://www.independentsciencenews.org/news/gmo-golden-rice-offers-no-nutritional-benefits-says-fda/) stated:

> The biotech industry and its supporters have promoted GMO Golden Rice for decades as an urgently needed solution to vitamin A deficiency. But, in a surprising twist, the US Food and Drug Administration (FDA) has concluded its consultation process on Golden Rice by informing its current developers, the International Rice Research Institute (IRRI), that Golden Rice does not meet the nutritional requirements to make a health claim. Originally developed by Syngenta, Golden Rice GR2E is now funded by the Gates Foundation. Thus FDA's letter states: "Based on the safety and nutritional assessment IRRI has conducted, it is our understanding the IRRI concludes that human and animal food from GR2E rice is not materially different in composition, safety, or other relevant parameters from rice-derived food currently on the market except for the intended beta-carotene change in GR2E rice. "But the letter from FDA goes further. It asserts that: "the concentration of β-carotene in GR2E rice is too low to warrant a nutrient content claim."

This is an example of how GMO advocates and dissenters present their points of view. Isn't a university supposed to do an independent analysis? Again, there are more foxes in this henhouse. The problem I have is that CALS is presenting one point of view and not including the opposing arguments on the subject. A university should be open and include a rounded presentation of both sides. What is suspect is that the Advancement for Science faculty does only marketing, and this does not include their own testing. It just relies on other sources. The testing should include evaluation of heirloom, natural, or hybrid seeds as well as GMO seeds by evaluating the costs to the farmer. It may appear to an outsider that the university is marketing for money. To me, this is contrary to what a university should do. It also leaves a question about the ethics of the university having this department on campus. Following are other articles debating information published by the Advancement of Science, along with some opposing arguments.

The Advancement of Science (http://allianceforscience.cornell.edu/) includes testing data from an Italian team of scientists to justify Cornell's program in Africa (internet 2012):

> "It concluded that genetically engineering has increased yields and reduced toxins in maize. They said that the meta-analysis provided strong evidence that GE maize (corn) contains lower levels of naturally-occurring mycotoxins, which are dangerously poisonous and potentially carcinogenic in both people and animals. The occurrence of toxins was reduced by around a third using GMO corn because of fewer fungal infections on the corn. Monsanto said that thanks to the lower prevalence of insect attacks in insect-resistant

GE-Bt maize it made the genetically engineered maize on average inherently safer and more productive than non-GE alternatives."

"In the Promise of GMOs: Mycotoxins" by Anastasia Bodnar, posted in *Science & Society*, (https// www.biofortified.org/2014/02/mycotoxins/) stated:

That a 2010 review of 23 studies of mycotoxin in corn found that 19 of these studies came to the conclusion that Bt maize is less contaminated with mycotoxins than the conventional variety in each case. With regard to mycotoxins, the verdict is promise met."

This sounds good for GMOs but in the course MICRB 106, "Elementary Microbiology, Problems with Bt" (https://online.science.psu.edu/microb106_wd/node/6150/) (3/18/18) at Penn State University, Eberly College of Science, asked:

"So if Bt is so safe why not put the gene into everything? Two problems are associated with Bt corn. For example, one is the fact that Bt corn is not approved for consumption in humans by the FDA, and another issue with the use of Bt plants is the effect on other insects species that are not causing a problem. Bt corn can also produce the pesticide in its pollen. There are concerns the pollen may interact with other plants and confer this insecticide gene to another, intended plant species. By doing this GMOs also can cause a lack of diversity."

The FIOA request by US Right to Know in the spring of 2014 showed how Monsanto retooled their public relations and lobbying strategy to include a rarified group of advocates: professors with credentials. The *Boston Globe* reported that a Monsanto executive told Harvard professor Calestous Juma to write a paper about how GMOs are needed to feed Africa. He did, and a Monsanto marketing company pumped it out over the internet. He also wrote a book called *The Fresh Harvest* advocating the use of GM plants.

"Cornell Student Who Took on Bill Gates, Monsanto Plans to Expose Their Agenda Even Further in Blockbuster New Project" is an article on the internet on AltHeealthworks by Nick Meyer, from February 1, 2018 (https://althealthworks.com/15100/cornell-student-who-took-on-bill-gates-monsanto-plans-to-expose-their-agenda-even-further-in-new-film-project/):

Now, Robert Schooler is preparing to unleash what could be his most important project to date. "Hey Cornell, remember me? Your beloved hippie student who can't stand the fact that you're so cozy with Monsanto and the Biotech GMO industry?" Schooler asks in a video announcing plans for the aforementioned new film project. "That we need GMOs to solve world hunger?" "Remember when midway through (their pro-Biotech) course I learned that all the professors making these wild claims along with the deans of the Ag school, were all copied in emails from Monsanto, their PR firms and other biotech corporations?" "Remember when I decided to host my own independent GMO course at Cornell, free from Monsanto influence? "Well that's why I've decided to create a documentary film about my experiences, well more like an open letter to you and also to Bill Gates, Bill Nye and Neil DeGrasse Tyson … and everyone else who considers themselves to be pro-GMO." Schooler hopes his first film, titled GMO WTF (which stands for Grow More Organic Wholesome Tasty Food), will receive the funding it needs through its GoFundMe page.

An article posted by Sustainable Pulse on September 24, 2016, titled "New York Farmers Ask Cornell University to Evict Alliance for Science over GMO Bias," (https://sustainablepulse. com/2016/09/24/new-york-farmers-ask-cornell-univ/) stated:

> 67 New York State organic farmers sent a letter to Dean Boor of CALS asking them to evict the Alliance for Science over their biased and unscientific attitude towards GMOs. It said that Cornell Alliance for Science (CAS) had been spreading propaganda for genetic engineering under the cover of creating a "balanced" view of biotechnology. They said that CAS does not do research itself, but serves as a communication channel, hosts a speaker series and provides funding to train "Global Fellows" from third world countries to spread genetic engineering to their home countries by providing them with prestige that comes with association with "a high caliber expert institution" such as Cornell. This provides policy support to influence home governments.

There are also other comments in the letter. The article should be read to get its full impact.

The CALS website (https://cals.cornell.edu/) states as its principles:

> The College of Agriculture and Life Sciences is a pioneer of purpose-driven science and Cornell University's second largest college. We work across disciplines to tackle the challenges of our time through world-renowned research, education and outreach. The questions we probe and the answers we seek focus on three overlapping concerns: natural and human systems; food, energy and environmental resources; and social, physical and economic well-being. The Cornell CALS experience empowers us to explore the boundaries of knowledge, supported by the leading minds of today and surrounded by the leading minds of tomorrow.

Talk about a statement that needs to be rewritten if the Alliance for Science stays in the school.

On the Food and Water Watch, Tim Schaub on August 24, 2014 (http://www.foodandwaterwatch. org/blogs/is-cornell-the-go-to-university-for-industry-science/) posted:

> Cornell University announced last week that it is embarking on a multi-million dollar campaign to "depolarize the charged debate" around GMOs. Can you guess who's behind this effort? The biotech industry and its supporters. The website for this project, the Cornell Alliance for Science, is pretty sparse, but it does note its pro-GMO partners, including the International Service for the Acquisition of Agri-biotech Applications (ISAAA), which is funded by Monsanto, CropLife, and Bayer. Food & Water Watch detailed the enormous amount of industry research coming out of our public land-grant universities in our 2012 report, Public Research, Private Gain. Cornell is no stranger to this science-for-sale approach. Earlier this year, Cornell economist William Lesser took money from a biotech front group to produce a questionable analysis showing that GMO labeling will be very costly for consumers. The study reflected his personal opinions, not those of Cornell, GMO supporters began publicizing the findings of "the Cornell study" in their campaign to defeat state-labeling initiatives around the country. Independent studies, meanwhile, show that GMO labeling will not increase costs significantly — and perhaps not at all.

The CALS, Alliance for Science website (allianceforscience.cornell.edu) noted:

> The two following comments by Dr. Godfrey Asea while assessing a project in Africa: He stated: That "In all cases the GMO version is better protected and has better yields." "It's the same story in all the trials," he noted, pointing to rows of experimental non-GM and GM maize growing next to each other at the confined field trial (CFT) site down a dusty road in Namulonge. The maize plants labeled "GMO" were tall and green, while the non-GMO versions were riddled with insect damage and much smaller, displaying yellowing leaves and smaller seed cobs. The hybrids were identical except for the introduced genes, Asea explained. "We have done our research, now we have to make sure it reaches the farmer," Asea added. "This is the fourth trial. I think we have enough results. Once the regulatory environment allows us to move to the next stage, I think we are ready. Within a year or two we should have something ready for the farmer."

To date, I have not been able to find a field test, but they should be available. Note that the testing was done by Monsanto, and this brings into question its reliability. Also, knowing Monsanto's history, would they hire private contractors that would give negative results? Also, what were the dates of the test trials, and would all of them be available under the Freedom of Information Act? The USDA would be available to read them, and this would be better than hobnobbing all the time with big ag. Some other issues are as follows:

1. In the Dr. Asea case, notice that there is no data provided. They just ask you to just believe. Was the non-GMO testing area treated with the same fertilizer, and was it chemical or organic? Were both test plots in the same area with the same soils? Were they watered the same or just dependent on natural rains? What were the yields and what was the cost of production? How much organic matter and humus was in the existing soil?

2. With GMO production, the small farmer is committed to chemical input expenses and buying seeds from Monsanto. This eliminates the buying and producing seeds for crops that are indigenous to the area.

3. With Monsanto's leadership, pesticides and herbicides would be used, which would add to the production costs and environmental damage. They would also prevent the utilization of agroecology, restoration, and regeneration.

4. How their system fits into the overall food chain is not mentioned.

5. Are there weed and pest problems in the test plots?

6. Again, this is the promotion of a monocropping system lacking diversity and use of perennials.

7. The winner is Monsanto, and the loser is the subsistence farmer. At least Monsanto provides a living for genetic bioengineers, and that is a plus.

With organic agriculture and the use of natural systems, the farmer can utilize their own seeds from year to year and not be obligated to Monsanto and their high input costs.

At this point, to anyone thinking of donating to an agricultural school at a university that recommends chemical fertilizers, pesticides, and herbicides and trains students in advocacy of agribusinesses, I would recommend reading *The Vandana Shiva Reader* (AL77) by Vandana Shiva. She shows the damage that chemical companies have done to developing countries throughout the world, especially India.

> "Over 280,000 Indian farmers, mainly in the areas that are growing Bt cotton, have committed suicide because they became so indebted to Monsanto and other chemical companies." Now the government has passed a ban on GM crops and seeds as well as BT cotton. She explains "how global chemical companies have created hunger by monocropping. A study comparing traditional polycultures with industrial monocultures show that a polyculture (increased diversity of crops) can produce 100 units of food from 5 units of inputs, whereas an industrial system requires 300 units of input to produce 100 units. The 295 units of wasted inputs could have provided 5,900 units of additional food. This is a recipe for starving people, not for feeding them. (P 48)[117]. In the case of meat exports, for every $1 earned, India is destroying $15 worth of ecological functions performed by farm animals for sustainable agriculture." (p. 49)[118]

Any donor or student activist should review the courses being taught at the university, and this can be found on the internet. For a comparison, look up the courses being taught at Washington State University. If we don't do anything and keep the status quo, then who is to blame? There is something wrong when you have a marketing department advocating one system, and it is separated from the rest of the agricultural school. If you advocate a process, it should be tested on campus. Monsanto is only interested in comparing yields and not in the facts.

I can understand that a university would want to be able to present all sides of a topic or field of endeavor, and that is what it should do. But the Alliance for Science goes beyond this and is just being a field monitor for a large corporation. In a way, it is very disappointing, and I guess it is capitalism in action. Is money really worth doing this? It is hard for me to write this, as I am a former graduate of CALS, but in good conscience, I have to do so. CALS is rated quite high on the national level due to the number of different departments in various fields. However, there are few or no classes in organic farming or agroecology. There is a long-distance class in organic gardening, and there are courses in pest and weed management. Chemical fertilizers, amendments, pesticides, and herbicides are still offered for use, with little mention of innovative products on the market today. This becomes a one-sided story. However, Cornell as a university is probably the best in the country in sustainability research and topics offered in various sustainable subject matters.

Since the Alliance for Science is working in Africa, I would like to present the following information and strategies for developing countries to use when working overseas. IFOAM Organics International has been working with farmers throughout the world, and they have their activities available on their website (https://www.ifoam.bio/). They also have available on the website a publication titled "Best Practice Guideline for Agriculture & Value Chains." Their emphasis is on establishing programs that are sustainable and include all of the activities found on the Best Practice Agriculture & Value Chain diagram. The dialogue includes the following subjects that they are using to evaluate best practices.

Ecology: Water, Soil, Animal Husbandry, Atmosphere, Energy, Biodiversity

Society: Equity & Gender, Right Livelihood, Labor Rights, Safety & Hygiene

Culture: Community, Food Security & Sovereignty, Product Quality

Accountability: Holistic Management, Transparency & Reporting, Participation

Economy: Investment, Local Economy & Resilience, Markets & Trade, Materials/Waste/Contaminants

Any work advocating agricultural studies in developing countries should be sure that what is being recommended there in terms of agricultural production benefits the indigenous farmer and the country and not corporations in the United States or in other countries. We should build self-reliance, not dependency. The information provided by the ETC Group should be reviewed in detail to understand what approach should be used.

The culture of each country should be studied, and of course, this varies from site to site. If plant seeds are introduced, they should be adaptable to the local soils and climate. They should be able to produce their own seeds and not be dependent on buying new ones each year. They should contribute their knowledge of natural systems so that any production of crops follows these systems. Especially important is not encouraging them to grow cash crops, making them dependent on the market. Another interesting website is Action in Africa (http://www.actioninafrica.com/). A book to consider reading is *The Natural Way of Farming* by Masanobu Fukuoka (AL29):

> Ever since I began proposing a way of farming in step with nature, I have sought to demonstrate the validity of five major principals: no tillage, no fertilizer, no pesticides, no weeding, and no pruning. Even organic farming, which everyone is making a fuss over lately, is just another type of scientific farming. Of course, in a sense, natural farming will never be perfected. It will not see general application in its true form, and will serve as only a brake to slow the mad onslaught of scientific agriculture. I have created, together with the insects in the fields, a new strain of rice I call "Happy Hill." This is a hardy strain with the blood of wild variants in it, yet it is also one of the highest yielding strains of rice in the world. If a single head of Happy Hill were sent across the seas to a country where food is scarce another sown over a ten square yard area, a single grain would yield 5,000 grains in one year's time. In the fourth year it could sow 7,000 acres. This could become the seed rice for an entire nation. (p. 1–3)[119] Who needs golden rice with all its problems?

Another book on the subject, *Farmer First* (AL19), states:

> "The audience is wide because the topic is basic and the content challenging. Resource-poor farming in the Third World presents intractable problems. Probably well over a billion people depend for their livelihoods on the complex, diverse and risky forms of agriculture which have been poorly served by agricultural research. This failure has been met by two responses: "more of the same" through conventional generation and transfer of technology; and the development of new approaches and methods in which farmers participate. Robert Booth noted that in his general experience that a vast majority of research workers prefer to do research about a problem rather than research to solve

a problem. Thus, biological scientists keep busy, and happy breeding new varieties, developing disease control systems, or new store designs, while the socko-economists undertake their surveys and describe systems but all leave the actual solving of farmers' (clients) problems to someone else, and hence we hear of poor extensive services and backward farmers. This, to my mind, is passing the buck. Farmers often dictate important points overlooked by research workers." (p. 9)[120]

The logical approach when working with farmers is to try to determine what they have been doing in their present farming practices and the reasons. Find out what they designate as problems and then determine various options for fixing problems. If a disease is prevalent, then both conventional and regenerative solutions should be evaluated, ones that the farmer could afford, without additional input costs. A local variety of plants, although less productive, should be used. Many times, this is a healthier alternative. Buying GM crops is not an indigenous way because they do not allow the farmer to use natural methods, and the farmer is under their control in terms of plant selection and input costs. They also get toxins and super weeds for their money, as a bonus. Generally, a study of natural systems through agroecology is the best answer. This is then adapted to what the farmer has available in turns of inputs within his own cultural restraints. The use of perennials and diversified flowering plants, crop rotations, and soil improvement programs are other options that do not cost much money. The ideal solution would be to form local business enterprises to supply whatever is needed.

Know the Enemy: We as a society should do more than just state what problems are confronting us; we should offer solutions. It wouldn't be so bad if it was just Monsanto we were worried about, but add President Trump and his cohorts on top of it. An article by Christina Sarich of Natural Society, "Who are really the Top Shareholders of Monsanto," (http://naturalsociety.com/who-are-really-the-top-shareholders-of-monsanto/) said:

"The real owners of Monsanto stock are institutions, and the people who hide behind these institutions, not individuals like Gates and Grant. Five investment funds are the top shareholders in Monsanto, with the Vanguard Group, Inc. at the top. Furthermore, the Federal Reserve is comprised of 12 banks, represented by a board of only seven people, which comprises representatives of the "big four," ... which in turn are present in all other entities. Or that according to a report that was released last summer, the global elite have up to $ 32 TRILLION dollars stashed in offshore banks around the globe, which can fund lawsuit after lawsuit against the people who are tired of being poisoned. It means that seven people and their overlords are likely poisoning the entire planet through biotech, Big Ag, Big Pharma, and Big Banks while showing its net income was $ 2.27 billion dollars at the end of FY August 31, 2017."

The main thing to do now is continue lawsuits against Monsanto or the new corporation between Monsanto and Bayer. The other thing is to see what companies Monsanto or Bayer owns or partially owns and what foods contain glyphosate.

Alternative Daily on November 9, 2015, provided a list titled "68 Monsanto-Owned Companies to Boycott" (https://www.thealternativedaily.com/monsanto-owned-companies-to-boycott/). You should try to get GM foods labeled and find out if your representative or senator is for or against this. You might even give them this book. Vote accordingly. See if you can vote representatives, senators, and governors in the state houses that would present a state mandate for GM labeling. Just know what the person you are voting for believes and what they could do to correct problems you are concerned with. You can also start buying nutritional food, reduce or eliminate smoking and sugars, and limit the purchase of processed foods. Stop using chemicals and get an organic program established for your landscaping. Get something done and help others while doing it.

The main thing is to recognize what is going on in our governments (city, state, federal), corporations, and financial institutions and not be deceived by their claims of helping the American people. It is a shame that we spend as much time and money electing some of the members of Congress that we do. We desperately need the right kind of change in government, a change that will take us into a transition period that recognizes that greed, political influence, and inequality are not what we need. We need to vote for our children so they will not have a life of chaos and live in a society that is failing.

An article on August 10, 2018, by Aaum Hedlund Law on Organic Consumers.org, titled "Monsanto to pay $289.2M in Landmark Roundup Lawsuit Verdict" (https://www.organicconsumers.org/blog/monsanto-roundup-trial-verdict) noted the following:

> A San Francisco jury returned a verdict today in the case of a former groundskeeper with terminal cancer against Monsanto Company, ordering the agrochemical giant to pay $39.2 million in compensatory damages and $250 million in punitive damages for failing to warn consumers that exposure to Roundup weed killer causes cancer. Dewayne "Lee" Johnson filed the lawsuit (case no. CGC-16-550128) against St. Louis-based Monsanto Co. on Jan. 28, 2016, alleging exposure to the Roundup herbicide he sprayed while working as a groundskeeper for the Benicia Unified School District caused him to develop non-Hodgkin lymphoma (NHL). After eight weeks of trial proceedings, the jury found unanimously that Monsanto's glyphosate-based Roundup weed killer caused Mr. Johnson to develop NHL, and that Monsanto failed to warn of this severe health hazard. Importantly, the jury also found that Monsanto acted with malice, oppression or fraud and should be punished for its conduct. Monsanto Co. continues to refuse to warn consumers of the dangers of its multi-billion-dollar product Roundup despite the world's foremost authority on cancer—the International Agency for Research on Cancer (IARC)—listing glyphosate as a probable carcinogen in 2015. Monsanto-Bayer is now appealing this decision.

The entire article should be read to obtain the full impact of this decision, and it further establishes the case against Monsanto. An impact of this decision is explained in an article published on the internet by Sustainable Pulse on August 26, 2018, titled "Vietnam Set to Increase Legal Pressure on Monsanto for Millions of Agent Orange Victims"

(https://sustainablepulse.com/2018/08/26/vietnam-set-to-increase-legal-pressure-on-monsanto-for-millions-of-agent-orange-victims/?utm_source=newsletter&utm_medium=email&utm_campaign=gmos_and_pesticides_global_breaking_news&utm_term=2018-08-30).

Our Failing Society

The following books and articles are about all the corruption we have now and how it relates to past failing societies.

An article on Resilience by Richard Heinberg (www.resilence.org/stories/2018-01-18/old-age-societal-decline/) noted:

> "That societies have failed due to invasion by foreign marauders (and sometimes the diseases they brought); others have succumbed to resource depletion/ pollution, unforeseeable natural catastrophe, or class conflict." Those who get beyond denial and cynicism often arrive at an attitude of compassionate engagement. We may not be able to prevent collapse, but we can still make life better for ourselves and other potential survivors as events unfold. We can make our community more resilient, protect vulnerable people and other creatures, and devote ourselves to creating places and moments of beauty. Achieving a "good" civilizational death would entail minimizing damage to ecosystems and exhaustion of natural resources, so that human survivors would have the biophysical basis for recovery. It would also require minimizing human births prior to collapse so as both to conserve resources and reduce the sum total of human suffering during the decline and fall, since collapse always entails a reduction in carrying capacity.

William Ophuls's book *Immoderate Greatness: Why Civilizations Fail* (CE61) describes what we will face in the future:

> I argue to the contrary (that technology will save us) that industrial civilization will yield to the same "passions" that have produced the "same results" in all previous times. There is simply no escape from our all -too-human nature. In the end, mastering the historical process would require human beings to master themselves, something they are very far from achieving. (This is why democracy, considered by some to be an asset in the struggle against the forces that challenge industrial, is in fact a liability). Commanding history would also require them to overcome all the natural limits that have defeated previous civilizations. As will be shown, this is unlikely. Hence our civilization will decline and fall. (p. 1–2)[121]

Many of the books noted at the end of this book in the reference section describe the problems leading up to our present situation. To begin, I would recommend (CE45) to understand the present economic situation and to offer solutions. Other books are (CE25), (E7), (CE46), (CE34), and (SC50). I will only briefly note the present environmental and economic problems because they are noted in the books and articles.

We have had a capitalist society in the United States since the beginning of the Industrial Revolution. The continual growth of the population, consumerism, and inequality will deplete our natural resources. These resources may not be available or will be available at extractive prices, and this will make them so expensive or of such inferior quality that they become non-feasible to obtain (e.g., tar sands oil). There is a need to remove or simplify regulations if they are cumbersome and do not increase efficiency and clarity. They should not allow rules that impede fairness and give corporations illicit advantages. This just increases inequality and cynicism. Again, the "draining of the swamp" just made firmer ground for the elite to stand on.

The Spirit Level (CE11) details why our economy and growth are increasing inequality and other problems.

> What is essential if we are to bring a better society into being is to develop a sustained movement committed to doing that. "Policy changes will need to be consistently devoted to this end and over several decades and that requires a society which knows where it wants to go. The initial task is to gain a widespread public understanding of what is at stake. It must be taken up and pursued by a network of equality groups meeting to share ideas and action everywhere, in homes and offices, in trade unions and political parties, in churches and schools and many other locations. They should be concerned with the various issues which are related to equality and they need to be coupled with the urgent task of dealing with global warming and other situations that causes inequality." (p. 269)[122]

The book details what is causing inequality now and provides solutions.

Inequality is becoming more evident in the use of cell phones and gaming devices because they are expensive and not easily available to everyone. Kids and adults of all ages are using them, and marketers are continually saying that you must have the latest one out. With this are the questions "How many friends do you have on Facebook?" and "How many tweets do you send that could be critical of other people?" This also relates to bullying in schools. Indeed, corporate power is the elephant in the living room. This means not getting by without paying a fair amount of money for a sustainability fund when they use the earth's resources or cause pollution. These resources are presently free for most corporations, and preventing pollution is not a hot topic (at least at the EPA or with the news media).

The book *Scarcity* (E43) explains:

> That as a result of our ever-increasing exploitation, since the inception of our industrial revolution over 200 years ago, economically viable supplies associated with the vast majority of the earth's non-replenishing nonrenewable natural resources (NNRs) are becoming increasingly scarce, both domestically (US) and globally. In fact, NNR scarcity had become epidemic by 2008, immediately prior to the recession, to the extent that there are not enough economically viable NNRs to perpetuate our industrial lifestyle paradigm going forward. The Great Recession in 2008 marked the peak in American societal wellbeing; the U.S. will never again be able to obtain sufficient economically viable NNR supplies-domestic and foreign combined- to enable continuous increases in its economic output (GDP) level and societal wellbeing level. (p. 81)[123]

It further shows charts and information on social wellness projections and extensive information on economic dynamics. The prevailing view now is that our predicament can and will be fixed through fiscal manipulations.

Drawdown (E40)[124] is an excellent source of information concerning what could be done now to reduce climate warming and extraction. It is easy reading and should be part of school curriculums throughout the United States. It is also an excellent source for finding references for additional books about the environment. In just the energy section, it has information on wind turbines, micrograms, geothermal, solar farms, rooftop solar, wave and tidal, concentrated solar, biomass, nuclear, cogeneration, micro wind, methane digesters, in-stream hydro, waste-to-energy, grid flexibility, energy storage-utilities, energy storage-distribution, and solar water.

A contrasting view of what has been presented so far was printed in the McKinsey & Company quarterly report, "The future is now: How to win the resource revolution" by Scott Nyquist, Matt Rogers, and Jonathan Woetzel in October 2016 (https:// www.mckinsey.com/business-functions/ sustainability-and-resource-p). Part of that report is as follows:

> "While our estimates of energy-efficiency opportunities were more or less on target, the overall picture looks quite different today. Technological breakthroughs such as hydraulic fracturing for natural gas have eased resource strains, and slowing growth in China and elsewhere has dampened demand. Since mid-2014, oil and other commodity prices have fallen dramatically, and global spending on many commodities dropped by 50 percent in 2015 alone. Some of the biggest impact on resource consumption could come from analytics, automation, and Internet of Things advances."

These are some interesting concepts, but they are not taking into account all the problems of exponential growth, inequity, and the reduction of natural resources and waste associated with some technologies.

The books *Shrinking the Technosphere* (E38)[125] and *Dark Age America* (CE45)[126] give contrasting viewpoints to what was stated in the McKinsey report. The article and books should be read to put their views in full context. There is a viewpoint that technology will fix what we need to stay in a society of diminishing returns and limited options. These books question if this reliance on technology would be feasible. By saying that technology will save us, some people use it to keep the status quo and not do anything for the environment.

Simon Black—Where We Are

Right after the State of the Union, Simon Black, author of the daily newsletter "Sovereign Man," sent out an interesting daily newsletter (https://mail.google.com/mail/u/0/?ui=2&ik=5c1b887df d&jsver=n51S-ZIkXE …) (January 31, 2018). This is part of the letter:

> "Bear in mind the US government is already nearly $21 trillion in the hole and spending hundreds of billions of dolls each year just to pay interest on the debt and it hit a new high of $ 458,542,287,311. That's about 15% of federal government tax revenue … just to pay interest. On top of that, the government spent another $2.15 trillion on Social Security and medicare, and $720+ billion on defense spending. Total: 3.3 trillion. So before they paid for anything else they were hundreds of billions of dollars in the hole. The Federal Highway Fund and the Disability Insurance fund have been bailed out within the last two years. In 2016 its long term liabilities amount to $46.7 trillion." (Source-Treasury Department.)

There is more information in the letter. You can sign up to receive a daily newsletter from Sovereign Man. The financial information is very enlightening.

In the book *Prosperity without Growth* (CE25), Tim Jackson discusses different methods of sustainable living without relying on capitalist methods of growth. In doing this, he offers the following advice:

> Equally, it's clear that changing the social logic of consumption cannot simply be relegated to the realm of individual choice. In spite of a growing desire for change, it's almost impossible for people to simply choose sustainable lifestyles, however much they would like to. Even highly-motivated individuals experience conflict as they attempt to escape consumerism. And the chances of extending this behavior across society are negligible without changes in the social structure. Structural changes of two kinds must lay at the heart any strategy to address the social logic of consumerism. The first will be to dismantle or correct the perverse incentives for unsustainable (and unproductive) status competition. The second must be to establish new structures that provide capabilities for people to flourish, and particularly to participate fully in the life of society, in less materialistic ways. (p. 153)[127]

This is what I am attempting to do in the PDP.

On July 22, 2012, Reuters showed that the "Super rich hold $32 trillion in offshore havens" (https://www.reuters.com/article/us-offshore-wealth/super-rich-hold-32-trillion-in-offshore-havens-idUSBRE86L03U20120722):

> Rich individuals and their families have as much as $32 trillion of hidden financial assets in offshore tax havens, representing up to $280 billion in lost income tax revenues. The research was carried out for pressure group Tax Justice Network, which campaigns against tax havens, by James Henry, former chief economist at consultants McKinsey & Co. He used data from the World Bank, International Monetary Fund, United Nations and central banks. The report also highlights the impact on the balance sheets of 139 developing countries of money held in tax havens by private elites, putting wealth beyond the reach of local tax authorities. The research estimates that since the 1970s, the richest citizens of these 139 countries had amassed $7.3 to $9.3 trillion of "unrecorded offshore wealth" by 2010. Private wealth held offshore represents "a huge black hole in the world economy," Henry said in a statement.

I thought most corporations were ethical, but it's no surprise that there are exceptions to this. The purpose of a corporation is to make money for stockholders. But must it be done unethically by using tax havens, squandering natural resources (and also not including it in their costs of doing business), causing more inequality by increasing executive salaries with golden parachute retirement packages, encouraging consumption, using unhealthy products (e.g., Coca-Cola), squashing worker rights, banking and financial scandals, and many other questionable practices? This, of course, does not include all corporations, because there are some with high standards of sustainability.

Articles in this section could go on and on, but I think I have made the point throughout the book that we are in a failing society. It is not the Republican Party or Democratic Party; it is both that need to change. A too liberal or too conservative Supreme Court can make decisions that last for years and upset balances in our society. We also need a leader who quits praising himself with lies and false promises that shouldn't be filled (perhaps with a few exceptions). We need a political process where each voting district (if possible) does not protect one party over another so there are just a few districts that can determine election results. Mainly, we need an ethical Congress. They are one of the few organizations that earned their poor popularity ratings by doing nothing or very little.

This book details many problems occurring in our society, but hopefully it offers some solutions as well. An example for agriculture would be what to do with our agricultural food chain. The subsidy situation should offer more assistance to agroecological and restorative farming for educational, promotional, and research uses, rather than individual farmers' production of goods. Small farmers should do some of their own research and share it. In areas devoted to monocropping, there should be more native grasses, flowers, and nitrogen-fixing plants used for diversity and soil restoration. Management of meat production should be taken out of the feedlots and reduced to allow for the fallowing of land for crop rotations and use of perennials. Use of corn for ethanol should be reduced or eliminated. Some of the land not be used for making ethanol or feeding cows could be planted with legumes and native grasses to begin to restore the soil. A little crop rotation wouldn't hurt. Hopefully this would not be that big a problem if we use cars less often. Getting the soil to be more productive is the first step. Another first step would be the reduction or elimination of GMO crops, chemical fertilizers, pesticides, and herbicides. The chemical companies should go back to making sustainable products.

Another solution is to lower the number of lobbyists, especially those coming from government agencies. "Number of registered active lobbyists in the United States from 2000 to 2017" (https://www.statista.com/statistics/257340/number-of-lobbyists-in-the-us/) noted:

> Presently in 2016 there are 11,143 lobbyists (Statista Market Research). Doing this would open up the Washington DC housing market so there could be more affordable housing. This would also save money. Statista noted "In 1999 $1.45 billion dollars was spent on lobbyists and that increased to $3.15 billion dollars in 2016. Colleges should start to think about starting courses in "How to be a Lobbyist" in order to cover their shortfalls. In 2017 (Open Secrets) the pharmaceutical industry spent $279,113,483 on lobbying." Just think how much a pill this is costing the consumer. This may also include some kickbacks to doctors and politicians, I don't know. An encouraging sign is the student protests against Congress for not passing stricter (or any) gun laws. The National Rifle Association (NRA) did spend $5,122,000 for lobbyists.

The internet can be used to answer questions, and it is up to you to choose what responses you want to read. This is one of the best ways to use the internet. In one example, I asked on the internet if Paul Ryan received any money from the Koch family after the tax bill passed. One answer was from Snopes, which is a fact-checking site. You can see the article by asking the question (Snopes-Did Paul Ryan receive money from the Koch family after the tax bill passed) (https://www.snopes.com/fact-check/koches-contributed-ryan-after-tax/):

"Thirteen days after the house passed their version of the tax bill the Charles and Elizabeth Koch donated $ 247,000 each to Paul Ryan's fundraising campaign "Team Ryan" according to filings from ProPublica. The article shows where the money is going because most of the money went to "Team Ryan" which is a joint fundraising committee. Most of the money could not have gone to Ryan's campaign committee because the most money that the campaign committee could legally receive is $10,000, $ 5,000 from each of them." So, Paul Ryan and the House republicans all benefited.

One question to ask is, if people are so dissatisfied with Congress, why do they keep voting for the same people all of the time? Look it up on the internet and see if you agree with the answers.

A good summary of our failing society is found in two articles on Resilience by Richard Heinberg, "Getting Past Trump: This is how Democracies Die (Part 1)" (resilience.org/ stories/2018-03-07/getting--past-trump-this-is-how-democracies-die-part-1/)   and "Getting Past Trump (Part 2): The Russia Connection" (resilience.org/stories/2018-03-13/ getting-past-trump-part-2-the-russia-connection/).

The failing society applies not only to the United States but also the world. This is brought to light by the book *The New Confessions of an Economic Hit Man* (CE59)[128] by John Perkins. It describes how corrupt our world governments, financing institutions like the World Bank, corporations, and individuals have been (and are), taking advantage of people and other nations, especially in developing countries. In chapter 43, "Who are Today's Economic Hit Men?" and chapter 44, "Who are Today's Jackals?" he provides insights about our present politicians, Walmart (overseas tax havens and relying on the government to pick up some employee benefits), and several corporations. The jackals are the war machines that kill civilians.

In chapter 46, "What You Can Do," and chapter 47, "Things To Do," he offers insights as alternatives to what is happening. As he states:

> Out of the top ten international arms producers, eight are American. The arms industry spends millions lobbying Congress and state legislatures, and it defends its turf with an efficiency and vigor that its products don't always emulate on the battlefield. The F-35 fighter-bomber, for example-the most expensive weapons system in US history-will cost $1.5 trillion and it doesn't work. It's over budget, dangerous to fly, and riddled with defects. And yet few lawmakers dare challenge the powerful corporations who have shoved this lemon down our throats. (p 268)[129]Today's revolution is much bigger than the American Revolution. It is bigger than the agricultural or industrial revolutions. It is nothing less than a consciousness revolution.[130] (p 292)

Defense Spending: In Release No: NR-192-17, on May 23, 2017, the US Defense Department issued a budget (https://www.defense.gov/News/News-Releases/News-Release-View/Article/1190216/dod-releases-fiscal-year-2018-budget-proposal/) that stated in part:

> Today President Donald J. Trump sent Congress a proposed defense budget request of $639.1 billion, $574.5 billion in the base budget and $64.6 billion in the Overseas Contingency Operations (OCO) budget. This budget request is $52 billion above the defense budget cap in the Budget and Control Act (BCA) of 2011. This funding is required to continue to rebuild war fighting readiness and will restore program balance by fixing the holes created by previous budget cuts. Since enactment of the BCA, the world has become more dangerous. Over this period, the military has become smaller and training, maintenance, and modernization have been deferred, resulting in degraded war fighting readiness. This budget request reverses that degradation and starts restoring the readiness of our armed forces to meet the challenges of today and the future. To do so, it is essential that the defense sequestration caps be reversed. As Secretary Mattis recently told members of Congress, the BCA (Budget Control Act) and sequestration have "done more damage to our readiness than the enemies in the field."

Perhaps this says more about our failing societies in the world than anything I could have written.

Summary—Where We Are Now

Are we the America that is presented to us by our government? Can we keep doing what we have always done without changing our style of living? The present government was elected by the American people because they wanted a change from the what they considered Wall Street politics. Well, we got a big change, and look at what happened. I've tried in this book to describe what is good and bad in this world while offering solutions along the way. This is by describing how the pilot demonstration project could be a start to show people what is occurring around us and at the same time offering a solution. The first step is for us to get together and demand our rights and the rights of children to come. To emphasize this, I am including a summary using various topics.

Government and Politics

The articles on the Koch brothers and what they are attempting to do with their political agenda should be read by every American. I do not espouse the highest admiration for the Democratic and Republican Parties, and the Progressives are small but represent the average American. But what is hard to understand is the lack of ethics by Congress and the president. It is beyond my comprehension how anyone can say they speak for America when they accept money from people like the Koch brothers in order to allow them to do what they do to our government with their political contributions and philosophies. Since they pollute and try to reduce environmental safety laws, there are, to my knowledge, very few Republicans speaking out about these activities. Which is more important, receiving money so you can stay in office or feeling good about your ethics and responsibilities? President Trump is such a questionable example, using as many lies as he does. As long as you have to have so much money to run and stay in politics, it is hard for other people who have democratic ideals and limited means to run for office.

It seems that the majority of people do not care to understand what is happening within our political structure. We have become victims of technology, advertising, and platitudes of the elite. There is a need for political reform in wasteful defense spending, election spending, catering to special interests, and continual greed that affects everyone. Even the Supreme Court is getting on the bandwagon with the likes of the "Citizen United" decision. This is another door opening for corporation hijinks. Politicians seem to feel it is more important to spend money and time to get elected. Just think what a pleasure it would be to have a short election period like the British do. This, however, would cause a hardship for the media, due to lack of advertising revenues. They would have to have more drug and automobile ads.

We do not have much time left to correct our political system and enact environmental reforms. I wonder if people in other countries would be so willing to come here after reading this book. This is a harsh statement, but it borders on reality. This could be a partial answer to our immigration problems.

Environment

We have to decide if we want to clean up our act by recognizing climate change, the overuse of natural resources, the issue of handling and reducing waste, and the role of diversity, air, and water pollution. When we have to start paying more for our ignorance, it may be too late. One of the most important things we can learn is how natural systems work. We need to stop fighting them and enjoy the peace that this can bring.

To provide a summary for some of the main concerns that are facing us environmentally, I refer to an article on Acres USA by Graeme Sait, "The Soil Solution," from June 2015 (http://www. acresusa.com/media/downloads/June15_Sait.pdf?mc_cid=0c84189f21&mc_eid= e061d282b):

> There are five core threats that need to be urgently addressed, and they all relate back to the soil. "Loss of Topsoil." What is driving this dramatic loss? Basically, it comes down to the massive decline in organic matter following the industrial, extractive experiment in agriculture. What is driving this dramatic loss? We have now lost two-thirds of our humus. "Ocean Acidification." The CO_2 becomes carbonic acid in the ocean and, as a result, our seas have become increasingly acidic. "Ocean Warming." Ocean warming is possibly the most urgent issue at present. This can cause melting of the permafrost to release methane. Methane is a greenhouse gas that is 23 times more potent in thickening the heat-trapping blanket that warms our world compared to CO_2. "Food Security". GMOs can be very productive when given the proper fertilizers and growing conditions, but they can really struggle in challenging conditions. They do not have resilience. "Declining Nutrition". The lack of food nutrition is ongoing due to the decline of minerals in the soils. This is caused by poor farming practices by agribusinesses.

This is an extensive article and should be read to understand what we have to do to correct our present and prevent the problems noted above before it is too late.

Culture and Society

The silent illnesses that are increasing in our society, such as anxiety, depression, suicide, exalting one's self, greed, and drug use, are a reflection of where we are going. We need to reverse this by working together to obtain a purpose in our lives. This could be the start of a healing process.

One of our main concerns should be the growing inequities in our society. We need to develop solutions to reduce this problem. Just handing out money is not the answer. We need to encourage methods to help people develop a purpose and feel that they are treated with dignity and respect. The pilot demonstration project demonstrates how jobs can be created so there is a chance for everyone to be more self-sufficient, so they can have dignity regardless of who they are. Everyone has to be more innovative and not just concerned with the trivialities of social media and consumption. Also, we have to be sure that people have more electronic privacy and are not constantly tracked by social media and more. Now people are being targeted with ads, and their preferences are known, so they are swamped with specific election and other messages. Hacking may get so prevalent that we won't be able to use the internet for financial transactions. Think what that would do to society.

I have not mentioned the rash of school shootings, but it is becoming a major social problem. Congress says that it will do something, but the National Rifle Association's campaign donations are a powerful incentive to not do anything about strengthening our gun laws. What is wrong with strengthening our background checks, preventing the sale of bump stocks, putting restrictions on open gun sales in gun shows, and preventing the sale of assault weapons? As far as I can tell, this is not an infringement on the second amendment. Remember, they did not have assault weapons when the Bill of Rights was written. How many hunters use assault weapons to hunt game? That would not be hunting; it would be cruelty to animals.

One of the unknowns in our society is war. It has been going on for ages, and it looks like it will continue for a long time. With the weapons we have available, civilization may be partially destroyed in a short period of time. Seeking power and going to war are bedfellows. War should be unnecessary, but it probably never will be stopped. It doesn't make sense to me that a country feels that it has to be the best in prestige and power or try to overpower another country because that country has resources you didn't have. Negotiating and bartering are always options. Think about what the world would be like if we didn't have war and did not need enormous defense budgets. I don't think anyone will ever know.

Agriculture and Food Chain Landscaping

I have shown in the book the myths and lies that are presented in advertising and how the support of our present system of agribusiness (conventional) food production has harmed our environment. However, there are many things that happen that hurt small farmers that are associated with agribusiness. One of these is the use of farm equipment. Advertising promotes the largest and most sophisticated farming equipment, and this creates a burden of price most independent farmers can't afford. Secondly, the dealers have adopted Monsanto's mentality of operating procedure by putting digital controls on the equipment. This makes them more expensive and almost impossible for the farmer to repair. So, the farmer has to get the equipment repaired by the dealer, which could be many miles away. This is expensive to the farmer but is another profit source for the dealer. Gone are the days when the farmer could easily buy replacement parts or make some equipment parts on the farm. The farmer is trapped in the system, and the smaller farmers have to hope they do not have violent storms that wipe out their crops. Notice that storms are getting more intense, and many environmentalists think this is due to more carbon dioxide and methane in the air.

It has been shown in the book that the average farmer has a profit on one dollar of food costs of 2.5 percent (12.5 percent gross). Compare this to the gross cost to a distributor of over 30 percent of the food dollar. The distributor does not have to worry about food waste because of weather, but they do have some food waste because of having to travel long distances to deliver food to market. This is what happens when you do not farm locally.

Now take the case of Neversink Farms in the Catskills in New York (YouTube) (www.neversinkfarm. com/pages/contact-us). Conor Crickmore has this ecological farm grossing over $350,000 in an area of one and a half acres. This is due to knowing what you are doing, using no-till practices, and not needing large equipment. His market is local for the most part. Besides that, he is willing to share how to do it. The crops are diversified, and he uses sustainable practices, including producing healthy soils. This should make any agribusiness farm envious. This farm is unique, and this production quantity could be copied on many small farms. Producing this much food in a small space would eliminate the need for farming that uses large acreage for growing corn for feedstock and ethanol production. Other crops are available for biofuel use. Restorative agriculture could be used to produce what we need.

The six biggest problems (among many more) in agriculture are the monocropping methods of big agribusiness, the structure of the food chain, soil degeneration and erosion, lack of nutrition of food, the chemical companies and GMOs as presently used, tilling, lack of diversity, and misunderstanding the benefits of agroecology and using natural systems. Probably the biggest problem is the treatment of the small farmer by agribusinesses and lack of fair and lower-interest bank funding when they need it to get started.

Energy and Natural Renewable Resources

The drawing down of our natural resources, overuse and higher costs of fossil fuels, lack of a sustainable energy plan, inadequate and outdated urban planning and electrical grids, inefficient uses of energy, and lack of innovation in certain areas are just some of our energy problems at this time. Right now, we are so dependent on fossil fuels that we will have to make substantive changes in how we use our energy supplies. The structure of our society is energy based, and if we do not reduce our economic consumption, we will have to relearn how to be hunter-gatherers. The US needs an energy plan in order to proportion and estimate our energy needs in a time when our electrical grid is becoming outmoded.

Economics

This has been discussed extensively in this book as well as in the books included in the reference list, so all I can say now is pray heavily, eat lightly, and read a lot. We cannot discuss economics in isolation because it is intertwined with all of the other conditions that determine what we do. It becomes systems orientated and not just a lineal projection of thinking.

Urban Planning and Housing

Presently, we do not design our housing, businesses, or communities for future contingencies. This is one of the reasons I wrote this book. I hope it provides enough ideas so that new approaches can be designed for this transition period and the future. Look into the future to determine what we should be doing now to make communities and housing available for all people in the future. Lack of foresight can lead to bitter consequences. The lack of affordable housing must be addressed now. If we don't, our future social costs will be staggering, and we could easily become a nation of chaos.

Summary Analysis

The articles that are shown in this book are excerpts taken from the original books being described (from the reference list) and articles from magazines or the internet. The intent is to have you read what interests you most in order to understand what is happening in our society. Much of the book is controversial to those who espouse neoliberalism. Hopefully the information provided can change minds or provide additional reference material for those who agree with this thinking. The format was designed to encourage people to join many of the internet platforms that were mentioned. The main purpose of the pilot demonstration project is to show how to design and construct an enterprise that can be used to make people aware of our present social situation, beyond just writing about it. For example, we have to show how the present loss of safety and environmental regulations is destructive rather than a benefit. Our courts and Congress have to help in doing this. We cannot keep going backward just for the benefit of a few.

Many corporations and cities are recognizing climate change and destruction of nonrenewable resources, while others (oil companies, Big Pharma, and agribusinesses) ignore it for their own gain. The disappointing part of what is happening in America today is the rampant corruption of both political parties. The greed of some corporations add to this plight. Voting will mean very little unless our system starts to get cleaned up.

Monsanto and other chemical companies are some of the largest culprits because of the health problems and degradation of soil that they are spreading around the world. The pharmaceutical companies and agribusinesses are keeping us from being healthier, and there is a lack of oversight from the FDA, USDA, and EPA. Depression and loneliness are common now for many people because they do not have an opportunity to develop a sense of purpose. The media is dumbing down the news and emphasizing only news that seems to have a short-term consistency. Look at the time spent on "entertainment activities and celebrities." Short-term news seems to be the most popular, so that is what is provided.

The PDP community would be an alternative to the present situation, offering a way to show that a viable informative program is a better way forward, one offering different choices and viewpoints. This will happen through sharing and collaboration and fixing our society using bottom-up solutions. There are so many projects that need to be accomplished in our society. Let's hope we quit governing by soundbite diplomacy and backward thinking and strive to provide a purpose for the country to lead us into a better future. It will be a future with less consumerism and lower defense budgets, one that will emphasize sharing and collaboration with one another.

We tend to live for now instead of evaluating the future. Greed, corruption, and the seeking of power are slowly making what we are doing a pathway for destruction for later generations. In 2017, the United States had damage from extreme storms and fires of over $300 billion. This further damages our infrastructure and leads to excessive debt. Satellites shows what is happening relative to climate change, but this is not acknowledged by parts of our federal government. We are destroying ourselves with our agricultural practices, and the destruction of natural diversity is reaching an all-time high. Most people do not understand that this is happening. Time spent on social media becomes a false social crutch that leaves us empty, and the inequality among economic groups is continuing at an exponential rate, further accelerating our social and economic problems.

Another problems in the United States is that colleges and universities are graduating students with all-time-high debt loads, with many students ill equipped for the future. Doctors are trained with little knowledge of nutrition and no understanding of what our food chain is doing to our food. Many times, nutrition can contribute to ill health when the wrong foods are consumed. Poor diets can cause diabetes and other diseases, and this means more medical costs and shorter life spans. Without ceilings on campaign expenditures, we are electing people with money who are caught up in the power struggle of politics, and corporations want fewer regulations so they can increase their profits at the expense of the environment and public safety. Labor unions, which did not adjust to current needs, have been weakened, and the poor keep having less representation in Congress. The present non-immigration policies emphasize exclusion and not the collaboration that is needed between all parties involved. This leaves an uncertain future for families, and the continual policy of "who is the best" regarding military power could lead to our destruction faster than we thought possible. These are just a few of the problems that need to be fixed before it is too late. We need to work together and develop innovative ideas to reduce polarization and build a bottom-up society. Finally, our sense of purpose should change from our present habits to one of helping our earth for everyone that will be born in the future.

The purpose of the following reference list in the book is to give readers options to delve into the various subjects in greater detail and to make the book titles easier to access to review individual subjects. The older books listed show when the subject of survival became evident in our society. The information collected will be used (when applicable) in determining what can occur in the proposed pilot development project. Other suggestions are welcome in order for the project to reach its potential. Each book usually has a list of publications that the author has written, and this can expand the reading list. In this book, I tried to show ways that communities can become more self-sufficient. We need more people to join the parade.

REFERENCES AND RESOURCES

Note: The following references and resources are shown for references noted in the study. Many books should be read on your own in order to fully understand what a writer is trying to say. The book or reference paper will be noted one time and then referenced with parentheses if used more than one time. The subject reference titles are in caps. Many authors have written more than one book, and these can be sourced also, because they are usually found in the book. The list is provided in order to present books in certain areas of interest, and many of them could fit in many different categories but are listed in just one.

Agriculture and Landscape

(AL1) *Whitewash*, (2017), Carey Gillam

(AL2) *Soil Biology Primer*, (2000), Elaine R. Ingham (Beginning Concepts)

(AL3) *The Lean Farm—How to Minimize Waste & Increase Efficiency*, (2015), Ben Hartman

(AL4) *Planting in a Post-Wild World—Designing Plant Communities for Resilient Landscapes*, (2015), Rainer and West

(AL5) *Mycorrhizal Planet—How Symbiotic Work with Roots to Support Plant Health*, (2017), Michael Phillips

(AL6) *Sustainable Agriculture*, (2016) Carol Hand

(AL7) *Restoration Agriculture—Real-World Permaculture for Farmers*, (2013), Mark Shepard

(AL8) *Lentil Underground—Renegade Farmers and the Future of Food in America*, (2015), Liz Carlisle

(AL9) *Garden Revolution—How Our Landscapes Are a Source of Environment Change*, (2016), Weaner/Christopher

(AL10) *Stuffed and Starved—The Hidden Battle for the World Food System*, (2012), Raj Patel

(AL11) *Landscape Planning—Environmental Applications*, (1991), William M. Marsh

(AL12) *Growing a Revolution—Bringing Our Soil Back to Life*, (2016), David Montgomery

(AL13) *Transition to an Agro-Ecology—For a Food Secured World*, (2016), Jelleke de Nooy van Tol

(AL14) *The Concise Guide to Self-Sufficiency*, (2007), John Seymou

(AL15) *The Third Plate—Field Notes on the Future of Food*, (2014), Dan Barber

(AL16) *Building Inside Nature's Envelope—New Construction/Preservation Programs*, (2000), A. Wasowski

(AL17) *The Edible City-Resource Manual—Controlled Growing Environments*, (1981), Richard Britz

(AL18) *Ending Hunger—An Idea Whose Time Has Come*, (1985), The Praeger (Hunger) Project

(AL19) *Farmer First—Farmer Innovation and Agricultural Research*, (1989), edited by Chambers, Pacey, and Thrupp

(AL20) *The Dirt Cure—Growing Healthy Kids with Food Straight from the Soil*, (2016), Maya Shetreat-Klein, MD

(AL21) *The Organic Farming Manual—A Comprehensive Guide to Running an Organic Farm*, (2010), Ann Hansen

(AL22) *Forks Over Knives—The Plant Based Way to Health*, (2011), T. Collin Campbell and Caldwell B. Esselstyn Jr.

(AL23) *Biomimicry—Innovation Inspired by Nature*, (1997), Janine M. Benyus

(AL24) *The Unsettling of America, Culture and Agriculture*, (2015), Wendell Berry

(AL25) *Organic Management for the Professional—The Natural Way*, (2012), Howard Garrett and John Ferguson

(AL26) *Earth Medicine—Earth Foods—Plant Remedies, Drugs and Natural Foods of the N. A. Indians*, (1972), M. Weiner

(AL27) *Who Will Feed Us?—3rd Edition—The Peasant Food Web vs. The Industrial Food Chain*, (2017), Internet-etc Group

(AL28) *The Minimalist Gardener*, (2017), Patrick Whitefield

(AL29) *The Natural Way of Farming—The Theory and Practice of Green Philosophy*, (1985), Masanobu Fukuoka

(AL30) *Agroecology—The Ecology of Sustainable Food Systems*, 2nd edition, (2007), Stephen R. Guessman

(AL31) *Secrets of the Soil—A Fascinating Account of Recent Breakthroughs*, (1989), Peter Tompkins and Christopher Reed

(AL32) *Building Soils for Better Crops—Sustainable Soil Management*, 3rd edition, (2014), Magdoff and Van Es, (SARE)

(AL33) *Foodopoly—The Battle Over Food and Farming in America*, (2012), Wenonah Hauter

(AL34) *How Plants Work—The Science Behind the Amazing Plants Do*, (2015), Linda Chalker-Scott

(AL35) *Teaming with Microbes—The Organic Gardener's Guide to the Soil Food Web*, (Revised-2010), Lowenfels and Lewis

(AL36) *The Dorito Effect—The Surprising New Truth About Food and Flavor*, (2015), Mark Schatzker

(AL37) *Permaculture Design—A Step-by-Step Guide*, (2012), Aranya

(AL38) *The Concise Guide to Self-Sufficiency*, (2007), John Seymour and Will Sutherland

(AL39) *Vertical Gardening—Grow Up, Not Out, for More Vegetables and Flowers in Much Less Space*, (2011), Derek Fell

(AL40) *The Encyclopedia of Natural and Disease Control*, (1984), Roger B. Yepsen Jr.

(AL41) *Eat to Beat Disease—Foods Medicinal Qualities*, (2016), Catherine J. Frompovich

(AL42) *Food Forensics—The Hidden Toxins Living in Your Food and How You Can Avoid Them*, (2016), Mike Adams

(AL43) *The Organic Farming Manual—Guide to Running an Organic Farm*, (2010), Ann Larkin Hansen

(AL44) Books by Howard Garrett—The Dirt Doctor, Dallas, Texas

(AL45) *Biodynamic Greenhouse Management*, (1990), Heinz Grotzke

(AL46) *Organic Gardener's Composting*, (2015), Steve Solomon

(AL47) *Wildlife Friendly Plants—Make Your Garden a Haven for Beneficial Insects, Birds*, (2004), Rosemary Creeser

(AL48) *Waterwise Plants for Sustainable Gardens—200 Drought Tolerant Choices*, (2011), Lauren and Scott Ogden

(AL49) *100 Plants to Feed the Bees—Provide a Healthy Habitat to Help Pollinators Thrive,* (2016), The Xerces Society

(AL50) *Therapeutic Landscapes—An Evidence-Based Approach to Designing Healing Gardens,* (2014), Marcus and Sachs

(AL51) *Farmacology—Total Health from the Ground Up,* (2013), Daphne Miller, MD

(AL52) *Four-Season Harvest—Organic Vegetables from Your Home Garden all Year Long,* (1999), Eliot Coleman

(AL53) *Rodale's Annual Garden—Flowers, Foliage, Fruits and Grasses for One Summer Season,* (1998), Peter Loewer

(AL54) *How to Grow More Vegetables—Than You Ever Thought Possible on Less Land,* (2006 or later), John Jeavons

(AL55) *The Truth About Organic Gardening—Benefits, Drawbacks, and the Bottom Line,* (2008), Jeff Gillman

(AL56) *The Soil Will Save Us—How Scientists and Farmers are Healing the Soil to Save the Planet,* (2014), K. Ohlson

(AL57) *What a Plant Knows—A Field Guide for the Senses,* (2012), Daniel Chamovitz

(AL58) *All New Square Foot Gardening—Grow More in Less Space,* (2005), Mel Bartholomew

(AL59) *Geotherapy—Innovative Methods of Soil Fertility Restoration,* Goreau, Larson, and Campe

(AL60) *Real Food Fake Food—Why You Don't Know What You Are Eating and What You Can do About It,* (2016), Olmstead

(AL61) *Science For Sale—U.S. Government Uses Powerful Corporations to Support Government Policies,* (2014), D. Lewis

(AL62) *Bringing Nature Home—How You Can Sustain Wildlife with Native Plants,* (2014), Douglas Tallamy

(AL63) *FDA—Failure, Deception, Abuse—The Story of Out-of-Control Government Agency,* (2010), Life Extension Foundation

(AL64) *Merchants of Doubt—How a Handful of Scientists Obscured the Truth,* (2010), Naomi Oreskes and Erik Conway

(AL65) *Poisoning Our Children: Pesticide Residue,* (2018), Andre' Leu

(AL66) *Global Eating Disorder—We Can No Longer Afford Cheap Food,* (2014), Gunnar Rundgren

(AL67) *The Living Landscape—Designing for Beauty and Biodiversity in the Home Garden,* (2014), Rick Darke and D. Tallamy

(AL68) *Stand Together or Starve Alone—Unity and Chaos in the U.S. Food Movement,* (2017), Mark Winne

(AL69) *Our Daily Poison—From Pesticide to Packaging—How Chemicals Have Contaminated the Food Chain,* (2013), M. Robin

(AL70) *Recollected Essays,* (1998 reprint), Wendell Berry

(AL71) *What's Making Our Children Sick?—How Industrial Food Is Causing an Epidemic of Chronic Illness,* (2017), Dr. Perro and Adams

(AL72) *The Hidden Half of Nature—The Microbial Roots of Life and Health,* (2016), David Montgomery and Anne Bikle

(AL73) *Tragic Failures—How and Why We Are Harmed by Toxic Chemicals,* (2017), Carl F. Cranor

(AL74) *Food: What the Heck Do I Eat?,* (2017), Dr. Mark Hyman

(AL75) The Plant Paradox—The Hidden Dangers in "Healthy Foods" That Cause Disease and Health Gain, (2018), Dr. Steven Gundy

(AL76) Who Really Feeds the World?—The Failures of Agribusiness and the Promise of Agroecology, (2016), Vandana Shiva

(AL77) The Vandana Shiva Reader, (2015), Vandana Shiva

(AL78) Your Successful Farm Business—Production, Profit, Pleasure, (2017), Joel Salatin (plus other books and on youTube)

(AL79) The Omnivore's Delight—A Natural History of Four Meals, (2006), Michael Pollan

(AL80) Food, Inc.—How Industrial Food Is Making Us Sicker, Fatter, and Poorer, (2009), edited by Karl Weber

(AL81) Traditional Nutrition—Healthy Diets from Around the World, (2015), Ben Hirshberg

(AL82) An Agricultural Testament, (1956, 1972, 2010), Sir Albert Howard

(AL83) Call of the Reed Warbler: A New Agriculture, A new Earth, (2018), Charles Massy

Capitalism and Economics (Including Local Currencies)

(CE1) Post-Capitalist Entrepreneurship—Startups for the 99%, (2017), Boyd Cohen

(CE2) The High Price of Materialism, (2002), Tim Kasser

(CE3) Seven Bad Ideas—Economics, (2014), Jeff Madrick

(CE4) What Comes After Money?, (2011), Daniel Pinchbeck, Ken Jordan

(CE5) The Systems View of Life—A Unifying Vision, (2014), Fritjof Capra and Pier Luigi Luisi

(CE6) WTF—Work the Future Today, (2017–2018), Whitney Vosburgh and Charlie Grantham

(CE7) Race, Class and Gender in a Diverse Society, (1997), Diana Kendall

(CE8) Thinking in Systems, (2008), Donella H. Meadows

(CE9) Limits to Growth—30 Year Update, (2004), Donella H. Meadows

(CE10) Poverty and the Underclass—Changing Perceptions of the Poor in America, (1994), William A. Kelso

(CE11) The Spirit Level—Why Greater Equality Makes Societies Stronger, (2009), R. Wilkinson and K. Pickett

(CE12) Living Within Limits—Ecology, Economics, and Population Taboos, (1993), Garrett Hardin

(CE13) Paradigms in Progress—Life Beyond Economics, (1992), Hazel Henderson

(CE14) The Tipping Point—How Little Things Can Make a Big Difference, (2002), Malcolm Gladwell

(CE15) Exponential Organizations—Why New Organizations are Faster and Cheaper, (2014), Salim Ismail, Malone

(CE16) Credo, (2015), Brian Davey (out-of-print e-book from Smashwords, excellent)

(CE17) Naked Economics—Undressing the Dismal Science, (2010), Charles Wheelan

(CE18) Green with Envy—Why Keeping up with the Joneses is Keeping us in Debt, (2006), Shira Boss

(CE19) Systems Thinking for Social Change—Guide to Solve Complex Problems, (2015), David Peter Stroh

(CE20) The Value of Nothing—How to Reshape Market Society and Redefine Democracy, (2009), Raj Patel

(CE21) The End of the Nation State—The Rise of Regional Economies, (1995), Kenichi Ohmae

(CE22) Cannibals with Forks—The Triple Bottom Line of 21st. Century Business, (1998), John Elkington

(CE23) *Common Wealth—Economics for a Crowded Planet,* (2008), Jeffrey D. Sachs

(CE24) *Economics as if People Mattered,* (1973), E. F. Schumacher

(CE25) *Natural Capitalism—Creating the Next Industrial Revolution,* (1999), Paul Hawken, Amory Lovins, L. Lovins

(CE25) *Prosperity Without Growth—2nd Edition—Economics for a Finite Planet,* (2017), Tim Jackson

(CE26) *Beyond the Limits—Confronting Global Collapse, Envisioning a Sustainable Future,* (1992), Donella Meadows

(CE27) *The Creative Edge—Fostering Innovation Where You Work,* (1987), William C. Miller

(CE28) *Jump the Curve—50 Essential Strategies to Stay Ahead of Emerging Technologies,* (2008), Jack Uldrich

(CE29) *The Price of Civilization—Reawakening American Virtue and Prosperity,* (2012), Jeffrey D. Sachs

(CE30) *Flash Foresight—How to See the Invisible and Do the Impossible,* (2011), Dan Burrus

(CE31) *Predictably Irrational—The Hidden Forces that Shape our Decisions,* (2008), Dan Ariely

(CE32) *Age of Greed—The Triumph and the Decline of America, 1970 to Present,* (2011), Jeff Madrick

(CE33) *Everyday Survival—Why Smart People Do Stupid Things,* (2008), Laurence Gonzales

(CE34) *Why Nations Fail—The Origins of Power, Prosperity, and Poverty,* (2012), D. Acemoglu and J. Robinson

(CE35) *The End of Growth—Adapting to our New Economic Reality,* (2011), Richard Heinberg

(CE36) *An Aging Population, an Aging Planet, and a Sustainable Future,* (1995), edited by Ingman, et al.

(CE37) *Democracy at Work—A Cure for Capitalism, (2012), Richard Wolff*

(CE38) *Peasant Versus City-Dwellers—Taxation and the Burden of Economic Development,* (1992), R. Sah, J. Stiglitz

(CE39) *America the Impossible—Manifesto for a New Economy,* (2012), Jams Gustave Speth

(CE40) *Cities and the Wealth of Nations—Principals of Economic Life,* (1984), Jane Jacobs

(CE41) *Why the West Rules-For Now—The Patterns of History and What They Reveal About the Future,* (2010), Morris

(CE42) *Reshaping the World for the 21st Century—Society and Growth,* (2002), Virginia R. Smith

(CE43) *The Nearly Free University and the Emerging Economy,* (2013), Charles Hugh Smith

(CE44) *Ecological Economics,* (2010), Herman F. Daly and Joshua Farley

(CE45) *Dark Age America—Climate Change, Cultural Collapse and the Hard Future Ahead,* (2016), John M. Greer

(CE46) *Capitalism at the Crossroads—Next Generation Business Strategies for a Post-Crisis World,* (2010), Stuart Hart

(CE47) *The Divide—A Guide to Global Inequality and its Solutions,* (2017), James Hickel

(CE48) *The American Jubilee—A National Nightmare is Closer than You Think,* (2017), Porter Stansberry

(CE49) *The Rise and Fall of the Third Reich,* (1959), William L. Shirer

(CE50) *Beyond Growth—The Economics off Sustainable Development,* (1996), Herman E. Daly

(CE51) *Elite Thinking,* (not out for publication yet), Trump administration

(CE52) *The Third Industrial Revolution—How Lateral Power Is Transforming Energy and Economy,* (2011), J. Rifkin

(CE53) *Designs for the Pluriverse,* (2018), Arturo Escobar

(CE54) *The Bet,* (2013), Paul Sabin

(CE55) *Democracy in Chains—The Deep History of the Radical Rights Plan for America,* (2017), Nancy McLean

(CE56) *Dark Money—Billionaires Behind the Radical Right,* (2017), Jane Meyer

(CE57) *Energy and the Wealth of Nations—Understanding the Bisop,* (2018), Dr. Charles Hal

(CE58) *It's Even Worse Than You Think—What the Trump Administration Is Doing to America,* (2018), David Cay Johnston

(CE59) *The New Confessions of an Economic Hit Man,* (2016), John Perkins

(CE60) *Small Is Beautiful—Economics as if People Mattered,* (1973), E.F. Schumacher

(CE61) *Immoderate Greatness: Why Civilizations Fail,* (2012), William Ophus

(CE62) The Lessons of History, (2010), Will and Aerial Durant

(CE63) *Moyers on Democracy,* (2008), Bill Moyers

(CE64) *The Value of Everything—Making and Taking in the Global Economy,* (2018), Mariana Mazzucato

(CE65) *How Democracies Die,* (2018), Steven Levitsky and Daniel Ziblat

(CE66) *The Wizard and the Prophet—Two Remarkable Scientists and Their Dueling Visions to Shape Tomorrow's World,* (2018), Charles Mann

(CE67) *Edge of Chaos—Why Democracy Is Failing to Deliver Economic Growth—and How to Fix It,* (2018), Dambisa Moyo

(CE68) *Everything Trump Touches Dies—A Republican Strategist Gets Real About the Worst President Ever,* (2018), Rick Wilson

(CE69) *Can Democracy Survive Global Capitalism?,* (2018), Robert Kuttner

(CE70) *Us vs. Them—The Failure of Globalism,* (2018), Ian Bremmer

(CE71) *Fear—Trump in the White House, (2018), Bob Woodward*

(CE72) *From Uneconomic Growth to a Steady—State Economy,* (2014), Herman E. Daly

Environment

(E1) *Replenish—The Virtuous Cycle of Water and Prosperity,* (2017), Sandra Postel

(E2) *Political Ecology—An Integrative Approach to Geography and Environment,* (2003), Zimmer, Bassett

(E3) *Dirt—The Erosion of Civilizations,* (2012), David R. Montgomery

(E4) *Futures by Design—The Practice of Ecological Planning,* (1994), edited by Doug Aberley

(E5) *The Natural Advantage—An Organic Way to Grow Your Business,* (2001), Alan Heeks

(E6) *Eco-City Dimensions—Health Communities, Healthy Planet,* (1997), Mark Roseland

(E7) *The Ecology of Commerce—A Declaration of Sustainability,* (1993), Paul Harkin

(E8) *Silent Spring,* (2002), Rachel Carson and Linda Lear

(E9) *Our Ecological Footprint—Reducing Human Impact on the Earth,* (1998), M. Wackernagel and W. Rees

(E10) *The Next American Metropolis—Ecology, Community, and the American Dream,* (1993), Peter Calthorpe

(E11) *The Sense of Place,* (1981), Fritz Steele

(E12) *The Quality of Life Concept—A Potential New Tool for Decision Makers,* (1971), US government—EPA

(E13) *Ecology and the Politics of Scarcity-Revisited,* (1992), William Ophuls and Steven Boyan Jr.

(E14) *The Post Carbon Reader—Managing the 21ˢᵗ Century Sustainability Crises,* (2010), Heinberg, Lerch

(E15) *The Power of Geography—How Territory Shapes Social Life,* (1989), edited by J. Wolch and M. Dear

(E16) *Concepts of Ecology, Second Edition, (1976), Edward J Kormondy*

(E17) *From Eco-Cities to Living Machines—Principals of Ecological Design,* (1994), Nancy and John Todd

(E18) *Resilience Thinking—Sustaining Eco-Systems and People in a Changing World,* (2006) B. Walker and D. Salt

(E19) *Focus on Global Features—People and the Environment in Change,* (1990), N. Hutchinson and C. Bonnor

(E20) *Collapse—How Societies Choose to Fail or Succeed,* (2005), Jared Diamond

(E21) *Nature's Services—Societal Dependence on Natural Ecosystems,* (1997), edited by Gretchen C. Daily

(E22) *Environmental and Natural Resource Economics,* (1992), Tom Tietenberg

(E23) *The Greenpeace Book of Water,* (1995), Klaus Lanz

(E24) *BioLogic—Designing with Nature to Protect the Environment,* (1994), David Wann

(E25) *Effective Financing of Environmentally Sustainable Development,* (1996), Ismail Serageldin, W. Bank

(E26) *A Sand Country Almanac—Essays on Conservation,* (1966), Aldo Leopold (a classic)

(E27) *Ultimate Security—The Environmental Basis of Political Stability,* (1993), Norman Myers

(E28) *Rooted in the Land—Essays on Community and Place,* (1996), Wes Jackson—Land Institute

(E29) *Vital Signs—2000—The Environmental Trends that are Shaping our Future,* (2000), Worldwatch Institute

(E30) *Full House—Reassessing the Earth's Population Carrying Capacity,* (1994), Lester R Brown and Hal Kane

(E31) *Plowing the Sea—Nurturing the Hidden Sources of Growth in the Developing World,* (1997), Fairbanks/Lindsay

(E32) *God's Last Offer—Negotiating for a Sustainable Future,* (1999), Ed Ayres

(E33) *The Environmental Sourcebook—Issues, Organizations, Periodicals, Grants, (1992), Edith C. Stein*

(E34) *Making Development Sustainable,* (1994), World Bank Group

(E35) *Economic Values and the Natural World, (*1993), David W. Pearce

(E36) *Vanishing Borders—Protecting the Planet in the Age of Globalization,* (2000), Hilary French—Worldwatch

(E37) *The Long Emergency—Surviving the Converging Catastrophes of the 21ˢᵗ Century,* (2005), James Howard Kunstler

(E38) *Shrinking the Technosphere—Getting a Grip on the Technologies that Limit our Autonomy,* (2016), Dmitry Orlov

(E39) *The Meaning of Human Existence,* (2014), Edward O. Wilson

(E40) *Drawdown—The Most Comprehensive Plan Ever Proposed to Reduce Global Warming,* (2017), edited by Paul Harkin

(E41) *Walden—Black and White Classics,* (2014), Henry David Thoreau

(E42) *Wilderness Essays,* (2012), John Muir

(E43) *Scarcity—Humanity's Final Chapter,* (2012), C.O. Clugston

(E44) *This Changes Everything Capitalism vs. the Climate, (*2014), Naomi Klein

(E45) *Understanding Sustainable Development—Second Edition,* (2015), John Blewitt

(E46) *Extreme Cities—The Peril and Promise of Urban Life in the Age of Climate Change,* (2017), Ashly Dawson

(E47) *Introduction to Environmental Studies,* (1980), Jonathan Turk

(E48) *People, Land and Time—Introduction to the Relations Between Landscape, Culture and Environment,* (2014), Roberts, Atkins

(E49) *What Do You See—A Learner's Guide with Poetry,* (2016), George Hunt

(E50) *The Hidden Life of Trees—What They Feel, How They Communicate,* (2015), Peter Wohlleben

(E51) *Unprecedented Crime—Climate Science Denial and Game Changes for Survival,* (2016), Peter Carter and E. Woodworth

(E52) *The Sixth Extinction—An Unnatural History,* (2015), Elizabeth Kolbert

(E53) *The End of Nature,* (2006), Bill McKibben

(E54) *Eaarth—Making a Life on a Tough New Planet,* (2011), Bill McKibben

(E55) *Deep Ecology—The Wealth of Communities and the Durable Future,* (2007), Bill McKibben

Sharing and Culture

(SC1) *Sharing Cities—A Case for Truly Smart and Sustainable Cities,* (2015), Duncan McLaren and Julian Agyeman

(SC2) *The Monochrome Society, (*2001), Amitai Etzioni

(SC3) *Culture Matters—How Values Shape Human Progress,* (2000), L. Harrison, Samuel P. Huntington

(SC4) *The Theory of Share Tenancy, (*1969), Steven N. S. Cheung

(SC5) *Creating Successful Communities—A Guidepost to Growth Management Strategies,* (1990), Mantell, Harper

(SC6) *Building Communities from the Inside Out—Finding and Mobilizing a Communities Assets,* (1993), McKnight

(SC7) *Open Space Technology—A User's Guide,* (1992), Harrison Owen

(SC8) *Freedom to Build—Where Dwellers Are in Control, Their Homes Are Better,* (1972), J. Turner and R. Fichter

(SC9) *The Successful Volunteer Organization—Non-Profit and Community Groups,* (1981), Joan Flanagan

(SC10) *Building a Win-Win World—Life Beyond Global Economic Warfare,* (1996), Hazel Henderson

(SC11) T*he Cultural Creatives—How 50 Million People are Changing the World,* (2000), Paul Ray and Sherry Anderson

(SC12) *The Talent Solution—Aligning Strategy and People to Achieve Extraordinary Results,* (1998), Ed Gubman

(SC13) *Culture Shift,* (2004), Ted Brannen

(SC14) *The Millennium Organization,* (1994), Harrison Owen

(SC15) *Social Business Excellence—How to Compete, Win and Expand Through Collaboration,* (2012), Afshar and Martin

(SC16) *Creating Wealth—Growing Local Economies with Local Currencies,* (2011), Gwendolyn Hallsmith and Bernard Lietaer

(SC17) *Toward Sustainable Communities—Resources for Citizens and Their Governments,* (1998), Mark Roseland

(SC18) *The Stork and the Plow—The Equity Answer to the Human Dilemma,* (1995), Paul and Anne Ehrlich, G. Daily

(SC19) *What Then Must We Do?—Straight Talk About the Next American Revolution,* (2013), Gar Alperovitz

(SC20) *The Mesh—Why the Future of Business is Sharing,* (2010), Lisa Gansky

(SC21) *What's Mine is Yours—The Rise of Collaborative Consumption,* (2010), Rachel Botsman and Roo Rogers

(SC22) *The Economics of HappineSS—Building Genuine Wealth,* (2007), Mark Anielski

(SC23) *Cities Fit to Live In and How We Can Make Them Happen—Urban Renaissance,* (1971), Walter McQuade

(SC24) *The Key to Sustainable Cities—Meeting Human Needs Transforming Community Systems,* (2003), G. Hallsmith

(SC25) *Managing Community Growth—2nd edition,* (2004), Eric Damian Kelly

(SC26) *Cognitive Surplus—Creativity and Generosity in a Connected Age,* (2010), Clay Shirky

(SC27) *EarthEd—Rethinking Education on a Changing Planet,* (2017), Worldwatch Institute

(SC28) *Bowling Alone—The Collapse and Revival of American Community,* (2000), Robert D. Putnam

(SC29) *The Coming Anarchy—Shattering the Dreams of the Post Cold War,* (2000), Robert D. Kaplan

(SC30) *People, Land, and Community,* (1997), edited by Hildegarde Hannum (Schumacher Society)

(SC31) *Crowd Storm—The Future of Innovation, Ideas, and Problem Solving,* (2013), S. Abrahamson, P. Ryder, B Unterberg

(SC32) *Thinkertoys—2nd edition—A Handbook of Creative-Thinking Techniques,* (2006), Michael Michalko

(SC33) *The Ecology of Hope—Communities Collaborate for Sustainability,* (1997), Ted Bernard and Jora Young

(SC34) *Community Planning for an Aging Society—Designing Services and Facilities,* (1976), Lawton, Newcomber

(SC35) *Work and Human Behavior,* (1968), Walter S. Neff

(SC36) *The Urban Underclass,* (1991), edited by Christopher Jencks, Paul E. Peterson

(SC37) *Enough—Why the World's Poorest Starve in an Age of Plenty,* (2009), Roger Thurow and Scott Kilman

(SC38) *Why Do Ruling Classes Fear History?—And Other Questions,* (1997), Harvey Kaye

(SC39) *The Language of Landscape,* (1998), Anne Whiston Spirn

(SC40) *The Magic of Dialogue- Transforming Conflict into Cooperation,* (1999), Daniel Yankelovich

(SC41) *The Channeling Zone—American Spirituality in an Anxious Age,* (1997), Michael F. Brown

(SC42) *Culture and Truth—The Remaking of Social Analysis,* (1993), Renato Rosaldo

(SC43) *Cultural Anthropology,* (1995), Jacobs and Stern

(SC44) *The Careless Society—Community and its Counterfeits,* (1995), John McKnight

(SC45) *Improving Poor People—The Welfare State, the Underclass, and Urban Schools as History*, (1995), M. Katz

(SC46) *The War Against the Poor—The Underclass and Antipoverty Policy*, (1995), Herbert J. Gans

(SC47) *Anthropology—7th edition*, (1974), William A. Haviland and Cynthia K. Mahmood

(SC48) *The Runaway Species—How Human Creativity Remakes the World*, (2017), Anthony Brandt and David Eagleman

(SC49) *Money—Understanding and Creating Alternatives to Legal Tender*, (2001), Thomas H. Grecco Jr.

(SC50) *The End of Money and the Future of Civilization*, (2009), Thomas H. Grecco Jr.

(SC51) *Exponential Organizations—Why New Organizations Are 10 Times Better, Faster Than Yours*, (2014), Salim Ismail

(SC52) *Anthropology—7th edition*, (1994), William A. Haviland

(SC53) *Culture Shock—A Biblical Response to Today's Most Divisive Issues*, (2015), Chip Ingram

(SC54) *Beyond Culture and The Silent Language*, (1977), Edward T. Hall

(SC55) *Patterns of Culture—Analysis of our Society Related to Primitive Cultures*, (1934), Ruth Benedict

(SC56) *The Art of Happiness—A Handbook for Living*, (1998), His Holiness the Dalai Lama and Howard C. Cutler, MD

(SC57) *An Open Life*, *(1988), Joseph Campbell*

(SC58) *Myths, Dreams, and Mysteries—The Counter Between Contemporary Faiths and Archaic Realities*, (1957), M. Eliade

(SC59) *Megatrends—Ten New Directions Transforming Our Lives*, (1982), John Naisbitt

(SC60) *Megatrends for Women*, (1992), Patricia Aburdene and John Naisbitt

(SC61) *Understanding Media—The Extensions of Man*, (1964–1994), Marshall McLuhan

(SC62) *Future Man—An Optimistic Look into the Future and What It Holds for Society*, (1980), Chris Morgan

(SC63) *Social Anthropology—An Alternate Introduction*, (1989), Angela P. Cheater

(SC64) *Free Play—The Power of Improvisation in Life and the Arts*, (1990), Stephen Nachmanovich

(SC65) *Ritual of the Wind—North American Indian Ceremonies, Music and Dance*, (1977), Jamake Highwater

(SC66) *Humankind—What we Know About Ourselves, Where We are Headed, Behavior*, (1978), Peter Farb

(SC67) *Four Futures—Life After Capitalism*, (2016), Peter Frase

(SC68) *Generation Me—Why Today's Young Americans are More Confident, Assertive, and More Miserable*, (2014), J. Twenge

(SC69) *No Logo*, (2009), Naomi Klein

(SC70) *The Runaway Species—How Human Creativity Remakes the World*, *(2017)*, Anthony Brandt and David Eagleman

(SC71) *500 Social Media Marketing Tips—The #1 Marketing Bestseller*, (2016–2017), Andrew Macarthy

(SC72) *Creativity—The Magic Synthesis*, (1976), Silvano Arieti

(SC73) *Drawing on the Artist Within—A guide to Innovation, Invention, Imagination and Creativity*, (1986), Betty Edwards

(SC74) *Focus on Global Futures—People and Environment in Change,* (1990), Nick Hutchinson and Chris Bonno

(SC75) *People, Land and Time—An Historical Introduction to Landscapes, Culture and Environment,* (1998), Atkins, Simmons

(SC76) *The More of Less—Finding the Life you Want Under Everything You Own,* (2016), Joshua Becker

(SC77) *Money and Work Unchained,* (2017), Charles Hugh Smith

(SC78) *Get a Job, Build a Real Career, and Defy a Bewildering Economy,* (2014), Charles Hugh Smith

(SC79) *Why Our Status Quo Failed and is Beyond Reform,* (2016), Charles Hugh Smith

(SC80) *Lost Connections—Uncovering the Real Cause of Depression,* (2018), Johann Hart

(SC81) *Emotional Intelligence 2.0—Succinctly Explains how to Deal with our Emotions Creatively,* (2009), Dr. Travis Bradbury

(SC82) *Post-Capitalism—A Guide to our Future,* (2017), Paul Mason

(SC83) *Mountain Fragrance—Journeys and Encounters in Korea,* (2009), Rita Taylor, Green Review Publishing, Korea

(SC84) *Academically Adrift: Limited Learning on College Campuses,* (2010–2011), Richard Arum and Josipa Roksa

(SC85) *Why Does College Cost So Much,* (2014), Robert Archibald and David H. Feldman

(SC86) *Green with Envy—A Whole New Way to Kook at (Un) Happiness,* (2006), Shira Boss

(SC87) *The Spirit of Community—The Reinvention of American Society,* (1993), Amitai Etzioni

(SC88) *The Price of Everything—Solving the Mystery of Why We Pay What We Do,* (2011), Eduardo Porter

(SC89) *Collapse—How Societies Choose to Fail or Succeed,* (2005), Jared Diamond

(SC90) *Frenemies: The Epic Disruption of the Ad Business (and Everything Else),* (2018), Ken Auletta

(SC91) *The Mechanical Bride—Folklore of Industrial Man,* (1951), Herbert Marshall McLuhan

(SC92) *Get a Job, Build a Real Career and Defy a Bewildering Economy,* (2014), Charles Hugh Smith

(SC93) *Janesville—An American Story,* (2017), Amy Goldstein

(SC94) *Think Like a Commoner: A Short Introduction to the Life of the Commons,* (2014), David Collier

(SC95) *Squeezed—Why Our Families Can't Afford America,* (2018), Alissa Quart

(SC96) *Contagious—Why Things Catch On,* (2013), Jonah Berger

(SC97) *loneliness—Human Nature and the Need for Social Connections,* (2008), John T. Cacioppo and William Patrick

(SC98) *The Case Against Education—Why the Education System Is a Waste of Time and Money,* (2018), Bryan Caplan

Urban Planning

(UP1) *Maker City—A Practical Guide for Reinventing Our Cities,* (2017), Hirshberg, Dougherty, Kadanoff

(UP2) *The Community Resilience Reader—Essential Resources for an Era of Upheaval,* (2017), Edited by Daniel Lerch

(UP3) *The Permaculture City—Regenerative Design for Urban, Suburban and Town Resilience,* (2015), Toby Hemenway

(UP4) *Scale—The Universal Laws of Growth, Innovation and Sustainability,* (2017), Geoffrey West

(UP5) *The New Urbanism—Toward an Architecture of Community,* (1994), Peter Katz

(UP6) *Better Not Bigger—How to take Control of Urban Growth,* (2007), Eben Fodor

(UP7) *Sustainable America—A New Consensus—For a Healthy Environment,* (1996), President's Council on S.D.

(UP8) *Cities Fit to Live In—And How We Could Make Them Happen,* (1971), edited by Walter McQuade

(UP9) *Rural Environmental Planning for Rural Communities,* (1991), Sargent, Lusk, Rivera, Varela

(UP10) *The Millennial City—A New Urban Paradigm for 21st-Century America,* (2000), edited by Myron Magnet

(UP11) *The Timeless Way of Building,* (1980), Christopher Alexander

(UP12) *Boundaries of Home—Mapping for Local Empowerment,* (1993), edited by Doug Aberley

(UP13) *Collaborative Communities—CoHousing, Central Living, Shared Facilities,* (1991), Dorit Fromm

(UP14) *Urban Development—Theory, Fact and Illusion,* (1988), J. Vernon Henderson

(UP15) *Tomorrow by Design—A Regional Design Process for Sustainability,* (1996), Philip H. Lewis Jr.

(UP16) *Suburban Nation—The Rise of Sprawl and the Decline of the American Dream,* (2000), Duany, Plater-Zyberk, Speck

(UP17) *Understanding Sustainable Development,* (2006), John Blewitt

(UP18) *Introduction to Sustainable Development,* (2007), Peter P. Rodgers

(UP19) *Changing Course—A Global Business Perspective on Development and the Environment,* (1992), S. Schmidheiny

(UP20) *How Buildings Learn—What Happens After They are Built,* (1994), Stewart Brand

(UP21) *Strategies for Safe and Sustainable Communities—Short Subjects for Design Professionals,* (2003), LARBF

(UP22) *Design for Mountain Communities—A Landscape and Architectural Guide,* (1990), Sherry Dorward

(UP23) *Green by Design—Creating a Home for Sustainable Living,* (2003), Angela M. Dean

(UP24) *Land Development Handbook—Planning, Engineering and Surveying,* (1996), Dewberry and Davis

(UP25) *Regenerative Design for Sustainable Development,* (1994), John Tillman Lyle

(UP26) *Form Function and Design,* (1960), Paul Jacques Grillo

(UP27) *Visual Research Methods in Design,* (1991), Henry Sanoff

(UP28) *Green Metropolis—Why Living Smaller, Living Closer and Driving Less are Keys to Sustainability,* (2009) Owen

(UP29) *Design with Nature,* (1969), Ian L. McHarg

(UP30) *The New Science of Cities,* (2013), Michael Batty

(UP31) *Good Neighbors: Affordable Family Housing,* (1995), Tom Jones, William Pettus, AIA, Michael Pyator, FAIA

(UP32) *Climatic Design—Energy-Efficient Building Principals and Practices,* (1983), Donald Watson, FAIA, and Kenneth Labs

(UP33) *Process Architecture, #3,* (1977), Community Design by the People, edited by Jules Gregory and David Lewis

(UP34) *An Introduction to Sustainable Development,* (2008), Peter P. Rogers, Kazi F. Jalal, and John A Boyd

(UP35) *Can a City be Sustainable?* (2016), State of the World, Worldwatch Institute

(UP36) *The Death and Life of Great American Cities,* (1961), Jane Jacobs

(UP37) *The New Localism—How Cities can Thrive in the Age of Populism,* (2018), Bruce Katz and Jeremy Novak

(UP38) *LID—Low Impact Development—A Design Manuel for Urban Areas,* (2010), University of Arkansas

(UP39) *Landscape Ecology Principals in Landscape Architecture and Land-Use Planning,* (1996), Dramsted

(UP40) *Design, When Everybody Designs—An Introduction to Design for Social Innovation,* (2015), Ezio Manzini

(UP41) *Welcome to Your World—How the Built Environment Shapes Our Lives,* (2017), Sarah Willams Goldhagen

Magazines

There are many magazines that are available in written or digital form that can also be used for recently updated information. They can easily be found on the internet by asking for different categories of information. Some can be found free on Issuu and other sites. *New Internationalist, In These Times, Acres USA,* and *Yes* magazine are examples that specialize in the type of material that is in this book. On their websites, they usually show past magazine articles and a variety of topics. An excellent example would be all of the articles in the mental health issue of *Yes* magazine (fall 2018).

Internet

Some of the most pertinent data is found by searching on the internet. Reports and current articles can be found by asking certain questions on Google or other search engines. Many articles have blue letters within the article, and by tapping on them, you get additional information on the subject noted or links to other sites. Government agencies or nonprofit organizations publish digital reports that provide in-depth information. Many of them have updated survey information (example: Pew Foundation). Two important sites are Resilience and Peak Prosperity Weekly. Resilience is produced by the Post Carbon Institute. Both of these sites obtain their information from other sites on the internet but also have their own articles. How you frame questions is important, and it may take several different questions before the information you want is obtained, and several different opinions on a subject should be reviewed. Personally, I do not use Twitter or Facebook. However, some blogs are interesting when evaluating articles. Wikipedia is another source for review.

Some of the best sources for information are the podcasts shown on YouTube. Just put in a person's name or topic. They also have TED Talks. For urban farmers, Neversink Farms (www. neversinkfarm.com) is excellent, and this is a property that has revenues of $350,000 a year on one and a half acres. They started a few years ago with $30,000.

One example on YouTube is a series of presentations in a nine-part series, *GMOs Revealed* (www. youtube.com/channelUCIifmNfDiMwBmt295S5KbLg). This is an excellent source of information.

> (Partial information) GMOs and its associated pesticides were touted to feed the world but in 2013 U.S. farms contributed only 2.3 percent of the food supply to the countries with the most starving people. They stated that it is a form of technology when paired with greed and politics becomes a catastrophic mess experiment that harms people using it. Ninety percent of Americans now test positive for glyphosate. With this problem we are destroying topsoil and the way we are producing food with GMOs the planet will be left unsustainable for us and our children. Only 20% goes into the human food chain and 40% in the making of animal food. Meat products are not exempt. The article also show what glyphosate does to our bodies chemically.

Earlier in this book, it was noted that the inert ingredients in Roundup contained arsenic and heavy metals. A large majority of the people in the United States want GMOs in foods labeled, and like gun laws, Congress does not do anything.

Another way of finding reliable information is to ask the question "What are credible sources on the internet?" One example is the pdf "Credible Resources on the Internet." If you have any questions about this list, want to suggest additions, or need to report a broken link, please contact Jason Price, director of the Library, at 806-457-4200 ext. 787 or email jprice@fpctx.edu.

For example, another article by Richard Heinberg, from Resilience, that is critical for understanding what is happening to our environment, especially showing the acceleration of our social-economic and earth system trends, is "Human Predators—Human Prey—Part 2," from August 28, 2018 (https://www.resilience.org/stories/2018-08-28/human-predators-human-prey-part-2/).

Methodology

I apologize for not listing some of the hundreds of books not included. Many of the authors have written more than one book, and these should be reviewed also. One of the easiest means of reviewing books is Amazon. It is easy to look inside and find the table of contents and then click on a chapter to get an idea of what the author is presenting in the book. Often, authors refer to other books as references, and this is a valuable way to obtain additional information. Reviewing some of these books leads to an expansion of the topic or insight into another idea.

I have provided the necessary information for accessing the articles from the internet, magazines, YouTube and other sources. This is to encourage the reader to read the articles in their full text.

WHY THIS BOOK

I created this book to make information available to the public about all the books I have collected and enjoyed over the years and secondly as a means of being, in a small way, a contributor to society. This book would not be possible without the help of quite a few people I have known over the years who have helped me understand and look at nature around me and appreciate its capabilities. I also had the fortune of traveling to Ireland, Jamaica, Dominican Republic, China, Thailand, Mexico, Canada, Greece, Cypress, Lebanon, and South Korea. My wife, Louise, who was a professor, taught a course in Lebanon for six months, and my daughter, Patricia, was a professor in South Korea for eight years. Now my son, Greg, is trying to keep me in line, which is not an easy task.

The format for the book was designed so people can have access to information on the internet and know what books would be interesting to read. They then can understand what is happening in our society and be able to find pathways to make viable changes in fields they are interested in. Utilizing the book in this manner, it becomes much larger in terms of expanding one's knowledge; it then becomes a directory of what actions to take to make things better. My goal was to get people to understand more of what is happening, see and enjoy nature, and not spend so much of their time on smartphones and social media. They are useful but should not be a crutch. The constant pursuit of money, greed, and corruption discourages people from having faith in our political system. Changing these distorted symbols of democracy has to be one of our first goals. However, reducing the arms race might be up there with them. The question is, do we kill ourselves now or later when we have destroyed the earth's ecological balance and used up its "free" resources? I hate to leave this up in the air with our present administration.

A transitional period for this project does not mean that it is a transition from capitalism to communism, a socialist society, or another type of society. It is a transition from the twenty-first century to a period when civilization changes to become sustainable in its use of natural resources and collaborative social dynamics, or it is destroyed by our ignoring what could happen to us. I believe we cannot become a postcapitalist society without corporations, but they must exist to help themselves and society and not be structured as they are now. Their first purpose now is to make money for investors, but should not this include a triple bottom line and sustainability requirements as a part of a final legal structure? Workers should also be a part of the management structure in some way. Politics must also change with limitations on methods of funding. Laws to reduce inequality will add stability to our social structure and should be a corporate goal. Generally, money given out to people and businesses should provide work opportunities whenever possible, including restructuring of subsidies so that they benefit society as a whole. If corporations do not change along these lines, then we will need a world without them. I hope by reading this book and others, it will encourage people to be more innovative and caring in how we as a society live.

The *Huffington Post* had the following article on March 16, 2014: "Ten Examples of Welfare for the Rich and Corporations," by Bill Quigley (https://www.huffingtonpost.com/bill-quigley/ten-examples-of-welfare-for-the-rich-and-corporations_b_4589188.html). These are only a few examples among many.

> 1) A New York Times study by Louise Story calculated that state and local government provide at least $80 billion in subsidies to corporations. 2) The Cato Institute (a radical right organization) estimates that federal subsidies to corporations cost taxpayers almost $100 billion every year. 3) The USGAO thru the tax code gives corporations special tax breaks from a tax of 35% to an actual tax break of 13 percent. 4) Tax breaks for hedge fund managers costs taxpayers an estimated $83 billion annually. 5) Univ. Of Illinois documents that taxpayers pay about $243 billion each year in indirect subsidies to the fast food industry because taxpayers have to pay$ 243 billion to pay for public benefits for their workers. 6) The home mortgage deduction cost taxpayers $70 billion per year and the CBPP estimates that 77 percent of the benefit goes to homeowners with incomes over $100,000 per year. 7) The bailout of Wall Street was billions of dollars. 8) If banks are involved in criminal activities they can write off a majority of the fine. 9) The Federal Revenue code also has many other tax breaks for the rich and corporations and these are the reasons for thousands of lobbyists. Due to the lowering of the capital gains tax, while maintaining the same tax loopholes, some corporations may not pay any taxes. Some of the subsidies are applicable, hopefully for small businesses, but others for large corporations with money it amounts to greed.

Common Dreams on February 19, 2010, noted that an unpublished report from the United Nations estimated that the biggest corporations cause $2.2 trillion in environmental damage, and if they were held financially accountable, they would lose one-third of their profits (author: Juliette Jowit) (https://www.commondreams.org/news/2010/02/19/worlds-top-firms-cause-22-trillion-environmental-damage-report-estimates).

Later this year, another huge UN study, dubbed the "Stern for nature" after the influential report on the economics of climate change by Sir Nicholas Stern, will attempt to put a price on such global environmental damage and suggest ways to prevent it. The corporations not only get subsides (like Amazon, oil companies, Tyson, etc.), but they also cause pollution and use up natural resources that they don't pay for. For this, we allow the Trump administration to eliminate safety and environmental regulations.

> The report, led by economist Pavan Sukhdev, is likely to argue for abolition of billions of dollars of subsidies to harmful industries like agriculture, energy and transport, tougher regulations and more taxes on companies that cause the damage.

Since we are discussing the rich and corporations, a question to look up on the internet is the number of lies President Trump has told since he has been in office. FactCheck.org (a project of the Annenberg Public Policy Center) published an article by Lori Robertson, November 30, 2017, titled "Trump likely Benefits from Tax Bills" (https://www.factcheck.org/2017/11/trump-likely-benefits-tax-bills/). Some of the benefits are billions of dollars. It would be nice if there were electoral finance reforms where more people from either party with democratic principles could run for office. Maybe we need more people to understand what they are.

Trump, November 29: "This is going to cost me a fortune, this thing, believe me. Believe me—this is not good for me." Look up various articles on the internet to get other information about the Trump family and new pass-through taxes and alternative minimum tax legislation. This is one of the reasons he does not release his tax return information.

In comparison, people in the lower 80 percent get a small reduction in taxes in the 2018 tax bill. The hidden crime in this is that mainstream media does not seem too concerned. They are kept busy by the small Trump daily distractions. What if a newspaper or magazine published information on each congressman or senator, detailing each one's funding and voting record? Also district maps could show locations of party voters to evaluate gerrymandering. This may not make a difference, however, due to the large number of Republican judges in the states and local communities. There has to be continual information about what each member is doing in order to hold them accountable.

Now, wherever we look, we see the erosion of the democracy that our founding fathers envisioned. America now has the largest inequality gap of any country in the world, and with the present administration, this inequality is continuing to grow exponentially. Our political system, especially on the Republican side of the aisle, is being controlled by outside money contributions whose sole purpose is to follow the libertarian doctrine of the radical Right. Greed takes many forms, and we are seeing most of them now. Politics is controlled by corporations and the Koch brothers. The election of Donald Trump is just speeding up the process. The strategy is simple. You make people think that change is needed and then pass out tidbits of information through lies and deceptions. Granted, the Democrats have not helped the cause of justice because they are also mired in their own form of inconsistency and greed. Our last election was a case of voting against rather than voting for. In this book, I am not only noting what problems we are facing as a nation; I am also suggesting solutions. The main solution is to recognize what is happening in our society and not be led by false propaganda. The pathway to a future that has hope is creating a nation that is truly democratic, where all people are recognized as vital components to its success. The following two books discuss how our democracy is being affected.

The first book is *Moyers on Democracy* by Bill Moyers. The book is a compilation of his speeches up to 2008. It describes how democracy was slowly being usurped by the government and corporations up to that time. The book is a lesson in what democracy should be and what we need to know to recognize what is happening. This is a tall order because of the present mood within our nation. The polarization of thought can be reduced only by developing collaboration and understanding how to establish a democracy for all of the people in America. One crime of our present administration is the loss of human resources, which does not allow people to reach their true potential. Any proposed answers are complex and difficult to ascertain, and it will take many different attempts at trying to better our social dilemmas just to get started. The first step is to be informed about what is happening to our democracy and then correcting the policies.

Doing nothing will put our future children at risk socially and environmentally. No wonder we are a nation of anxiety. These are just brief excerpts from the book:

> Our democracy has prospered most when it was firmly anchored in the idea that "We the People"—not just a favored few—would identify and remedy common distempers and dilemma and win the gamble out forebears undertook when they espoused the radical idea that people could govern themselves wisely. (p. 5)[131]

> Here is the real political story, the one most politicians won't even acknowledge: the reality of the anonymous, disquieting daily struggle of ordinary people, including not only the most marginalized and vulnerable Americans but also young workers, elders and parents, families and communities, searching for dignity and fairness against long odds in an amoral market world. (p. 14)[132]

> Those of us in this room and kindred spirits across the nation must confront the most fundamental liberal failure of the current era: the failure to embrace a moral vision of America based on the transient faith that human beings are more than the sum of their material appetites, our country is more than an economic machine, and freedom is not license but responsibility—the gift we have received and the legacy we must bequeath. (p. 21)[133]

The second book I would like to mention should be read in order to understand what is happening in our country and to learn of the dangers it exposes. The author, Nancy MacLean, is an award-winning author and the William H. Chafe Professor of History and Public Policy at Duke University. *Democracy in Chains—The Deep History of the Radical Right's Stealth Plan for America* is extensively researched and fills one with trepidation as to what can occur if something is not done soon to correct what is happing in America. If you do not read the full book, read the conclusion, "Get Ready." Due to copyright restrictions, I can only comment on a few passages from the book, but even these should encourage people to vote and voice their opinions in a movement to bring back our democracy. Otherwise, we will be controlled by money and the Koch brothers advocating the expansion of rights, allowing corporations to expand and control our economy.

> Presently we are a nation that stands at 138th of 172 democracies in the world in voter turnout. Now ALEC (American Legislative Exchange Council) a radical right organization, had legislators introduce 180 bills to restrict who could vote and how. (p. 231)[134]

> Today the big lie of the Koch sponsored radical right is that society can be split between the makers and takers. Mitt Romney remarked at a donor meeting that "47 percent" of voters were, in effect, leeches on "productive " Americans. (p. 211)[135]

> By 2014, only 8 of 278 Republicans were willing to acknowledge that man-made climate change is real. If the Koch-network-funded academics and institutions were not in the conversation, the public would have little doubt that the evidence is overwhelming. Sadly, these campaigns are working and the opinion in America concerning the burning of fossil fuels being man-made and causing climate change dropped from 71 percent in 2007 to 44 percent in 2011. (p. 217)[136]

The Koch brothers and their institutions are affecting judges and courts, education facilities increasing inequality, health systems, decreased unionization (Janus decision) and many other parts of our society. The change that people were wanting is being tilted in the wrong direction and many refuse to acknowledge this regardless of evidence otherwise.

The book also lists some articles on the internet to show what is happening to our rights. Other information noted in the *New York Times* headlined an investigative report on DealBook, October 31, 2015, by Jessica Silver Greenberg and Robert Gebeloff, titled "Arbitration Everywhere, Stacking the Deck of Justice" (https://www.nytimes.com/2015/11/01/business/dealbook/arbitration-everywhere-stacking-the-deck-of-justice.html)

> On Page 5 of a credit card contract used by American Express, beneath an explainer on interest rates and late fees, past the details about annual membership, is a clause that most customers probably miss. If cardholders have a problem with their account, American Express explains, the company "may elect to resolve any claim by individual arbitration." Those nine words are at the center of a far-reaching power play orchestrated by American corporations, an investigation by The New York Times has found. By inserting individual arbitration clauses into a soaring number of consumer and employment contracts, companies like American Express devised a way to circumvent the courts and bar people from joining together in class-action lawsuits, realistically the only tool citizens have to fight illegal or deceitful business practices. Among the class actions thrown out because of the clauses was one brought by Time Warner customers over charges they said mysteriously appeared on their bills and another against a travel booking website accused of conspiring to fix hotel prices.

Remember, in most cases, the courts have ruled in favor of the corporations. This is because courts in the federal, state, and local governments have been filled with conservative judges. The book also lists many other institutions and liberties that have been altered by Koch money, not the least being our present Trump administration. The Koch brothers' philosophy has becomes Trump's philosophy. Thus, where we go from here will determine our future.

America needs a new way of helping people other than what we are doing now. "Make America great again," the slogan of the present administration, is not the answer. Now more than ever, our society needs to prevent what the Trump administration and the Koch brothers are doing to our fragile democracy. Their libertarian beliefs demonstrate that they are intent on establishing their own rules of helping the elites at the expense of other people, especially the poor. Their beliefs that they are entitled to all the benefits that they are accumulating by present political practices. Many times, these practices were allowed to occur by devious means. The radical Right believes that most of the people who obtain benefits are "takers" of the tax money that is collected from the rich. They feel that they are due their money because it is rightfully theirs and they have "earned" it. This is why they do not like any regulations on corporations that prevent them from obtaining more money. Many corporations, especially in the mining and oil industries, pollute the air and water and consume natural resources without paying for them. This also includes passing laws that favor corporation growth, while prohibiting laws helping the people and unions. Their rhetoric of helping all the people rings a little hollow. This is evidenced by an analysis of the 2018 tax bill. There has to be an innovative approach to help people to better themselves with dignity. I try to show several ways of doing this. Unless people lack food and shelter or are in dire circumstances, money should be used to provide job opportunities, especially within their own communities. Sharing and collaborative neighborhoods where neighbors help to fix up communities is just one way to do this. Use of local currencies, establishing their own banking systems, consuming less, farmers' markets, reducing inequities, establishing low-cost vocational educational facilities, and reducing the need to travel long distances to work are just a few ideas. This can then be a start toward creating a democracy for all of the people and not just a few.

Finally, I am writing this book to help all the people described in the book *Squeezed*[137] (SC95) as well as other people in the middle classes and those in poverty who are trying to make a sustainable living in our present economy. She describes how many middle-class families are being squeezed to the point that they are heavily in debt and have many different social problems that they have to confront. In several areas of the United States, earning over $100,000 is not sufficient for living where they are located, due to social and economic circumstances.

There are problems including getting pregnant and losing your job because of it and of being hypereducated. Some people have accumulated large student loan debts that they have a difficult time paying off because they cannot obtain enough income to substantiate what they studied in college. This is especially true of adjunct teachers and people who have obtained degrees from for-profit schools. Other chapters in the book describe outlasted life at the bottom of the top, extreme high costs of day care, immigration families, moonlighting, the second act industry (when older people go back to college for studies that still do not help them), high cost of housing, the rise of 1 percent television, and the introduction of robots. She not only describes problems but also offers solutions.

Some of the solutions could be incorporated into the design of the proposed pilot demonstration project. One example would be day care facilities. Since many of the people in the community will be living or working in the PDP an on-site day care facility is critical to its success. This would reduce transportation costs, and the costs of day care can be reduced by bartering services and certain goods. Older people could earn money by babysitting at the day care facility, in the child's home, or in their home. Several people could work together if necessary to reduce long hours. The pilot demonstration project will have its own work-study, low-cost educational facilities, and this could be offered during the day and with night classes. Attendance costs would not include transportation costs. People should also establish their own values and not be concerned about keeping up with the Joneses. Be yourself and establish your standards of value. Remember, excessive consumption is not the pathway to take.

If you would like additional information or have suggestions to make the project stronger or provide funding, I can be reached at georgehunt200@gmail.com.

An awareness must be developed of the problems we have now and will have in the future. This is not about sitting home but being somewhere and getting the word out using social media in a positive way. The following poem was taken from my previous book, *What Do You See—A Learner's Guide with Poetry*[138] (E49), and is a brief summation of what is happening now.

A Child's Political Primer

The political process is something to behold
Just watching it as it begins to unfold
The many things you have to learn
Is to study politics and try to discern
The rules you need to get ahead
And how to be a leader and not just be led
This process has many a precedent
On the way to becoming a president
You may start by being a mayor
Or even a more active player
Male or female, it does not really matter
As long as your hand is not in the platter
The first thing you have to learn
Is what you give and what you get
So that you become all the more set
To serve the people, you know, the one percent
But don't say this is what you meant
The "American People" is the best phrase
To allow you to get the most praise
The second thing you have to learn
Is that you say one thing and yet do another
And give jobs to your brother
The third thing you have to learn
Is the study of hypocrisy
This may take all the time you are there
Or it may come without any great despair
This is the study of being insincere
By telling people what they always want to hear
Education is not a prerequisite for a hypocrite
Because you learn it bit by bit
For there isn't any difference from where I stand
Because all good works seem to have a brand
This is done in order to stay
Serving the people every other day
And the perks increase bit by bit
The longer that you can sit In the chamber where you meet
And hope you will not suffer defeat
All of this one may learn
As to how you can return
The art of being a hypocrite does not come automatically
Until you have learned political practicality
If you are new at the game

Others may treat you with disdain
Earmarks you will try to kill
But put it in another bill
Hypocrisy is but a hidden pretense
To promote programs that do not make sense
Or to insist that your agenda is right
And that the budget is oh so tight
While all along it doesn't do, what the people wanted it to
The corporations are represented
Because they are being presented
As people like you and I
See this and only sigh
That some day politicians may be
Just people like you and me
The fourth thing you have to learn
Is stand on principal and not compromise
Because anything else would not be wise
Even though the principal is weak
And there won't be allowed even a tweak
You make it appear that you are strong
And that the other party's wrong
For the party you know is the principal thing
If one votes the other way, against the party line
They might be in trouble in a short period of time
The fifth thing you have to learn
Is the ability to talk and not say a thing
For no amount of reckoning this could bring
An analysis of problems are a concern
That is something you don't have to learn
Practicing sound bites is quite a chore indeed
How else then can one hope to succeed?
All this learning is costly you know
Money must be spent campaigning in the snow
So the people's business takes the back seat
In order that you are the one that they keep
All this learning is an art and a special thing
So no telling then what tomorrow will bring.

—George Hunt from the book *What Do You See*

AFTERWORD

With the Trump administration in office, it is difficult to write a book with current information. It seems we are continually in a downhill crisis. At this time, the end of August 2018, the Manafort and Cohen situations have ended in convictions, we have tariff problems to work out, the Russian investigation is still awaiting a conclusion, and we face a host of other problems. Pruitt has been fired and replaced by Anthony R. Wheeler, who was a former coal industry lobbyist, and he is continuing with the same destructive environmental policies. Now Hurricane Lane is hitting Hawaii, and there are early wildfires in the west, along with Hurricane Florence hitting the Carolinas. The water temperature in the ocean by San Diego is 9. 5°F higher than normal. This is warm enough that a hurricane could come this far north. These global warming conditions are accelerating exponentially each year, yet the federal government is doing nothing about it. In fact, the Sierra Club and other organizations are continually suing the government because of the executive orders that are reducing pollution restrictions of the coal processing and for allowing mining and oil drilling in our national parks and monuments.

To understand how this has been an ongoing problem for many years, two books by Bill McKibben, one of the nation's leading environmentalists, should be read. They are *Eaarth* (E54)[139] and *Deep Economy* (E55).[140] The books are exceptionally well written and explain the consequences of what is happening on the earth from a social and environmental aspect. It also offers many solutions. Until we as a society recognize that our greed, social inequities, political ineptitudes, and misunderstandings are causing problems, our grandchildren will become victims of a totally different world. If you aren't convinced by this book, then those two books should be read as soon as possible. As a nation, we are hurting not only ourselves but other nations as well. Examples of this are noted in *Deep Economy,* with special emphasis on how big agribusiness is enriching the rich and hurting small farmers and other countries. This is further helped by giving the largest share of subsidies to these large agribusinesses so they can underprice their products and destroy small farmers throughout the world. The chemicals they are selling cause fatal diseases and ruin lives. The Trump administration is allowing this to continue under the guise of simplifying regulations that affect our environment, health, and safety. Until political reforms are made in political spending, continuation of gerrymandering districts in the states, corruption practices, and excessive entitlements for the rich, there is little hope for change for the better.

Unless we recognize the problems of how we are creating unmanageable climate change, rapid soil deterioration, and other environmental and social problems, we will continue in the path of our past history that led to the destruction of civilizations. We are living in complex civilizations that frustrate basic human needs.[141] The key word here is complex. We need to simplify our lives, beginning with helping and sharing with one another. Hopefully we can recognize what we are doing in time to prevent the possible consequences. The greed that we are displaying now can be a death wish for those people who will be living in the future. Knowing this and not doing anything about it will then become our legacy.

Now that I have proposed the establishment of the pilot demonstration project, the question becomes, "What is next?" First, we need to obtain suggested solutions from everyone out there who wants to see change. We need to get rid of labels such as liberal, conservative, and and socialism because labels limit the abilities of people or parties to accept or agree to compromises. In most cases innovators do not use specific labels because doing so allows them more freedom to evaluate the different options of any problem. We also should think of how to start or attach to a movement in the direction of preserving the earth and our society. A book that may help is *Contagious* (SC96)[142] by Jonah Berger. As a Wharton professor, he's studied how ideas spread, what drives word of mouth, why online content goes viral, and how social influence shapes everything from the cars we buy to the names we give our children. He uses six basic principles to drive all sorts of things to become contagious.

If I get a positive response to what is presented in this book, I will attempt to obtain funding and select a team to work with to find a site and begin the design process. This entire process will be documented to be used for educational purposes. In conjunction with the site design, an economic and market study will be presented for funders. Hopefully we can get to this stage in the near future. I also hope to obtain ideas from many of the authors I have mentioned. As they say in the design professions, "It is time to get an idea on the ground."

APPENDIX—SLIDESHOW

This is a graphic presentation for the Pilot Demonstrating Project and is used to explain project options.

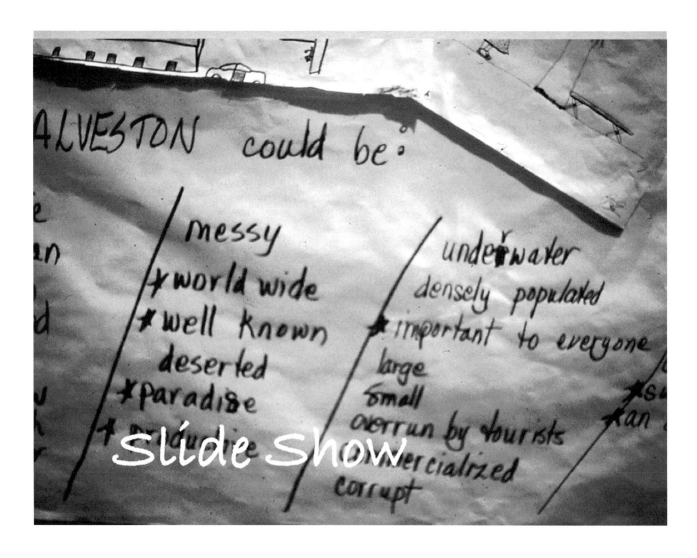

What are Sustainable Communities?

The term "**sustainable communities**" has various definitions, but in essence refers to **communities** planned, built, or modified to promote **sustainable living**. **Sustainable communities** tend to focus on environmental and economic **sustainability**, urban infrastructure, social equity, and municipal government.

Sharing

The uses shown on the plan are discussed in detail in the book and they will be just listed here. The number of housing units will vary because some of the triplex and student housing buildings could be used for other than just housing uses.

Housing Units:

- ○ Duplex - D
- ○ Triplex - T1
- ○ Triplex - T2
- ○ Triplex - T3
- ○ Student Housing - SH
- ○ Staff or Homeless Housing - S-H
- ○ Student Housing or Elderly - SH-E

Other Uses:

- ○ Retail - R
- ○ Restaurant - R2
- ○ Bank - B
- ○ Medical Clinic - M
- ○ IT and Study Center - IT
- ○ Administration & Library - A-R
- ○ Parking - P
- ○ Training Building - Agriculture - TCA
- ○ Training Building - Construction - TCC
- ○ Greenhouses - GH
- ○ Storage & Maintenance - SM
- ○ Farmers & Flea Market - FM
- ○ Regenerative Farming Research - RF
- ○ Agriculture Research & Production - AG
- ○ Community Building - CB
- ○ Community Park - CP

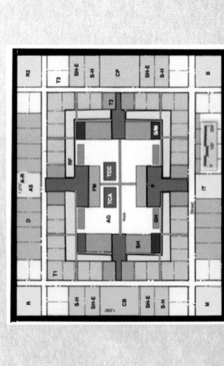

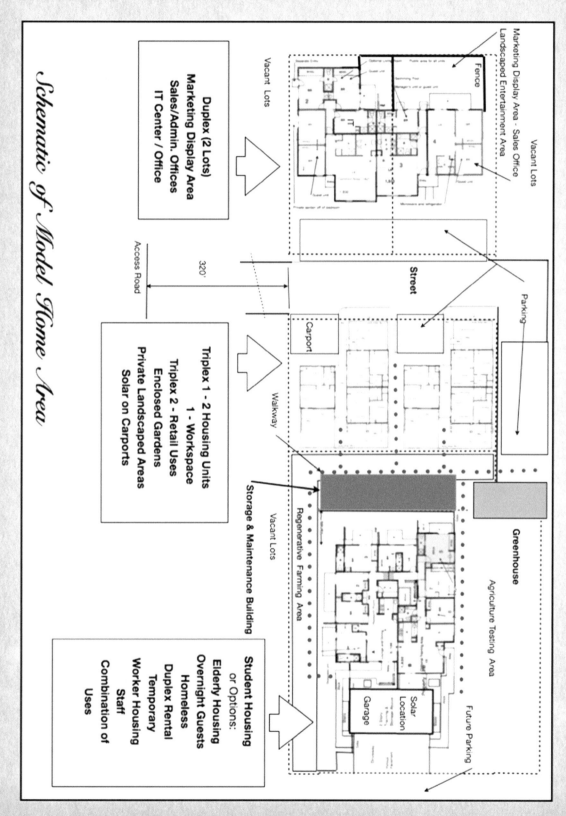

Schematic of Model Home Area

Duplex (2 Lots)
Marketing Display Area
Sales/Admin. Offices
IT Center / Office

Marketing Display Area - Sales Office
Landscaped Entertainment Area

Vacant Lots

Vacant Lots

Fence

Street

320'

Access Road

Parking

Carport

Walkway

Triplex 1 - 2 Housing Units
1 - Workspace
Triplex 2 - Retail Uses
Enclosed Gardens
Private Landscaped Areas
Solar on Carports

Vacant Lots

Regenerative Farming Area

Storage & Maintenance Building

Greenhouse

Agriculture Testing Area

Garage

Solar Location

Future Parking

Student Housing
or Options:
Elderly Housing
Overnight Guests
Homeless
Duplex Rental
Temporary
Worker Housing
Staff
Combination of
Uses

3

GOAL 1: A SUSTAINABLE COMMUNITY

In developing a sustainable community it is better to make it be as self-sufficient as possible. This is especially true as we are going into a transitioning society when there will be drastic changes caused by our using up of our natural resources. This slide program will not go into these details, but just show what potentially can be done from a design standpoint. My book points out all of the social ramifications during this time going into the future. For now it is unknown if we will completely reduce capitalism as we know it now.

On page 15 is a schematic plan that was an example for a project on an island in the Caribbean. This plan has most of the components in it to make it almost self-sufficient. It has within it a community similar to what is shown on page 10 of this slide program and in my book. It is the area labeled for a self-sufficient community.

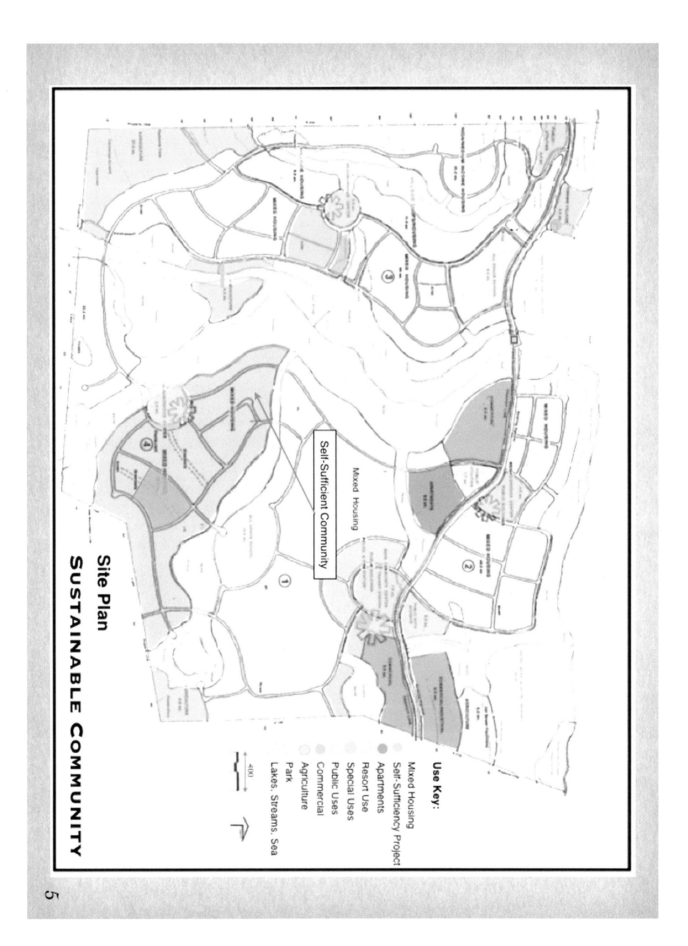

Site Plan
SUSTAINABLE COMMUNITY

Self-Sufficient Community

Mixed Housing

Use Key:
Mixed Housing
Self-Sufficiency Project
Apartments
Resort Use
Special Uses
Public Uses
Commercial
Agriculture
Park
Lakes, Streams, Sea

400

5

- 225 -

TRIPLEX

Number 1 is the typical triplex unit with each unit being about 500 sf in area. The pink shows how A & C units could be made larger during the design stage. A unit could just have the bath room and the area could be used as work space, office, play room, artist's studio, business etc. Figure 3 shows it as a community a community room in an enlarged unit. Also removing part of a wall in units B & C can make it a single family. Figure 2 shows how two units can become one unit. These units are the larger units.

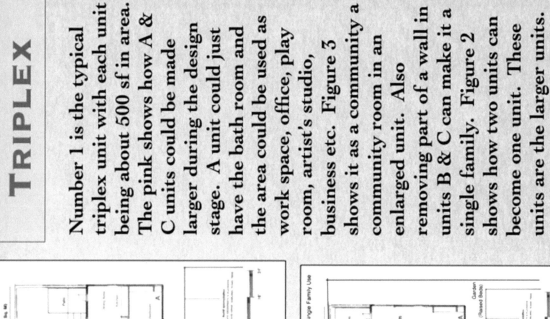

USE OF ADD-ON UNITS

The add-on building concept is used to easily add an addition on to an existing structure. This is shown as an option prior to the sale of a house.

Use of Add-On units for Ownership or Rental Housing

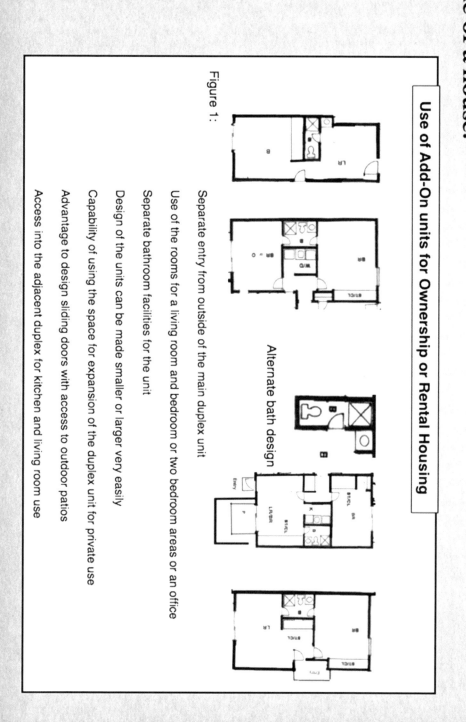

Alternate bath design

Figure 1:

Separate entry from outside of the main duplex unit

Use of the rooms for a living room and bedroom or two bedroom areas or an office

Separate bathroom facilities for the unit

Design of the units can be made smaller or larger very easily

Capability of using the space for expansion of the duplex unit for private use

Advantage to design sliding doors with access to outdoor patios

Access into the adjacent duplex for kitchen and living room use

Building 9 is a building that could be used for student housing, elderly or the homeless. Bedrooms 2, 5, and 6 cold be add on units. The green units would be for managers or staff. The white area is a common area for bedrooms 3, 4, 5 and 6. Bedroom 7 could also be a guest room if not needed by the manager or an office.

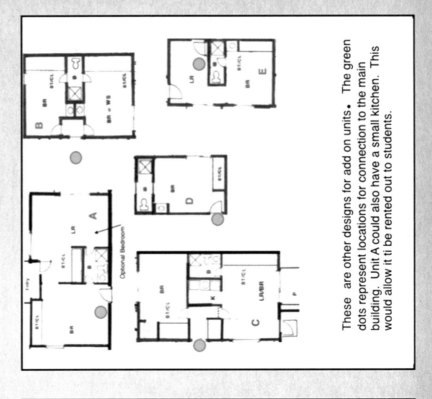

These are other designs for add on units. The green dots represent locations for connection to the main building. Unit A could also have a small kitchen. This would allow it ti be rented out to students.

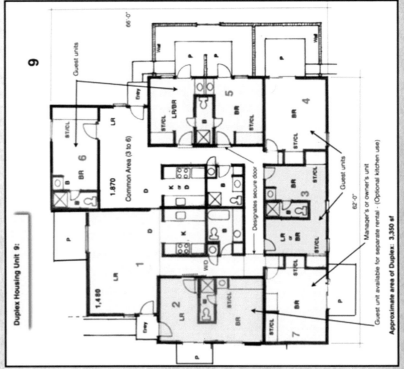

Duplex Housing Unit 9:

Approximate area of Duplex: 3,350 sf

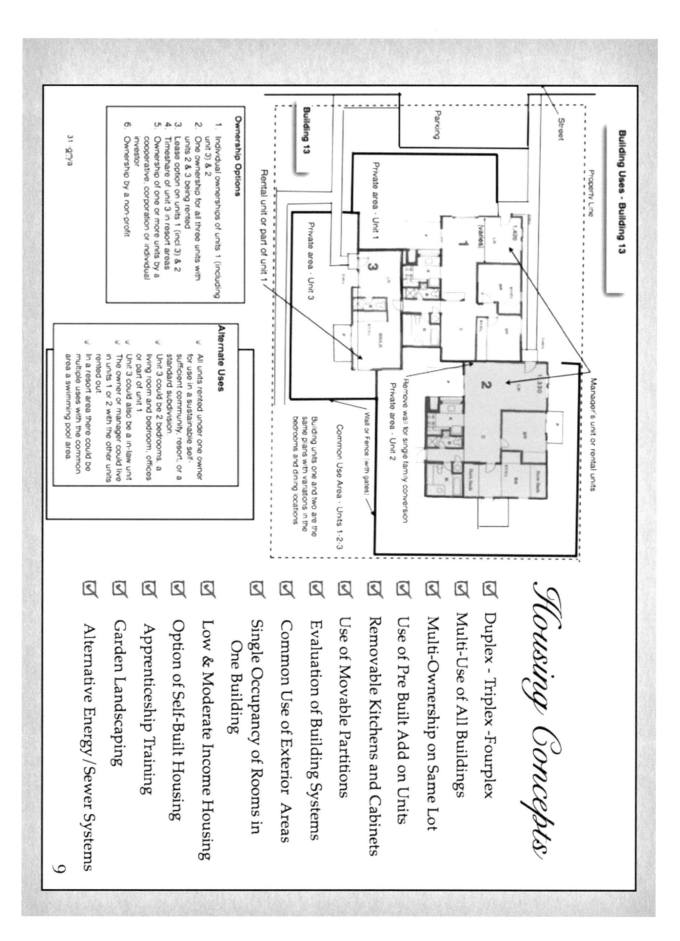

Property Line

Street

Parking

Building 13

Private area - Unit 1

Private area - Unit 3

Rental unit or part of unit 1

Manager's unit or rental units

Remove wall for single family conversion

Private area - Unit 2

Wall or Fence (with gates)

Common Use Area - Units 1-2-3

Building units one and two are the same plans with variations in the bedrooms and dining locations

Ownership Options

1. Individual ownerships of units 1 (including unit 3) & 2
2. One ownership for all three units with units 2 & 3 being rented
3. Lease option on units 1 (incl 3) & 2
4. Timeshare of unit 3 in resort areas
5. Ownership of one or more units by a cooperative, corporation or individual investor
6. Ownership by a non-profit

31 פרק

Alternate Uses

☑ All units rented under one owner for use in a sustainable self-sufficient community, resort, or a standard subdivision.

☑ Unit 3 could be 2 bedrooms.

☑ Unit 3 could be 2 bedrooms, a living room and bedroom, offices or part of unit 1.

☑ Unit 3 could also be a in-law unit

☑ The owner or manager could live in units 1 or 2 with the other units rented out.

☑ In a resort area there could be multiple uses with the common area a swimming pool area.

Housing Concepts

☑ Duplex - Triplex - Fourplex

☑ Multi-Use of All Buildings

☑ Multi-Ownership on Same Lot

☑ Use of Pre Built Add on Units

☑ Removable Kitchens and Cabinets

☑ Common Use of Exterior Areas

☑ Use of Movable Partitions

☑ Evaluation of Building Systems

☑ Single Occupancy of Rooms in One Building

☑ Low & Moderate Income Housing

☑ Option of Self-Built Housing

☑ Apprenticeship Training

☑ Garden Landscaping

☑ Alternative Energy / Sewer Systems

9

The add-on unit in this plan is shown in green. It adds two bedrooms or a bedroom and a small living room. It can be part of the original design or be added at a later date. The slab, footing, plumbing and electrical would be constructed originally when the house was built. It would be covered with tile or other material like outdoor carpet. The house would be designed originally for this addition so the roof would match. It can be used for now as an outdoor patio. The add on also has an exit door in case it was used for rental or in-laws/guests. The kitchen in blue would be removed for conversion to single family. Other conversions are noted.

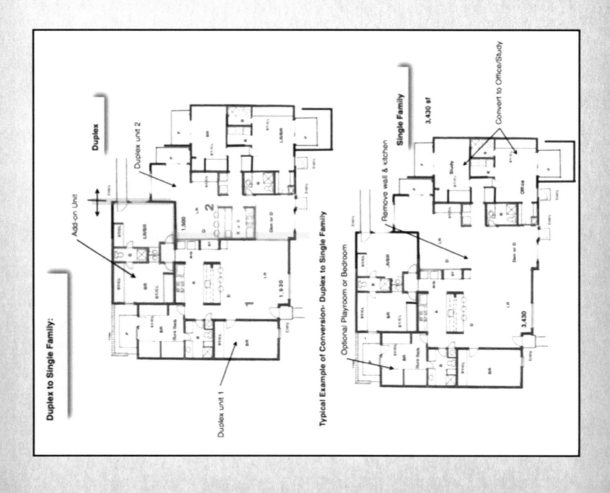

Buildings 3 and 5 represent two other building designs that could be adapted for student housing, elderly and the homeless. Unit 4 in building 3 could be used as a study area or other work function such as a studio. The interior walls could be deleted and it would open it up as a multi purpose room. Several add-on units are located in both buildings.

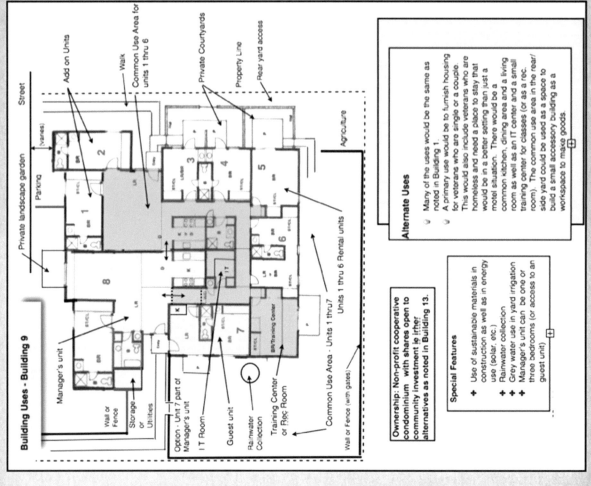

Building 9 is a large duplex which could easily be a single family. The red area could be suitable also for student housing or a separate business as an elderly home. Room 7 can be an add-on as well as the yellow rooms in the building below. This building also is changeable from a duplex to a single family dwelling. There are also options for different types of ownership on one lot.

Alternate Uses

- Many of the uses would be the same as noted in Building 1.
- A primary use would be to furnish housing for veterans who are single or a couple. This would also include veterans who are homeless and need a place to stay that would be in a better setting than just a motel situation. There would be a common kitchen, dining area and a living room as well as an IT center and a small training center for classes (or as a rec. room). The common use area in the rear/side yard could be used as a space to build a small accessory building as a workspace to make goods.

Special Features

- Use of sustainable materials in construction as well as in energy use (solar, etc.)
- Rainwater collection
- Grey water use in yard irrigation
- Manager's unit can be one or three bedrooms (or access to an guest unit)

Ownership: Non-profit cooperative condominium with shares open to community investment ie if/ther alternatives as noted in Building 13.

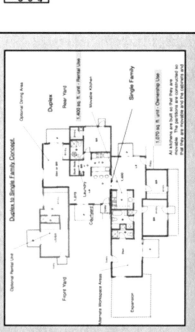

Building Uses - Building 1:

Note:

The manager's unit could also be used as a teaching center and the two bedrooms could be smaller classrooms. This could be done to expand the number of class topics.

The number of land uses could change according to the occupancy and uses of some of the triplex units.

Land Uses:

D - 8 Buildings - 16 units
T1 - 32 Buildings - 96 units
T2 - 8 Buildings - 24 units
T3 - 16 Buildings - Mixed Uses Housing or Businesses
SH - 4 Buildings - 24 to 40 Students

Maximum Number of Housing or Student Units - 190

Density: 6.4 units per acre

Model homes will be constructed first for pre-sales

Student Housing and Medical Housing

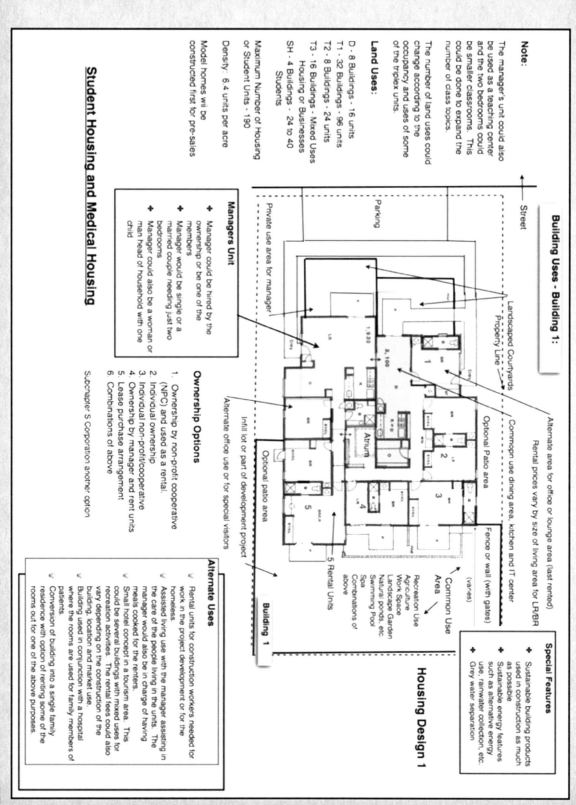

Street

Parking

Private use area for manager

Managers Unit

+ Manager could be hired by the ownership or be one of the members
+ Manager would be single or a married couple needing just two bedrooms
+ Manager could also be a woman or man head of household with one child

Alternate office use or for special visitors

Ownership Options

1. Ownership by non-profit cooperative (NPC) and used as a rental.
2. Individual ownership
3. Individual non-profit/cooperative
4. Ownership by manager and rent units
5. Lease purchase arrangement
6. Combinations of above

Alternate for office or lounge area (last rented)

Rental prices vary by size of living area for LR/BR

Landscaped Courtyards
Property Line

Common use dining area, kitchen and IT center

Optional Patio area

1,939

2,100

Atrium

Optional patio area

5 Rental Units

Building 1

Fence or wall (with gates)
(varies)

Common Use Area

Recreation Use
Agriculture
Work Space
Landscape Garden
Natural ponds, etc.
Swimming Pool
Spa
Combinations of above

Alternate Uses

w Rental units for construction workers needed for work in the project development or for the homeless.

w Assisted living use with the manager assisting in the care of the people living in the units. The manager would also be in charge of having meals cooked for the renters.

w Small hotel concept in a tourism area. This could be several buildings with mixed uses for recreation activities. The rental fees could also vary depending on the construction of the building, location and market use.

w Building used in conjunction with a hospital where the rooms are used for family members of patients.

w Conversion of building into a single family residence with option of renting some of the rooms out for one of the above purposes.

Subchapter S Corporation another option

Special Features

+ Sustainable building products used in construction as much as possible
+ Sustainable energy features such as alternative energy use, rainwater collection, etc.
+ Grey water separation

Housing Design 1

13

HURRICANE VILLAS

This building was designed to be as sustainable as possible from an architectural and landscape standpoint. It is powered by a separate solar or wind turbine located in the area of the red dot. The lower part of the door can be sealed against water coming into the unit. It also has an organic garden for food.

This is a villa that was designed for buildings in hurricane zones. Its shape is resistant to wind and does not have a roof overhang. The foundation is 3' high above ground level and on an area surrounded with walls, so it can be set up 5' to 8' high above sea level.

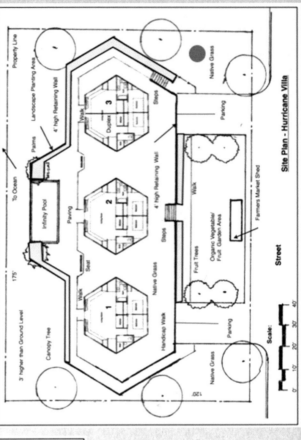

Site Plan - Hurricane Villa

Residence - Villa

EDUCATION BUILDING

The building is designed as a teaching center. It can have two or four rooms depending if the collapsable walls are used. There is space available for storage, computer equipment or closets. The wall in the center is a space for video screens. It can have two classrooms and two living quarters or any combination. Instructors or students could also stay there if they were guest speakers.

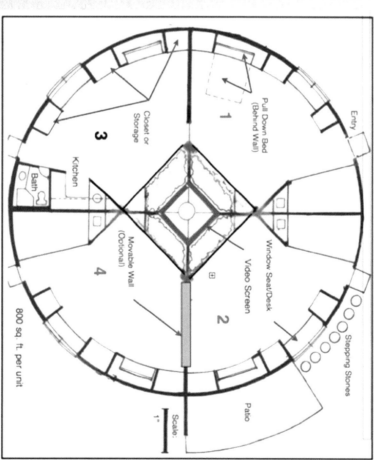

Entry

Pull Down Bed
(Behind Wall)

1

Closet or
Storage

3

Kitchen

Bath

Window Seat/Desk

Video Screen

Movable Wall
(Optional)

4

2

Stepping Stones

Patio

800 sq. ft. per unit

Scale:

1"

TINY HOME PLANNING

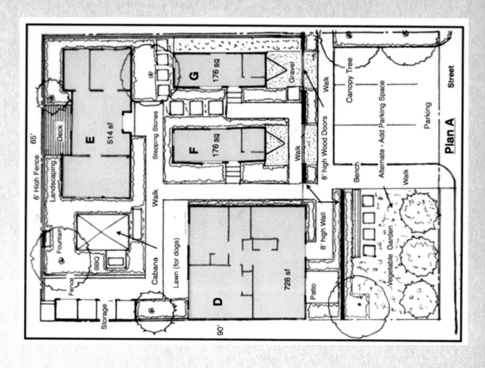

Plan A

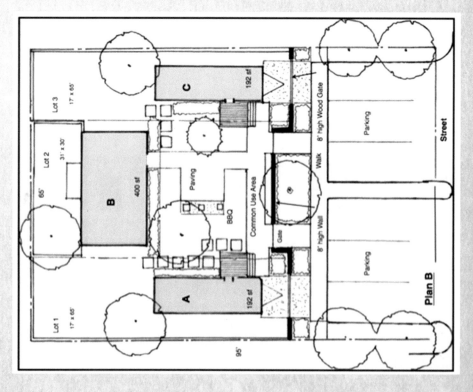

Plan B

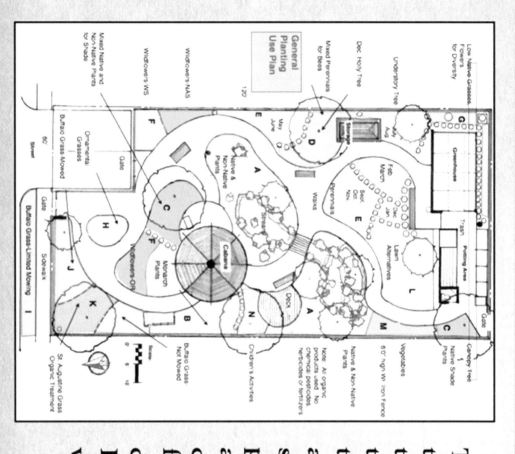

Triplex lots will be one of the proposed housing and this is one of the concepts that can be use in place of a triplex. It is demonstration and educational garden showing native landscape plants, a water feature and areas for vegetables. It also can be used for social functions and a learning center for school students. It is an example of the versatility of the project.

17

SUMMARY

"For Our Future - Which One?"

ENDNOTES

1 Dambisa Moyo, *Edge of Chaos - Why Democracy is Failing to Deliver Economic Growth and How to Fix it.* (London, Great Britain: Little, Brown, 2018)

2 Carey Gilliam, *Whitewash* (Island Press, 2017).

3 Manual, Univ. of Arkansas Architecture Department UADC, *LID—Low Impact Development* (Fayetteville, Arkansas: University of Arkansas Press, 2019).

4 Manual, Univ. of Arkansas Architecture Department UADC, *LID—Low Impact Development* (Fayetteville, Arkansas: University of Arkansas Press, 2019).

5 Toby Hemenway, *The Permaculture City* (White River Junction, Vermont: Chelsea Green, 2015).

6 Sarah Williams Goldhagen. *Welcome to Your World—How the Built Environment Shapes our Lives* (New York, New York: HarperCollins, 2017),292.

7 Worldwatch Institute, *EarthEd—Rethinking Education on a Changing Planet* (Washington, DC: Island Press, 2017.)

8 Mark Shepard, *Restoration Agriculture—Real World Permaculture for Farmers* (Austin, Texas: Acres U.S.A, 2013).

9 William Vitek and Wes Jackson (editors), *Rooted in the Land—Essays on Community and Place* (Berkeley, California: Counterpoint, 1996).

10 Ben Hartman, *The Lean Farm—How to Minimize Waste and Increase Efficiency* (White River Junction, Vermont: Chelsea Green, 2015).

11 Jelleke de Nooy van Tol, *Transition to an Agro-Ecology—For a Food Secured World* (Bloomington, Indiana: AuthorHouse UK, 2016).

12 Maya Shetreat-Klein, MD, *The Dirt Cure—Growing Healthy Kids with Food Straight from the Soil* (New York, NY: Atria Paperback-Simon & Schuster, 2016).

13 Mike Adams, *Food Forensics—The Living Toxins Living in Your Food and How You Can Avoid Them* (Dallas, Texas: Ben Bella Books Inc., 2016).

14 Larry Olmsted, *Real Food—Fake Food—Why You Don't Know What You Are Eating* (Chapel Hill, North Carolina: Algonquin Books of Chapel Hill, 2016).

15 Bruce Katz and Jeremy Novak, *The New Localism—How Cities Can Thrive in an Age of Populism* (Washington, DC: The Brookings Institute, 2018).

16 Dr. Charles Hall and Kent A. Klitgaard, *Energy and the Wealth of Nations* (Springer, New York: Springer Science + Business Media LLC2012, 2018).

17 Dmitry Orlov, *Shrinking the Technosphere—Getting a Grip on the Technologies That Limit Our Autonomy* (government of Canada, 2016), 116.

18 Dmitry Orlov, *Shrinking the Technosphere—Getting a Grip on the Technologies That Limit Our Autonomy* (government of Canada, 2016), 120.

19 Dmitry Orlov, *Shrinking the Technosphere—Getting a Grip on the Technologies That Limit Our Autonomy* (government of Canada, 2016), 124–125.

20 Steven Levitsky and Daniel Ziblatt, *How Democracies Die* (New York, New York: Crown-Penguin Random House, 2018).

21 Steven Levitsky and Daniel Ziblatt, *How Democracies Die* (New York, New York: Crown-Penguin Random House, 2018), 231.

22 Charles Hugh Smith, The *Nearly Free University and the Emerging Economy* (Berkeley, California: Oftwominds. com, 2013), 15.

23 Charles Hugh Smith, The *Nearly Free University and the Emerging Economy* (Berkeley, California: Oftwominds. com, 2013), 21–23.

24 Charles Hugh Smith, The *Nearly Free University and the Emerging Economy* (Berkeley, California: Oftwominds. com, 2013), 72.

25 David Peter Stroh, *Systems Thinking for Social Change—Guide to Solve Complex Problems* (White River Junction Vermont: Chelsea Green, 2015), 21–22.

26 David Peter Stroh, *Systems Thinking for Social Change—Guide to Solve Complex Problems* (White River Junction Vermont: Chelsea Green, 2015), 206–207.

27 Richard Arum and Josipa Roksa, *Academically Adrift: Limited Learning on College Campuses* (Chicago, Illinois: Chicago University Press, 2010–2011).

28 Worldwatch Institute, *EarthEd—Rethinking Education on a Changing Planet* (Washington, DC: Island Press, 2017).

29 David Caplan, *The Case Against Education—Why the Education System Is a Waste of Time and Money* (Princeton, New Jersey: Princeton University Press, 2018) 215.

30 David Caplan, *The Case Against Education—Why the Education System Is a Waste of Time and Money* (Princeton, New Jersey: Princeton University Press, 2018), 255.

31 David Caplan, *The Case Against Education—Why the Education System Is a Waste of Time and Money* (Princeton, New Jersey: Princeton University Press, 2018), 255.

32 David Caplan, *The Case Against Education—Why the Education System Is a Waste of Time and Money* (Princeton, New Jersey: Princeton University Press, 2018), 255.

33 David Caplan, *The Case Against Education—Why the Education System Is a Waste of Time and Money* (Princeton, New Jersey: Princeton University Press, 2018), 255.

34 Mark Anielski, *The Economics of HappineSS—Building Genuine Wealth* (Gabriola Island, BC, Canada: New Society Publishers, 2007).

35 Jean M. Twenge, *Generation Me—Why Today's Young Americans Are More Confident, Assertive, and More Miserable* (New York, NY: Atria Books).

36 Johann Hari, *Lost Connections—Uncovering the Real Cause of Depression* (New. York, New York: Bloomsbury Publishing Plc., 2018), 64.

37 Joshua Becker, *The More of Less—Finding the Life You Want Under Everything You Own* (Colorado Springs, Colorado: WaterBook Press, 2016), 47.

38 Joshua Becker, *The More of Less—Finding the Life You Want Under Everything You Own* (Colorado Springs, Colorado: WaterBook Press, 2016), 58–61.

39 Eduardo Porter, *The Price of Everything—Solving the Mystery of Why We Pay What We Do* (New York, New York: Penguin Group, 2011), 3–4.

40 Eduardo Porter, *The Price of Everything—Solving the Mystery of Why We Pay What We Do* (New York, New York: Penguin Group, 2011), 64.

41 Thomas H. Grecco Jr. and Karen Kearney, *Money—Understanding and Creating Alternatives to Legal Tender* (White River Junction, VT: Chelsea Green, 2001), 13.

42 Thomas H. Grecco Jr., *The End of Money and the Future of Civilization* (White River Junction, Vermont: Chelsea Green, 2009), 230.

43 Gwendolyn Hallsmith and Lietaer, *Creating Wealth—Growing Local Economics with Local Currencies* (Gabriola Island, BC, Canada: New Society Publishers, 2011).

44 William Ophuls, *Immoderate Greatness—Why Civilizations Fail (*North Charleston, South Carolina: Create Space Independent Publishing, 2012).

45 Mariana Mazzucato, *The Value of Everything—Making and Taking in the Global Economy* (United Kingdom: Allen Lane-Penguin, 2018), back cover.

46 Ashly Dawson, *Extreme Cities—The Peril and Promise of Urban Life in the Age of Climate Change* (London, England: Verso Books, 2017).

47 Naomi Klein, *This Changes Everything, Capitalism vs. the Climate* (New York, New York: Simon and Schuster, 2014).

48 Donella H. Meadows and Jorden Randers, *Limits to Growth—30-Year Adjustment* (White River Junction, Vermont: Chelsea Green, 2004), 144.

49 Dmitry Orlov, *Shrinking the Technosphere—Getting a Grip on the Technologies That Limit Our Autonomy* (government of Canada, 2006).

50 William Ophuls, *Immoderate Greatness—Why Civilizations* Fail (North Charleston, South Carolina: Create Space Independent Publishing, 2012).

51 Mathis Wackernagel and William Rees, *Our Ecological Footprint—Reducing Human Impact on the Earth* (Gabriola Island, BC, Canada: New Society Publishers, 1998).

52 Peter Frase, *Four Futures—Life After Capitalism* (Verso Books and Jacobin Magazine, 2016).

53 Daniel Lerch and Sarah Byrnes, editors, *The Community Resilience Reader—Essential Resources for an Era of Upheaval* (Washington, DC: Island Press, 2017), 262.

54 Daniel Lerch and Sarah Byrnes, editors, *The Community Resilience Reader—Essential Resources for an Era of Upheaval* (Washington, DC: Island Press, 2017), 264.

55 Lisa Gansky, *The Mesh—Why the Future of Business Is Sharing* (New York, New York: Penguin Portfolio, 2010).

56 Rachel Botsman and Rogers, *What's Mine is Yours—The Rise of Collaborative Consumption* (New York, New York: HarperCollins, 2010).

57 John Perkins, *The New Confessions of an Economic Hit Man* (Oakland, California: Berrett-Koehler Publishers, 2016).

58 Eben Fodor, *Better Not Bigger—How to Take Care of Urban Growth* (Gabriola Island, BC, Canada: New Society Publishers, 2007), 8.

59 Eben Fodor, *Better Not Bigger—How to Take Care of Urban Growth* (Gabriola Island, BC, Canada: New Society Publishers, 2007), 9.

60 E. F. Schumacher, *Small Is Beautiful—Economics as if People Mattered* (New York, New York: HarperCollins, 2010), 178.

61 Toby Hemenway, *The Permaculture City* (White River Junction, Vermont: Chelsea Green, 2015), ix–x.

62 Boyd Cohen, *Post-Capitalist Entrepreneurship—Startups for the 99%* (Boca Raton, Florida: CRC Press, 2017).

63 Gwendolyn Hallsmith, *The Key to Sustainable Cities—Meeting Human Needs, Transforming Community Systems* (Gabriola Island, BC, Canada: New Society Publishers, 2003).

64 Gwendolyn Hallsmith, *The Key to Sustainable Cities—Meeting Human Needs, Transforming Community Systems* (Gabriola Island, BC, Canada: New Society Publishers, 2003), back cover.

65 Naomi Klein, *No Logo* (New York, New York: St. Martin's Press, 2009).

66 Ken Aulettta, *Frenemies: The Epic Disruption of the Ad Business (and Everything Else)* (New York, New York: Penguin Books, 2018), 184–185.

67 Marshall McLuhan and Lewis H. Lapham, *Understanding Media—The Extensions of Man* (Cambridge, Massachusetts: MIT Press, 1964–1994), 194.

68 Marshall McLuhan and Lewis H. Lapham, *Understanding Media—The Extensions of Man* (Cambridge, Massachusetts: MIT Press, 1964–1994), 202.

69 Marshall McLuhan, *The Mechanical Bride: Folklore of Industrial Man* (Berkeley, California: Gingko Press, 1951–2008), xi.

70 Arturo Escobar, *Designs for the Pluriverse* (Durham North Carolina: Duke University Press, 2018).

71 Enzio Manzini, *Design, When Everybody Designs—An Introduction to Design for Social Innovation* (Cambridge, Massachusetts: MIT Press, 2015).

72 Arturo Escobar, *Designs for the Pluriverse* (Durham North Carolina: Duke University Press, 2018), 184–185.

73 Enzio Manzini, *Design, When Everybody Designs—An Introduction to Design for Social Innovation* (Cambridge, Massachusetts: MIT Press, 2015), 31.

74 Enzio Manzini, *Design, When Everybody Designs—An Introduction to Design for Social Innovation* (Cambridge, Massachusetts: MIT Press, 2015), 35.

75 Enzio Manzini, *Design, When Everybody Designs—An Introduction to Design for Social Innovation* (Cambridge, Massachusetts: MIT Press, 2015), 192.

76 Richard Wolff, *Democracy at Work—A Cure for Capitalism* (Chicago, Illinois: Haymarket Books, 2012).

77 Charles Hugh Smith, *Money and Work Unchanged* (Berkeley, California: Oftwominds.com, 2017), 2.

78 John Perkins, *The New Confessions of an Economic Hit Man* (Oakland, California: Berrett-Koehler Publishers, 2016), 291.

79 Edward O. Wilson, *The Meaning of Human Existence* (New York, New York: Liveright Publishing, 2015), 150–151.

80 Jane Meyer, *Dark Money—Billionaires Behind the Radical Right* (New York, New York: Penguin Random House, 2017), xxii.

81 David Kay Johnston, *It's Even Worse Than You Think—What the Trump Administration Is Doing to America* (New York, New York: Simon and Schuster, 2018).

82 Charles Hugh Smith, *Get a Job, Build a Real Career, and Defy Bewildering Economy* (Berkley, California: Oftwominds.com, 2014), 24.

83 Charles Hugh Smith, *Why Our Status Quo Failed and Is Beyond Reform* (Berkeley, California: Oftwominds.com, 2016), 3, 24.

84 Charles Hugh Smith, *Why Our Status Quo Failed and Is Beyond Reform* (Berkeley, California: Oftwominds.com, 2016), 5, 24.

85 Charles Hugh Smith, *Why Our Status Quo Failed and Is Beyond Reform* (Berkeley, California: Oftwominds.com, 2016), 4, 79.

86 Stephen Schmidheiny and BCSD, *Changing Course: A Global Business Perspective on Development and the Environment* (Cambridge, Massachusetts: MIT Press, 1992), 84.

87 Peter Wohlleben, *The Hidden Life of Trees—What They Feel, How They Communicate* (Berkeley, California: Greystone Books, 2015), foreword.

88 Paul Mason, *Post Capitalism—A Guide to Our Future* (New York, New York: Farrar, Straus and Giroux (Penguin), 2017), xii.

89 Paul Mason, *Post Capitalism—A Guide to Our Future* (New York, New York: Farrar, Straus and Giroux (Penguin), 2017), 143.

90 Paul Harkin (editor), *Drawdown—The Most Comprehensive Plan Ever Proposed to Reduce Global Warming* (New York, New York: Penguin-Random House, 2017).

91 Eben Fodor, *Better Not Bigger—How to Take Care of Urban Growth* (Gabriola Island, BC, Canada: New Society Publishers, 2007), 9.

92 Eben Fodor, *Better Not Bigger—How to Take Care of Urban Growth* (Gabriola Island, BC, Canada: New Society Publishers, 2007), 131.

93 David Peter Stroh, *Systems Thinking for Social Change—Guide to Solve Complex Problem* (White River Junction, Vermont: Chelsea Green, 2015), 32.

94 Janine M. Benyus, *Biomimicry—Innovation Inspired by Nature* (New York, New York: William Morrow and Company-Quill, 1997), 288.

95 Rita Taylor, *Mountain Fragrance—Journeys and Encounters in Korea* (Green Review Publishing Co., 2009), 1.

96 Rita Taylor, *Mountain Fragrance—Journeys and Encounters in Korea* (Green Review Publishing Co., 2009), 89.

97 Kristin Ohlson, *The Soil Will Save Us: How Scientists, Farmers, and Foodies Are Healing the Soil to Save the Planet* (Des Moines, Iowa: Rodale (Hearst), 2014.

98 Jared Diamond, *Collapse—How Societies Choose Fail or Succeed* (New York, New York: Penguin Group, 2005).

99 Richard Heinberg and Daniel Lerch (editors), *The Post Carbon Reader—Managing the 21st Century's Sustainability Crisis* (Healdsburg, California: Watershed Media), xv–xvi.

100 Dambisa Moyo, *The Edge of Chaos—Why Democracy Is Failing to Deliver Economic Growth—and How to Fix It* (New York, New York: Hachete Book Group), 218, 219.

101 William Ophuls, *Immoderate Greatness—Why Civilizations Fail (*North Charleston, South Carolina: Create Space Independent Publishing, 2012).

102 Ian Bremmer, *Us vs. Them* - The Failure of Globalism, (New York, New York, Portfolio/Penguin, 2018, p6)

103 Jelleke de Nooy van Tol, *Transition to an Agro-Ecology—For a Food Secured World* (Bloomington, IN: AuthorHouse UK, 2016).

104 Stephen R. Guessman, *Agroecology—The Ecology of Sustainable Food Systems,* 2nd edition (Boca Raton, Florida: CRC Press, 2007).

105 Mark Shepard, *Restoration Agriculture—Real World Permaculture for Farmers* (Austin, Texas: Acres USA, 2013), 154–159.

106 Carey Gilliam, *Whitewash* (Island Press, 2017).

107 Andre Leu, *Poisoning Our Children—People's Guide to the Myths of Safe Pesticides* (Greeley, Colorado: Acres USA, 2018).

108 Rick Darke and Douglas Tallamy, *The Living Landscape: Designing for Beauty and Biodiversity in the Home Garden* (Portland, Oregon: Timbe Press, 2014).

109 Rick Darke and Douglas Tallamy, *The Living Landscape: Designing for Beauty and Biodiversity in the Home Garden* (Portland, Oregon: Timbe Press, 2014), 112.

110 Gunnar Rundgren, *Global Eating Disorder—We Can No Longer Afford Cheap Food* (Mountain View, California: Creative Commons Attribution, 2014), 92.

111 Gunnar Rundgren, *Global Eating Disorder—We Can No Longer Afford Cheap Food* (Mountain View, California: Creative Commons Attribution, 2014), 349.

[112] Paul Harkin (editor), *Drawdown—The Most Comprehensive Plan Ever Proposed to Reduce Global Warming* (New York, New York: Penguin-Random House, 2017), 118–120.

[113] Karl Weber (editor), *Food, Inc.—How Industrial Food Is Making Us Sicker, Fatter, and Poorer—And What You Can Do About it.* (Philadelphia, PA: Public Affairs Perseus Books Group, 2009).

[114] Ben Hirshberg, *Traditional Nutrition* (publisher not listed, www.BenHirshberg.com, 2015), 91–95.

[115] Joel Salatin, *Your Successful Farm Business—Production, Profit, Pleasure* (Swoope, Virginia: Polyface, Inc.).

[116] Michael Pollan, *The Omnivore's Dilemma—A Natural History of Four Meals* (New York, New York: Penguin, 2006).

[117] Vandana Shiva, *The Vandana Shiva Reader* (Lexington, Kentucky: University of Kentucky Press, 2015), 48.

[118] Vandana Shiva, *The Vandana Shiva Reader* (Lexington, Kentucky: University of Kentucky Press, 2015), 49.

[119] Masanobu Fukuoka, *The Natural Way of Farming—The Theory and Practice of Green Philosophy* (Tokyo, Japan: Japan Publications, 1985), 1–3.

[120] Robert Chambers et al. (editors), *Farmers First—Farmer innovation and agricultural research* (Southampton Row, London: Intermediate Technology Publications, 1989), 9.

[121] William Ophus, *Immoderate Greatness—Why Civilizations Fail* (publisher not listed, 2012), 1–2.

[122] Richard Wilkenson and Kate Pickett, *The Spirit Level—Why Greater Equality Makes Societies Stronger* (New York, New York: Bloomsbury Press, 2009), 269.

[123] Christopher Clugston, *Scarcity—Humanity's Final Chapter?* (Port Charlotte, Florida: Booklocker, 2012), 81.

[124] Paul Harkin (editor), *Drawdown—The Most Comprehensive Plan Ever Proposed to Reduce Global Warming* (New York, New York: Penguin-Random House, 2017).

[125] Dmitry Orlov, *Shrinking the Technosphere—Getting a Grip on the Technologies That Limit Our Autonomy* (government of Canada, 2016).

[126] Michael Greer, *Dark Age America—Climate Change, Cultural Collapse and the Hard Future Ahead* (Gabriola Island, BC, Canada: New Society Publishers, 2016).

[127] Tim Jackson, *Prosperity Without Growth—Economics for a Finite Planet* (Washington, DC: Earthscan, 2011), 153.

[128] John Perkins, *The New Confessions of an Economic Hit Man* (Oakland, California: Berrett-Koehler Publishers, 2016),

[129] John Perkins, *The New Confessions of an Economic Hit Man* (Oakland, California: Berrett-Koehler Publishers, 2016), 268.

[130] John Perkins, *The New Confessions of an Economic Hit Man* (Oakland, California: Berrett-Koehler Publishers, 2016), 292.

[131] Bill Moyers, *Moyers on Democracy* (New York, New York: Doubleday, 2008), 5.

[132] Bill Moyers, *Moyers on Democracy* (New York, New York: Doubleday, 2008), 14.

[133] Bill Moyers, *Moyers on Democracy* (New York, New York: Doubleday, 2008), 21.

[134] Nancy MacLean, *Democracy in Chains—The Deep History of the Radical Right's Stealth Plan for America* (New York, New York: Penguin, 2018), 231.

[135] Nancy MacLean, *Democracy in Chains—The Deep History of the Radical Right's Stealth Plan for America* (New York, New York: Penguin, 2018), 211.

[136] Nancy MacLean, *Democracy in Chains—The Deep History of the Radical Right's Stealth Plan for America* (New York, New York: Penguin, 2018), 217.

[137] Alissa Quart, *Squeezed—Why Our Families Can't Afford America* (New York, New York: Ecco-Harper Collins, 2018).

[138] George Hunt, *What Do You See?--A Learner's Guide with Poetry* (Bloomington, Indiana: Xlibris, 2016), 29-31

[139] Bill McKibben, *Eaarth—Making a Life on a Tough New Planet* (New York, New York: St. Martin's Press, 2010).

[140] Bill McKibben, *Deep Economy—The Wealth of Communities and the Durable Future* (New York, New York: Henry Holt and Company, 2007).

[141] William Ophuls, *Immoderate Greatness—Why Civilizations Fail (*North Charleston, South Carolina: Create Space Independent Publishing, 2012).

[142] Johan Berger, *Contagious—Why Things Catch On* (New York, New York: Simon and Schuster Paperbacks, 2013).

INDEX

A

AARP, 67

"Abdominal Obesity Linked to Anxiety and Depression" (Mercola), 72

Abrams, Amanda, 105

Academically Adrift: Limited Learning on College Campuses (Arum and Roksa), 56

Acres USA magazine, 191

ad blocker, 95, 101

ad filter, 101

additional park and recreation areas, in PDP, 37

add-on units, 20, 227

administration and research library, in PDP, 26

administration facilities and library, in PDP, 32

"Adolescence research must grow up" (Leen), 126–127

Advancement for Science, 174, 175–176

"Advantages and Disadvantages of Business Cooperatives" (Johnston), 92

advertising
    and drug industry, 95–99
    and marketing, 94–101

"Advertising–The Art of Capitalism" (Zaykova), 94

affordable housing
city governments as not receiving many applications for, 89
    lack of, 79, 193
    limitations of solutions for, 11
    need for, 11
    options for in PDP, 21
    problems of, 124–125
    provision of, 40
    "The Affordable Housing Issue," 124

agribusiness, 114, 144, 155, 156, 158, 159, 166, 168, 169, 171, 172, 179, 191, 192, 193, 194

agricultural and regenerative or restoration crops for research, in PDP, 27

agricultural biodiversity, 147–148

agricultural greenhouses, in PDP, 27

agricultural inputs, control of, 161

agricultural myths, 155

agricultural resources, as being used up, 160

agriculture
    and construction class buildings, in PDP, 27
    and food chain landscaping, 192–193
    and landscaping at the crossroads, 143–171

research and production, as major component of PDP, 39

research and production, as part of teaching curriculum, 57

research and production, in PDP, 33

Agriculture, Food, and Human Values Society, 175

agroecology, 13, 71, 144–145, 152, 153, 156, 161, 167, 168, 179, 181, 193

Agroecology, The Ecology of Sustainable Food Systems (Gliessman), 144, 170

AI (artificial intelligence), 42, 78, 119

Airbnb, 39, 40, 43

"The alarming statistics that show the U.S. economy isn't as good as it seems" (Long), 79–80

Alliance for Excellent Education, 63

Alliance for Science (Cornell University), 172–182

alternate lifestyle/worldview, as needed to prevent chaos, 100

Alternative Daily, 181–182

AltHealthworks, 176

Amazon, 89, 143

amenities, of PDP, 13

American Academy of Pediatrics, 68

American Revolution Center, 61

"America's best scientists stood up to the Trump administration," 128

"America's Version of Capitalism Is Incompatible with Democracy" (Levitz), 138

Angus, Jan, 152

Anielski, Mark, 66

antidepressants, 72, 126

anxiety
    causes of, 61, 79
    problem of, 69–70, 72

Apiroux, Joel, 145

APNAN, 149

Appleby, Julie, 97

Arbab, Farzam, 128

"Arbitration Everywhere, Stacking the Deck of Justice" (Greenberg and Gebeloff), 214

"The Arctic is full of toxic mercury" (Mooney), 151–152

artificial intelligence (AI), 42, 78, 119

Arum, Richard, 56

Atarexik, 104

Audubon Center (Dallas), 153

Auletta, Ken, 94–95

Aziza, Sarah, 117

B

bank
    in PDP, 25
    scandals in, 136
Barber, Dan, 170
Baum Hedlund Law, 182
Bayer, 138, 161, 169, 177
Bayer-Monsanto, 14, 108–109, 139, 140, 181, 182
The Bears of Blue River (Major), 85
Beaton, Caroline, 66
Becker, Joshua, 74
Benyus, Janine, 132
Berry, Wendell, 170
"Best Practice Guidelines for Agriculture & Value
    Chains" (IFOAM Organics International),
    179–180
*Better Not Bigger—How to Take Control of Urban
    Growth* (Fodor), 87, 131
"beyond organic" farming, 170
Big Brother (TV series), 101
Big Pharma, 69, 95, 96–97, 98, 181, 194
Bill and Melinda Gates Foundation, 172, 173
Biomimicry (Benyus), 132
Biopharm America, 109
"Biophysical Limits" (Ophuls), 141–142
Bitonio, Jo, 92
Black, Simon, 135–136, 186–187
Blasi, Joseph, 115
Bodnar, Anastasia, 176
Boston Globe, 176
Bowen, Linda, 107
Breen, Howard, 123–124
Bremmer, Ian, 142
Brown, Ellen, 108
Brown, Gabe, 135, 170
Brown's Ranch (Bismarck, North Dakota), 170
Bua, Adrian, 117
building design, options for, 16–17
building materials, options for, 19, 38
building uses
    building 1, 233
    building 9, 228, 232
    building 13, 229
    buildings 3 and 5, 231
    overview, 222
Burnett, Derek, 69

C

CALS (College of Agriculture and Life Sciences)
    (Cornell University), 172–182
"Can farming save Puerto Rico's future? As climate
    change alters how and where food is grown,

Puerto Rico's agro-ecology brigades are a
    model for sustainable farming" (Lim), 124
Capital Home Care Cooperative, 130
capitalism, social problems and, 69
capitalist society
    greed as mantra for, 100
    with improving technology to solve problems, 82
    as our present situation, 81–82
Caplan, Bryan, 60, 61
CARMA, 111
Carrington, Daimian, 114
carrying capacity, 83
*The Case Against Education–Why the Education System
    is a Waste of Time and Money* (Caplan), 60–62
CBD (Convention on Biological Diversity), 147–148
CBPP (commons-based peer production), 92
celebrities, emphasis on, 101
Center for Agroecology and Sustainable Food Systems
    (CASFS), 144
Center for Media and Democracy (CMD), 111
Centers for Disease Control and Prevention (CDC), 73
The Chain (Industrial Food Chain), 159–168
changing conditions, responding to, 42
Changing Course, 119
Charles G. Koch Charitable Foundation, 111
chemicals, cautions with, 129
children, "Genetically Modified Children" (film),
    139–140
Choudhry, Izza, 49–50
Chron, 92
CIRSPR, 109
climate change, 10, 14, 43, 61, 69, 78, 79, 81, 82, 102,
    111–112, 118, 119, 122, 123–124, 128, 137, 139,
    158, 159, 160, 163, 166, 191, 194
CMD (Center for Media and Democracy), 111
CNN, 81
Coca-Cola, 106
"Coca-Cola Sued for Alleged Deceptive
    Marketing," 106
Colbert, Steven, 10
collaboration, in PDP, 75–76. *See also* sharing/
    collaboration
Collapse (Diamond), 135
college dropouts, examples of, 62
"College Enrollment Dips as More Adults Ditch
    Degrees for Jobs" (Farber), 57
College of Agriculture and Life Sciences (CALS)
    (Cornell University), 172–182
College of Design at North Carolina State
    University, 40
Common Dreams, 139, 211
commons-based peer production (CBPP), 92

community and personal purposes, importance of, 64–80

community and recreation building, in PDP, 34

community branch bank, in PDP, 31

community building, in PDP, 28

community commons concept, formation of, 89–90

community development, resources for, 104–142

community park, in PDP, 28, 34

Community Resilience Reader, 84

compassion, need for, 73

computers and iPhones, 113

Congress
    approval rating of, 81
    Koch's contributions to, 143
    need for ethical Congress, 187
    as needing to set better example, 68

Conrow, Joan, 172–173

consumer price index (CPI), 9

Consumer Reports, 100

consumerism
    and discontent, 118
    reductions in, 74–75

Convention on Biological Diversity (CBD), 147–148

Cooper, Rosemary, 84

cooperatives, 17, 37, 41, 47, 52, 53, 57–58, 71, 75, 77, 78, 85, 89, 91–92, 103, 117, 130, 131, 156

"Coping with Depression and Overeating" (Gotter), 72–73

corn, "It's Time to Rethink America's Corn System" (Foley), 146

Cornell Chronicle, 172–173

"Cornell Student Who Took on Bill Gates, Monsanto Plans to Expose Their Agenda Even Further in Blockbuster New Project" (Meyer), 176

Cornell University, 172–182

"Corporate Greed: These Companies Deceived America For Profit–And You Probably Helped Them" (Burnett), 69

corporations, 108, 114–115, 119, 143, 187. *See also specific corporations*

cost analysis, 19, 38

Cox, Anne, 113

CPI (consumer price index), 9

Cranor, Carl, 121

Creating Wealth–Growing Local Economics with Local Currencies (Hallsmith and Lietaer), 77

CREDO, 110

Crickmore, Conor, 170, 192–193

crop pollinators, care for, 162

cultural diversity, 164–165

culture and economics, 105

culture and society, main concerns about, 191–192

Cunningham, Nick, 116

D

Daily Kos, 105, 110

Daily Reckoning, 125

Dark Age America–Climate Change, Cultural Collapse and the Hard Future Ahead (Greer), 186

Dark Money–Billionaires behind the Radical Right (Mayer), 112

Dawson, Ashley, 118

de Nooy van Tol, Jelleke, 144

"Declining Majority of Online Adults Say the Internet Has Been Good for Society" (Smith and Olmstead), 106–107

Deep Economy (McKibben), 218

deep learning, 42

Defarge, Nicolas, 145

defense spending, 185, 189, 190

democracy
    "America's Version of Capitalism Is Incompatible with Democracy" (Levitz), 138
    need for gatekeeper for, 9
    saving of, 47

Democracy at Work–A Cure for Capitalism (Wolff), 103

Democracy in Chains–The Deep History of the Radical Right's Stealth Plan for America (MacLean), 213

demonstration, described, 12

"Depressed? Anxious? Blame Neoliberalism" (Hart), 71–72

depression
    causes of, 61, 79
    and eating, 70, 72
    housing for people who need help with, 16
    problem of, 11, 69–70
    recognizing adolescent depression, 72
    use of antidepressants, 126

"Depression in Teens" (Mental Health America), 72

design
    as always changing, 103
    incorporation of sustainable design features, 18–19
    options for building design, 16–17
    systems design, 51, 131
    transition design, 102–103

"Designing the Future of Learning for All Kids" (Scheidegger), 55

Designs for the Pluriverse (Escobar), 102, 127

Design–When Everybody Designs (Manzini), 102, 103

Detroit, Michigan, housing in, 12

development approval, conventional method of obtaining, 87–89

Diamond, Jared, 135

"Dieting Does Not Work" (Wolpert), 120

diets, 120

"Dirt Poor: Have Fruits and Vegetables Become Less Nutritious?" (Pool), 120–121

The Dirt Cure—Growing Healthy Kids with Food Straight from the Soil (Shetreat-Klein), 38

discontent, consumerism and, 118

"Disembedding grain: Golden Rice, the Green Revolution, and heirloom seeds in the Philippines" (Stone and Glover), 175

diversity
    agricultural biodiversity, 147–148
    cultural diversity, 164–165
    food diversity, 160–161
    as key to success, 11, 152
    loss of organic diversity, 158
    social diversity, 12

Dixon, Arlene, 64

"Dr. Charles Hall: The Laws of Nature: Trump Economics," 44–45

Drawdown—The Most Comprehensive Plan Ever Proposed to Reduce Global Warming (Harkin), 130–131, 158, 186

Drug Enforcement Agency (DEA), 139

drug industry. *See also* Big Pharma
    advertising and, 95–99
    "60 Minutes just laid out the ugliest truth about the opioid crisis" (Lopez), 138–139
    "The drugs do work: anti-depressants should be given to a million more Britons, largest ever review claims" (Getty), 126

Drugwatch, 98
    "The dumbing down of society—the constant urge to be plugged in" (White and Cox), 113

duplex plans, 13, 16, 18, 24, 29, 30, 32, 33, 39, 40, 230

E

Eaarth—Making a Life on a Tough New Planet (McKibben), 218

EarthEd (Worldwatch Institute), 52, 57

Eco Watch Community, 169

Ecologist, 173

economic and market feasibility studies, 41

economic development options, 81–86

"Economic Numbers Are Less Than Meets the Eye" (Rickards), 125

Economic Policy Institute, 143

economics, as intertwined with all other conditions, 193

Economics Foundation, 117
    The Economics of Happiness (Anielski), 66

Edelman, Marc, 127

Edge of Chaos (Moyo), 8, 141

education, training, and financing, in PDP, 57–63

education, training, and workshops
    as main objective of PDP, 49
    as major component of PDP, 13
    education building, 235

education potential, procedures, and methods, 49–63

Edwards, Chris, 133

Ehrlich, Paul R., 158
    "EIA: U.S. Oil Abundance for Now—But Don't Peek behind That Curtain, Shale Reality Check: Drilling into the U.S. Government's Rosy Projections for Shale Gas and Tight Oil Production through 2050" (Heinberg and Hughes), 116

elderly housing, 13, 16, 21, 24, 29, 30, 40, 44

election process, 9

"Elementary Microbiology, Problems with Bt" (Penn State University), 176

"Empowering a Life-Destroying Cartel" (Welch, Shiva, Meyer, and Brown), 108

The End of Money and the Future of Civilization (Greco), 77

energy, and natural renewable resources, 193

Energy and the Wealth of Nations (Hall), 44

energy sources, in PDP, 36–37

entrepreneurship, 55

environment
    main concerns about, 191
    resources for, 130–131

environmental messaging, 100

Environmental Working Group, 169

EPA. *See* US Environmental Protection Agency (EPA)

equipment storage and maintenance buildings, in PDP, 27

EROI (energy return on investment), 44

Escobar, Arturo, 102, 127

ETC Group, 158–168, 180

Eudaemonia, Umaie Haque, 124

evaluation study, use of, 19

Extreme Cities—The Peril and Promise of Urban Life in the Age of Climate Change (Dawson), 81

F

Facebook, 113

FactCheck.org, 211–212

Farber, Madeline, 57

"Farewell to Development" (Escobar), 127

Farm Bill (2018), 157

Farmer First—Farmer Innovation and Agricultural Research (Chambers, Pacey, and Thrupp), 180–181

farmers market/flea market, 13, 17, 26, 27, 28, 32, 33, 131, 215

Faux, Jeff, 143
FDA. *See* US Food and Drug Administration (FDA)
"Fearless Cities" (Gellaly and Riveria), 117
feedback loops, 131
"Find out if your doctor takes payments from drug companies—New government data show more than 500,000 U.S. physicians have industry ties," 96
Fire and Fury (Ivins), 10
Firefox, 101
fisheries, safeguarding of, 160
food
    access problems with, 156
    consumption of, 164
    costs of, 155–156
    processing and preservation of, 163
    production of, 158, 159
    sources of, 159
Food, Inc. (Weber ed.), 169
Food and Environment Reporting Network, 124
Food and Water Watch, 177
food diversity, 160–161
Food Forensics—The Hidden Toxins Living in Your Food and How You Can Avoid Them (Adams), 38
food loss, 163–164
food nutrition, 120–123, 147
forest/forest foods, protection of, 161
for-profit, leadership of PDP by, 38, 43, 44
Fortune magazine, 57, 106
fossil carbon, 163
Four Futures, 83
"fox in the henhouse" policy/agencies, 9, 95
Frenemies: The Epic Disruption of the Ad Business (and Everything Else) (Auletta), 94–95
The Fresh Harvest (Juma), 176
Fukuoka, Masanobu, 180
funding/financing, for PDP, 41, 42
"The future is now: How to win the resource revolution" (Nyquist, Rogers, and Woetzel), 186

G

"The Gap: The Affordable Housing Gap Analysis 2017," 125
Garden Earth, 150
Gates, Bill, 173
GDP (gross domestic product), 9
Gebeloff, Robert, 214
Gellaly, Jerry, 117
Generation Me (Twenge), 67
"Genetically Modified Children" (film), 139–140
genuine progress indicator (GPI), 9
Genuine Wealth, 66

George, Steve, 81
George R. Hunt Associates/Natural Regenerative Technologies, 33
gerrymandering, 9–10
Get a Job, Build a Real Career and Defy a Bewildering Economy (Smith), 114–115
"Getting Past Trump (Part 1): This is How Democracies Die" (Heinberg), 188
"Getting Past Trump (Part 2): The Russia Connection" (Heinberg), 188
Getty, Laura Donnelly, 126
Gillam, Carey, 9
Gliessman, Stephen R., 144, 170
Global Eating Disorder (Rundgren), 155–156
Global Footprint Network, 82
Global Research News Hour, 108
global warming, 20, 43, 69, 71, 111, 130, 151, 158, 184
globalism, 141, 142
globalization, 143, 163
Glover, Dominic, 175
glyphosate, 110, 112, 122, 145, 147, 153, 169, 181, 182, 209. *See also* Roundup
"GMO Golden Rice Offers No Nutritional Benefits Says FDA" (Wilson), 175
GMOs, 25, 109, 112, 138, 139, 140, 145–146, 147, 149, 157, 158, 160, 161, 165, 171, 172, 173, 174, 175, 176, 177, 178, 179, 181–182, 187, 191, 193, 209
GMOS Revealed, 209
"Goodby to Golden Rice? GM Trait Leads to Drastic Yield Loss and 'Metabolic Meltdown'" (Wilson), 174
Google, 101, 113
Gorelick, Steven, 122
Gotter, Ana, 72–73
governance
    conventional method of obtaining development approval, 87–89
    formation of community commons concept, 89–90
    pilot demonstration governance, 90–92
    solidarity economy, 90
government
    cleaning up of, 100
    subsidies from, 144
government offices, in PDP, 31
GPI (genuine progress indicator), 9
grassroots empowerment, 117
"Grassroots Guide to Federal Farm and Food Programs," 157
Graves, Lisa, 111
"A Great Irony—The U.S. Federal Reserve" (Martinson), 119–120
Greco, Thomas, 77

greed, biology of, 113–114
Greenberg, Jessica Silver, 214
greenhouses, in PDP, 32–33
gross domestic product (GDP), 9
growth problem, reduction of/solution to, 88
Guardian, 114, 128, 129, 173

H

Hall, Charles, 44
Hallsmith, Gwendolyn, 90
happiness, requirements for, 109
Hari, Johann, 69–70
Harkin, Paul, 130–131
Harkinson, Josh, 76–77
harm-benefit analysis (for technology), 45–46
Hart, Johann, 71–72
Hartll, Brett, 151
Healthline, 72–73
Heard Museum (Dallas), 153
Heinberg, Richard, 116, 183, 188, 209
Hemenway, Toby, 88
Hertsgaard, Mark, 158
The Hidden Life of Trees—What They Feel, How They Communicate (Wohlleben), 129
"High School Dropouts More Likely to Go to Prison" (Choudhry), 49–50
"Higher Education Solutions" (Smith), 51
Hightower Lowdown, 89, 111
The Hill, 151
Hirshberg, Ben, 170
"Home Care Cooperatives and the Future of Work" (Ingalls), 130
home health care industry, 130
Homeless Services eBook, 69
homelessness, people who are experiencing, 11, 13, 21, 24, 29, 30, 31, 40, 43, 44, 53, 71
Horovitz, Bruce, 97
Horsch, Rob, 172
Household Survival Budgets, 107
housing
    affordable housing. *See* affordable housing
    costs of, 135–136
housing and land-use improvements
    description, 20–22
    option 1, 23–28
    option 2, 29–35
housing construction, methods of, 38
"How Big Pharma Manipulates the Public Good" (Song and Penn Wharton PPI), 98
"How Black Lives Matter" (King), 118
How Democracies Die (Levitsky and Ziblatt), 47

"How Much Money Do People Need to Be Happy?" (Kopf), 66
"How polluters are writing the rules at the EPA" (Hartll), 151
"How Societies Collapse: The Eerie Parallels between Rome, Nazi Germany, and America" (Eudaemonia), 124
"How the Nation's Only State-Owned Bank Became the Envy of Wall Street" (Harkinson), 76–77
"How Unregulated Household Chemicals Harm Us" (Miller), 121
HUD (US Department of Housing and Urban Development), 11
Huffington Post, 65, 66, 113–114, 211
Hughes, David, 116
"Human Predators—Human Prey—Part 2" (Heinberg), 209
"Humans just 0.01% of all life but have destroyed 83% of wild animals—study" (Carrington), 114
Humus: The Essential Ingredient and Mastering Mineral Balance in the Soil (video), 168
Hunt, George, vii, 216–217
hurricane villas, 234

I

IFOAM Organics International, 179–180
illness, cure for, 126
immigration, 81, 105–106, 110, 140, 190, 215
Immoderate Greatness—Why Civilizations Fail (Ophuls), 78, 82, 141–142, 183
"In the Age of AI" (Veronese), 119
"In the Promise of GMOS: Mycotoxins" (Bodnar), 176
In These Times magazine, 71–72
Independent Science News for Food and Agriculture, 174, 175
Indian Health Service (IHS), 133
"Indian Lands, Indian Subsidies, and the Bureau of Indian Affairs" (Edwards), 133
"Indicators of Economic Progress: The Power of Measurement and Human Welfare," 47
Industrial Food Chain (The Chain), 159–168
"Inefficient Productivity or Productive Inefficiency?" (Rundgren), 150
inequality, 8, 10, 11, 47, 55, 61, 71, 81, 83, 100, 117, 137, 182, 183, 184, 186, 194, 210, 212, 214
inequity, 68, 87, 100, 140, 185, 191
INFRC, 149
Ingalls, Reed, 130
in-ground agricultural research, in PDP, 28
innovation
    inspired by nature, 132
    who really innovates? 165–166

internet, 106–107
iPhones, computers and, 113
"Iroquois Great Law of Peace," vii
irrigation, 19, 27, 36, 150, 154, 162
"Is There a Cure for Greed?" (Selby), 113–114
It's Even Worse Than You Think—What the Trump Administration Is Doing to America (Johnston), 113
"It's Time to Rethink America's Corn System" (Foley), 146
Ivins, Molly, 10

J

Jackson, Tim, 118, 187
Jackson, Wes, 170
Jamaica, as example, 16, 64
Japan, agricultural arable land areas in, 45
job trend predictions and student debt, 53–57
jobs, 114–115
John Bunker Sands Wetland Center, 153
Johnson, Jon, 70
Johnston, David Cay, 113
Johnston, Kevin, 92
Jowit, Juliette, 211
Juma, Calestous, 176
Juric, Sam, 66–67

K

Kaiser Health News, 97
Katz, Bruce, 43
Kauffman Foundation, 54–56
The Key to Sustainable Cities (Hallsmith), 90
Khullar, Dhruv, 65
Kim, Sharon, 65
King, Jamilah, 118
Klein, Naomi, 81, 94
Koch brothers, 9, 111–112, 122, 143, 187–188, 213, 214
Koch Exposed (Center for Media and Democracy), 111
Koch Industries, 111, 115
Kopf, Dan, 66
Kruse, Douglas L., 115
Kurtzman, Daniel, 141
Kyusei Nature Farming, 149
"Kyusei Nature Farming and Technology of Effective Microorganisms—Guidelines for Practical Use" (Sangakkara ed.), 149

L

Land Institute, 170
land uses
    and housing, description, 20–22
    and housing, option 1, 23–28
    and housing, option 2, 29–35
    summary of, 37–42
landscaping
    agriculture and at the crossroads, 143–171
    maintenance of, 18, 40
    planning and maintenance of, why use natural systems for, 152
Larkin, Molly, vii
"Latest Update on Toxicity of Popular Weed Killer and Proposed Rule for Labeling of GMOs" (Mercola), 112
lawns, 12, 18, 36, 152, 154
League of Woman Voters, 9
The Lean Farm, 28
Leen, Nina, 126–127
legal naturehood, 129
Levitsky, Steven, 47
Levitz, Eric, 138
LID—Low Impact Development—A Design Manual for Urban Areas (University of Arkansas), 18–19
life on Earth, assessment of, 114
Lim, Audrea, 124
Limits to Growth—30-Year Adjustment (Meadows and Randers), 82
"A Little-Known Cause of Millennial Job Burnout" (Beaton), 66
livelihoods, protection of, 165
livestock
    breeding of, 160
    health of, 160
"Living in a Rapidly Changing Society: Transition to Maturity" (Arbab), 128
The Living Landscape: Designing for Beauty and Biodiversity in the Home Garden (Darke and Tallamy), 154, 155
lobbyists, 68, 99, 111, 122, 143, 187, 211
local currencies, 13, 17, 25, 27, 58, 74, 76–77, 127, 215
"Localization, Essential Steps to Economic Happiness" (Norberg-Hodge), 143
Long, Heather, 73, 79–80
Longreads, 118
"Look at the Shocking Student Loan Debt Statistics for 2018," 56
Lopez, Linette, 138–139
Lost Connections (Hari), 69–70
low-income households/areas, 12, 38–39, 42, 50, 55, 64, 95, 107–108, 122, 125
LucidEnergy, 78

M

MacLean, Nancy, 213
Maguire, Robert, 111

Major, Charles, 85
"Major Study Shows Species Loss Destroys Essential Ecosystems" (Angus), 152
"The man who stopped the desert" (Hertsgaard), 158
Manzini, Ezio, 102, 103
Margill, Mari, 129
marketing
advertising and, 94–101
resources for, 115
Martinson, Chris, 44, 119–120
Mason, Paul, 130
master-planned communities, 12
Mayer, Jane, 112
McKendrick, Joe, 54
McKibben, Bill, 218
McKinsey & Company, 186
McLuhan, Marshall, 99–100
McMansions, 12
The Meaning of Human Existence (Wilson), 109
The Mechanical Bridge: Folklore of Industrial Man (McLuhan), 99–100
media, role of, 8, 10
medical clinic, 16, 25–26, 31
medical housing, 16, 30
Medical News Today, 70
meeting/entertaining building, in PDP, 32
meetups, 40
"Men, Power, and Sexual Harassment–Why Powerful Men Sexually Harass Women" (Bowen), 107
Mental Health America, 72
Mercola, Joseph, 72, 112, 118, 123, 139–140, 149
The Mesh–Why the Future of Business Is Sharing (Gansky), 84
Method, 119
Meyer, Nick, 108, 176
microbes, care for, 162
MicroLife, 109
millennials, research on, 67
Miller, Bettye, 121
Miller, Emily, 98
Miller, Ethan, 90
Mirimichi (weed killer), 109
MIT Technology Review, 78
mixed auto uses, in PDP, 31
model home sales area, 43, 223
Momaday, N Scott, 172
Monbiot, George, 126
Mondragon Corporation (Spain), 92
Money (Greco), 77
"Money and Work Unchained" (Taggert), 105
monocropping, 129–130, 154, 171, 178, 179, 187, 193

Monsanto, 9, 69, 108, 110, 118, 130, 135, 140, 144, 145, 146, 147, 149, 157, 161, 168, 169, 172, 173, 175, 176, 177, 178, 179, 181, 182, 192, 194. See also Bayer-Monsanto
"Monsanto Relied on These 'Partners' to Attack Top Cancer Scientists," 110
"Monsanto to pay $289.2M in Landmark Roundup Lawsuit Verdict" (Organic Consumers.org), 182
Montgomery, David R., 155
Mooney, Chris, 151–152
moral education, 128
The More of Less (Becker), 74
Morin, Rebecca, 140
Mother Jones, 76–77, 174
Mountain Fragrance (Taylor), 132
Moyers, Bill, 212–213
Moyers on Democracy (Moyers), 212–213
Moyo, Dambisa, 8, 141
MSS Research, 47
multi-use of buildings and products
benefits of, 17
as major component of PDP, 12–13

N

Nadasen, Premilla, 68
"NAFTA's Impact on U.S. Workers" (Faux), 143
National Center for Education Statistics (NCES), 49
National Family Farm Coalition, 157
National Geographic, 137
National Organic Standards Board (NOSB), 148
National Sustainable Agriculture Coalition (NSAC), 157
Native Americans
nature and, 132–133
poverty among on reservations, 133–134
social challenges among, 134–135
Native News, 138
natural renewable resources, energy and, 193
natural resources
reducing use of, 19, 43
reductions in, 45
Natural Society, 181
natural systems, 33, 37, 38, 59, 129, 130, 131, 144, 148, 152, 153, 155, 178, 180, 181, 191, 193
The Natural Way of Farming (Fukuoka), 180
nature
diversity as key to success of, 11
innovations in, 132
and Native Americans, 132–133
using processes of as guidelines, 7
Nature Ecology and Evolution, 122
NCES (National Center for Education Statistics), 49
Nearly Free University (NFU), 51, 52

"Neighborhood Newsletter," 26
neoliberalism, problems of, 71–72
Neversink Farm (New York), 32, 170, 192–193
   The New Confessions of an Economic Hit Man
      (Perkins), 87, 108, 188
New Internationalist, 118, 119
   The New Localism–How Cities Can Thrive in the
      Age of Populism (Katz and Nowak), 43
"New Normal" approach, 144, 147
"New York City Files $500 Million Lawsuit Against
      Drug Companies Over Opioid Deaths," 96–97
"New York Farmers Ask Cornell University to Evict
      Alliance for Science over GMO Bias" (Sustainable
      Pulse), 177
New York Times, 65, 99, 149, 214
NIMBY ("not in my backyard") thinking, 87
NJ Med survey, 50–51
No Logo (Klein), 94
Non-GMO Project–GMO Facts, 145
nonprofit
      governing framework for, 17
      leadership of PDP by, 38, 41, 43–44
      PDP developer as, 91, 92
Norberg-Hodge, Helena, 143
NOSB (National Organic Standards Board), 148
"not in my backyard" (NIMBY) thinking, 87
Nowak, Jeremy, 43
NSAC (National Sustainable Agriculture Coalition), 157
"Number of registered active lobbyists in the United
      States from 2000 to 2017," 187
nutrition, resources for, 131
Nyquist, Scott, 186

O

Obama, Barack, 139
Ohlson, Kristin, 135
Okada, Mokichi, 149
Olmstead, Kenneth, 106–107
The Omnivore's Dilemma (Pollan), 171
Ophuls, William, 78, 141–142, 183
opioid epidemic, 45, 96–97, 138–139
Organic Consumers.org, 182
organic farming, 144, 150, 155, 179, 180
"organic" label, 118
organic landscape planting and maintenance, 153
Organisation for Economic Co-operation and
      Development (OECD), 63
Orlov, Dmitry, 45
Our Ecological Footprint, 82
"Our laws make slaves of nature. IT's not just humans
      who need rights" (Margill), 129

"Out of Hand: Farmers face the consequences of a
      consolidated seed industry" (National Family
      Farm Coalition), 157
overnight accommodations/facilities, in PDP, 34, 39, 40

P

parking, in PDP, 26, 32
Participation City (London), 105
partisan politics (United States), 8, 9, 104–105
PCE (personal consumption indicator), 9
PDP (Pilot Demonstration Project). *See* Pilot
      Demonstration Project (PDP)
Peak Prosperity Weekly, 104, 138
Peasant Food Web (PFW), 159, 166
Penn Wharton PPI, 98
pensions, 79
      "Perfect Storm Global Financial System Showing
         Danger Signs" (Evans-Pritchard), 25
      "The Perilds of GMO Research–Scientist Speaks
         Out" (Advancement for Science), 174
periodiCALS, 172
Perkins, John, 108, 188
      The Permaculture City (Hemenway), 19, 88
permit, for PDP, 41
persons with handicaps, units designed for, 40–41
pets, 40
Pew survey, 43, 106–107
PFW (Peasant Food Web), 159, 166
"Pharmaceutical Industry Ethics" (Thomas), 98
pharmaceutical medicine, 95–99. *See also* Big Pharma
Philip Morris, 139, 140
Phillpott, Tom, 174
Pilot Demonstration Project (PDP)
      activities needing to occur for PDP to proceed,
         41–42
      as breakthrough opportunity for depression
         research, 70–73
      description, 16–22
      goals of, 11, 65, 84
      introduction, 7–9
      location of, 38, 40
      project information and direction, 43–48
      purpose of, 11, 12
      reasons for creating, 12
      slideshow, 220–237
      summary of, 12–14
platform cooperatives, 89, 92, 117
Poisoning Our Children: Pesticide Residue (Leu), 151
policy changes, needed, 166–167
Political Economy Research Institute, 111
political spending, need for limits on, 9
Pollan, Michael, 170, 171

Polluter Watch, 111
Polyface Farm (Swoope, Virginia), 170, 171
Pool, Martin, 120–121
Porter, Edurado, 74–75
Post Capitalism (Mason), 130
Post Carbon Institute, 137
Post Carbon Reader–Managing the 21st Century Sustainability Crisis, 137–138
Post-Capitalist Entrepreneurship–Startups for the 99% (Cohen), 89–90
postcapitalist society
    as goal, 7, 8
    transition into, 46–48
poverty
    elimination of, 83
    growth of, 69
    help for people in, 68
    on reservations, 133–134
"Poverty and Child Health in the United States," 68
"Prescription drug costs are up, so are TV ads promoting them" (Horovitz and Appleby), 97
    The Price of Everything: Solving the Mystery of Why We Pay What We Do (Porter), 74–75
    "The Price of Prisons, 2015," 50
prisons, as innovative learning systems, 50
product labeling, 118, 146
"Prospect of shale wave looms over resurgent oil prices" (Seskus), 116
Prosperity without Growth (Jackson), 187

Q

Quartz, 66
Queally, Jon, 139
Quigley, Bill, 211

R

racism, 81, 118, 142
Reader's Digest, 69
The Readout, 109
Real Food Fake Food–Why You Don't Know What You Are Eating and What You Can Do about It (Olmstead), 38
refugees, and PDP community projects, 21
"Regenerative Agriculture–The Next Big Thing" (Mercola), 118
regenerative farming production and research, in PDP, 33
renewable energy applications, 17, 36–37, 41–42, 46
renewable materials, running out of, 7
"Requiring Prices in Drug Ads: Would It Do Any Good? Is It Even Legal?" 99
Resilience (website), 104, 183, 188, 209

"Resistance Is Complex" (*Nature Ecology and Evolution*), 122
restaurant, in PDP, 25
Restoration Agriculture (Shepard), 27, 146, 170
retail store, in PDP, 25
retail uses, in PDP, 31
Reuters, 187
Rickards, James, 125
Riveria, Marios, 117
Rodale Institute, 150
Rogers, Matt, 186
Roksa, Josipa, 56
Rooted in the Land, 27
Roundup, 110, 112, 122, 140, 145, 146–147, 168, 169, 172, 182, 209. *See also* glyphosate
"Roundup for Breakfast? Weed Killer Found in Kids' Cereals, Other Oat-Based Foods" (Eco Watch Community), 169
Rundgren, Gunnar, 150, 155–156
Ryan, Paul, 187–188
"Ryan Zinke Is Opening Up Public Lands. Just Not at Home" (Turkowitz), 149

S

"Sacrifice Zones in Rural and Non-Metro USA: Fertile Soil for Authoritarian Populism" (Edelman), 127
Sait, Graeme, 168, 191
Salatin, Joel, 170
San Francisco Chronicle, 69
Sangakkara, Ravi, 149
Sarich, Christina, 181
Sawadogo, Yacuba, 158
Scarcity–Humanity's Final Chapter? (Clugston), 184
Schaub, Tim, 177
Scheidegger, Julie, 55
Schematic Land Use Plan, 15, 16, 18
Schleicher, Andreas, 63
Schoen, John E., 56
Schumacher, E.F., 88
Science & Society, 176
"Science of Loneliness" (Juric), 66–67
Scientific American, 120–121, 146, 155
SCORE mentoring program, 39
seed companies, 157. *See also* Monsanto
Sekai Kyusei Kyo, 149
Selby, John, 113–114
self-help housing, 39
Seralini, Gille-Eric, 145
Seskus, Tony, 116
Seven Pillars Institute, 98
seventh-generation principle, 3
sewage system, in PDP, 35–36

sexual harassment and power, 107
shale production, 116
sharing urban villages, 105
sharing/collaboration
    benefits of, 88
    in cities, 117
    as guiding principles of PDP, 16
    how it works, 84
    importance of, 11, 13, 68, 70
Shepard, Mark, 146, 170
Shiva, Vandana, 108, 179
Shrinking the Technosphere (Orlov), 45, 82, 186
silvicultural system, 158
site analysis, 42
site plan, 16, 75, 91, 225
    "60 Minutes just laid out the ugliest truth about
        the opioid crisis" (Lopez), 138–139
    "68 Monsanto-Owned Companies to Boycott"
        (Alternative Daily), 181–182
Slideshare, 92
Small Business Administration, 39
Small Is Beautiful (Schumacher), 88
smart housing concepts, 11
"A Smarter Smart City" (Wolke), 46
Smith, Aaron, 106–107
Smith, Charles Hugh, 51, 104, 105, 114–115
Snopes, 187–188
social activities, PDP as designed around, 13
social cohesion, importance of, 11
social diversity, 12
"Social Isolation Looms Large as More Adults Live
    Alone–Loneliness Is a Greater Health Threat
    than Obesity" (AARP), 67
social problems, and capitalism, 69
society
    as collapsed and in chaos, 83
    as failing, 183–189
    as out of balance, 140
    with reduced consumption and minimal
        nonrenewable resources, 82
soil food web, 144, 148, 153
    "The Soil Solution" (Sait), 191
    The Soil Will Save Us (Ohlson), 135
soils
    amendments to, 18, 33, 147
    deterioration/erosion of, 10, 14, 44, 45, 62, 71, 79,
        102, 112, 130, 147, 193, 194, 209, 218
    development of regenerative soils, 33, 135
    food nutrition and, 120–123
    grazing animals and soil vitality, 168
    gut microbiome and soil biome, 38
    improvement of, 144–145, 153, 155, 156, 181,
        187, 191

lawns as requiring more bacteria in, 152
    organic methods of landscaping, 36
    safeguarding of, 162
    used by builders, 12
solid waste disposal, in PDP, 37
solidarity economy, 85, 90
    "Solidarity Economy–Key Concepts and Issues"
        (Miller), 90
Song, Grace, 98
South Korea, lands and culture of, 132
South San Antonio, as example, 64
Sovereign Man (Simon Black), 79, 135–136, 186–187
species loss, 152
    *The Spirit Level–Why Greater Equality Makes
        Societies Stronger* (Wilkenson and
        Pickett), 184
    Squeezed–Why Our Families Can't Afford America
        (Quart), 215
staff, in PDP, 30
"State of Entrepreneuership 2017," 55
Stern, Nicholas, 211
Stone, Glenn Davis, 175
Stone Barnes Center for Food and Agriculture, 170
storage and maintenance buildings, in PDP, 33
stormwater, in PDP, 36
Stroh, David Peter, 54, 131
student debt, 56–57
student housing, 13, 16, 17, 23–24, 30, 32, 40, 44, 52
Student Loan Hero, 56
"Suicide rising across the U.S." (CDC), 73
Summer, Mark, 105
"Super rich hold $32 trillion in offshore havens"
    (Reuters), 187
support mechanisms, governance, as major
    component of PDP, 13–14
sustainability, 124
sustainable community
    defined, 221
    as goal 1, 224
sustainable consumption, requirements of, 84
sustainable design features, incorporation of, 18–19
sustainable farming, 124, 149
Sustainable Pulse, 110, 145, 146, 177
systems design, 51, 131
Systems Thinking for Social Change (Stroh), 54, 131

T

Taggert, Adam, 105
"Take Action: Oppose the House Farm Bill," 157
Taylor, Rita, 132
technology
    changes in, 78
    harm-benefit analysis for, 45–46

technology (or innovative) study center
as part of education focus in PDP, 51, 52–53
in PDP, 26, 31
"Technology and Its Discontents" (Gorelick), 122
Techwood, 17
"Ten Examples of Welfare for the Rich and
Corporations" (Quigley), 211
"10 tips for turning employees into 'intrapreneurs'"
(McKendrick), 54
"A third of Bangladesh under water as flood
devastation widens" (George), 81
The Third Plate (Barber), 170
"37 Million Bees Found Dead after Planting Large
GMO Corn Field," 138
This Changes Everything (Klein), 81
Thomas, Rachel, 98
ThoughtCo, 107, 141
"3 Big Myths about Modern Agriculture"
(Montgomery), 155
Time magazine, 61
tiny home planning, 236
"Today's Young Adults Want to Redesign Capitalism.
But into What?" (Blasi and Kruse), 115
"The Town That Found a Potent Cure for Illness:
Community" (Monbiot), 126
toxic chemicals, 121, 129
Toxic Release Inventory, 111
Tradition Town movement, 127
Traditional Nutrition (Hirshberg), 170
Tragic Failures (Cranor), 121
training center (agriculture), in PDP, 32
transition design, 102–103
transition period
cause of, 10
length of, 47–48, 102
PDP as necessary for, 16
Seven Guiding Principles of Transition, 127
Transition to Agro-Ecology (de Nooy van Tol), 38, 144
transportation, options for, 40
triplex plans, 12–13, 17, 18, 20, 21, 23–24, 26, 27,
29–30, 31, 32, 33, 34, 35, 39, 40, 43, 52, 64, 72,
226, 237
Trump, Donald, 8, 9, 10, 47, 67, 68, 78, 79, 100, 104,
110, 113, 127, 140, 143, 169, 181, 211, 212
"Trump likely Benefits from Tax Bills" (Robertson),
211–212
"Trump nominates member of hate group to oversee
refugee resettlement," 110
"Trump praises Texas AG's lawsuit to repeal DACA"
(Morin), 140
Turkowitz, Julie, 149
Twain, Mark, 141
Twenge, Jean M., 67

U

"The Ultimate Guide to GMOs: Discovering the
Myths and Truths about Genetically Modified
Organisms" (Mercola), 149
"Undergraduate Retention and Graduation Rates," 49
Understanding Media (McLuhan), 99
unemployment, 50, 79, 125, 134, 137, 143
"The unhappy states of America: Despite an improving
economy" (Long), 73
United Way study "UW-(ALICE)," 107
Universal by Design (College of Design at North
Carolina State University), 40–41
University of California at Santa Cruz, 144, 170
"Unprecedented Crime" (Breen), 123–124
urban growth, 87, 131
urban planning and housing, 193
urban populism, 43
US Constitution, 47
US Department of Agriculture (USDA), 109, 112, 144,
178, 194
US Department of Housing and Urban Development
(HUD), 11
"U.S. Drug Prices vs. the World" (Miller), 98
US Environmental Protection Agency (EPA), 9, 114,
134, 151, 154, 169, 184, 194
US Federal Reserve, 119–120
US Food and Drug Administration (FDA), 9, 95, 97, 98,
174, 175, 176, 194
"US Judge Gives Green Light to Misleading Roundup
Label Lawsuit against Monsanto," 146
US Right to Know, 176
US Solidarity Economy Network, 90
US Supreme Court, Citizens United decision, 190
Us vs Them—The Failure of Globalism (Bremmer), 142
"UW-(ALICE)" United Way study, 107

V

value, meaning of, 79
*The Value of Everything—Making and Taking in the
Global Economy* (Mazzucato), 79
The Vandana Shiva Reader (Shiva), 179
Vera Institute of Justice, 50
Veronese, Roberto, 119
"Vietnam Set to Increase Legal Pressure on Monsanto
for Millions of Agent Orange Victims"
(Sustainable Pulse), 182
"A visit to one of Trump's child-gulags reveals
prison conditions and propaganda posters"
(Summer), 105
Voskoboynik, Daniel Macmillen, 119

W

walkways, in PDP, 34
"Wall Street freaked out about CRISPR again" (Biopharm America), 109
war games, 101
Washington Post, 68, 73, 79–80, 151–152
waste (in food), 163–164
water
    in PDP, 35
    shortages of, 136–137
wasting of, 162–163
WaterSense, 154
"We Should Be Talking about the Effect of Climate Change on Cities" (Dawson), 118
Weber, Karl, 169
Welch, Craig, 137
Welch, Michael, 108
Welcome to Your World—How the Built Environment Shapes Our World (Goldhagen), 20
What Do You See—A Learner's Guide with Poetry (Hunt), 215, 216–217
"What Foods Are Good for Depression?" (Johnson), 70
What's Mine Is Yours—The Rise of Collaborative Consumption (Botsman and Rogers), 84
White, Crystal, 113
White, William, 25
Whitewash (Gillam), 9, 147
"Who are really the Top Shareholders of Monsanto?" (Sarich), 181
"Who Will Feed Us" (ETC Group), 158–168
"Why America Can't Take Its Entrepreneurial Spirit for Granted," 54–55
"Why Cape Town Is Running out of Water" (Welch), 137
"Why Does a College Degree Cost so Much" (Schoen), 56
"Why is Cornell University hosting a GMO propaganda campaign?" (*Ecologist*), 173
"Why is the Gates foundation investing in GM giant Monsanto? 173
"Why Is the Shale Industry Still Not Profitable?" (Cunningham), 116
Why Our Status Quo Failed and Is beyond Reform (Smith), 115
"Why Urban Villages Are on the Rise around the World" (Abrams), 105
"Why Workers' Rights Are Good for the Economy" (Bua), 117
"Why You Should Never Chase Your Passion" (Kim), 65
Wi-Fi, 123
"Wi-Fried—Is Wireless Technology Dooming a Generation to Ill Health? That External Interference Can Disrupt Your Body's Natural Bioelectric Signals" (Mercola), 123
Wild Farm Alliance, 157
wildlife and educational centers, PDP as working with, 153
Wilson, Allison, 174, 175
Wilson, Edward O., 109
Wise, Bob, 63
Woetzel, Jonathan, 186
Wolff, Richard, 103
Wolke, Elizabeth, 46
Wolpert, Stuart, 120
work, 114–115
"Worker Cooperatives Offer Real Alternatives to Trump's Retrograde Economic Vision" (Aziza), 117
worker-cooperative model, 130
workers' rights, 117
workers' self-directed enterprise (WSDE), 103
workshops, in PDP, 13, 32, 49
work-study programs, use of, 62
World Class: How to Build a 21st-Century School System (Schleicher), 63
Worldwatch Institute, 57
Worst Pills-Best Pills, 95

Y

Yes magazine, 115, 124
young people, 126
Your Successful Farm Business—Production, Profit, Pleasure (Salatin), 170

Z

Zaykova, Alla, 94
ZD Net, 54
Ziblatt, Daniel, 47
Zinke, Ryan, 149
zoning ordinances, 11, 29, 41, 44, 87, 90, 103

Printed in the United States
By Bookmasters